D1561171

KOINE

Mediterranean Studies
in Honor of R. Ross Holloway

edited by
Derek B. Counts and Anthony S. Tuck

Oxbow Books
Oxford and Oakville

Joukowsky Institute Publication 1

General series editor: Prof. John F. Cherry

Joukowsky Institute for Archaeology and the Ancient World

Brown University, Box 1837/60 George Street, Providence, RI 0212, USA

Published by
Oxbow Books, Oxford, UK

© Oxbow Books and the individual authors, 2009

ISBN 978 1 84217 379 4

This book is available direct from

Oxbow Books, Oxford, UK
(Phone: 01865-241249; Fax: 01865-794449)

and

The David Brown Book Company
PO Box 511, Oakville, CT 06779, USA
(Phone: 860-945-9329; Fax: 860-945-9468)

or from our website

www.oxbowbooks.com

A CIP record for this book is available from the British Library

Library of Congress Cataloging-in-Publication Data

Koine : Mediterranean studies in honor of R. Ross Holloway / edited by Derek B. Counts and Anthony S. Tuck.
   p. cm. -- (Joukowsky Institute publication ; 1)
 From the Joukowsky Institute for Archaeology and the Ancient World, Brown University.
  ISBN 978-1-84217-379-4
 1. Mediterranean Region--Antiquities. I. Counts, Derek B. II. Tuck, Anthony S. III. Holloway, R. Ross, 1934- IV. Brown
University. Artemis A.W. and Martha Sharp Joukowsky Institute for Archaeology and the Ancient World.
  DE60.K65 2009
  938--dc22
                        2009040534

*Cover: Reverse of silver stater (10.82 g) from Cnossus mint (Crete) with stylized representation
of the Labyrinth (ca. 320–270 BC). RISD Museum Inv. No. 40.015.371. Museum of Art, Rhode Island School of Design.
Museum Appropriation Fund. Photography by Erik Gould.*

Printed in Great Britain by
Gomer Press, Llandysul, Wales

Contents

SECTION I: A VIEW OF CLASSICAL ART: ICONOGRAPHY IN CONTEXT

SECTION II: CROSSROADS OF THE MEDITERRANEAN: CULTURAL ENTANGLEMENTS ACROSS THE CONNECTING SEA

SECTION III: COINS AS CULTURE: ART AND COINAGE FROM SICILY

SECTION IV: DISCOVERY AND DISCOURSE: ARCHAEOLOGY AND INTERPRETATION

Acknowledgements

This genesis of this volume can be traced back to a late night conversation on a snow-covered porch in South Boston in January of 2005. Gainfully employed and established in the field, we set ourselves to the task of honoring our mutual advisor at Brown's Center for Old World Archaeology and Art, R. Ross Holloway.

As anyone who has ventured into the abyss of edited volumes can attest, a project such as this can only be realized through the diligence of colleagues. In that regard, we were particularly fortunate to have a patient and attentive group of contributors who rode the ebb and flow of progress without complaint and responded to our inquiries promptly. We take this opportunity to thank them for their contributions.

We have benefited from the help of numerous people over the last several years, all of whom provided essential help in preparing, assembling, and producing this volume. The patient, insightful guidance of the editorial staff of Oxbow Books, including Ian Stevens, Val Lamb, Clare Litt and David Brown, has been deeply appreciated. The Joukowsky Institute for Archaeology and the Ancient World provided generous financial support for the project and we are pleased to see this volume appear as the first in the Institute's newly constituted monograph series; we especially thank Professors John Cherry, editor of the monograph series, and Sue Alcock, director of the JIAAW for their interest in the project and efforts to see it to completion. In addition, we thank the anonymous reviewers whose suggestions and comments added considerable strength to the volume.

The onerous task of editing the volume would not have been possible if not for the assistance and talents of Julia Gaviria, Jennifer Mimno, Katherine P. Iselin, Nevin, Lisa Marie Smith, Elisabetta Cova, and Michele Kunitz. The cover image, from the fine collections of ancient art housed in the Museum of Art of the Rhode Island School of Design, was generously provided by Gina Borromeo, with the assistance of Melody Ennis.

We would also like to thank the University of Wisconsin-Milwaukee Department of Art History and the University of Massachusetts Amherst Department of Classics, as well as our respective Deans, for constant academic and financial support throughout this project.

Finally, we recognize the unwavering support of our respective families and proudly dedicate the volume to our children, who provided both levity and laughter along the way.

About the Editors

Derek B. Counts is Associate Professor of Classical Art and Archaeology in the Department of Art History at the University of Wisconsin-Milwaukee. Under the mentorship and guidance of R. Ross Holloway, he received his Ph.D. in Old World Archaeology and Art from Brown University; he holds additional degrees in Classics from Davidson College (A.B.) and the University of Georgia (M.A.). Counts is Associate Director of the Athienou Archaeological Project at the site of Athienou-*Malloura* in Cyprus, where he has been excavating for the last fifteen years. He has published extensively on the archaeology of cult in Cyprus and the eastern Mediterranean during the first millennium BCE, with a particular emphasis on Cypriote votive sculpture and its associated iconography. His current research explores divine representation in Cypriote sanctuaries. At present, he is preparing a monograph that considers the intersection of cult and cultural identity in the formation of communities using a broad theoretical model largely informed by postcolonial critiques of culture contact. His research and excavations have been funded by the National Endowment for the Humanities and the National Science Foundation and he serves on the editorial boards of the *Bulletin of the American Schools of Oriental Research* and the *Cahier du Centre d'Études Chypriotes*.

Anthony S. Tuck is Assistant Professor of Classical Archaeology in the Department of Classics at the University of Massachusetts Amherst. He received his Ph.D. from Brown University under the direction of R. Ross Holloway, studying issues related to Etruscan burial practices. Today, Tuck is the Director of excavations at the site of Poggio Civitate, an Etruscan site spanning the dynamic years of the 8th through 6th centuries BCE. He publishes on range of issues related to the social development and burial practices of the Iron Age and early Etruscan periods and recently completed a volume examining the tombs of the necropolis of Poggio Civitate, Poggio Aguzzo. He also supervised the construction of a comprehensive, publically available digital archive of all materials related to the history of excavations at Poggio Civitate. In addition to his work in early Italy, he also studies the ancient phenomenon of songs that encode information related to patterns in textile production of Central Asia and Western Europe. His is a co-founder of the University of Massachusetts Amherst's Center for Etruscan Studies and is the Co-Editor of the on-line journal, *Rasenna*. He also serves on the advisory board of the Etruscan Foundation and on the editorial board of the Foundation's journal, *Etruscan Studies*.

List of Contributors

Susan Heuck Allen earned an A.B. in History from Smith College and an M.A. and Ph.D. in Classical Archaeology from the University of Cincinnati and Brown University, respectively. She teaches at Smith College and is a visiting Scholar at Brown University. She has excavated in Greece, Cyprus, and Israel and swam the Hellespont, from Asia to Europe in 1997. She chairs the Archives and the Women in Archaeology Committees of the Archaeological Institute of America. Her research focuses on the history of archaeology and the classical tradition. In 1999, she published *Finding the Walls of Troy* (University of California Press); an edited volume, *Excavating Our Past* (AIA, 2002), examines the history of the AIA. Other areas of research concern the Hellespont through history, pioneering American women in archaeology, and American archaeologists of the OSS Greek Desk in World War II, the subject of her next book.
Susan_Heuck_Allen@.brown.edu

Carmen Arnold-Biucchi is curator of numismatic collections at the Harvard Art Museum and Lecturer on the Classics. Previously she worked for the Editorial Center of the *Lexikon Iconographicum Mythologiae Classicae* in Basle, Switzerland and for many years was the Margaret Thompson curator of Greek coins at The American Numismatic Society in New York. Her publications include entries for the *LIMC*, articles on Sicilian and Hellenistic numismatics, *The Randazzo Hoard 1980 and Sicilian Chronology* (Numismatic Studies 18, New York, 1990), *Alexander's Coins and Alexander's Image* (Cambridge, MA 2006).

Harvard Art Museum, Arthur M. Sackler Museum Department of Ancient and Byzantine Art and Numismatics, 12 Quincy Street Cambridge, MA 02138
biucchi@fas.harvard.edu

Barbara A. Barletta is a Professor of Ancient Art History at the University of Florida. She has long been interested in the Greeks of southern Italy and Sicily. Her first book, *Ionic Influence in Archaic Sicily: The Monumental Art* was published by Studies in Mediterranean Archaeology (Paul Åströms Förlag, 1983). Since then, she has continued to explore both sculpture and architecture in this region. Her second book, *The Origins of the Greek Architectural Orders* (Cambridge University Press, 2001), examined architecture in a regional manner, but throughout the Greek world. More recently, she has focused on fifth-century Athens and is currently working on the publication of the Temple of Athena at Sounion.

School of Art and Art History P.O. Box 115801 University of Florida Gainesville, FL 32611
barletta@ufl.edu

Malcolm Bell, III is Professor Greek Art and Archaeology at the University of Virginia. He has served as Professor-in-charge at the American Academy in Rome, as Andrew W. Mellon Professor at the Center for Advanced Study in the Visual Arts at the National Gallery of Art, and since 1980 as director or co-director of the U.S. excavations at Morgantina in Sicily. He has written on Greek painting, sculpture, and architecture, and maintains an interest in Greek terracottas. He is preparing studies of the agora and city plan of Morgantina, and of Thomas Jefferson's collaboration with Benjamin Henry Latrobe in the designing of the University of Virginia.

433 North First Street Charlottesville, VA 22902
mb2s@virginia.edu

Larissa Bonfante is Professor Emerita of Classics, at New York University. She is the editor of *Etruscan Life and Afterlife* (Wayne State University Press, 1986) and *The World of Roman Costume* (University of Wisconsin Press, 1994). Her publications also include *Etruscan Mirrors in the Metropolitan Museum of Art* (L'Erma di Bretschneider, 1997), *Etruscan Myths* (University of Texas Press, 2006), and the forthcoming *Images and Translations, Greek, Etruscan and Barbarian* (The Jerome Lectures). With her father, the linguist Giuliano Bonfante, she is the author of *The Etruscan Language. An Introduction* (second edition, Manchester University Press, 2002). She is a member of the Istituto di Studi Etruschi, the Archaeological Institute of America, the German Archaeological Institute, and the American Philosophical Society.

New York University Silver Center #503 New York NY 10003
larissa.bonfante@nyu.edu

Elisabetta Cova is Assistant Professor of Classics in the Department of Foreign Languages and Linguistics at the University of Wisconsin-Milwaukee. She graduated in 'Lettere Classiche' from the University of Bologna (Italy) with a thesis on Roman domestic architecture and received her Master of Philosophy in Archaeology at the University of Cambridge (UK). Her research interests include Pompeii and the Roman *domus;* she is currently working on a monograph on the *alae* of Pompeian houses. She is also a senior staff member of the Athienou Archaeological Project (AAP) in Athienou, Cyprus, where she is charged with the publication of the late Roman/early Byzantine settlement, as well as a small corpus of inscriptions excavated from the sanctuary nearby.

Department of Foreign Languages and Linguistics/Classics, PO Box 413, University of Wisconsin-Milwaukee, Milwaukee, WI 53201
covae@uwm.edu

Owen Doonan is Associate Professor of Art History at California State University, Northridge. Doonan is an archaeologist and ancient art historian specializing in the cultures of the Mediterranean and the Black Sea. He focused on early Sicilian Architecture and society in his Ph.D., under Holloway, at Brown University's Center for Old World Archaeology and Art in 1993. He became interested in Turkey and the Black Sea while teaching Archaeology and Art History at Bilkent University in Turkey. Since 1996 he has led the Sinop Regional Archaeological Project, the land survey and excavation component of the Black Sea Trade Project. His book *Sinop Landscapes: Exploring Connection in the Hinterland of a Black Sea Port* was published in 2004 by the University of Pennsylvania Museum Press.

Program in Art History, Art Department, California State University, Northridge, 18111 Nordhoff St., Northridge, CA 91330–8300
owen.doonan@csun.edu

Stephen L. Dyson is Park Professor of Classics at the University at Buffalo and past president of the Archaeological Institute of America. He received a B.A. at Brown University, a Diploma in Classical Archaeology at Oxford, and an M.A. and Ph.D. at Yale. His research areas include the Roman Countryside, the Development of the Roman Frontier, the City of Rome, and the History of Classical Archaeology. His books include *The Creation of the Roman Frontier* (Princeton University Press, 1985), *Community and Society in Roman Italy* (Johns Hopkins University Press, 1992), *Ancient Marbles to American Shores* (University of Pennsylvania Press, 1998), *The Roman Countryside* (Duckworth, 2003), and *In Pursuit of Ancient Pasts* (Yale University Press, 2006).

341 MFAC, Classic Department University at Buffalo Buffalo, N.Y. 14260
cldyson@buffalo.edu

Maria Beatriz Borba Florenzano is Professor of Classical Archaeology at the University of São Paulo, Brazil. She has written on Greek numismatics and on the role of coinage in ancient economies. She is currently engaged in studies of the ancient Greek city and is director of the *Labeca*, laboratory for the study of the ancient city at the Museu de Arqueologia e Etnologia, University of São Paulo, Brazil (www.mae.usp.br/labeca).

Museu de Arqueologia e Etnologia. University of São Paulo, Brazil, Av. Professor Almeida Prado, 1466, Cidade Universitária, 05508–900 S.P., S.P., Brasil
florenza@usp.br

L. Peter Gromet is an Associate Professor in the Department of Geological Sciences at Brown University. He earned a B.S. from SUNY Stony Brook (1972) and a Ph.D. from the California Institute of Technology (1979) in the fields of geology and geochemistry. He became acquainted with the archaeological community through interactions with Frances Van Keuren, and has greatly enjoyed contributing geological and mineralogical observations to marble and limestone provenance determinations. He is delighted to have this opportunity to participate in a volume honoring Brown colleague R. Ross Holloway.

Department of Geological Sciences, Brown University, Providence, RI USA 02906
L_Gromet@brown.edu

Angela Murock Hussein is a consultant for research and publications at the Supreme Council for Antiquities in Egypt. She received her Ph.D. in Old World Archaeology from Brown University in 2004. Her research interests focus on the interregional interaction among the cultures of the Ancient Eastern Mediterranean and North Africa. She taught at a number of Universities and colleges in the Northeast. She is currently on the publication team of the Minoan site of Mochlos, Crete and is pursuing research on Egyptian trade contacts with the Mediterranean.

Supreme Council for Antiquities, 3 El Adl Abu Bakr St., Zamalek, Cairo, Egypt
anginegypt@verizon.net

Martha Sharp Joukowsky is Professor Emerita of Old World Archaeology and Art and Anthropology at Brown University. She is a veteran of 40 years of archaeological fieldwork in Lebanon, Turkey, Greece, Italy, Hong Kong, and currently at the Petra Great Temple, Jordan, which she rediscovered in 1993. She has published 200+ articles and nine books, including the *Petra Great Temple, Volume II, Brown University Excavations 1993–2007* (Petra Exploration Fund, 2007). She was president of the Archaeological Institute of America and vice-president of the American Schools of Oriental Research. Joukowsky has received numerous awards from the World Monuments Fund, the National Science Foundation, Brown University's President's and Rosenberger Medals, and the King Hussein Medal.

5061 Cotton Valley, Christiansted, VI 00820, USA
Martha_Joukowsky@brown.edu

Natalie Kampen recently retired as Barbara Novak Professor of Art History at Barnard College. She completed a Ph.D. in Art History with Ross Holloway and Rolf Winkes at Brown and has taught in the field and in Women's Studies at the University of Rhode Island, and at Barnard College and Columbia University since 1969. Her work has concentrated on the sculpture of the Roman Empire with occasional diversions in the art of other periods in the West. Her most recent book is *Family Fictions in Roman Art* (Cambridge University Press, 2009). She retired in the winter of 2009 and hopes to write on Roman provincial art in the future.

49 Shadow Farm Way Wakefield, RI 02879
nbk6@columbia.edu

John Kenfield is Associate Professor Art History at Rutgers University, where he has taught since 1971. Kenfield received his B.A. in Classics with honors (1966), as one of Holloway's first students. Again following Holloway's lead, Kenfield received graduate training in Classical Archaeology at Princeton University, studying with E. Sjoqvist, K. Weitzman, H. Thompson, D. Thompson, E. Harrison, R. Stillwell and T. Leslie Shear, Jr. His early publications range from an examination of early Greek armor as sculpture to the iconography of the 4th cent. A.D. New Catacomb on the Via Latina in Rome. Kenfield co-directed excavations of a Roman courtyard villa at Castle Copse in Wiltshire and published its mosaics and wall paintings. Kenfield is a recipient of the Rome Prize at the American Academy in Rome. His current research interests include archaic terracotta architectural sculpture at Morgantina and elsewhere.

Department of Art History, Rutgers University, Voorhees Hall, 71 Hamilton Street, New Brunswick, NJ 08901
john.kenfield@gmail.com

Susan S. Lukesh started excavating with Holloway in the early 1970s as a graduate student and continued to work with him on all subsequent excavations up to his retirement. Her interests in pottery and pottery design as well as artifact record keeping informed her subsequent work in record management, image handling and computer efforts in general. Her pursuit of an M.L.S. was specifically driven by evolving scholarly communication, especially how the Internet and digital communication are changing the way the academic community functions. Today she oversees faculty affairs for the Middle East campus of Weill Cornell Medical College in Qatar, a location that allows ready access to parts of the world that have held great interest since graduate school.

susanslukesh@gmail.com

Christofilis Maggidis is the Chr. Roberts Associate Professor of Archaeology at Dickinson College and Field Director/Assistant to the Director of excavations at Mycenae. He received his B.A. from Athens University (Greece) in 1988 and his Ph.D. from the University of Pennsylvania in 1999. From 1997–1999, he was a Postdoctoral Fellow at the Center for Old World Archaeology and Art at Brown University. He is an active field archaeologist with long field experience (Thera, Idaean Cave and Archanes in Crete, Glas, and Mycenae) and has received several honorary distinctions, fellowships, and research grants. His publications comprise fifteen articles in Prehistoric Aegean and Classical archaeology and three forthcoming books. He has presented papers at many international conferences and has given invited lectures all over the world.

Keck Archaeology Lab, Department of Archaeology, 10 Dickinson Ave., P.O. Box 1773, Dickinson College, Carlisle PA 17013, U.S.A.
maggidic@dickinson.edu

Jodi Magness is the Kenan Distinguished Professor for Teaching Excellence in Early Judaism in the Department of Religious Studies at the University of North Carolina at Chapel Hill. She received her B.A. in Archaeology and History from the Hebrew University of Jerusalem and Ph.D. in Classical Archaeology from the University of Pennsylvania. Magness' books include *The Archaeology of Qumran and the Dead Sea Scrolls* (Eerdmans, 2002), *The Archaeology of the Early Islamic Settlement in Palestine* (Eisenbrauns, 2003), *Debating Qumran: Collected Essays on Its Archaeology* (Peeters, 2004), and *Jerusalem Ceramic Chronology circa 200–800 C.E.* (Sheffield Academic Press, 1993). She currently co-directs excavations in the late Roman fort at Yotvata, Israel.

Department of Religious Studies CB #3225 University of North Carolina at Chapel Hill Chapel Hill, NC 27599–3225
magness@email.unc.edu

Clemente Marconi is the James R. McCredie Professor of Greek Art and Archaeology and University Professor at the Institute of Fine Arts of New York University. Among his areas of interest are the Art and Archaeology of Ancient South Italy and Sicily. He is the Director of the Institute of Fine Arts Excavations on the Akropolis of Selinunte. His last two books are *Greek Painted Pottery: Images, Contexts, and Controversies* (Brill, 2004) and *Temple Decoration and Cultural Identity in the Archaic Greek World* (Cambridge University Press, 2007).

Institute of Fine Arts - NYU, 1 East 78th Street, New York, NY 10021
cm135@nyu.edu

Brian E. McConnell is Associate Professor of Art History and Classical Archaeology, Department of Visual Arts & Art History at Florida Atlantic University. He holds degrees in Classical Archaeology from Dartmouth College and Brown University. He has worked extensively in Sicily as an external collaborator of the Soprintendenze at Agrigento and now Catania on projects relating to pre- and proto-historic, Classical, and later antiquity. The present contribution represents a gelling of experience in the Mediterranean and an avid interest in the archaeology of North America, which stems from fieldwork in the territory of Mineo (Catania). At FAU, Dr. McConnell teaches a range of topics that integrate ancient and more recent art, as well as visual and other media.

Department of Visual Arts & Art History, School of the Arts, Dorothy F. Schmidt College of Arts & Letters, Florida Atlantic University, 777 Glades Road, Boca Raton, Florida 33431
mcconnel@fau.edu

Naomi J. Norman is the Editor-in-Chief of the *American Journal of Archaeology* and Associate Professor of Classics in the Department of Classics at the University of Georgia. She is a specialist in Greek architecture and Roman Carthage where she has directed excavations since 1982. Her most recent project is the excavation of the Yasmina cemetery. These projects have focused on the southwest quadrant of the Roman city – an area of the city which is dominated by two public entertainment complexes, the Roman circus and amphitheater – and have enlarged our understanding of that district of the city. She is currently writing a book on the archaeology of Roman Carthage and is working on publishing the results of the Yasmina excavation project.

Department of Classics, Park Hall, University of Georgia, Athens GA 30602–6203
nnorman@uga.edu

Peter Nulton teaches in the Department of the History of Art and Visual Culture at the Rhode Island School of Design. He received his B.A. in Classical Languages and Art History at Fordham University, and completed his doctorate in 2000 under Holloway at the Center for Old World Archaeology at Brown University. His book, *The Sanctuary of Apollo Hypoakraios and Imperial Athens*, was published by the Center for Old World Archaeology and Art in 2003. He is an alumnus of the American School of Classical Studies in Athens and a former Fulbright Fellow.

History of Art and Visual Culture, Rhode Island School of Design, 2 College St., Providence, RI 02903
pnulton@risd.edu

Spencer Pope is an Assistant Professor in the Department of Classics at McMaster University in Hamilton, Ontario. His research interests include Greek Colonization and acculturation in Western Greece, Greek Urbanism and Greek Numismatics. He has excavated in Sicily at Paliké (Rocchicella di Mineo), Il Faraglione on Ustica and at Naxos (Giardini Naxos). He is presently preparing a study of urbanism in colonial and inland Sicily.

Department of Classics, Togo Salmon Hall, McMaster University, 1280 Main Street West, Hamilton, Ontario, L8P 1V3 Canada spope@mcmaster.ca

Keith Rutter is Professor Emeritus and former Head of the Classics Department at the University of Edinburgh before his retirement in 2004. He has published widely on the coinages and history of South Italy and Sicily in the Greek period. His publications include *Campanian Coinages 475–380 BC* (Edinburgh University Press, 1979) and *Greek Coinages of Southern Italy and Sicily* (Spink & Son, 1997). He was editor-in-chief of the Italian volume of the third edition of *Historia Numorum* (British University Press, 2001).

Department of Classics, University of Edinburgh David Hume Tower, Edinburgh EH8 9JX Scotland UK K.Rutter@ed.ac.uk

H. A. Shapiro is the W. H. Collins Vickers Professor of Archaeology and Professor of Classics at Johns Hopkins University. He has been a Fellow of the American School of Classical Studies, the Alexander von Humboldt Foundation, and the John Simon Guggenheim Memorial Foundation. His publications include *Art and Cult under the Tyrants in Athens* (Philipp von Zabern, 1989); *Myth into Art* (Routledge, 1994); and numerous articles on Greek mythology, religion, and iconography. He was most recently co-editor of the exhibition catalogue *Worshiping Women: Ritual and Reality in Classical Athens*, for the Onassis Cultural Center (New York, 2008).

Department of Classics, The Johns Hopkins University, 3400 North Charles St. Baltimore, MD 21218 ashapir1@jhu.edu

Rebecca Sinos is Professor of Classics at Amherst College. She received an A.B. from the College of William and Mary and an M.A. and Ph.D. from the Johns Hopkins University. As a graduate student she spent a year at the American School of Classical Studies at Athens. Since then she has been teaching Greek art and archaeology, Greek and Latin language and literature, Greek history, and Greek mythology. She first met Ross through his generous friendship to Amherst College, where he had studied Classics as an undergraduate. Her research interests include Greek iconography, religion, and vase painting.

Department of Classics AC# 2257, Amherst College P.O. Box 5000, Amherst, MA 01002-5000   rhsinos@amherst.edu

Barbara Tsakirgis is Associate Professor of Classics and Art History at Vanderbilt University where she serves as Chair of the Department of Classical Studies. Tsakirgis received her Ph.D. from Princeton University where she began studying the Hellenistic houses at Morgantina for her dissertation. She has studied houses throughout the Greek world and has written on both their architecture and how the occupants used the domestic space. Her current research is the publication of the houses excavated around the Athenian Agora. Tsakirgis has served on the Governing Board of Archaeological Institute of America and currently sits on the board of the Nashville Parthenon.

Department of Classical Studies, PMB 0092, 230 Appleton Place, Nashville, TN 37203-5721 barbara.tsakirgis@vanderbilt.edu

Frances Van Keuren is Professor of Art History in the Lamar Dodd School of Art at the University of Georgia. She received her A.B. in Greek, with a Latin minor, from Vassar College in 1968. In 1973, she was the first student to receive a Ph.D. in Classical Archaeology with R. Ross Holloway as her dissertation director. Throughout her graduate studies and her professional career, he has been an unfailing supporter and friend, suggesting her dissertation topic of the frieze from the Hera I temple at Foce del Sele and other research projects, such as the coinage of Heraclea Lucaniae and the investigation of the marbles of the altars and sarcophagi from the Licinian tomb in Rome.

Lamar Dodd School of Art, 270 River Road, University of Georgia Athens, GA 30602–7676 USA   Fvankeur@aol.com

Rudolf Winkes is Professor Emeritus of Classical Archaeology, History of Art and Architecture, and Old World Archaeology and Art at Brown University. Winkes is co-founder of the former Center for Old World Archaeology and Art. His areas of expertise include Roman portraiture, Greek sculpture, portraiture, Roman painting, and Greek & Roman crafts, the impact of Greek and Roman culture on later periods and the art of emerging Christianity. He has previously directed excavations on the island of Corfu and is currently working at the Celtic-Roman site of Tongobriga, a Portuguese National Monument. His publications include *Roman Paintings and Mosaics, Museum of Art, Rhode Island School of Design* (Providence, 1982); *Livia, Octavia, Iulia - Porträts und Darstellungen* (Louvain, 1995); and *Kerkyra, Small finds from the Palaiopolis* (Providence, 2004).

Joukowsky Institute for Archaeology and the Ancient World Box, 1837 70 Waterman Street Providence, RI 02912 Rudolf_Winkes@brown.edu

The Making of Archaeology at Brown: A Tribute

Rudolf M. Winkes

R. Ross Holloway and I have been colleagues for many decades, through which the field of archaeology has changed dramatically. At the time when we began to teach, archaeology had been taught at Brown University since the mid 19th century, when the Manning Chapel was used as a plaster cast museum. However, there was little growth in the discipline at Brown until Charles Alexander Robinson revived it somewhat with his course on Alexander the Great. Robinson hired Holloway in the hopes of building this field up in the Department of Classics.

I first came to Brown in the fall of 1969 as visiting assistant professor. Holloway, a professor of Classics, was on sabbatical that semester. I was hired by the former Art Department, which had just started an ambitious new graduate program in Art History. As so often is the case in universities, we experienced program rivalries between our departments.

At some point during my visiting semester I walked down College Hill and introduced myself at the Museum of Art at the Rhode Island School of Design. There I met Tony Hackens, a close collaborator of Holloway's (and with whom Holloway founded the monograph series *Archaeologia Transatlantica*), and soon to be mine as well. I finally met Ross the following year. At the time he had just been given some office space for his studies in archaeology, which was on the top floor of the Cabinet building. Coincidentally, the building is next door to 70 Waterman Street, which was to become later the address for Old World Archaeology and Art. At the time most of the Cabinet building housed the University Printing Services, while 70 Waterman St. was the place everybody went to have the Brown ID photos taken in the University Photo Lab.

From the beginning Holloway helped his junior colleagues in the same field. At the time, friction existed between some of the faculty of the two departments of Art History and Classics over where Classical archaeology should be taught. Ironically Holloway, who had a Ph.D. in Art History was in the Classics department, while I, with my Ph.D. in Classical archaeology, resided in Art History. It was not until my tenure came through four and a half years later (making me less vulnerable) that Holloway came to my office in the List Art Building. I will never forget that moment of opportunity, which was to be the spark that brought archaeology into a new age at Brown. Ross said to me: "Now that your tenure is certain, how about getting together?" What a surprise to the two departments!

Holloway soon negotiated a new space at 70 Waterman Street and indicated that there were other rooms available. I asked to have an office there as well, thinking it would benefit the field of Classical archaeology. The art historians wanted me to keep my office at the List Art Building, but I felt that I should follow Ross's example and move to a new space. At the time it seemed to us an important symbol that Classical archaeology at Brown should have the distinct space it deserved as a field. After all, we were only following the example of European institutions, having studied the evolution of our field in the 19th and 20th centuries. We, therefore, began to conquer space at 70 Waterman St. We did so year after year, room by room, with arguments that certain projects needed more space. Professors of Sociology and the Mao Writing Project gradually found happier neighbors in other buildings and archaeology became the sole occupant.

We spent many exhausting hours, days, months, and years using diplomacy and making compromises before being able to create the Center for Classical Archaeology and Art in 1978. Thankfully, a very influential member of the Corporation and lifetime member of the Archaeological Institute of America, John Nicholas Brown, spoke on our behalf at a Corporation meeting. While enhancing archaeology at Brown, Holloway, even more than I, was diligent about keeping some members of the Corporation informed about the growth of the field. Later our annual newsletter was very helpful in that respect.

One might ask: "Why call it a Center?" At the time an Institute at Brown University had to be endowed and could not have academic instructional programs. There were also Programs, but a Program seemed a politically unwise choice, since Programs were mostly structures within and under the authority of departments. A Center, however, could have several programs and was independent. We first began to create a graduate program within the Center, keenly aware of the fact that we did not have big undergraduate enrollments, which were routinely checked in annual budget conferences. Holloway had known George Parker, who gave us the endowment. We sat down and planned how we could make the utmost use out of it; naturally hoping that one day Parker might continue with other endowments. We, therefore, created the Parker Visiting Scholar Program. It brought many scholars to campus, which turned out to be of greatest benefit for the new graduate program as it made us friends with academics in many countries. We had visitors from North America, as well as various countries in Europe and the Mediterranean; the atmosphere could not have been more international. We created exchanges with institutions in numerous countries and on three continents. When we started our graduate program, we also created our colloquia series; most of the speakers were (due to lack of funds) the graduate students who were made to talk about their dissertation projects. We also brought the graduate students under the same roof with the professors. Before its renovation, 70 Waterman St. consisted of an oblong downstairs space. This space was later turned into a lobby and the secretarial office. Here the students had their old metal desks and ugly plastic chairs, which Holloway and I bought in old warehouses and carried over by ourselves. And there was that infamous day, when a graduate student jumped up scared by a vermin and we had to call the exterminator to remove the rats.

We created the Center thanks to the support of a group of friends, despite reservations by some in the Development Office. We organized an inaugural meal as a thank you for these friends. Now some academics would take the opportunity to spend money in an elegant restaurant. We believed that we were much smarter, since donors prefer to give for the benefit of graduate students and not the bellies of professors. We therefore staged a catered dinner in the old building with tables with white linen cloths and nice plates. The event took place in the most run down room of the building. We could not have planned the miraculous result of this dinner any better: the mother of an important member of the Corporation was seated next to an administrator. Flakes of paint fell from the decrepit ceiling onto her plate. She looked up and told the administrator that he must do something to improve the state of this building. He promised he would.

The next milestone in the history of the Center was when Holloway returned from a trip to New York, having met a couple that had great interest in Brown, especially in its archaeology. Arte and Martha Joukowsky had both studied and subsequently met at Brown. Martha was a very successful archaeologist who was teaching a course on methods of fieldwork at Hunter College and had excavated at various sites and published on methods of excavation. Soon after, we invited her to come and give a talk. One thing led to another and soon Martha was commuting and teaching the fieldwork methods course at Brown. This course became enormously popular campus-wide with incredibly long waiting lists. The Brown President also took keen interest in the Joukowskys, but for him archaeology was

not as high a priority as for us. Seeing the support we received he started to call us a "white elephant." Unfortunately, the president stepped in on one occasion to prevent the "white elephant" Center from receiving an endowment from a member of the Corporation as the money was, according to him, more needed in other areas.

When Arte Joukowsky retired from his business, he and Martha decided to move to Providence. With Martha employed as full time faculty member and Arte as member of the Corporation, they both became intensely involved with Brown. They have done so much for so many in the university community. In order to recognize Martha's particular expertise and contributions we changed the name of the Center from Classical to Old World Archaeology and Art. The Joukowsky Foundation paid for the renovation of 70 Waterman St. Ross and I took turns that summer to ensure that one of us was always present during the entire construction project so that everyone's expectations were met. The Joukowskys also generously funded graduate student summer travel, dissertation support, and excavations. What were in the beginning annual contributions soon became an endowment, which did so much good for so many years for numerous people.

As our program grew, so did our library. Holloway had already worked hard on building up the archaeological collection. When I came to Brown, there was a substantial library for Classical archaeology due to acquisitions going back many generations. The History of Art had been given a huge library allocation in order to build up the new program. At the time, it was common in most departments for professors to mark books in antique book catalogues for acquisition and these catalogues were circulated in departments. Some of our colleagues in both departments were not as eager as we were to do this extra work. Taking advantage of this opportunity allowed for archaeology books to be bought in abundance. Ross enticed his friend Billy Mayer to give us money for books; I was able to acquire the library of my Ph.D. advisor Walter Gross for very little money for Brown. Ross's numismatic friend Albert Harkness and some others donated valuable coins collections, while I managed a similar result with the late Captain Lewis on Block Island. Harkness' friend John Slocum also gave us a valuable collection of coin catalogues. Thus the story of building up the field went on.

After Martha retired, the Joukowskys endowed all of what existed and more in the most generous of terms. Archaeology at Brown is now far beyond our wildest dreams. Oue home at 70 Waterman St. has been replaced with a new home in Rhode Island Hall on the main campus, now called the Artemis A.W. and Martha Sharp Joukowsky Institute for Archaeology and the Ancient World.

On a personal note, I was a beneficiary of Ross's presence in my life. For years we usually began our days in his office. Here we walked and talked about the fields of archaeology.

It has been a wonderful journey with a colleague who can talk about the turtles on Aeginetan coins, inscriptions on the Acropolis (he studied after all with Raubitschek), Greek vases, grandfather Parthenon, the Parthenon frieze and its relationship to the Erechtheion, Alexander, Hieron, the tombs of the princes of Troy, the princes on the Ara Pacis, Aegean trade or the Arch of Constantine, early Rome and the Etruscans; Ross has always been very eager and excited to share his thoughts long before publishing them. So many colleagues all over the world have recognized R. Ross Holloway and in our generation he remains the first and only archaeologist at Brown who received the Gold Medal of the Archaeological Institute of America.

Curriculum vitae of R. Ross Holloway

Elisabetta Cova

Education and Degrees

The Roxbury Latin School, diploma magna cum laude, 1952
A.B., summa cum laude, Amherst College, 1956
M.A., University of Pennsylvania, 1957
M.A. and Ph.D., Princeton University, 1960
M.A., ad eundem gradum, Brown University, 1969
L.H.D., Honoris Causa, Amherst College, 1976
Doctor Philosophiae et Litterarum Honoris Causa, Catholic University of Louvain, 1997

Teaching and Professional Positions

Princeton University (1963), Visiting Assistant Professor of Art and Archaeology
University of North Carolina, Chapel Hill (1963–1964), Assistant Professor of Classics and Archaeology
Brown University (1964–2006), Assistant Professor of Classics, 1964–1967, Associate Professor of Classics 1967–1969, Professor of Central Mediterranean Archaeology, 1970–2006, Elisha Benjamin Andrews Professor, 1990–2006, Director, Center for Old World Archaeology and Art, 1978–87, 1994–2000
International Center for Numismatic Studies, Naples, Italy (1980–1986), President
American Academy in Rome (2005), Professor in Charge of the School of Classical Studies

Academic Honors and Lectureships

Phi Beta Kappa, 1955
Rome Prize Fellowship, American Academy in Rome, 1960
Fellow of the American Academy in Rome, 1962
Charles Eliot Norton Lecturer, Archaeological Institute of America, 1989–90
Gold Medal for Distinguished Archaeological Achievement, Archaeological Institute of America, 1995
John and Penelope Biggs Resident in the Classics, Washington University, St. Louis, 1997
Elected Memberships in Learned Societies
Sodalizio tra Studiosi dell'Arte, Rome, Socio Effettivo, 1962
Deutsches Archäologisches Institut, Korrespondierendes Mitglied, 1967
American Numismatic Society, Fellow, 1979
Royal Numismatic Society, London, Fellow, 1984
Société royale de numismatique de Belgique, membre honoraire, 1985
Istituto Italiano di Preistoria e Protostoria, Socio Straniero, 1986
Istituto Nazionale di Studi Etruschi ed Italici, Florence, Socio Straniero, 1995

Editorial Work

Editorial Board, *Journal of Field Archaeology*, 1974–1994
Editorial Board, *American Journal of Archaeology*, 1985–1994

General Editor

Catalogue of the Classical Collection (Rhode Island School of Design. Museum of Art)
  Classical Sculpture, by B. S. Ridgway (1972).
  Classical Bronzes, by D. G. Mitten (1975).
  Classical Jewelry, by T. Hackens (1976).
  Classical Vases: Excluding Attic Black-figure, Attic Red-figure and Attic White Ground, by A. H. Ashmead and K. M. Phillips, Jr. (1976),
  Roman Paintings and Mosaics, by R. Winkes (1982).
  Ancient Greek Coins, by R. R. Holloway (1998).

Co-Editor (with T. Hackens) and Editor (after 1998)

Archaeologia Transatlantica: A Series in Mediterranean Archaeology
  1. *Italy and the Aegean, 3000–7000 B.C.*, by Ross Holloway (1981).
  2. *Crossroads of the Mediterranean*, edited by T. Hackens, N. D. Holloway, and R. R. Holloway (1984).
  3. *Prehistoric Aphrodisias*, by M. S. Joukowsky, and others (1986).
  4. *Les statuettes anthropomorphes crétoises en bronze et en plomb, du IIIe millénaire au VIIe siècle av. J.-C.*, by C. Verlinden (1984).
  5. *The Age of Augustus*, edited by R. Winkes (1985).
  6. *Inscriptions inédites relatives à l'histoire et aux cultes de Rhodes au IIe et au Ier s. av. J.-C.: Rhodiaka*, by V. Kontorini (1983).
  7. *Love for Antiquity: Selections from the Joukowsky Collection*, edited by R. Winkes and T. Hackens (1985).
  8. *Le bâtiment de scène des théâtres d'Italie et de Sicil: étude chronologique et typologique*, by C. Courtois (1989).
  9. *L'Égée et la Méditerranée orientale à la fin du deuxième millénaire: témoignages archéologiques et sources écrites*, by J. Vanschoonwinkel (1991).
  10. *The Greek Geometric Warrior Figurine: Interpretation and Origin*, by Michael Byrne (1991).
  11. *The Age of Pyrrhus*, edited by T. Hackens and others (1992).
  12. *La Muculufa II*, by B. E. McConnell and others (1995).
  13. *Livia, Octavia, Iulia: Porträts und Darstellungen*, by R. Winkes (1995).

14. *Ustica I*, by R. R. Holloway, S. S. Lukesh, and others (1995).
15. *Ancient Greek Coins*, by R. R. Holloway (1998).
16. *Myth, Sexuality and Power: Images of Jupiter in Western Art*, edited by F. Van Keuren (1998).
17. *Interpretatio Rerum: Archaeological Essays on Objects and Meaning by students of R. R. Holloway*, edited by S. S. Lukesh (1999).
18. *Miscellanea Mediterranea*, edited by R. R. Holloway (2000).
19. *Ustica II*, by R. R. Holloway and S. S. Lukesh (2001)
20. *The Villa of Livia ad Gallinas Albas: A Study in the Augustan Villa and Garden*, by J. C. Reeder (2001).
21. *The Sanctuary of Apollo Hypoakraios and Imperial Athens*, by P. E. Nulton (2003).
22. *Samnium: Settlement and Cultural Change*, edited by H. Jones (2004).

Bibliography

A note on the bibliography: publications have been grouped according to four broad categories: I. Field archaeology; II. Ancient art and architecture; III. Numismatics; and IV. Roman history. Within each category, references have been divided into (A) books and monographs and (B) articles and notes, and listed in chronological order.

I. Field Archaeology

IA. BOOKS AND MONOGRAPHS, INCLUDING FINAL PUBLICATIONS

(1970a) *Satrianum: The Archaeological Investigations Conducted by Brown University in 1966 and 1967*. Providence, Brown University Press.

(1973a) *Buccino: The Eneolithic Necropolis of San Antonio and Other Prehistoric Discoveries Made by Brown University in 1968 and 1969*. Rome, De Luca.

(1975a) Buccino: the Early Bronze Age Village of Tufariello, with N. P. Nabers, S. S. Lukesh, E. R. Eaton, N. B. Hartmann, G. Barker, H. McKerrall, W. L. Phippen, and G. Leuci. *Journal of Field Archaeology* 2, 11–81.

(1981a) *Italy and the Aegean, 3000–700* B.C. Louvain-la-Neuve, Institut supérieur d'archéologie et d'histoire de l'art, Collège Erasme. Archaeologia Transatlantica 1.

(1984a) *Crossroads of the Mediterranean*, with T. Hackens and N. D. Holloway (eds.). Providence and Louvain-la-Neuve, Center for Old World Archaeology and Art, Brown University and Institut supérieur d'archéologie et d'histoire de l'art, Collège Erasme. Archaeologia Transatlantica 2.

(1990a) *Rome's Alpine Frontier. Proceedings of the Conference Held at the Center for Old World Archaeology and Art, Brown University, Providence, Rhode Island, September 27th 1986.* (ed.) Providence, Art and Archaeology Publications.

(1990b) *La Muculufa, The Early Bronze Age Sanctuary: The Early Bronze Age Village (Excavations of 1982 and 1983)*, with M. S. Joukowsky, J. Léon and S. S. Lukesh. Providence, Center for Old World Archaeology and Art, Brown University. Reprint of *Revue des archéologues et historiens d'art de Louvain* 23 (1990), 11–67.

(1991a) *The Archaeology of Ancient Sicily*. London, Routledge. Italian trans. *Archeologia della Sicilia Antica*. Turin, Società

Editrice Internazionale (1995). Second English edition (2000) London, Routledge.

(1994a) *The Archaeology of Early Rome and Latium*. London, Routledge.

(1994b) *The Age of Pyrrhus. Proceedings of an International Conference Held at Brown University April 8th–10th, 1988*, with T. Hackens, N. D. Holloway, G. Moucharte (eds.). Providence and Louvain-la-Neuve, Center for Old World Archaeology and Art, Brown University and Institut supérieur d'archéologie et d'histoire de l'art, Collège Erasme. Archaeologia Transatlantica 11.

(1995a) *La Muculufa II: Excavation and Survey of the Regione Siciliana, Soprintendenza ai Beni Culturali ed Ambientali di Agrigento in Collaboration with Brown University* by B. E. McConnell and other contributors, with T. Hackens (eds.). Providence and Louvain-la-Neuve, Center for Old World Archaeology and Art, Brown University and Institut supérieur d'archéologie et d'histoire de l'art, Collège Erasme. Archaeologia Transatlantica 12.

(1995b) *Ustica I: The Results of the Excavations of the Regione Siciliana Soprintendenza ai Beni Culturali ed Ambientali Provincia di Palermo in Collaboration with Brown University in 1990 and 1991*, with S. S. Lukesh and other contributors. Providence and Louvain-la-Neuve, Center for Old World Archaeology and Art, Brown University and Institut supérieur d'archéologie et d'histoire de l'art, Collège Erasme. Archaeologia Transatlantica 14.

(2001a) *Ustica II: The Results of the Excavations of the Regione Siciliana, Soprintendenza ai Beni Culturali ed Ambientali Provincia di Palermo in collaboration with Brown University in 1994 and 1999*, with S. S. Lukesh. Providence, Center for Old World Archaeology and Art, Brown University. Archaeologia Transatlantica 19.

IB. ARTICLES AND NOTES

IB1. MORGANTINA

(1963a) A tomb group of the fourth century B. C. from the area of Morgantina. *American Journal of Archaeology* 67, 289–91.

IB2. ATHENS

(1966a) Exploration of the Southeast Stoa in the Athenian Agora. *Hesperia* 35, 79–85.

(1966b) Music at the Panathenaic festival. *Archaeology* 19, 112–19.

IB3. SATRIANUM

(1967a) Excavations at Satrianum, 1966. *American Journal of Archaeology* 71, 59–62.

(1968) Excavations at Satrianum, 1967. *American Journal of Archaeology* 72, 119–20.

(1971a) Torre di Satriano. In D. Adameseanu (ed.) *Popoli anellenici in Basilicata*, 92–95. Naples, La buona stampa.

IB4. BUCCINO

(1969a) Excavations at Buccino: 1969. *American Journal of Archaeology* 73, 199–200.

(1970b) Excavations at Buccino: 1970. *American Journal of Archaeology* 74, 145–48.

(1971b) Excavations at Buccino: 1971. *American Journal of Archaeology* 75, 151–54.

(1973b) Excavations at Buccino: 1973. *American Journal of Archaeology* 77, 411–12.

(1973c) The Eneolithic necropolis of San Antonio, Buccino (Italy). In M. V. Garasanin, A. Benac, and N. Tasic (eds.) *Actes du VIII Congrès International des Science Préhistoriques et Protohistoriques, 1971*, 428–31. Belgrade, Union internationale des sciences préhistoriques et protohistoriques.

(1974a) Excavations at Buccino: 1974. *American Journal of Archaeology* 78, 156–57.

(1974b) Buccino. In G. B. Modesti, B. d'Agostino and P. Gastaldi (eds.) *Seconda Mostra della Preistoria e della Protostoria nel Salernitano*, 43–49. Salerno, P. Laveglia.

(1974c) The sanctuary at San Mauro, Buccino. *American Journal of Archaeology* 78, 25–32.

(1975b) Excavations at Buccino: 1975. *American Journal of Archaeology* 79, 371–72.

(1976a) Ricerche preistoriche a Buccino (Salerno). In *Atti della XVII Riunione Scientifica dell' Istituto Italiano di Preistoria e Protostoria*, 141–50. Florence, Istituto italiano di preistoria e protostoria.

(1976b) Gaudo and the east. *Journal of Field Archaeology* 3, 143–58.

IB5. TRENTINARA

(1978a) Trentinara, an Apennine site near Paestum, with S. S. Lukesh and N. P. Nabers. *Journal of Field Archaeology* 5, 133–44.

IB6. LA MUCULUFA

(1983a) Primi saggi di scavo a La Muculufa, Butera. *Sicilia Archeologica* 6, 33–44.

(1984–1985) Scavi archeologici del periodo castellucciano a 'La Muculufa' (Butera). *Kokalos* 30–31, 483–88.

(1985a) La Muculufa: un santuario-villaggio della prima età del bronzo. *Orizzonte Sicilia* 6, 20–26.

(1986a) Scavi archeologici a La Muculufa e premesse per lo studio della cultura castellucciana. In N. Bonacasa and G. Castellana (eds.) *Atti della Seconda Giornata di Studi sull'Archeologia Licatese e della Zona della Bassa Valle dell'Himera, 1985*, 69–90. Licata, Soprintendenza ai beni archeologici Agrigento.

(1988a) Mining La Muculufa, with M. S. Joukowsky and S. S. Lukesh. *Archaeology* 41, 40–47.

(1996a) La Muculufa: un centro sul fiume Salso e il suo raggio di contatti, with S. S. Lukesh, L. Maniscalco and B. E. McConnell. In D. C. Genick, *L'antica età del bronzo in Italia. Atti del Congresso Nazionale, Viareggio, 9–12 gennaio 1995*, 291–303. Florence, Octavo.

IB7. USTICA

(1991b) Ustica: report on the excavations of the Bronze Age site of Faraglioni, 1990, with S. S. Lukesh. *Archäologischer Anzeiger*. 359–65.

(1991c) Ustica: rinvenimento di una scultura della media età del bronzo. *Sicilia Archeologica* 24, 81–85.

(1991d) Ustica, località Faraglioni: villaggio della media età del bronzo. In *Di terra in terra: nuove scoperte archeologiche nella provincia di Palermo*, 186–94. Palermo, Museo archeologico regionale di Palermo.

(1992a) Ustica: report on the excavations of the Bronze Age site of Faraglioni, 1991, with S. S. Lukesh. *Archäologischer Anzeiger*, 553–60.

(1993a) Bronze casting molds from Ustica. *Archivio per l'Antropologia e l'Etnologia* 123, 379–90.

(1993b) Ustica: the development of a middle Bronze Age town in the Tyrrhenian basin. *Journal of Ancient Topography* 3, 7–16.

(1993c) Gettoni in terracotta provenienti dagli scavi di Ustica. *Rivista Italiana di Numismatica e Scienze Affini* 95, 189–91.

(1993d) Ustica, I Faraglioni. Le mura dell'insediamento della media età del bronzo, with C. Gifford. *Quaderni dell'Istituto di Archeologia della Facoltà di Lettere e Filosofia dell'Università di Messina* 8, 5–9.

(1993–1994) Ustica, località Faraglioni: villaggio della media età del bronzo. Campagne di scavo 1990 e 1991. *Kokalos* 39–40, 1177–781.

(1996b) Ustica: report on the excavations of the Bronze Age site of Faraglioni, 1994, with S. S. Lukesh. *Archäologischer Anzeiger*. 1–6.

(1997a) Ustica. *Enciclopedia dell'arte antica*, Supp. 2 1971–1994. Rome. 914–15.

(1997b) Ustica, località Faraglioni: perchè castello? with S. S. Lukesh. In *Archeologia e Territorio*, 455–60. Palermo, G. B. Palumbo.

(2000a) Ustica: report on the excavations of the Bronze Age site of I Faraglioni, 1999, with S. S. Lukesh. Uploaded February 2000, http://brown.edu/Departments/Joukowsky_Institute/resources/papers/ustica/report.html.

(2002) The non-fraud of the Middle Bronze Age stone goddess from Ustica: a reverse Piltdown hoax, with S. S. Lukesh. *Antiquity* 76, 4–8.

(2003a) Ustica: il castello della media età del bronzo in località "I Faraglioni." In *Atti della XXXV Riunione Scientifica, 2000*, 239–46. Florence, Istituto italiano di preistoria e protostoria.

(2009) Domestic and ritual meals at Ustica. In D. Palermo, A. Pautasso and M. Cultraro (eds.) *Cibo per gli uomini cibo per gli dei. Archeologia del pasto rituale. Atti della Riunione Scientifica (Piazza Armerina, 4–8 maggio 2005)*. Padua, Ausilio Editore.

IB8. OTHER

(1971c) Archaeological news from south Italy. *American Journal of Archaeology* 75, 75–81.

(1974d) Exploration of inland southern Italy. *Journal of Field Archaeology* 1, 67–80.

(1980a) The later prehistory of the Italian peninsula. *Journal of Field Archaeology* 7, 353–57.

(1982a) The princely burial of Roscigno (Monte Pruno), Salerno with N. P. Nabers. *Revue des archéologues et historiens d'art de Louvain* 15, 97–163.

(1983b) Archaeology as a discipline. *Journal of Field Archaeology* 10, 387–88.

(1985b) Synoicism in Bronze Age Sicily. In C. Malone and S. Stoddart (eds.) *Patterns in Protohistory, Papers in Italian Archaeology* 4, 389–98. Oxford, British Archaeological Reports, International Series 245.

(1988b) Saxa loquuntur. In A. Stazio and R. Vitale (eds.) *Un secolo di ricerche in Magna Grecia. Atti del ventottesimo convegno di studi sulla Magna Grecia*, 423–25. Taranto, Istituto per la storia e l'archeologia della Magna Grecia.

(1989a) Un vase castellucien au musée de Princeton, with S. S. Lukesh. *L'Anthropologie* 93, 317–20.

(1990c) The geography of the southern Sicels. In J.-P. Descoeudres (ed.) *EUMOUSIA: Ceramic and Iconographic Studies in Honour of Alexander Cambitoglou* (Mediterranean Archaeology Supp. 1), 147–54. Sydney, Meditarch.

(1990d) Koine and commerce in the Sicilian Bronze Age. *Mediterranean Historical Review* 5, 3–13.

(1992b) Italy and the central Mediterranean in the crisis years. In W. A. Ward and M. S. Joukowsky (eds.) *The Crisis Years: the 12th Century B.C.*, 40–45. Dubuque, Kendall/Hunt Publishers.

(1993e) Koine e commercio nell'età del bronzo siciliano. In *Storia e Archeologia della Media e Bassa Valle dell'Himera. Atti della Terza Giornata di Studi sull'Archeologia Licatese e della Zona della Bassa Valle dell'Himera*, 45–52. Palermo, Soprintendenza ai beni archeologici Agrigento.

(1993f) Where did the Greeks learn to write? with N. D. Holloway. *Archaeological News* 18, 1–5.

(1993g) Aedes Minervae in Foro Boario. *Revista do Museu de Arqueologia e Etnologia* 3, 97–103.

(1994–95) Cneve Tarchunies Rumach. *Classica* 7–8, 101–10.

(1999a) *La cité antique* of Fustel de Coulanges and its modern critics. *Revue des Archéologues et Historiens d'art de Louvain* 32, 2–5.

(2000b) The classical Mediterranean, its prehistoric past and the formation of Europe. Uploaded, February 2000, http://brown.edu/Departments/Joukowsky_Institute/resources/papers/classicalmed/report.html.

(2001b) Nuragic tower models and ancestral memory. *Memoirs of the American Academy in Rome* 46, 1–9.

(2005a) Urbanism, Etruscan, Italic and Latin in the light of recent developments. In P. Attema, A. Nijboer, and A. Zifferero (eds.) *Community and Settlements from the Neolithic to the Early Medieval Periods, Papers in Italian Archaeology* 6, 32–36. Oxford, British Archaeological Reports, International Series 1452.1.

(2005b) Fortifications with towers in Bronze age Sicily. In R. Giglia (ed.) *Megalai Nesoi: Studi dedicati a Giovanni Rizza per il suo ottantesimo compleanno*, 299–306. Catania, Consiglio nazionale delle ricerche I.B.A.M.

(2006a) A Castelluccian vase in the Boston Museum of Fine Arts and the problem of the "Proto-Castelluccian" pottery. In *Studi di protostoria in onore di Renato Peroni*, 361–64. Florence, All'insegna del giglio.

II. Ancient Art and Architecture

IIA. BOOKS AND MONOGRAPHS

(1973d) *A View of Greek Art*. Providence, Brown University Press.

(1974e) [reprint] *A View of Greek Art*. New York, Harper Torch Books.

(1975c) *Influences and Styles in the Late Archaic and Early Classical Greek Sculpture of Sicily and Magna Graecia*. Louvain-la-Neuve, Institut supérieur d'archéologie et d'histoire de l'art.

(1998a) *The Hand of Daedalus*. Three lectures delivered at Washington University in St. Louis, MO as the John and Penelope Biggs Resident in Classics. Uploaded December 1999, http://brown.edu/Departments/Joukowsky_Institute/resources/papers/daedalus/index.html.

(2000c) *Miscellanea Mediterranea*, (ed.). Providence, Center for Old World Archaeology and Art, Brown University. Archaeologia Transatlantica 18.

(2004a) *Constantine and Rome*. New Haven and London, Yale University Press.

IIB. ARTICLES AND NOTES

(1958) The date of the Eleusis relief. *American Journal of Archaeology* 62, 403–408.

(1960a) Tindari, last colony of the Sicilian Greeks. *Archaeology* 12, 246–50.

(1963b) Seurat's copies after the antique. *Burlington Magazine* 105, 282.

(1965a) Conventions of Etruscan painting in the Tomb of Hunting and Fishing at Tarquinia. *American Journal of Archaeology* 69, 341–47.

(1966c) Architettura sacra e matematica pitagorica a Paestum. *La Parola del Passato* 21, 60–64.

(1966d) The tomb of Augustus and the princes of Troy. *American Journal of Archaeology* 70, 171–73.

(1966e) The Archaic Acropolis and the Parthenon frieze. *Art Bulletin* 48, 223–26.

(1967b) Panhellenism in the sculptures of the Zeus temple at Olympia. *Greek, Roman and Byzantine Studies* 8, 93–101.

(1969b) Architect and engineer in Archaic Greece. *Harvard Studies in Classical Philology* 80, 281–90.

(1971d) The recutting of the Gorgon metope of Temple C at Selinus. *American Journal of Archaeology* 75, 435–36.

(1972) Il Maestro di Olimpia: la testimonianza dei documenti. *Colloqui del Sodalizio* seconda serie 1, 46–58.

(1973e) Una matrice di testa silenica proveniente dagli scavi di Buccino. *Acta Instituti Romani Regni Sueciae* 32, 143–47.

(1977a) Flying high at Paestum: a reply. *American Journal of Archaeology* 81, 554.

(1979a) La sculpture archaïque dans un livre récent de synthèse: B. S. Ridgway, The Archaic Style in Greek Sculpture, Princeton University Press, 1977. *Revue des archéologues et historiens d'art de Louvain* 12, 199–204.

(1980b) Figure alate e corazzate in Etruria. In *Philias charin. Miscellanea di studi classici in onore di Eugenio Manni*, 1–6. Rome, "L'Erma" di Bretschneider.

(1980c) La canthare d'argent de Roscigno (Monte Pruno, Salerno), with N. P. Nabers. *Aurifex* 1, 64–81.

(1984b) Who's who on the Ara Pacis Augustae. In N. Bonacasa, A. Di Vita, and G. Barone (eds.) *Alessandria e il mondo ellenistico-romano. Studi in onore di Achille Adriani*, 625–28. Rome, "L'Erma" di Bretschneider.

(1985c) Le programme de la décoration sculpturelle du Temple 'C' de Sélinonte. *Revue des archéologues et historiens d'art de Louvain* 17, 7–15.

(1985d) The spolia of the Arch of Constantine. *Quaderni Ticinesi di Numismatica e Antichità Classiche* 14, 261–74.

(1986b) An alabaster kouros in Chicago. *American Journal of Archaeology* 90, 33.

(1986c) The bulls in the Tomb of the Bulls at Tarquinia. *American Journal of Archaeology* 90, 447–52.

(1986d) Selected antiquities from the Navarra Collection, Licata. *Revue des archéologues et historiens de l'art de Louvain* 19, 11–49.

(1987a) Reflections on the Arch of Titus. *L'Antiquité Classique* 55, 183–91.

(1987b) The model of the column of Trajan. *Revue des archéologues et historiens d'art de Louvain* 20 (Hommages à Jazeps Trizna), 63–66.

(1988c) Early Greek architectural decoration as functional art. *American Journal of Archaeology* 92, 177–83.

(1988d) The state of the Severe style: new evidence and old problems. *Quaderni Ticinesi di Numismatica e Antichità Classiche* 17, 55–80.

(1988e) Gli eroi di Riace sono siciliani? *Sicilia Archeologica* 21, 23–30.

(1989–1990) Il cubicolo della villa romana di Boscoreale nel Metropolitan Museum di New York. *Rendiconti della Pontificia Accademia Romana di Archeologia* 62, 105–19.

(1992c) Why korai? *Oxford Journal of Archaeology* 11, 267–74.

(1995c) The Severe style and the Severe style period. In N. Bonacasa (ed.) *Lo stile severo in Grecia e in Occidente. Aspetti e problemi*, 43–47. Rome, "L'Erma" di Bretschneider.

(1998b) An Attic red figure chous with heroes in the Museum of Art, Rhode Island School of Design. In L. H. Lesko (ed.) *Ancient Egyptian and Mediterranean Studies in Memory of William A. Ward*, 129–32. Providence, Dept. of Egyptology, Brown University.

(1998c) Marriage and death: a lebes gamikos by the Pan Painter in Providence. In Frances Van Keuren (ed.) *Myth, Sexuality and Power: Images of Jupiter in Western Art*, 1–8. Providence and Louvain-la-Neuve, Center for Old World Archaeology and Art, Brown University. Archaeologia Transatlantica 16.

(1999b) Peisistratus' House. *Quaderni Ticinesi di Numismatica e Antichità Classiche* 28, 1–13.

(2000d) The Parthenon frieze again. *Quaderni Ticinesi di Numismatica e Antichità Classiche* 29, 1–20.

(2000e) The mutilation of statuary in Classical Greece. In R. R. Holloway (ed.) *Miscellanea Mediterranea*, 77–82. Providence, Center for Old World Archaeology and Art, Brown University. Archaeologia Transatlantica 18.

(2003b) The Arch of Constantine and the emperor's enemies. *O Qui Complexus et Gaudia Quanta Fuerunt. Essays presented to Michael C. J. Putnam by his Brown colleagues on the occasion of his 70th Birthday*, 119–32. Providence: Brown University.

(2003c) Three lekythoi by the Pan Painter in Providence. *Archeologia del Mediterraneo. Studi in onore di Ernesto De Miro*, 401–404. Rome,"L'Erma" di Bretschneider.

(2006b) The Arch of Constantine and the emperor's enemies at Rome. In C. Mattusch, A. Donohue, and A. Brauer (eds.) *Common Ground: Archaeology, Art, Science, and Humanities. Proceedings of the XVIth International Congress of Classical Archaeology, Boston, August 23–26, 2003*, 26–29. Oxford, Oxbow Books.

(2006c) The Tomb of the Diver. *American Journal of Archaeology* 110, 365–88.

(2006d) The development of Etruscan tomb painting to the mid-fifth century B.C. *Ocnus* 14, 143–56.

(2008a) Was Pausanias right concerning Perithoos in the west pediment of the Temple of Zeus at Olympia? In S. E. Thompson and P. Der Manuelian (eds.) *Egypt and Beyond, Essays Presented to Leonard H. Lesko upon his Retirement from the Wilbour Chair of Egyptology at Brown University*, 167–70. Providence, Dept. of Egyptology and Ancient Western Asian Studies, Brown University.

(2008b) The painting of ancient sculpture. *American Journal of Archaeology* 112, 347–51.

(Forthcoming) An unpublished terracotta from the Malophoros sanctuary at Selinus. In *Festschrift für Prof. Dr. Andreas Furtwängler*.

III. Ancient Numismatics

IIIA. BOOKS AND MONOGRAPHS, INCLUDING CATALOGUES

(1960b) *The Elder Turtles of Aegina*. Dissertation, Princeton University.

(1961) *Sylloge Nummorum Graecorum, The Burton Y. Berry Collection*, Part I. Collaborator of Margaret Thompson. New York, American Numismatic Society.

(1969c) *The Thirteen-Months Coinage of Hieronymos of Syracuse*. Berlin, Walter De Gruyter.

(1973f) *Catalogue of the Frederick M. Watkins Collections, Coins*. Fogg Art Museum. Cambridge, Harvard University.

(1977b) Translation of G. Giacosa, *Women of the Caesars*. Bellinzona, Edizioni Arte e Moneta.

(1978b) *Art and Coinage in Magna Graecia*. Bellinzona, Edizioni Arte e Moneta.

(1981b) *Wheaton College Collection of Greek and Roman Coins*, with J. D. Bishop. New York, American Numismatic Society.

(1982b) *The Coinage of Terina*, with G. K. Jenkins. Bellinzona, Edizioni Arte e Moneta.

(1989b) *Ripostigli del museo archeologico di Siracusa*. Rome, Istituto italiano di numismatica.

(1989c) *Morgantina Studies II: The Coins*, with T. V. Buttrey, K. T. Erim, T. Groves. Princeton, Princeton University Press.

(1998d) *Catalogue of the Classical Collection, Museum of Art, Rhode Island School of Design. Ancient Greek Coins*. Providence and Louvain-la-Neuve, Center for Old World, Archaeology and Art, Brown University and Institut supérieur d'archéologie et d'histoire de l'art, Collège Erasme. Archaeologia Transatlantica 15.

IIIB. ARTICLES AND NOTES

(1960c) Numismatic notes from Morgantina II: half coins of Hieron II in the monetary system of Roman Sicily. *American Numismatic Society, Museum Notes* 9, 65–73.

(1961) Monete provenienti dagli scavi di Morgantina e già attribuite ad Hiempsal II. *Annali dell'Istituto Italiano di Numismatica* 8, 35–38.

(1962a) Eagle and fulmen on the coins of Syracuse. *Revue belge de numismatique* 108, 5–28.

(1962b) The crown of Naxos. *American Numismatic Society, Museum Notes* 10, 1–8.

(1964) Damarete's lion. *American Numismatic Society, Museum Notes* 11, 1–11.

(1965b) Monetary circulation in central Sicily to the reign of Augustus as documented by the Morgantina excavations. In

Congresso Internazionale di Numismatica, Rome, 1961, Vol. 2, 135–50. Rome, Istituto italiano di numismatica.

(1969d) Alexander the Molossian and the Attic standard in south Italy. In *La circolazione della moneta ateniese in Sicilia e in Magna Grecia. Atti del 1° convegno del centro internazionale di studi numismatici, Napoli, 1967,* 1231–240. Rome, Istituto italiano di numismatica.

(1969–1970) The bronze coinage of the third Syracusan democracy (344–315 B.C.). *Annali dell'Istituto Italiano di Numismatica* 16–17, 129–42.

(1971e) A hoard of archaic Aiginetan coins from Crete. *American Numismatic Society, Museum Notes* 17, 1–21.

(1973g) Poseidonia-Paestum: relazioni tra monetazione d'argento e monetazione di bronzo. In L. Breglia (ed.) *La monetazione di bronzo di Poseidonia-Paestum. Atti del III Convegno del Centro Internazionale di Studi Numismatici, Napoli 19 - 23 aprile 1971,* 135–48. Rome, Istituto italiano di numismatica.

(1975d) Agyrio, Stiela, Entella, Nakone, Hippana ed Eluntion. In *Le emissioni dei centri siculi fino all'epoca di Timoleonte e i loro rapporti con la monetazione delle colonie greche di Sicilia. Atti del IV Convegno del Centro Internazionale di Studi Numismatici. Napoli, 9–14 aprile 1973,* 133–56. Rome, Istituto italiano di numismatica.

(1977c) La struttura delle emissioni di Siracusa nel periodo dei "signierende Künstler". *Annali dell'Istituto Italiano di Numismatica* 23, 33–38.

(1978c) La ricerca attuale sull'origine della moneta. *Rivista Italiana di Numismatica e Scienze Affini* 80, 7–14.

(1979b) L'inizio della monetazione del bronzo siracusana. In *Le origini della monetazione di bronzo in Sicilia e in Magna Grecia. Atti del VI Convegno del Centro Internazionale di Studi Numismatici, Napoli, 17–22 aprile 1977,* 23–44. Rome, Istituto italiano di numismatica.

(1979c) The bronze coinage of Agathokles. In O. Mørkholm and N. Waggoner (eds.) *Greek Numismatics and Archaeology: Essays in Honor of Margaret Thompson,* 87–95. Wetteren, NR.

(1980–1981) Alexander the Great's choice of coin types. *Annali dell'Istituto Italiano di Numismatica* 26–27, 57–60.

(1981c) Heads and tails. *Odyssey Magazine* 2, 20–21.

(1982c) Il problema dei pegasi in Sicilia. *Quaderni Ticinesi di Numismatica e Antichità Classiche* 11, 129–36.

(1984c) The date of the first Greek coins: some arguments from style and hoards. *Revue belge de numismatique* 130, 5–18.

(1987c) Sostratos Kalos. In *Studi per Laura Bregli* (Supplemento al n. 4, 1987, parte III del *Bollettino di Numismatica*), 9–12. Rome, Istituto Poligrafico e Zecca dello Stato.

(1987d) Tipologia ed arte delle monete di Neapolis. In A. Stazio, M. Taliercio, and V. Zagli (eds.) *La monetazione di Neapolis nella Campania antica. Atti del VII Convegno del Centro Internazionale di Studi Numismatici, Napoli, 20–24 aprile 1980,* 407–12. Naples, Arte tipografica.

(1987e) The coinage production of the Sicilian Greek mints of the sixth and fifth centuries B.C. In G. Depeyrot, T. Hackens, and G. Moucharte (eds.) *Rythmes de la production monétaire, de l'antiquité à nos jours. Actes du colloque international organisé à Paris du 10 au 12 janvier 1986 par la Monnaie de Paris, le Centre National de la Recherche Scientifique et le Séminaire de numismatique Marcel Hoc de l'Université Catholique de Louvain,* 11–20. Louvain: Séminaire de numismatique Marcel Hoc, Collège Érasme.

(1989d) Aes grave brunense. In G. Le Rider (ed.) *Kraay-Mørkholm Essays: Numismatic Studies in Memory of C.M. Kraay and O. Mørkholm,* 69–75. Louvain: Institut supérieur d'archéologie et d'histoire de l'art, séminaire de numismatique Marcel Hoc.

(1990e) Early roman coinage. *Dédalo* 28, 227–43.

(1991e) Syracusan coinage between Dion and Timoleon. *Quaderni Ticinesi di Numismatica e Antichità Classiche* 20, 57–62.

(1992d) The Romano-Campanian coinage. In T. Hackens, N. D. Holloway, R. R. Holloway, and G. Moucharte (eds.) *The Age of Pyrrhus. Proceedings of an International Conference Held at Brown University April 8th-10th, 1988,* 225–36. Providence and Louvain-la-Neuve, Center for Old World Archaeology and Art, Brown University and Institut supérieur d'archéologie et d'histoire de l'art, Collège Erasme. Archaeologia Transatlantica 11.

(1993h) Monete frazionali siracusani del quarto secolo. In A. Stazio, M. T. Mensitieri, and S. Ceccoli (eds.) *La monetazione dell' età dionigiana. Atti dell'VIII Convegno del Centro Internazionale di Studi Numismatici, Napoli 29 maggio-1 giugno 1983,* 325–29. Rome, Istituto Italiano di numismatica.

(1993i) Syracusan bronzes with the legend SURASOSIA. In *Proceedings of the XIth International Congress of Numismatics,* 83–84. Louvain-la Neuve, Association Professeur Marcel Hoc pour l'encouragement des recherches numismatiques.

(1995d) The lady of the denarius. *Quaderni Ticinesi di Numismatica e Antichità Classiche* 24, 207–15.

(1995e) Alcuni aspetti stilistici del quadrigato romano. In M. C. Caltabiano (ed.) *La Sicilia tra l'Egitto e Roma. La monetazione siracusana dell'età di Ierone II. Atti del Seminario di Studi, Messina 2–4 dicembre 1993,* 335–43. Messina, Accademia peloritana dei pericolanti.

(1996c) Further notes on the Early Bronze coinage of Syracuse. In R. G. Doty and T. Hackens (eds.) *Italiam Fato Profvgi Hesperinaque Venerunt Litora. Numismatic Studies Dedicated to Vladimir and Elvira Eliza Clain-Stefanelli,* 217–22. Louvain-La-Neuve, Département d'Archéologie et d'Histoire de l'Art, Séminaire de Numismatique Marcel Hoc.

(1999c) A drachm of Zankle with pellets indicating value in the Museum of Art, Rhode Island School of Design. In M. Amandry and S. Herter (eds.) *Travaux de numismatique grecque offert à Georges Le Rider,* 167–68. London, Spink.

(1999d) The early owls of Athens and the Persians. *Revue belge de numismatique* 155, 5–15.

(2000f) A group of Argive coins at Brown University. In S. Herter and C. Arnold-Biucchi (eds.) *Pour Denyse. Divertissements Numismatiques,* 75–82. Bern, Dr. Schüler.

(2000g) Remarks on the Taranto hoard of 1911. *Revue belge de numismatique* 146, 1–6.

(2004b) Why coins in Greece? In P.-A. Deproost and A. Meurant (eds.) *Images d'origines, origines d'une image,* 261–62. Louvain-la-Neuve, Academia-Bruylant.

(2007) The "Kainon" coinage. In G. Moucharte and P. Marchetti (eds.) *Liber Amicorum Tony Hackens,* 223–27. Louvain-la-Neuve: Association de numismatique professeur Marcel Hoc.

(Forthcoming) The coin finds at Ossaia and wider questions of the monetization of Italy in the imperial period.

IV. Roman History

(2008c) Who were the tribuni militum consulari potestate? *L'Antiquité Classique* 77, 107–25.

(Forthcoming) Praetor Maximus and consul. *Studi in onore di Giovanni Uggeri.*

(In progress) How did Rome acquire its double consulship?

V. Reviews

Fifty book reviews in *American Journal of Archaeology, Archaeology, Gnomon, American Historical Review, Classical World, Computers and the Humanities, The Classical Outlook, Bulletin of the American Schools of Oriental Research, Etruscan News.*

Excavating the Labyrinth: An Archaeology of a Career*

Derek B. Counts and Anthony S. Tuck

For those of us who dedicate a measure of our lives to reconstructing the past through discovery and discourse, we cannot fail to see a vast garden of forking paths and crossing intersections. In our allotted time within this landscape of objects and ideas, we trace upon that ground the avenues of ambition and greatness as well as those of simplicity and anonymity. As archaeologists it is our honor to endeavor to make sense of but a few of these avenues. Within this labyrinthine space, we pursue threads of meaning and pathways of understanding that might illuminate ancient practice and give voice to the past. As we map our paths of inquiry within this garden, the accidents of evidence and opportunity create connections to places and people mis-remembered by history or simply altogether forgotten. Indeed, the scholar we honor with this volume has dedicated a career to the consideration of and contribution to the great body of knowledge that informs our view of the past and connects us to those who created it. It is in R. Ross Holloway that a vast ancestry of ideas merges within a man. It is through him that pieces of what was lost to us, those nameless many whose experiences remain illustrated by the material expression of their lives, are made known again. The pathways reaching back to them, across the distance of time, are revealed to us.

We write these words as students of R. Ross Holloway. Our debt to him cannot be repaid with mere thanks. It was he who taught us how to look back into this past of such humbling complexity. It was he who reminded us that each rude and broken potsherd has a voice as clear and meaningful as that of the greatest monuments of imperial pretension. But we are most grateful for the example he set of such expansive generosity of intellect. No idea or insight, no matter how small or great, was ever discarded for want of interest. For Holloway, ancient monuments and objects should never be studied in isolation, nor should their biographies be preserved only by the opinions of a select few. Whether discussed over coffee in an office overburdened with books and offprints or communicated to colleagues and scholars across the world through the pages of his publications, Holloway continues to share his insights and inspirations, pointing out directions unanticipated and pathways of knowledge hitherto concealed. Whether as a colleague, mentor, or a scholar, an excavator or a writer, few careers have touched so many or borne witness to so much (see Winkes, this volume).

Over the arc of many years, Holloway has traced the courses of Mediterranean civilization from early prehistory to the rise of Christianity. Although the product of a Department of Fine Arts at Princeton University, he has always viewed his role as an archaeologist and social scientist as fundamental. In fact, Holloway's half century of scholarly activity (see Cova, this volume) is bracketed by the direction of major field excavations on the island of Ustica (Holloway 1995b; 2001a) and in the Agora of Athens (Holloway 1966a). Moreover, the intervening years witnessed full scale projects at four sites: Satrianum (Holloway 1970a, *inter alia*), Buccino (Holloway 1973a, *inter alia*), La Muculufa (Holloway 1990b, *inter alia*), and Trentinara (Holloway 1978a).

An Archaeology of a Career

The metaphor of a labyrinth-like garden of academic knowledge envisioned in the opening paragraph of this introduction mirrors the many intersecting paths of scholar-ship as it advances from idea to publication. The practice of archaeology embodies a multi-staged approach that begins with the conception of larger questions and the development a problem-oriented research design, followed by implement-ation and discovery through systematic fieldwork, collection and analysis, interpretation, and finally reaction. As an archaeologist as comfortable in the field as in the halls of academia, Holloway's own scholarly output reflects these myriad processes of archaeological pursuit and material culture analyses. The nature and scope of his publication record not only signals the rigors of scholarly inquiry, but also reflects the very evolution of the discipline of archae-ology over the past fifty years.

Perceiving the Problem

Holloway's approach to archaeological fieldwork and the interpretation of data from the field has always been predicated on the need for problem-oriented interpretive

---

* References to Holloway's publications correspond to the bibliography found in Cova, this volume.

models that confront the broader themes of cultural interaction and the exchange of ideas. He writes,

> But in the Bronze Age Mediterranean…there are suggestions of the contacts by single individuals made well beyond their immediate cultural provinces…The purposeful voyage enlarges and complicates the possibilities of cultural transmission, freeing it from a step-by-step transmission and placing it in the hands of the voyagers who may bypass numerous intermediaries between their home and their goals. At the same time that they extend and complicate cultural relationships, they dramatically reduce the time element in cultural transmission (Holloway 1981a, 20).

With the publication of *Italy and the Aegean: 3000–700 BC*, Holloway sought to understand central Mediterranean cultural transmission not as a product of confined cultural boundaries, but rather as a series of open-ended and dynamic processes exposing connections between landscapes and artifacts. Reconstructions of the *longue durée* of the Mediterranean have sought to emphasize that significant connections complement the diversity present and the complexity inherent in the cultural entanglements across the Mediterranean (Doonan, this volume). While it is true that such a holistic narrative of Mediterranean history has been widely criticized, few scholars have refuted the growing, related trend to view Mediterranean culture as unbounded and malleable. For Holloway, material culture, whether produced locally or imported from abroad, should never be accepted solely as a reflection of interaction, but rather it should be questioned and freed from the myopic views of diffusion and reception. Holloway's recognition of the significance of traditionally underappreciated indigenous cultures within the wider milieu of trans-Italian and trans-Mediterranean contact has provided a framework within which many later studies have been situated (e.g., the contributions by Hussein, Tsakirgis, and McConnell in this volume). Today, such thinking is central to innumerable discussions of economic, demographic and social complexity of the Mediterranean. And yet, the very ubiquity of this approach today underscores its profound and revolutionary impact at a time when the idea of the classical world was far more narrowly defined than it is now.

Theory into Practice

Perhaps more than any other actor engaged in the study of the ancient Mediterranean, the field archaeologist maintains a constant dialogue with the cultural processes and material products that gave foundation and shape to the societies of the past. While his scholarship consistently reveals the desire to shape research under the mantle of broader questions and pan-Mediterranean themes, Holloway has always insisted upon the primacy of field excavation and significance of scientific discovery, for it is within this body of data that the intentions of the past and the present co-exist (see Lukesh

and Joukowsky, this volume). More expansive, theoretically- and thematically-driven conclusions can only linger so long without the implementation of scientific testing. In the opening pages to his magisterial volume, *The Archaeology of Early Rome and Latium*, Holloway (1994a, 11) offers his perspective on the importance of archaeological work and the central role of excavation data in the formation of historical narratives:

> Archaeology deserves better than to remain the crutch for the tales of the annalists and their followers. Its own tale is no less fascinating, and it has one supreme advantage over the written tradition as we have it: its evidence is direct and uncontaminated. The following pages are an attempt to answer the call to turn archaeology into history.

Through his presentation of archaeological work in Iron Age Italy, Holloway brought to light novel bodies of evidence concerning the earliest form and development of the community that would become Rome and in so doing, pointed the way for new generations of scholars to add their own voice to this central concern of the ancient world. Holloway's own career in the field, which has seen more summers in Mediterranean lands than in his native New England, serves notice that while the theoretical approaches to social change and development provide the foundation of archaeological fieldwork, evidence for the answers we seek must first come from the ground and not the library.

Potsherds and Postholes

When one considers the various projects that Holloway has directed and compares the dates of fieldwork collection to the dates of corresponding analyses and final publication, it becomes clear that he has exemplified the model of prompt examination and publication of archaeological material. While conceptualizing research questions and implementing them through systematic excavation in the field form the basis for initial work, it is only after careful collection and analysis of the material record that the voice of the past may be heard. As Holloway himself has stressed, the artifactual data available to us represent unique moments, offering the archaeologist raw information that reflects, without bias, the cultural processes which led to its formation. In his recent essay "The Classical Mediterranean, its Prehistoric Past and the Formation of Europe", referenced in two contributions to the present volume (see Hussein and Luskeh), Holloway has provided an eloquent comment on the importance of the archaeological object and its context. He writes,

> …objects are also pointers to technology – and thus to verbally transmitted knowledge – to traditions – and thus to social continuity – to both utility and display – and thus not only to the working life of a community but also to creativity and the diplomacy of men's relations with neighbors and gods at home

and foreigners over the horizon. To keep in mind what is superficially missing in the physical record but was present in its creation opens our eyes to many things that in a literate society would be recorded but that with the judicious use of imagination can be recaptured even in the absence of the written word (Holloway 2000b).

The analysis of material culture through comprehensive and prompt publication, as well as specialized studies of artifacts, remain the primary vehicle for far-reaching syntheses of societal development and demise, serving as a starting point for historical, political, economic, and cultural narratives of prehistoric and classical Mediterranean civilizations. At a time when many of his contemporaries lingered in traditional culture-historical paradigms and selective collection and presentation, Holloway's insistence upon the systematic recovery of context and detailed, scientific analysis of all artifactual remains seems prescient. His final publications of the sites of Satrianum (Holloway 1970a) and Buccino (Holloway 1973a) not only stressed the contextual value of architecture and finds, but also incorporated emerging technologies and approaches to scientific analysis, from radiocarbon dating (a process less than a generation old at the time) and osteological studies at Buccino to infrared spectroscopy and X-ray fluorescence at Satrianum. The fact that such diverse approaches to the analysis of the physical past are standard practice in the field today reflects precisely how visionary their application was at the time. Moreover, Holloway's willingness to explore new avenues of inquiry is reflected in the range of perspectives taken by the contributors to this volume, fostered by Holloway as a teacher, mentor and colleague (compare, for example, the approaches of Nulton and Van Keuren to Graeco-Roman reliefs or the reading of imperial Roman topography by Norman and Dyson, in this volume). Indeed, for Holloway, the only sterile pathway to understanding the ancient world was the one not taken.

Interpretatio Rerum

The purpose of archaeological work is interpretation. The value of scientific discovery is made complete when material is taken out of its quantitative and 'raw' state and placed within a synthetic narrative. Holloway's excavations and detailed observations have provided the foundation for a series of explanatory models dealing with topics as diverse as early Bronze Age Mediterranean exchange (Holloway 1981a; 1984a; 1991a), Archaic Greek artistic form and expression (Holloway 1973d), the westward expansion of Greek culture into Magna Graecia (Holloway 1975c), and early Italic cultural formation processes (Holloway 1994a). The acknowledgement of multiple levels of meaning inherent in any object has often characterized Holloway's own search for interpretations that might take into account the complexity of ancient practice. For example, in *A View*

of Greek Art, Holloway (1973d, xxi) argued:

> The first duty of the historian of ancient art has been to ask when and where, to reconstruct the chronology…Success in these tasks has led to asking by whom, and as a result much of Greek art, at least, has been arranged by schools and attributed to masters known by their own names or by modern conventional designations. It has been less common, however, for the art historian to ask why – why did ancient style develop as it did, and why were monuments created in the form they assumed?

A View of Greek Art represented a break from the more traditional treatments of ancient art that had previously been published. By redirecting focus away from 'masters' and monolithic schools of style and the strict confines of chronologies and categories, Holloway emphasized the grace and simplicity of Greek art by considering the motive and motivation of the ancient viewer (see Bonfante, this volume). Throughout his career, Holloway has maintained this approach to the "holistic interpretation" of ancient objects and architectural monuments – an approach that is perhaps best witnessed in his treatment of numismatic evidence. Because of their intrinsic value and association with sovereignty and state functions, Holloway has long recognized that coins provide vital commentary on the economic and political strategies of ancient states and their leaders (Holloway 1969c; 1992d; 1999d; 2004b; see also Pope and Rutter, this volume). Nevertheless, the recognition of coins as a vehicle for understanding not only social history, but also art history characterizes much of Holloway's important work on numismatics (see Florenzano, this volume). As moveable objects and emblems marked with visual messages, Holloway has stressed that coins convey a range of symbols and ideologies through the medium of iconography and text. From the publication of *Art and Coinage in Magna Graecia* (Holloway 1978b) to the prefatory essay of his publication of the Greek coins of the Rhode Island School of Design (Holloway 1998d) two decades later, Holloway has stressed both the skill of numismatic craft and the achievement of the craftsman for objects otherwise cast aside as mass-produced and thus unable to speak to the individual.

Reading Old Problems Anew

Reevaluating prior interpretations by confronting old problems with new ideas and new ways of looking occupies a central place in archaeological discourse. Professor Larissa Bonfante aptly dedicates her contribution to the present volume to Holloway, who "has shown us things that were not visible." Much of Holloway's scholarship has been characterized by a constant willingness to look without assumption or prejudice on monuments already well considered by the academic community. Whether tackling the fundamental message(s) of ubiquitous Roman imperial monuments such as the Arch of Titus (Holloway 1987a; see also Magness and Norman, this volume) and the Arch of Constantine (Holloway 1985d; 2004a) or archaic Greek temple design and decoration (Holloway 1988c; see also Marconi, Maggidis, and Barletta, this volume), small details, overlooked or unconsidered by generations of scholars, have developed into new ways of thinking about the familiar. Reexamining the well-known dedications of archaic korai on the Athenian Acropolis, Holloway (1992c, 267) wrote:

> The Athenian korai are easily the most intensively studied group of archaic Greek sculptures, and among the authors of works devoted to them are three of the greatest names in classical archaeology of the past century: Payne (1936), Langlotz (1939), and Richter (1968)...A fundamental question raised by these elegant statues, however, is still unanswered: why was the kore type chosen so overwhelmingly for the major sculptural dedications of the late sixth and first two decades of the fifth century on the Athenian Acropolis?

From such simple observations, a spark of insight emerges that allows for the reshaping of old questions with new interpretations (e.g., Shapiro, Bell, Kenfield, and Kampen, this volume). Moreover, Holloway's unwavering attempts to reshape current debate have extended into his own research. His range of publications often reveals a sense of self-reflection that challenged him to revisit his own interpretations, often decades later, as witnessed in his reading of the Parthenon frieze (Holloway 1966e; 2000d) or the sculptures of the Temple of Zeus at Olympia (Holloway 1967b; 1972; 2008a). While many of Holloway's publications reflect his desire to challenge paradigms, this was never more evident than in the classroom. Many of the contributors to this volume will remember graduate seminars where nineteenth century tomes were dragged from their resting place in Brown University's John Hay special collections library and aggressively interrogated once again (consider Kampen's introductory words to her contribution for this volume). More often then not, this served to remind his students of the tradition to which they were indebted. Sometimes, conversations driven by new approaches in the discipline, by theories and methods imported from other disciplines, or by the critical addition of new data from the field would lead to a volley of new ideas across the table of the seminar room. Some such ideas would fall away, their brief half-life spent merely as foils for further argument. Others thrived and took root, growing into bodies of inquiry that sometimes gently pushed our thinking of the past in small and measurable ways, sometimes shaking our assumptions to their very foundations so that they might be rebuilt stronger. It is in this joyousness of debate that the paths of the scholar and the teacher become one again. Indeed no better reflection of this fact can be found than the dozens of subtle comments and citations throughout Holloway's own body of writing that recall and graciously thank the observations and ideas of students and colleagues alike.

In assembling this volume, we have sought to merge a career over a half century in breadth and scope with an editorial vision that brings together a chorus of scholarly contribution reflecting the interdependence of interpretive approaches. In doing so, we have simultaneously attempted to echo the core principles of Holloway's own unique perspective on ancient Mediterranean studies. Through broadly conceived themes, the four individual sections of this volume are an attempt to capture these many and varied trajectories of thought that have marked his career. Reflecting the spirit of Holloway's own substantial, admittedly and unapologetically eclectic, bibliography, the topics covered here take on questions dealing with a wide range of subjects - from prehistory to the Christian era. Some chapters represent fully developed treatments replete with extensive commentary and great detail, mirroring Holloway's own ability to synthesize and explicate in full-length volumes and long articles; others offer shorter comments and quick paced observations, akin to Holloway's numerous briefs and archaeological notes intended to spark further conversation and provoke dialogue. The individual chapters that follow mirror the breadth and depth of Holloway's own learning, but also represent the multiple paths of inquiry and interconnected stages of archaeological practice considered above. In fact, the value of these contributions lies in their rejection of singular, monolithic approaches to archaeological discourse. Yet, in spite of the wide scope of interests and methods they embrace, the collection of papers in each of the sections responds well to the four broad themes imposed upon them by the editors. To this end, we are especially grateful to our three distinguished colleagues (Allen, Sinos, and Arnold-Biucchi), who have provided synthetic overviews to sections of this volume. Their prefatory essays contextualize the invited contributions through their exposition of Holloway's place in the discipline, transforming this festschrift into an academic biography. In the end, we hope that this volume serves not only as a tribute to the career of Holloway and a reflection of the many lives his has touched, but also a lens through which the complex and impressive biography of such a scholar may be appreciated. Of the many and varied paths of thought Holloway's career has traced, we are honored to have walked with him on a few.

The *Oxford English Dictionary* defines «koine» as "a set of cultural or other attributes common to various groups." As students and colleagues of R. Ross Holloway, we come together with a shared sense of community and a common vision of how material culture illuminates the past. The intellectual threads of Holloway's own career have been woven into the contributions found in this volume and the various chapters serve not only as testimony to the significance of his research, but also as a witness to its influence on our own careers.

* * *

SECTION I
INTRODUCTION

A View of Classical Art: Iconography in Context

Susan Heuck Allen

R. Ross Holloway traces his interest in ancient art to sketching classes that he took at the Museum of Fine Arts, Boston when he was a young child. Asked whether his first interest in antiquity came from archaeology, art or classics, Holloway is quick to answer that it was archaeology, but that interest began so early that he cannot pinpoint the exact time. It may have been nurtured by the Explorers' Club at the Museum of Natural History in Boston where he gave his first archaeological lecture. Be that as it may, the first excavation for this student of iconography was far from the rarified world of ancient art. In fact, it took place in a pigpen in Scituate, Massachusetts with the Massachusetts Archaeological Society. Soon thereafter the Greek master at Roxbury Latin School opened Holloway's eyes to Greco-Roman antiquity, introducing him to the world of university scholarship which was to become his career and lifelong passion. This teacher handpicked him for Greek, the study of which ensured his membership in a very privileged club where he read Plato, Homer, Xenophon, and Thucydides.

Holloway showed his independent streak early on when, at a time when 12 out of 16 graduates of Roxbury matriculated at Harvard, he instead struck out for western Massachusetts and the greener pastures of Amherst College. At Amherst Holloway encountered his most important mentor, Professor Charles Hill Morgan (1902–1984), founder of the Department of Fine Arts as well as the Mead Art Museum and a scholar of vast interests who published books on Greek sculpture of the fourth century BC, as well as on Michelangelo and the Hudson River School. When the college disposed of its 19th century plaster cast collection, it was Morgan who salvaged a few and had Holloway work on the iconography of the Eleusis relief of Demeter and Kore for a senior essay; this research resulted in Holloway's first published article. According to Holloway, Morgan had an "amazing gift" to offer in "the style of his scholarship" which he chose to emulate.[1]

Holloway won a Fulbright Fellowship in his senior year at Amherst which gave him the opportunity to sample the wealth of archaeological activity at the University of Pennsylvania and its famous museum where he took seminars with the "enormously stimulating" Rodney Young. In turn, Dorothy Burr Thompson encouraged Holloway to migrate to Princeton where he began his doctoral work on the coins of Aegina, a dissertation topic on which he had settled during a summer fellowship at the ANS. Holloway first excavated in the Mediterranean at Morgantina, an ancient Greek city on the island of Sicily where a Princeton University team under the direction of Richard Stillwell in 1958 and 1959 and Eric Sjoqvist in 1961 and 1962 was turning up "bushels and bushels of coins." During this period, Holloway also attended a summer session of the American School of Classical Studies at Athens in 1958, but only after he had set foot on Sicily and lost his heart to the Central Mediterranean.

---

[1] All quotations in this essay come from the words of R. Ross Holloway in a taped interview with the author on February 18, 2009.

Bookended by seasons at Morgantina were two propitious years, 1960–62, which Holloway spent at the American Academy courtesy of the prestigious Rome Prize. At the Academy he discovered that opportunities for foreign excavations were far more ample in Italy than in Greece. Whole areas, such as Lucania, had been virtually unexplored. At a workshop on archaeology, photography, and illustration conducted by Dino Adamestianu, Holloway met his great collaborator, Tony Hackens of the University of Louvain. It was also during those years that he met Gisela Richter who had just retired to Rome in her late 70s after more than half a century at the Metropolitan Museum of Art where for over 20 years she had been Curator of Greek and Roman Art. Richter maintained a kind of salon in her ground floor apartment near the American Academy where, over tea and cakes, she introduced younger scholars to each other and provided friendship and moral support. Her prolific scholarship spanning Greece and Rome also set a powerful example for them and Richter's formative impact on Holloway and his scholarship is reflected by his dedication of his first book to her memory.

In 1964, after two years of teaching at Princeton and the University of North Carolina at Chapel Hill, Holloway joined the Classics Department at Brown University, whose larger-than-life Professor of Classics, Charles Alexander Robinson, had long wanted a Brown University excavation in Athens. Holloway was able to realize Robinson's dream only after his death, conducting a six-week season of excavations between the Agora and the lower slopes of the Acropolis under the auspices of Nicholas Platon, Ephor of the Acropolis.

In 1978, Holloway teamed up with Rolf Winkes and founded the Center for Old World Archaeology and Art. Around the same time, Martha Sharp Joukowsky joined the faculty at the Center, expanding the scope of its activities to the Middle East and providing a powerful role model for young women entering the field (see Winkes, this volume). Holloway was interested in the power of hero cults in Athens and surely, through his role as co-founder of the Center for Old World Archaeology and Art at Brown University, now called the Joukowsky Institute for Archaeology and the Ancient World, he qualifies as an *oikist*, the founder of a colony. An earlier festschrift, *Interpretatio Rerum: Archaeological Essays on Objects and Meanings* edited by S. S. Lukesh (Providence, 1999) included contributions on iconography from a number of participants in this volume who studied with Holloway at Brown University.

Professor Holloway's intellectual descendants from four decades of teaching are not limited to Rhode Island. His association with Malcolm Bell III dates to Holloway's years of teaching at Princeton and Chapel Hill, and John Kenfield to his first year of undergraduate teaching at Brown University in 1964. Peter Nulton and I were his graduate students from the 80s and 90s where we enjoyed fruitful interactions at the Center with Parker Fellows, such as Alan Shapiro and Naomi Norman, and Mellon professors, such as Jodi Magness. Countless Italian scholars, such as Clemente Marconi, also regard Holloway as their mentor although the relationship was of a less formal variety.

The essays of this chapter deal with iconography, from the painted vessel to the carved architectural relief, to Byzantine illuminations and mosaics. Several of the topics were inspired by the maverick thinking of Holloway's *A View of Greek Art* (1973), a survey of Greek monumental art in which he moved beyond the traditional trope of art historical discourse whose questions had focused upon when, where, and by whom to ask why. Contributors examine iconography, not as the product of some homogenizing and unifying cultural machine, but as the expression of individual cultural experiences negotiating difference and multiple levels of meaning. In his essay on Kleophrades's Tarquinia krater, often construed to be a mistake by the master who articulated a figure with two right hands, Bell argues that, in fact, the artist offered a visual metaphor to literal ambidexterity worthy of an exceptional athlete. Shapiro also examines the motive behind the iconography of a youth seated on an altar and posits a scene depicting Orestes as a suppliant in Athens during the festal days of the Anthesteria as an allusion to the hospitality of Athens even to the polluted. Just as Holloway foregrounded the ancient viewer and his motive over the grand and monolithic syntheses of Greek monumental achievement in the program of architectural sculpture on the Temple of Zeus at Olympia, Marconi explores the emotional impact of attraction and repulsion provoked by architectural sculpture during the archaic and classical eras in Greece. None of these essays could have been written without a keen appreciation of cultural literacy championed by Holloway.

More recently, Holloway has breathed new life into old Roman monuments through *Constantine and Rome* (2004) – a book which reexamines the urban landscape of Constantinian Rome as a reflection of the emperor's delicate negotiations between paganism and Christianity and their respective practitioners. Nulton transports us to this re-envisioned Roman world by his re-dating of relief sculpture from a late classical religious context in Athens to a neo-Attic home décor for the *literati* of the Julio-Claudian era as was common in contemporary Roman wall painting. In their contributions, both Norman and Magness consider Flavian monuments, both drawing on Holloway's 1987 article on the Arch of Titus. Norman argues persuasively for the Arch of Titus as a mnemonic device invoking both the triumph and the apotheosis of Titus when the emperor temporarily and then permanently achieved divine status. Hence the circle of imperial life was experienced and reactivated each time one approached the Campus Martius from the center of the city, either in a triumphal or funerary procession. Magness considers the irony of the core ideal of peace in the official construction of Vespasian's public image being founded on war as depicted in the iconography of the Arch of Titus, the Porta Triumphalis, and the Templum Pacis.

Finally, in his piece, Kenfield moves beyond the world of Late Antiquity to examine a Byzantine topic with an historian's eye, an insight for which he credits Holloway's own perspectives on art. His observations on early Byzantine angels brings us full circle to Holloway's days at Amherst where he was mentored by Charles Hill Morgan who had studied and published Byzantine material and to another Amherst professor, Sterling Lamprecht who, in the course on the panorama of western philosophy, taught Holloway to examine the epistemology and metaphysics of a civilization in order to understand how they saw their world.

Holloway's early interest in the power of images in expressing culture and the manipulation of cultural images to express power has born fruit and remained at the forefront of studies in ancient art and iconography. To this day, ancient Etruscan, Greek, and Roman iconography is approached through the lens of audience and reception, "the viewer's gaze," as well as through perspectives on ancient political propaganda and socio-economic hierarchies. The following chapters are a tribute to Holloway's own challenging gaze and supremely literary scholarship probing just how the ancients conceived their world and expressed their vision of it through visual records.

Looking back on the circumstances that led to his being awarded the AIA's Gold Medal, Holloway credits the strong mentorship of Morgan and the opportunities presented by the Rome Prize, as well as the support of his colleagues. Chief among them is his devoted wife, Nancy Degenhardt Holloway, a Bryn Mawr-trained classicist who catalogued his finds at Morgantina and Satrianum, and his daughters Susie and Ann, who illustrated his finds. Other long-term collaborators are Susan Lukesh in ceramics and cutting-edge computer applications, Ned Nabors in photography, architect Elise Elrick, and many more.

For Holloway, the greatest figures in archaeology were the nineteenth-century titans, Wilhelm Dörpfeld (1853–1940) and Paolo Orsi (1859–1935), who were able to organize, synthesize, and reach major conclusions succinctly. It can be honestly said that he truly has followed in their footsteps.

1

Early Greek Architectural Decoration in Function

Clemente Marconi

Did the Greeks pay attention to the images displayed on their buildings? How much attention did they pay? Was it simply a glance or was it something more? Before we even pose these questions, are we allowed to talk about the ancient viewer at all, and about the ancient viewing of Greek architectural sculpture? A recent treatment of the subject suggests a negative response to these last two questions (Ridgway 1999, esp. 12–19, 74–102). By insisting on the fact that Greek and Latin texts say little about Greek architectural sculpture, and by insisting on the relative visibility of architectural decoration, the author of this study concludes by arguing very strongly that "we can no longer recapture the ancient mentality, or even the ancient visual acuity and sensitivity, and that we tend to overreach in our interpretations because of our different experiences" (Ridgway 1999, 93).

Yet, there are several literary and visual sources that tell us about the ancient viewer and the ancient viewing of Greek architectural sculpture. These sources are critical for rethinking our approach to the whole issue of the reception of the figural decoration of buildings in the various phases of Greek culture.

At the turn of the nineteenth century, modern architectural theory had abandoned ornament and decoration, seeing it as a criminal, degenerate practice (one need only mention *Ornament and Crime* by Adolf Loos). As a consequence, the rejection of ornament and decoration became one of the main features of the Modern Movement (Brolin 2000; Frank 2000). At the same time, a crucial development of urban modernity has been that the modern city has been gradually absorbing every architectural object: in the modern city attention to architecture is dissolved into immediate use (Tafuri 1980, 79–102). One is reminded here of Walter Benjamin's reference in *The Work of Art in the Age of Mechanical Reproduction* to buildings as the object of a collective and distracted attention, and to the perception of architecture as tactile, through use, rather than optical (Heynen 1999, 95–118; Benjamin 2005).

I wonder how much the twentieth-century estrangement

from ornament and decoration on buildings and the twentieth-century distracted perception of architecture are responsible for current approaches to the issue of visibility of Greek architectural sculpture. Take the emphasis of modern scholarship on an apparently significant example of distracted viewing of architecture and architectural decoration from Classical antiquity: Pausanias's description of the Parthenon (1.24.5–7). In describing the Parthenon, Pasuanias offers only a brief reference to the subjects of the pediments and has no word of appreciation for the architecture and no word at all for the akroteria, the metopes, and the frieze that formed such a critical part in the sculptural adornment of that building. Can we take these omissions as evidence of a generalized, distracted viewing of architectural decoration in Classical antiquity, as they are sometimes taken? I exclude this last possibility, and for a variety of reasons. On the one hand, because these omissions concern the text of Pausanias's *Description of Greece*, not Pausanias's personal experience, and they do not reflect what he saw but what he thought was worth mentioning for a traveler, selecting among the many things visible on the Akropolis (on Pausanias's selective approach, see Arafat 1996, 31 *ff.*, 212; Beard 2003, 23–31 suggests that what Pausanias omits of the sculptural decoration of the Parthenon simply came low on his list of priorities in comparison with the Athena Parthenos). On the other hand, Pausanias himself provides sufficient evidence of concentration on architecture and architectural sculpture with his extended description of the Temple of Zeus at Olympia (5.10.2 *ff.*), which includes a detailed discussion of the building and its sculptural decoration.

It is not Pausanias, however, but the Archaic period that represents the focus of my essay, which is dedicated to the viewing of Greek architectural decoration and to the response to images on buildings (on response, see Freedberg 1989). Unlike other periods, in fact, our sources point to a strong, emotional reaction to these images, partly due to their placement in an elevated position, partly due to their subject and appearance, and partly due to the general belief of this period that images have the magic power to come alive. These sources consist of representations of architecture on vases, texts, and building models. I argue that these sources introduce us to the power of images on buildings to capture the attention of their public, to generate an emotional response, and to remain impressed in the memory of the viewer. Through these sources, we see Greek architectural decoration at work.

I begin my discussion with a well-known Athenian black-figure neck-amphora in London (British Museum B49: *CVA* London, British Museum 3, pl. 35 [155] 2a; Beazley 1956, 326; Oliver-Smith 1964, 235, fig. 4; 1969, 116–17, 134, no. 12, fig. 64; Boardman 1986, 94–96, fig. 1; Carpenter 1989, 88; Shapiro 1989, 59–60, pl. 29c; De Cesare 1997, 83, fig. 33, 84, 288, no. 413; Oenbrink 1997, 116–21, 384, D1) with a sanctuary depicted on one side and two horsemen followed by a warrior on the other (Fig. 1.1). Of unusual shape and style, this amphora has proved difficult to date, and proposals range from immediately after 550 BC (Schefold 1937, 38) to the beginning of the last decade of the sixth century (Oliver-Smith 1969, 116). The most plausible dating is the one suggested by Shapiro (1989, 60), to about 540–530, based on the similarities noted by Tiverios between this vase and Group E (Tiverios 1976, 116 n. 357).

Our attention is drawn to the representation of the sanctuary, which is apparently quite simple. At the sides

Fig. 1.1 *Amphora, British Museum B49 (Photo © British Museum).*

stand two tall tripods with birds perched on the rings of the handles (two swans on the left tripod and two doves on the right tripod). The two tripods flank a shrine (a baldachin – Wesenberg 1971, 84; Robertson 1975, 128; Weber 1990, 42–43, 165, B106 – rather than a temple or a *naiskos*, as it is often called), which is articulated with a stylobate, two columns carrying Aeolic capitals, and a tall architrave with a molding at the top. Upon the flat roof of this building, which has no frieze and no pediment, a lion crouches to the right so aggressively that it gives the impression of being ready to jump on the doves to the right. The tail of the beast curls up and overlaps the pattern framing the panel of the amphora above, a detail that increases the vividness of the image (for this expressive device, see Schapiro 1969, 228 *ff.*; Hurwit 1977, 9 *ff.*). Inside the shrine stands the statue of the divinity, shown fully frontal, with the head reaching to the ceiling and the feet overlapping the stylobate, as if, although still, the figure were coming out of the building. This divinity, who has long hair and no beard, wears a long chiton and a mantle upon its shoulders.

The divinity holds no attributes, and for this reason it has been subject to different identifications. It was first identified as a female deity, either Artemis or Kybele, the Mother of the Gods (Artemis or Kybele: H. B. Walters in *CVA* London, British Museum 3, on pl. 35 [155] 2a; Kybele: Schefold 1937, 38; Simon 1953, 81; Betancourt 1977, 147, no. 1; Naumann 1983, 117; Mertens-Horn 1986, 14–15; see Simon 1997, 756, no. 64). This second identification, definitely more plausible than the first, was based on the Aeolic capitals, taken as an allusion to the Anatolian origin of the cult of Kybele, and on the lion, often used as an attribute of the goddess as *Potnia therōn*. In more recent years, this divinity has been identified with Apollo (Bauchhenss-Thüriedl 1971, 100 n. 149; Tiverios 1976, 116 n. 357; Boardman 1986, 96; Shapiro 1989, 59; De Cesare 1997, 288, no. 413; Oenbrink 1997, 120–21). The divinity, in fact, has no female attributes, and the long hair, the long chiton, and the mantle are consistent with images of Apollo on Athenian vases of the Archaic period. Moreover, the lion had a strong association with Apollo, and Apollo had close ties with Asia Minor. Additionally, the tripods and the birds perching on their handles also had a strong association with Apollo. For all these reasons not only the divinity on our vase has been identified with Apollo but also the shrine has been taken for the Temple of Apollo in Delphi, or for the Temple of Apollo Pythios in Athens. In particular, for Shapiro our amphora would commemorate the construction of the Python in Athens attributed by Hesychios to Peisistratos. The Aeolic capitals of our shrine do not speak against this last identification, since the Aeolic style is documented in Attica during the Archaic period (Betancourt 1977, 99–112). Moreover, although Aeolic structures featured on vases generally represent minor constructions in perishable materials, particularly wood (Oliver-Smith

1964; Betancourt 1977, 145–51), our building appears to be an exception to that rule since it has proportions and characteristics that are in tune with stone architecture (Oliver-Smith 1964, 235; 1969, 116).

Whatever the identification of the shrine, it is evident that on our vase the image of the divinity stands for both the god itself and its cult image. Although at first glance one might infer from the absence of a base that the image of the divinity is the divinity in person, the stillness, frontality, and location of the figure at the center of the shrine leave no doubt that the image is intended to be a statue. In this regard, our representation is consistent with the general trend in Early Greek art to play with the idea, in the case of cult images, that the represented is not just in the image but is the image. One may mention the earliest representations of the rape of Kassandra, which show Ajax trying to separate the Trojan prophetess from the statue of Athena, and in which the goddess herself intervenes in defense of Kassandra, as if the prophetess were embracing not the statue of Athena but Athena herself (Connelly 1993; De Cesare 1997, 79–91; Oenbrink 1997, 340–44). Likewise, on our amphora the boundary is blurred between the cult-statue and the divinity that it represents.

A similar blurring of boundaries between representation and represented may also be at work with the image of the lion on top of the roof. This image of a crouching lion on top of a roof is particularly intriguing from the perspective of Archaic architectural decoration, considering the fact that in these years images of lions involved in fights with other beasts were often used for the decoration of pediments in Athens (on this subject, see Hölscher 1972; Müller 1978, 167–73; Markoe 1989). It is in Athens, actually, that the motif of the animal fight may have been used for the first time for the decoration of a pediment, since the earliest documented occurrence of an animal fight in this architectural context is on Temple H (570–560 BC) on the Acropolis. Both pediments of this building featured at their center a group of a lion and lioness intent at devouring a bull, while staring at the viewer (East pediment: Schuchhardt 1935–36, 87–88, fig. 14; West pediment: Dinsmoor 1947, 145–47). To the same years (570–560 BC) belongs the head of a lion from the Agora (Floren 1987, 242 n. 24), comparable in style and size to the head of the lioness from the West pediment of Temple H, and thus attributed to the decoration of the pediment of another, large building in that area. It remains unclear whether this last lion was already attacking or still confronting its prey. The latter was certainly the case on the small pediment of an *oikos* (560–540 BC) on the Acropolis featuring the representation of a lion and a boar confronting each other before the fight (Floren 1987, 243 n. 30). The importance of this subject on the Acropolis is confirmed by the fact that, toward the end of the sixth century, two lions devouring a bull were prominently featured at the center of one of the pediments of the so-called

Peisistratid Athenaion (510–500 BC), though it remains unclear whether they were on the front or the back of the building (Floren 1987, 245–47; Marszal 1998). The popularity of the subject in Athens throughout the end of the Archaic period is confirmed by its use outside the Acropolis, for a small pediment from the area of the Olympieion (500–490 BC) (Floren 1987, 243 n. 31), and for a small pediment from the area of the Agora (500–490 BC) (Floren 1987, 243 n. 29). In both cases, the lion, at the center of the composition, falls upon a bull lying on the ground. To this list of Athenian buildings of the Late Archaic period one may add the Temple of Apollo at Delphi (generally dated to 510 BC), built with the financial backing of the Athenian family of the Alkmeonids, and most likely carved by an Athenian sculptor. At the corners of the east pediment of this temple, two groups, one of a lion attacking a bull, the other of a lion attacking a stag, framed the central scene featuring the arrival of Apollo in his sanctuary (Floren 1987, 244–45; Childs 1993; Marconi 2007, 192–93). These representations of animal fights had an impact on Athenian vase painters, as proved by a black-figure hydria in Copenhagen that shows a fountain-house with an elaborate pediment decorated by two lions devouring a bull (Copenhagen, National Museum: Lund and Rasmussen 1994, 65; Pfisterer-Haas 2002, 37, fig. 41). This impact, however, went beyond the reproduction of pediments since it also affected the representation of animal fights at large. In fact, as first pointed out by Buschor (1922, 102), several representations of lions on Athenian vases suggest a dependence on those sculptural groups (see also Schefold 1937, 38; Markoe 1989, 94–95), and among them, our amphora stands out as the most intriguing case. There are several indications of the fact that our lion on the roof was inspired by the scenes of animal fighting on the pediments: its aggressive behavior, its placement right at the center of the roof, and, last but not least, the fact that the nonsense inscriptions inscribed at both sides of the beast are neatly arranged to suggest a pedimental facade (as pointed out by Boardman 1986, 96). It looks as if one of those lions in the pediments just mentioned had the power to come alive, in a blurring of boundaries between representation and represented that runs parallel to the one seen in the case of the cult-statue below.

With the amphora at the British Museum we are still not dealing with a case of animation of architectural decoration, since the lion is clearly a living being (although it should be emphasized that more than one author has taken the beast for a statue, starting with Gerhard 1840–58, IV, pl. 241.1–2; see also Collignon 1911, 43, fig. 19; Picard 1935–66, I, 422 fig. 118; Oliver-Smith 1964, 235; 1969, 117). However, with the next vase we are confronted with precisely that situation (Figs. 1.2–4). I am referring to the famous cup said to be from Vulci, now at the Metropolitan Museum (1989.281.62), attributed to the Amasis Painter and dated to about 540 BC

Fig. 1.2 *Cup, Metropolitan Museum of Art 1989.281.62 (Photo © Metropolitan Museum of Art).*

Fig. 1.3 *Cup, Metropolitan Museum of Art 1989.281.62 (Photo © Metropolitan Museum of Art).*

(Beazley 1971 67; Bothmer 1985, 217–20, no. 60, with earlier literature; Carpenter 1989, 46; Shapiro 1989, 44, 108–9, pl. 21b; Moore 2004, 39–40, figs. 7–8). One side of this cup shows four horses in their stables tied to columns, still wearing their halters, and being attended by youthful grooms before being harnessed (see Moore 2004, 39–40), and the other shows Poseidon in the company of a series of warriors, five hoplites and two archers, with two onlookers at the sides. The standard interpretation of this cup, which

goes back to 1965 (proposed by both Marjorie J. Milne [see Bothmer 1985, 219] and Jucker 1965–66, 42 n. 132), suggests a thematic connection between the two sides of the vase, both of which according to this hypothesis would illustrate the opening of the *Iliad* 13 (10 *ff.*), the Book dedicated to the battle at the ships. In the opening of Book 13, Poseidon, looking in the direction of Troy from the top of the mountain of Samothrace, sees the Greeks losing to the Trojans and decides to intervene in their support. Leaving

Fig. 1.4 *Cup, Metropolitan Museum of Art 1989.281.62. (Photo © Metropolitan Museum of Art).*

the island, the god goes to his palace at Aigai at the bottom of the sea, harnesses the horses under his chariot, and reaches Troy. There he appears in the battlefield in the likeness and with the voice of Kalchas, and first speaks to the two Ajaxes, and then the rest of the Greek army, rousing them to the fight. According to this passage in the *Iliad*, one side of our cup would represent the stables of Poseidon at Aiagai, and the other side would represent Poseidon in the battlefield. This last reading is compelling (the picture would be one of the few Homeric scenes on Athenian vases of the early and mid-sixth century; see Shapiro 1989, 44–45), in spite of the fact that Poseidon does not appear disguised as Kalchas, and it is tempting to identify the two hoplites at the sides of the god with the two Ajaxes (Simon 1976, 84, makes a systematic attempt to identify all the warriors on scene). At first glance, it appears more difficult to relate the stable scene to this same episode, since in the *Iliad* it is the god who personally takes care of harnessing the horses under his chariot. Stables, horses, and grooms attending the animals have, however, a strong connection with Poseidon, given the special ties of this god with horses: Poseidon was in fact honored as tamer of horses, and his cult as Hippios was widespread and included Attica (Burkert 1985, 138; Shapiro 1989, 108–11). This alone would be enough to connect the two sides of the cup. But there is more.

Let us focus in fact on the stable scene, and more precisely on the architecture of the building. It seems unlikely that this stable – something like a hypostyle hall – is a direct

copy of an existing building (Oliver-Smith 1969, 61–62). However, there is no question that the vase painter had the Doric order in mind, as indicated by the five columns without bases crowned by a Doric capital consisting of echinus and abacus, and by the frieze with triglyphs without incisions alternating with metopes. Still, we are far away from the canonical Doric forms developed during the course of the sixth century in monumental architecture (Barletta 2001, 54–83): the columns are in fact unfluted, between the abacus and the frieze there is an extra block, taller than the short abacus, the architrave is missing (and replaced, one would say, by the extra block), and the placement of the triglyphs in relation to the axis of the columns is not regular. The fact that the columns are particularly slender speaks in favor of a wooden structure. In this regard, the white echinus does not necessarily imply that the capitals are of stone (as suggested by Schefold 1978, 222), since, as shown by Oliver-Smith (1969, 16–17, 61), vase painters did not follow a strict color pattern as regards the materials of the buildings that they reproduced, such as white for stone and black for wood. The use of wood would account for the discrepancies between the painted building and contemporary, monumental Doric architecture. The assumption here is of course that representations of buildings on vases are faithful reproductions of contemporary, nonmonumental architecture, as regards individual architectural elements (as advocated, in particular, by Vallois 1908; Oliver-Smith 1964; Oliver-Smith 1969; Pedley 1987; there has been opposition to this approach: *e.g.*, Tarbell 1910). Be this as it may, there is no question that the painter of our vase had in mind the Doric order and a Doric frieze with its sequence of triglyphs and metopes: more precisely, a Doric frieze carrying a figural decoration. In fact, of the twenty-six metopes featured on the vase, one out of every two is decorated with a single figure. Moving from left to right one sees four birds, a squatting monkey, a panther, a hen, another monkey bending over, a swan, a lion, a hen, and a dog. An exception to this sequence appears at the far right, where two figures are represented on two contiguous metopes. The metope at the left shows an enigmatic figure identified as either a boy (Bothmer 1985, 217) or an ape (first by Hoffmann 1964, no. 24, and more recently by Moore 2004, 40) apparently climbing out of its metope and setting its left foot on the abacus of the capital below. The metope at the right shows a kneeling archer who is apparently taking aim at the retreating figure on the left. These last two figures resemble, although on a much smaller scale, two mysterious, small figures that appear in the stable scene below in connection with the two left-hand horses. One is an archer in eastern dress, who has jumped onto the back of the left horse and is preparing to shoot an arrow. The other is a naked boy, who is either lowering himself from the entablature onto the horse on the right or, quite the opposite, scaling the column. Much depends on what we make of the posture of this figure: his left foot is already set on the back of the horse, his right foot is still set against the shaft of the column, and both his hands are grasping the abacus of the capital. The similarities between the two pairs are striking; this is especially true of the two archers, who are both preparing to shoot. But this is also partially true in the case of the naked boy grasping the abacus on the left and of the figure leaving its metope on the right. What they have in common is that they both reach, however differently, toward capitals. It is because of these similarities that the two pairs of figures have sometimes been connected, suggesting that the pair on the left has just climbed down from the frieze (Schefold 1978, 222) and that the pair on the right will soon follow suit and take their places on the two right-hand horses (Bothmer 1985, 217). This is only one possibility, of course. As well, the precise identity and function of the two pairs remain unclear; the figures on the left, for example, have often been taken for demons engaged in protecting and calming down the horses (Schefold 1978, 222) or stirring up the already excited horses (Moore 2004, 60 n. 31). One thing, however, is sufficiently clear and matters to us here: that in at least one case, the figure climbing out of the metope, if not in all four, we are clearly dealing with animated architectural decoration (see Boardman 1974, 56; Simon 1976, 85). As first suggested by Hoffmann (1971, 112) and systematically pointed out by Schefold (1978, 222), our figures find their best parallel in the golden handmaids crafted by Hephaistos for his own palace: made in the semblance of living girls, with the power to come alive, and capable of moving to serve their lord, speaking, and thinking (Hom. *Il.* 18.417–20). The golden and silver dogs standing as guardians on either side of the door of the palace of Alkinoos, also fashioned by Hephaistos with cunning skill (Hom. *Od.* 7.91–95), are another parallel. It is precisely these two parallels that strongly support the view that we are not dealing with an ordinary stable but with the palace of a god, and the idea of a thematic link between the two sides of the cup.

Our cup is interesting not only because it illustrates the power of images serving as building decoration to come alive but also because it illustrates their power to capture the attention of the viewer. One figure on our cup is, in fact, gazing in wonder (as pointed out, again, by Schefold 1978, 222) at the figure slipping from its metope and reaching toward the abacus, and that is the bearded man at the far right, who is wearing a himation over a chiton and is holding a staff, and who has often been taken as the person in charge of the stable (Simon 1976, 84; Bothmer 1985, 217; Moore 2004, 40). The turning of his head and of his gaze from the grooms taking care of the horses toward the direction of the little, animated, architectural figure above his head can hardly be missed.

This turning of the head and of the gaze introduces us to the first literary source that I discuss in this essay: a passage of the eighth paean by Pindar, probably written for the Delphians in the 490s–480s. The background for this text is the myth of the first four temples at Delphi, for which Pindar's paean is the earliest source (see Sourvinou-Inwood 1979; Rutherford 2001, 216–32). Chronologically, the next relevant source for this myth is Pausanias's discussion of the history of the Temple of Apollo (10.5.9–12), which, along with the history of the oracle, opens his section on Delphi in Book 10. Pindar and Pausanias are the only known systematic accounts of this myth, while other passages from ancient authors contain references to one or more but not all of the first four temples (Arist., fgm. 3 Rose; Strabo 9.3.9; Philost. *V A*, 6.11; these texts are collected by Rutherford 2001, 231–32). Since the text of Pindar is only fragmentary, it is better to look at the version offered by Pausanias first. According to Pausanias, who says he is reporting the local tradition ("the Delphians say"), but who only mentions Pindar as a specific source, the first and most ancient temple of Apollo was in the form of a hut and was made of laurel, the branches of which were brought from the laurel in Tempe. The second temple was made by bees from beeswax and feathers, and was sent to the Hyperboreans by Apollo (no reference is made to the form of this building). As an alternative to the local tradition regarding this second temple, Pausanias reports two other versions: that the temple was built by a Delphian named Pteras, who gave his name to the building (a rationalizing version); and that the temple was built of the fern (*pteris*) that grows in the mountains (a version that Pausanias does not find acceptable). The third temple was made of bronze. Pausanias believes in the possibility of a bronze temple for Apollo, since he knows about the use of bronze as a building material, for which he lists mythical and historical parallels (the bedchamber made by Akrisios for his daughter Danae; the Temple of Athena Chakioikos at Sparta; the tiles of the roof of the Forum of Trajan in Rome). However, he cannot believe the rest of the story: that the temple was made by Hephaistos; that on top of its pediments stood golden singers (here Pausanias quotes Pindar and remarks that his Golden Charmers were simply an imitation of Homer's Sirens; see below); and that the temple disappeared, falling into a chasm in the earth or was melted by fire. After the bronze temple, Pausanias mentions the fourth temple of Apollo, made of stone, built by Trophonios and Agamedes, and burnt down in 548–547 BC. He ends his account by mentioning the temple standing in his own time (the Late Classical building), which he says was built by the Amphictyons, and claims that Spintharos of Corinth was the architect (it is remarkable how in his account, Pausanias omits the temple built in the Late Archaic period under the supervision of the Alkmeonids).

The fourth temple in this sequence, the one built by Trophonios and Agamedes, is traditionally identified with the seventh-century predecessor of the Late Archaic temple, known to us through a few architectural elements, which are large enough to suggest a monumental building made of poros (Courby 1927, 190–99; La Coste-Messelière 1969, 731–32; Maass 1993, 103–4). Sometime during the sixth century (not necessarily before the fire of 548–547 BC, as it is often assumed; see Càssola 1975, 102), the construction of this temple was described in the *Homeric Hymn to Apollo* (295–99): Apollo lays down the foundations, wide and very long, Trophonios and Agamedes build the stereobate (literally the "stone threshold") with stone, and finally the countless tribes of men build the walls with worked stones (I am following the translation and interpretation of the passage proposed by Càssola 1975; the traditional interpretation is: Apollo lays down the foundations, Trophonios and Agamedes add the *adyton*, and then men build around it with stones [Rutherford 2001, 225]).

This fourth temple might correspond to historical reality; however, there is little question that the entire story of the four temples of Apollo at Delphi is a figment of mythopoetic imagination, and it in not impossible that this myth was largely constructed by Pindar. In fact, as pointed out by Sourvinou-Inwood (1979) and Rutherford (2001), the sequence of building phases presented by this myth is structured according to a sequence of materials (laurel, wax and feathers, bronze, stone) and of craftsmen (absence of craft, animal craft, divine craft, heroic craft) that is clearly inspired by both the five-stage myth of the races in Hesiod's *Works and Days* (109 *ff.*; as regards the sequence of materials: gold, silver, bronze, iron) and by the recounting of the construction of the Temple of Apollo in the *Homeric Hymn to Apollo* (as regards the sequence of craftsmen: Apollo, Trophonios and Agamedes, and men). Yet, in spite of the blatant fictional nature of this myth, it is remarkable how many efforts have been made to identify a nucleus of truth in it, particularly for what concerns the first three buildings.

Thus, it is often assumed that the story about the laurel temple would reflect the memory of an eighth-century shrine made of laurel, cancelled from the archaeological record by later building construction at the core of the sanctuary (suffice here to mention Bérard 1971, 68–69; Sourvinou-Inwood 1979, 234–38; Gruben 2001, 75; Rutherford 2001, 225). This proposition is based primarily on the alleged parallel with the earliest Temple of Apollo Daphnephoros at Eretria, as restored by its Swiss excavators. This building, dated to 800–750, had an apsidal plan and was built of wood and other perishable materials upon a foundation of stone. The Swiss excavators suggested that its walls and roof were covered by panels made of laurel branches attached to a framework of wooden posts, and a similar structure has consequently been hypothesized in the case of Delphi. Although fascinating, this theory is very problematic, not least because of the problem of the circularity of the argumentation, given that the use of laurel branches in that restoration of the elevation of the Eretria building was itself

mainly based on the Delphic myth (see esp. Bérard 1971, 68–69; Auberson and Schefold 1972, 118–19; Auberson 1974, 60, 66). It is thus not surprising that in recent years the restoration has been regarded with increasing skepticism, and that a closer look at the archaeological evidence has led to an alternative restoration with reinforced mudbrick walls, which is now followed by the Swiss archaeologists working at the site (Coulton 1988, 60–62; Drerup 1993; Mazarakis Ainian 1997, 59–60; Barletta 2001, 25; S. Verdan in Ducrey et al. 2002, 131 n. 14; 2004, 228).

The second temple, the one made of wax and feathers, does not fare any better. In fact, the plural of the Greek name for feathers, *ptera*, has been linked to its other meaning of colonnade of a peripteral temple (E. L. Schwandner in Gruben 2001, 75; see Rutherford 2001, 218, 225–26). Herein lies the implication that the myth makes a reference to a peripteral temple, but the consequent, inevitable question is not posed as to whether wax was used as a building material, and bees employed as architects and masons, as the rest of the myth goes. In this context one may mention the suggestion by Rumpf (1964, 7–8) that the mythological temple at Delphi was reproduced as a real building in Delos, based on the discovery of wall blocks decorated with a honeycomb pattern. This theory is disproved by the fact that in Delos the use of this pattern was not limited to only one building, since it appears on both the Letoon (Bruneau and Ducat 2005, 222–24, no. 53), built *c.* 540 BCE, and on the so-called Monument aux hexagons (Bruneau and Ducat 2005, 205–6, no. 44, fig. 52), dated *c.* 500 BC (a similar pattern is found on a series of blocks reused in a house in the theater district; see Bruneau and Ducat 2005, 206). It is also disproved by the fact that this honeycomb pattern is found in several other places in and around the Aegean (Paros, Thasos, Sane, Erythrai), with a distribution that suggests that this decorative motif was characteristic of the architecture of the Cyclades (Hellmann and Fraisse 1979, 73–74, pl. X; Gruben 1997, 399; Hellmann 2002, I, 113; Bruneau and Ducat 2005, 206).

Also in the case of the third temple, there are those who believe that the story has a core of truth: namely, the use of bronze as a building material (La Coste-Messelière 1969, 732 n. 2; Maass 1993, 102; Gruben 2001, 75). This is a rationalizing interpretation of the myth that ultimately derives from Pausanias, and that seemingly finds support in the use of bronze for revetment in early Greek architecture (Drerup 1952; Philipp 1994; Normann 1996). However, the problem here is represented by the fact that the myth posits a temple with walls and pillars made entirely of bronze, not just covered with bronze plaques. Rather than corresponding to reality, this building closely corresponds to the Homeric description of the palace of Alkinoos, mentioned before, made by Hephaistos with bronze walls, and with dogs of gold and silver on either side of the door.

It is now time to focus on Pindar's version about this

third temple, starting with a full quotation of the best-preserved passage:

> But what was the pattern, O Muses, that the latter showed, through the artful strength of Hephaestus and Athene? Bronze were the walls, bronze pillars stood beneath, and six golden Charmers sang above the gable. But the sons of Cronus opened the ground with a thunderbolt and hid it, the most sacred of all works . . . astonished at the sweet voice, that foreigners wasted away apart from children and wives, hanging up their spirit as a dedication to the sweet voice. (Translation by Rutherford 2001, 213)

Pindar's description of the bronze temple differs from that of Pausanias in the fact that the temple is attributed to the craft of not only Hephaistos but also Athena. As suggested by Rutherford (2001, 219), a model for this cooperation may have been provided by Hesiod's account of the creation of Pandora, made by Hephaistos and clothed by Athena (*Theog.* 571–80; *Op.* 70–72). Moreover, I suggest that this inclusion of Athena may have also been motivated by the fact that the Late Archaic Temple of Apollo was built with the substantial contribution of the Athenian family of the Alkmeonids, who were put in charge of its reconstruction (along similar lines, Snell 1962, 5, has suggested that the prominent position of Athena in the paean was motivated by the fact that the poem was written for the Athenians or

for a city closely connected with Athens). This contribution by the Alkmeonids was well known to Pindar, who in praising a member of the Athenian family for his victory at the games in Delphi in 486 makes an explicit reference to it (*Pyth.* 7.9–12). It has been suggested that Pindar devised the eighth paean as a celebration of the new temple (Rutherford 2001, 231); in this context, the attribution of the bronze temple not only to Hephaistos but also to Athena would be an appropriate tribute to the family in charge of the reconstruction of the Late Archaic temple (Fig. 1.5).

The divine craftsmanship of the bronze temple gives an explanation for both the material and the supernatural character of the figural decoration of the building, which consists of six Charmers (*Kēledones*) made of gold and endowed with the power to sing. In placing these six Charmers above the gable (*aietos*), Pindar clearly took inspiration from the use of akroteria on temples (as first pointed out by Furtwängler 1882, 343), even though the repetition of the same subject at the top and the sides of both gables is not documented on Archaic buildings. However, the fact that these *Kēledones* are part-human, destructive, female monsters (Sourvinou-Inwood 1979, 245–46) closely reminds one of sphinxes, which were often used as lateral akroteria, including on the Late Archaic Temple of Apollo (Floren 1987, 244–45; the possibility of

Fig. 1.5 *Delphi, Late Archaic Temple of Apollo, east facade restored by F. Courby (From Courby 1927).*

the use of Sirens as akroteria in the Archaic period is not excluded, but it is problematic: see Danner 1989, 48).

This makes it all the more interesting for us to analyze here the powerful effect that these *Kēledones* would have had on their public, an effect that forced the intervention of the gods (Zeus and Poseidon?) who hid the building beneath the earth. From their position above the gable, the Charmers sang, and with their song (a paean?), like the Homeric Sirens (*Od.* 12.44), they entranced the strangers visiting Delphi, who ended up forgetting their families and lingering there in pleasure.

More precisely, according to Pindar's words, these visitors hang up (*anakrimnantes*) their souls as an offering to the voice of the *Kēledones,* in a metaphor that suggests, according to Rutherford (2001, 220), both religious dedication and psychological dependency. In fact, the term used by Pindar to connote the mental state of the strangers (*anakrimnantes*) indicates both emotional dependence (see Pl. *Ion* 536 A) and physical suspension (see Hdt. 5.77 on votive offerings hanging from the walls of the Akropolis; and Hdt. 5.95 on votive offerings hanging from the Temple of Athena at Sigeum), as if their hearts were at the same time engaged by the music and suspended, nailed onto the temple next to the akroteria (for *kremannumi* and *anakremannumi,* see Liddell et al. 1940; Chantraine 1968–1980).

If the text of Pindar tells us of a fatal attraction of architectural decoration for its public, another text introduces us to an opposite emotional response: repulsion. I am referring, of course, to a well-known fragment of a satyr drama by Aeschylus called *Theōroi ē Isthmiastai* (see esp. Fraenkel 1942, 244–45; Setti 1952; Snell 1956; Lloyd-Jones 1971, 541–56; Stieber 1994; Conrad 1997, 56–86; O'Sullivan 2000). It is primarily known through a series of papyrus fragments published by Lobel in 1941 (E. Lobel in Lobel et al. 1941, 14–22, no. 2162; further editions of this text are by Radt 1985, fgms. 78a–82; Diggle 1998, 11–15). Since *theōros* means not only "member of a sacred embassy" but also "spectator," before the publication of the fragments it was thought that in the drama of Aeschylus the satyrs were introduced as spectators of the Isthmian Games. However, since in the fragments an explicit mention is made of a votive offering to Poseidon, today the *communis opinio* is that the satyrs were brought on scene as members of a sacred embassy sent or led by Dionysos to the Sanctuary of Isthmia in honor of Poseidon. Also, since the preserved fragments contain a quarrel between Dionysos and the satyrs, and since these creatures are featured training for the games, it is also generally believed that prior to entering the stage, the satyrs, after reaching the sanctuary as members of the sacred embassy, had made the decision to abandon Dionysos, putting themselves under the protection of the sea god. For this reason, in the preserved text they should be understood as practicing for the games and not for the dances that they

were supposed to perform under the guidance of Dionysos (see Lloyd-Jones 1971, 543–46; Conrad 1997, 56–59).

Be this as it may concerning the prior events and the plot of this satyr drama (we might have preserved only one-seventh or one-eighth of the original text), what interests us here is the first scene preserved on papyrus (F 78a Radt). In this scene, the satyrs of the chorus are portrayed standing in front of the Temple of Poseidon and holding images representing themselves, which have been given to them by a character who is not named in the preserved lines and whose identification has thus been subject to much controversy (among the suggested names are Sisyphos, Daidalos, or Hephaistos). The images that the satyrs hold in their hands are so accurate in representing them that the satyrs spend several lines praising their mimetic qualities and the skill of their maker. These lines are particularly famous, and they have attracted considerable interest since their first publication, for a variety of reasons (Daidalos and the magic of images: Morris 1992, 217–20; the mimetic power of the new, Early Classical style: Else 1958, 78; Sörbom 1966, 41–53; Hallett 1986, 75–78; Stewart 1990, 142; the expressive power credited to portraiture in its early stages: Richter 1965, 32; Philipp 1968, 28; Stieber 1994). After praising their likenesses, the satyrs approach the temple of the god, saying that they are carrying the images as votive offerings (*euktaia*) to Poseidon, adding that the images will serve as an ornament for the divinity (*kosmon . . . tō theō*) and as a well-painted prayer (*kalligraptos euchē*). Then the satyrs proceed to nail the images high up on the building. From that position, they say, the images will keep away the visitors approaching the sanctuary.

This final remark is what interests us in the present context, since we are most likely dealing with the figural decoration of a temple, and with the description of the impact that it produces on its public. There is, in fact, a very good chance that the images that are the center of the action in this passage are satyr masks painted with bright colors (this was first suggested by Fraenkel 1942, 245; see also, among others, Snell 1956, 6; Green 1994, 45–46, 79; Conrad 1997, 64–65; O'Sullivan 2000, 357; Kaimio et al. 2001, 56–58; Steiner 2001, 47–48. The alternative identification of these images with painted *pinakes* reproducing the satyrs in full figure – advocated by Lobel in Lobel *et al.* 1941, 14; Krumeich *et al.* 1999, 142 *ff.*; Krumeich 2000 – is wrong, as I have argued in Marconi 2005a, 77–79; *contra* see also Kaimio *et al.* 2001, 57). There is also a very good chance that the act of nailing these masks high up on the building represents an allusion to the use of antefixes with satyr masks. These were particularly popular in Sicily, especially during Aeschylus's lifetime (525/24–456/55 BC). An intriguing coincidence indeed, since Aeschylus spent several years on the island (see Marconi 2005a).

As I have already mentioned, in this passage of the satyr drama, the satyrs' masks, placed high on the temple like antefixes, have the power to inflict a deep emotional shock on the visitors of the sanctuary. More precisely, to quote Aeschylus's words (in the translation by Lloyd-Jones 1971, 553–54), the satyrs say, "let each fasten up the likeness of his handsome face, a truthful messenger (*aggelon*), a voiceless herald (*kēruk' anaudon*) to keep off travellers (*emporōn kōlutora*); he'll halt strangers on their way (*epischēsei keleuthou tous xeno[us]*)."

The reason why the images will terrify the strangers is controversial (for Snell 1956, 7, followed by Faraone 1992, 37–38, the reason is that the visitors, seeing heads hanging from the temple, will believe that in the sanctuary visitors are decapitated; for Stieber 1994, 92, instead, the reason would be that the portraits of the satyrs are horrific), but what matters here, and is made clear by the text, is that the images will be, in fact, terrifying because of their appearance rather than their sound, voiceless as they are (one is reminded of Simonides's saying that "painting is silent poetry, and poetry painting that speaks"; see Plut. *Mor.* 346 *f*.; De Angeli 1988, 29, no. 6). Moreover, these images will not only terrify strangers; they will also stop them on their way to the sanctuary. Located high on the temple, these images have the power to engage, to transfix their public from some distance (this passage is the main evidence that we have for the so-called apotropaic function of images on temples; see esp. Hölscher 1972, 28; for a parallel interpretation of the role of these images in creating shock and a sense of awe in the worshipers, see Marconi 2004, 222; 2007, 216).

The texts by Pindar and Aeschylus describe two opposite responses to the figural decoration of buildings: attraction and repulsion. In both instances we are in the presence of a strong, emotional reaction. One should contrast this kind of response with the famous scene in the *Ion* of Euripides (184–218) where the handmaids of Kreousa are featured approaching the Temple of Apollo at Delphi and expressing their admiration for the images displayed on the building (see Zeitlin 1994). This passage by Euripides, which is still about seeing frightening creatures, such as the Hydra, the Chimaira, and the Giants, no longer describes strong emotions such as attraction or repulsion but rather the pleasure that the viewers take in identifying the subjects, and in matching those subjects with their mythological competence. Confusion is no longer allowed between representation and represented, which are now two clearly separate entities.

There is one more opportunity for us to experience the impact of buildings on their public during the Archaic period, and this is offered by building models (see Schattner 1990; Muller 2001). Although building models have traditionally been used as a source of information about the plan, elevation, and general appearance of profane and sacred buildings (one need only think of two famous models, the one from Perachora and the other from the Argive Heraion, which have been so critical for modern scholarship in

visualizing the architecture of the Geometric period), it has now become clear that ancient building models are not small-scale projects waiting to be transformed into real architectures but rather evocations of already existing buildings (Muller 2001). As such, building models are first-rate documents for the reception of Greek architecture.

Concerning the figural decoration of Archaic buildings, a primary document is represented by the well-known model from Sabucina (Fig. 1.6). This model was used by Professor Holloway in the opening of his important article on Greek temple decoration of 1988, an article that has taught us to look at the decoration of Archaic Greek buildings as a whole. It is with this model that I now end this essay in his honor.

The model from Sabucina, dating to the end of the sixth century, represents a small building standing on a tall, rounded base (Orlandini 1962, 103–6; Castellana 1983; Holloway 1988, 177–79; 1991, 78–79; Schattner 2001, 203–4, no. 24; Danner 2002, 70–71, E8; Panvini 2003, 75–76). It has been thought that this model was used in cult and that it was carried in processions, although it must be said that it appears too fragile to have served for that purpose. Speaking of this model in the language of Greek architecture

Fig. 1.6 *Model from Sabucina, Caltanissetta, Museo Archeologico Regionale (Photo by the author).*

– something we are allowed to do in consideration of the fact that the author of the building had Greek architecture in mind – the model features a prostyle building consisting of a small cella preceded by a porch. Of this porch, only the two external columns are represented; the central ones were probably omitted to allow for a full view of the large door leading into the cella. There are several interesting things about the elevation of this building, but also a number of strange things. Among the interesting things are the two narrow windows piercing the walls of both sides of the cella. Among the strange things are the two columns of the porch, which are fluted and bear rough, Doric-looking capitals but stand on bases. The main surprise, however, comes from the top of the building. The particular interest of the maker of the model in this part of the building is first revealed by the neat indication of the tiles of the roof, which has an interesting convex profile. It is the decoration of the building, however, that has caught most of his attention. This decoration consists first of three disk akroteria attached to the corners of both pediments, and of two large masks in the pediment above the main front of the building: a silen, based on the rendering of the ear, at the center of the left half; and a gorgoneion at the center of the right half. Above the pediments, the decoration continues with the forepart of a horse with a rider at the end of the ridgepole on the main front of the building, the forepart of a horse (in my view, not a second horse and rider group, as usually assumed, but most likely a winged horse, the wings badly damaged; there is in fact no evidence for bridles or the legs of the rider) in a similar position on the rear front of the building, and of a third figure on the ridgepole almost at the center of the roof, which has left almost no traces.

This model was found in the so-called *capanna-tempietto* (or *sacello* A), a sacred structure of circular plan, preceded by a small, irregular distyle-in-antis portico, dated to between the seventh century and the first half of the sixth century (De Miro 1977, 102–3; 1980–81, 561 *ff.*; 1983, 337–42; Romeo 1989, 34, no. 53; Panvini 2003, 43). This is interesting in consideration of the fact that building models were generally used in Archaic Greece as votive offerings (Schattner 1990, 191 *ff.*), and a similar function may be posited here. With its rectangular plan, our model offered a striking contrast to the architecture of the building where it was housed. It should also be pointed out that although between the mid-sixth century and the first half of the fifth century a new shrine (De Miro 1980–81, 565 *ff.*; Romeo 1989, 34–35, no. 54; Panvini 2003, 43) was built next to the old one with a rectangular plan (referred to as *oikos rettangolare* or *sacello* B) – one of the several shrines with a rectangular plan built in the native settlements of eastern and central-southern Sicily during these years (see Albanese Procelli 2003, 214–15; Palermo 2005, 120) – that building did not have a porch and was probably entered from the south flank. This means that the architecture of our building model was a stranger within its own town, and the same goes for at least part of its figural decoration, the equine akroteria, for example, which are not documented at the site (but gorgon and silen antefixes are, although they appear to be later than the model). It is thus inevitable to think that a temple in a Greek colony on the coast provided the inspiration for our model, although it should be noted that prostyle temples do not seem to have been popular in Archaic Sicily, where preference was accorded to distyle-in-antis fronts (Romeo 1989). The only buildings that might plausibly be restored as prostyles, in alternative to distyle in antis, are Temple M at Selinus (Pompeo 1999) and Temple A in via Minerva at Syracuse (Orsi 1918, 370–80; Romeo 1989, 12, no. 12; Marconi 2007, 52). Yet, it must also be acknowledged that – as indicated by the convex roof, which appears to be a compromise between a Greek pitched roof and a local thatched roof (De Miro 1983, 340) – inspiration was soon overwhelmed by the imagination of its maker.

This is where the figural decoration of our model might come in. Based on our present knowledge of the figural decoration of buildings in Archaic Sicily, we have to deal with the possibility that what we see on this model is not the faithful reproduction of the figural apparatus of a Greek temple but something like a bricolage of individual figural elements taken from their context and reassembled in ways unusual for the monumental architecture that provided the inspiration. Thus, if it is common in Sicilian temples of the Archaic period to have one large gorgoneion right in the middle of the pediment (Danner 2000; Marconi 2007, 214–22), the use of two masks placed at the center of the two halves of the pediment is not documented (I do not think that this possibility applies to a gorgoneion from Morgantina; Danner 1996, 36–37, F79). It looks as if the author of our model moved to the main facade antefixes that he saw along the flanks of small buildings like those at Gela, which has provided several examples of gorgon and silen antefixes (for a full bibliography on Sicilian antefixes, see Marconi 2005b, 213–14). Likewise, the combination on the facade of disk and horse-and-rider akroteria is not documented (Danner 1996). We are probably dealing with a native working from memory, the memory of the sacred architecture of the Greek cities of the coast. Seeing this superabundance of decorative elements, we can only agree with Holloway's comment that "with all its awkwardness this object has captured the essence of a colonial Greek temple of its day. This is not because the model reproduces any temple, but because it emphasizes, even exaggerates, the essential elements of architectural form and decoration of these buildings" (Holloway 1988, 177; see also 1991, 78). For the purpose of this essay, one would add that that essence, perceived and impressed in the memory, consisted primarily of images.

Acknowledgments

I would like to thank Derek Counts and Anthony Tuck for inviting me to contribute to this volume in honor of Professor Ross Holloway.

Works Cited

Albanese Procelli, R. M. (2003) *Sicani, Siculi, Elimi*. Milan, Longanesi.

Arafat, Karim W. (1996) *Pausanias' Greece*. New York, Cambridge University Press.

Auberson, P. (1974) La reconstitution du Daphnéphoréion d'Erétrie. *Antike Kunst* 17, 60–68.

Auberson, P. and Schefold, K. (1972) *Führer durch Eretria*. Bern, Francke.

Barletta, B. A. (2001) *The Origins of the Greek Architectural Orders*. Cambridge and New York, Cambridge University Press.

Bauchhenss-Thüriedl, Ch. (1971) *Der Mythos von Telephos in der antiken Bildkunst*. Würzburg, Triltsch.

Beard, M. (2003) *The Parthenon*. Cambridge, Mass., Harvard University Press.

Beazley, J. D. (1956) *Attic Black-figure Vase-Painters*. Oxford, Clarendon Press.

Beazley, J.D. (1971) *Paralipomena: Additions to Attic Black-figure Vase-painters and to Attic Red-figure Vase-painters*. Oxford: Clarendon Press.

Benjamin, A. (ed.) (2005) *Walter Benjamin and Art*. London and New York, Continuum.

Bérard, C. (1971) Architecture érétrienne et mythologie delphique. Le Daphnéphoréion. *Antike Kunst* 14, 59–73.

Betancourt, Ph. P. (1977) *The Aeolic Style in Architecture*. Princeton, Princeton University Press.

Boardman, J. (1974) *Athenian Black Figure Vases*. London, Thames & Hudson.

——— (1986) Leaina. In H. A. G. Brijder, A. A. Drukker, and C. W. Neeft (eds.), *Enthousiasmos. Essays on Greek and Related Pottery Presented to J. M. Hemelrijk*, 93–96. Amsterdam, Allard Pierson Museum.

Bothmer, D. von. (1985) *The Amasis Painter and His World*. Athens, Malibu, and New York, The J. Paul Getty Museum and Thames and Hudson.

Brolin, B. C. (2000) *Architectural Ornament: Banishment and Return*. New York, Norton.

Bruneau, Ph. and Ducat, J. (eds.) (2005) *Guide de Délos*. 4th ed., rev. M. Brunet, A. Farnoux, and J.-Ch. Moretti. Athens, École française d'Athènes.

Burkert, W. (1985) *Greek Religion*. Trans. John Raffan. Cambridge, Mass., Harvard University Press.

Buschor, E. (1922) Burglöwen. *Mitteilungen des Deutschen Archäologischen Instituts, Athenische Abteilung* 47, 92–105.

Carpenter, T. H. (1989) *Beazley Addenda*. 2nd ed. Oxford and New York, Oxford University Press.

Càssola, F. (ed.) (1975) *Inni Omerici*. Milan, Fondazione Lorenzo Valla and Arnoldo Mondadori.

Castellana, G. (1983) Il tempietto votivo fittile di Sabucina e la sua decorazione figurata. *Rivista di archeologia* 7, 5–11.

Chantraine, P. (1968–80) *Dictionnaire étymologique de la langue grecque*. 4 vols. Paris, Klincksieck.

Childs, W. A. P. (1993) Herodotos, Archaic chronology, and the Temple of Apollo at Delphi. *Jahrbuch des Deutschen Archäologischen Instituts* 108, 399–441.

Collignon, M. (1911) *Les statues funéraires dans l'art grec*. Paris, Leroux.

Connelly, J. B. (1993) Narrative and image in Attic vase painting. In Peter J. Holliday (ed.), *Narrative and Event in Ancient Art*, 88–129. Cambridge, Cambridge University Press.

Conrad, G. (1997) *Der Silen*. Trier, Wissenschaftlicher Verlag.

Coulton, J. (1988) Post holes and post bases in early Greek architecture. *Mediterranean Archaeology* 1, 58–65.

Courby, F. (1927) *La terrasse du temple*. 2 vols. Paris, de Boccard (*Fouilles de Delphes, École française d'Athènes* II.2).

Danner, P. (1989) *Griechische Akrotere der archaischen und klassischen Zeit*. Rome, Giorgio Bretschneider.

——— (1996) *Westgriechische Firstantefixe und Reiterkalyptere*. Mainz am Rhein, Philipp von Zabern.

——— (2000) Westgriechische Giebeldekorationen 1. *Römische historische Mitteilungen* 42, 19–105.

——— (2002) Westgriechische Giebeldekorationen 3. *Römische historische Mitteilungen* 44, 19–102.

De Angeli, S. (1988) Mimesis e techne. *Quaderni urbinati di cultura classica* 28, 27–45.

De Cesare, M. (1997) *Le statue in immagine*. Rome, L'Erma di Bretschneider.

De Miro, E. (1977) Nuovi santuari ad Agrigento e a Sabucina. *Cronache di archeologia e di storia dell'arte* 16, 94–104.

——— (1980–81) Ricerche archeologiche nella Sicilia centro-meridionale. *Kokalos* 26–27, 561–80.

——— (1983) Forme di contatto e processi di trasformazione nelle società antiche. Esempio da Sabucina. In *Forme di contatto e processi di trasformazione nelle società antiche*, 335–42. Pisa and Rome, Scuola Normale Superiore and École française de Rome.

Diggle, J. (1998) *Tragicorum Graecorum fragmenta selecta*. Oxford, Clarendon Press.

Dinsmoor, W. B. (1947) The Hekatompedon on the Athenian Acropolis. *American Journal of Archaeology* 51, 109–51.

Drerup, H. (1952) Architektur und Toreutik in der griechischen Frühzeit. *Mitteilungen des Deutschen Archäologischen Instituts* 5, 7–38.

——— (1993) Das sogenannte Daphnephoreion in Eretria. In Karin Braun and Andreas Furtwangler (eds.), *Studien zur klassischen Archaologie: Friedrich Hiller zu seinem 60. Geburtstag*, 3–21. Saarbrücken, Archaeological Institute of the Saarland University.

Ducrey, P. ed. (2004) *Eretria*. Athens, École suisse d'archéologie en Grèce.

Ducrey, P., Simon, P., and Verdan, S. (2002) Les activités de l'Ecole suisse d'archéologie en Grèce 2001. *Antike Kunst* 45, 124–32.

Else, G. F. (1958) "Imitation" in the fifth century. *Classical Philology* 53, 73–90.

Faraone, C. A. (1992) *Talismans and Trojan Horses*. New York and Oxford, Oxford University Press.

Floren, J. (1987) *Die griechische Plastik, 1*. Munich, Beck. (*Handbuch der Archäologie* 5).

Fraenkel, E. (1942) Aeschylus: New texts and old problems. *Proceedings of the British Academy*, 28, 237–58.

Frank, I. (ed.) (2000) *The Theory of Decorative Art*. New Haven and London, Yale University Press.

Freedberg, D. (1989) *The Power of Images*. Chicago, University of Chicago Press.

Furtwängler, A. (1882) Von Delos. *Archäologische Zeitung* 40, 321–64.

Gerhard, E. (1840–58) *Auserlesene griechische Vasenbilder*. 4 vols. Berlin, Reimer.

Green, J. R. (1994) *Theatre in Ancient Greek Society*. London and New York, Routledge.

Gruben, G. (1997) Naxos und Delos. *Jahrbuch des Deutschen Archäologischen Instituts* 112, 261–416.

——— (2001) *Griechische Tempel und Heiligtümer*. 5th ed. Munich, Hirmer.

Hallett, C. H. (1986) The origins of the Classical style in sculpture. *Journal of Hellenic Studies* 106, 71–84.

Hellmann, M.-Ch. (2002) *L'Architecture Grecque*. 2 vols. Paris, Picard.

Hellmann, M.-Ch. and Fraisse, P. (1979) *Le monument aux Hexagones et le portique des Naxiens*. Paris, de Boccard. (*Exploration archéologique de Délos* 32).

Heynen, Hilde (1999) *Architecture and Modernity: A Critique*. Cambridge, Mass., MIT Press.

Hoffmann, H. (ed.) (1964) *Fogg Art Museum of Harvard University. Norbert Schimmel Collection*. Mainz am Rhein, Philipp von Zabern.

——— (1971) *Collecting Greek Antiquities*. New York, Potter.

Holloway, R. R. (1988) Early Greek architectural decoration as functional art. *American Journal of Archaeology* 92, 177–83.

——— (1991) *The Archaeology of Ancient Sicily*. London and New York, Routledge.

Hölscher, F. (1972) *Die Bedeutung archaischer Tierkampfbilder*. Würzburg, Triltsch.

Hurwit, J. (1977) Image and frame in Greek art. *American Journal of Archaeology* 81, 1–30.

Jucker, H. (1965–66) Bronzehenkel und Bronzehydria in Pesaro. *Studia Oliveriana* 13–14, 1–128.

Kaimio, M. (2001) Metatheatricality in the Greek satyr-play. *Arctos* 35, 35–78.

Krumeich, R. (2000) Die Weihgeschenke der Satyrn in Aischylos' Theoroi oder Isthmiastai. *Philologus* 144, 176–92.

Krumeich, R., Pechstein, N., and Seidensticker, B. (eds.) (1999) *Das griechische Satyrspiel*. Darmstadt, Wissenschaftliche Buchgesellschaft.

La Coste-Messelière, P. de. (1969) Topographie delphique. *Bulletin de correspondance hellénique* 93, 730–58.

Liddell, H. G., Scott, R., and Jones, H. S. (1940) *A Greek-English Lexikon*. 9th ed. Oxford, Clarendon Press.

Lloyd-Jones, H. (1971) *Aeschylus 2*. Cambridge, Mass., Loeb Classical Library.

Lobel, E., Roberts, C. H., and Wegener, E. P. (eds.) (1941) *The Oxyrhynchus Papyri, 18*. London, Egypt Exploration Society.

Lund, J. and Rasmussen, B. B. (1994) *Antiksamlingen: Graekere, etruskere, romere: Nationalmuseets vijlednnger*. Copenhagen, Nationalmuseet.

Maass, M. (1993) *Das antike Delphi*. Darmstadt, Wissenschaftliche Buchgesellschaft.

Marconi, C. (2004) Kosmos: The imagery of the Archaic Greek temple. *Res. Anthropology and Aesthetics* 45, 209–24.

——— (2005a) I Theõroi di Eschilo e le antefisse sileniche siceliote. *Sicilia Antiqua* 2, 75–93.

——— (2005b) La decorazione figurata di età classica. In P. Minà (ed.), *Urbanistica e architettura nella Sicilia Greca,* 83–86, 213–14. Palermo, Regione Siciliana.

——— (2007) *Temple Decoration and Cultural Identity in the Archaic Greek World*. New York, Cambridge University Press.

Markoe, G. E. (1989) The "lion-attack" in Archaic Greek art: Heroic triumph. *Classical Antiquity* 8, 86–115.

Marszal, J. R. (1998) An epiphany for Athena: The Eastern pediment of the Old Athena Temple at Athens. In K. J. Hartswick and M. C. Sturgeon (eds.), *Stephanos: Studies in Honor of Brunilde Sismondo Ridgway,* 173–80. Philadelphia, The University of Pennsylvania Museum of Archaeology and Anthropology.

Mazarakis Ainian, A. (1997) *From Rulers' Dwellings to Temples*. Jonsered, Åström.

Mertens-Horn, M. (1986) Studien zu griechischen Löwenbildern. *Mitteilungen des Deutschen Archäologischen Instituts, Römische Abteilung* 93, 1–61.

Moore, M. B. (2004) Horse care as depicted on Greek vases before 400 BC. *Metropolitan Museum Journal* 39, 35–67.

Morris, S. P. (1992) *Daidalos and the Origins of Greek Art*. Princeton, Princeton University Press.

Muller, B. (ed.) (2001) *"Maquettes architecturales" de l'Antiquité*. Paris, de Boccard.

Müller, P. (1978) *Löwen und Mischwesen in der archaischen griechischen Kunst*. Zurich, Juris.

Naumann, F. (1983) *Die Ikonographie der Kybele in der phrygischen und der griechischen Kunst*. Tübingen, Wasmuth.

Normann, A. von. (1996) *Architekturtoreutik in der Antike*. Munich, Tuduv.

Oenbrink, W. (1997) *Das Bild im Bilde*. Frankfurt am Main and New York, Lang.

Oliver-Smith, P. (1964) Representations of Aeolic capitals on Greek vases before 400 BC. In Lucy Freeman Sandler (ed.), *Essays in Memory of Karl Lehmann*, 232–41. New York, Institute of Fine Arts, New York University.

——— (1969) Architectural elements on Greek vases before 400 BC. Ph.D. dissertation, New York University.

Orlandini, P. (1962) L'espansione di Gela nella Sicilia centro-meridionale. *Kokalos* 8, 69–121.

Orsi, P. (1918) Gli scavi intorno a l'Athenaion di Siracusa negli anni 1912–1917. *Monumenti Antichi*. 25, 353–762.

O'Sullivan, P. (2000) Satyr and image in Aeschylus' Theoroi. *Classical Quarterly* 50, 353–66.

Palermo, D. (2005) La ricezione dei modelli dell'architettura greca nel mondo indigeno: I luoghi di culto. In P. Minà (ed.), *Urbanistica e architettura nella Sicilia Greca*, 119–21. Palermo, Regione Siciliana.

Panvini, R. (ed.) (2003) *Caltanissetta. Il Museo Archeologico. Catalogo*. Palermo, Regione Siciliana.

Pedley, J. G. (1987) Reflections of architecture in sixth-century Attic vase-painting. In *Papers on the Amasis Painter and His World*, 63–80. Malibu, J. Paul Getty Museum.

Pfisterer-Haas, S. (2002) Mädchen und Frauen am Wasser:

Brunnenhaus und Louterion als Orte der Frauengemeinschaft und der möglichen Begegnung mit einem Mann. *Jahrbuch des Deutschen Archäologischen Instituts* 117, 1–79.

Philipp, H. (1968) *Tektonon Daidala*. Berlin, Hessling.

——— (1994) Chalkeoi toichoi—Eherne Wände. *Archäologischer Anzeiger*, 489–98.

Picard, Ch. (1935–66) *Manuel d'archéologie grecque: La sculpture*. 5 vols. Paris, Picard.

Pompeo, L. (1999) *Il complesso architettonico del tempio M di Selinunte*. Florence, Le Lettere.

Radt, S. (1985) *Tragicorum Graecorum fragmenta 3. Aischylos*. Göttingen, Vandenhoeck & Ruprecht.

Richter, G. M. A. (1965) *The Portraits of the Greeks*. 3 vols. London, Phaidon Press.

Ridgway, B. S. (1999) *Prayers in Stone*. Berkeley, Los Angeles, and London, University of California Press.

Robertson, M. (1975) *A History of Greek Art*. 2 vols. London, Cambridge University Press.

Romeo, I. (1989) Sacelli arcaici senza peristasi nella Sicilia greca. *Xenia* 17, 5–54.

Rumpf, A. (1964) Bienen als Baumeister. *Jahrbuch der Berliner Museen* 6, 5–8.

Rutherford, I. (2001) *Pindar's Paeans*. Oxford and New York, Oxford University Press.

Schapiro, M. (1969) On some problems in the semiotics of visual art: Field and vehicle in image-signs. *Semiotica* 1, 223–42.

Schattner, T. G. (1990) *Griechische Hausmodelle*. Berlin, Mann.

——— (2001) Griechische und großgriechisch-sizilische Hausmodelle. In B. Muller (ed.), *"Maquettes architecturales" de l'Antiquité*, 161–209. Paris, de Boccard.

Schefold, K. (1937) Statuen auf Vansebildern. *Jahrbuch des Deutschen Archäologischen Instituts* 42, 30–75.

——— (1978) *Götter- und Heldensagen der Griechen in der spätarchaischen Kunst*. Munich, Hirmer.

Schuchhardt, W. H. (1935–36) Die Sima des alten Athena-tempels der Akropolis. *Mitteilungen des Deutschen Archäologischen Instituts, Athenische Abteilung* 60–61, 1–111.

Setti, A. (1952) Eschilo Satirico 2. *Annali della Scuola normale superiore di Pisa* 21, 205–44.

Shapiro, H. A. (1989) *Art and Cult under the Tyrants in Athens*. Mainz am Rhein, Philipp von Zabern.

Simon, E. (1953) *Opfernde Götter*. Berlin, Mann.

——— (1976) *Die griechischen Vasen*. Munich, Hirmer.

——— (1997) Kybele. *Lexicon iconographicum mythologiae classicae* 8, 744–66.

Snell, B. (1956) Aischylos' Isthmiastai. *Hermes* 84, 1–11.

——— (1962) Pindars 8. Paian über die Tempel von Delphi. *Hermes* 90, 1–6.

Sörbom, G. (1966) *Mimesis and Art*. Stockholm, Svenska Bokførlaget.

Sourvinou-Inwood, Ch. (1979) The myth of the first temples at Delphi. *Classical Quarterly* 73, 231–51.

Steiner, D. (2001) *Images in Mind*. Princeton, Princeton University Press.

Stewart, A. (1990) *Greek Sculpture*. New Haven, Yale University Press.

Stieber, M. (1994) Aeschylus' *Theoroi* and realism in Greek art. *Transactions of the American Philological Association* 124, 85–119.

Tafuri, Manfredo (1980) *Theories and History of Architecture*. Trans. G. Verrecchia. New York, Harper & Row.

Tarbell, F. B. (1910) Architecture on Greek vases. *American Journal of Archaeology* 14, 428–33.

Tiverios, M. A. (1976) *Ho Lydos kai to ergo tou*. Athens, Hyperesia Demosieumaton.

Vallois, R. (1908) Études sur les formes architecturales dans les peintures de vases grecs. *Revue archéologique* 11, 359–90.

Weber, M. (1990) *Baldachine und Statuenschreine*. Rome, Giorgio Bretschneider.

Wesenberg, B. (1971) *Kapitelle und Basen*. Düsseldorf, Rheinland.

Zeitlin, F. I. (1994) The artful eye: Vision, ecphrasis and spectacle in Euripidean theater. In S. Goldhill and R. Osborne (eds.), *Art and Text in Ancient Greek Culture*, 138–96. Cambridge and New York, Cambridge University Press.

2

Ambidexterity in the Tarquinia Krater of the Kleophrades Painter

Malcolm Bell, III

Athletes are frequent subjects on the vases of the Kleophrades Painter. Some are depicted in black figure, as the artist held the contract for Panathenaic prize vases in the early fifth century BC, and on these the various athletic contests continued to be rendered in the traditional archaic technique (Bentz 1998, 138–42). Studies of athletes also appear on more than a dozen of the Kleophrades Painter's red-figure vases. One of the finest is the well-preserved calyx-krater in the Museo Archeologico Nazionale of Tarquinia (Figs. 2.1–4), where the careful and confident renderings of a javelin and discus thrower document the new style of the

early fifth century BC (inv. RC 4196; Ferrari 1988, 73–76). It was in these years of stylistic change immediately before and after 500 BC that the challenge of showing the body's responses to movement and gravity pushed artists to abandon the weightless figural schemata of the archaic for greater naturalism. The Kleophrades Painter's vase belongs to the mature phase of this transitional period. It was painted perhaps around the year 490 BC (Ferrari 1988, 75).

There are just two figures to a side. On one (see Figs. 2.1–2) a diskobolos stands with weight entirely on his right leg, his backward lean counterbalanced by his raised arms

Fig. 2.1 *Red-figure krater by the Kleophrades Painter, side A, discus-thrower and trainer; Tarquinia, Museo Archeologico Nazionale, RC 4196 (Photo Hirmer Verlag München).*

Fig. 2.2 *Same as Fig.2.1, detail of discus-thrower (Photo Hirmer Verlag München).*

Fig. 2.3 *Red-figure krater by the Kleophrades Painter, side B; akontist and trainer; Tarquinia, Museo Archeologico Nazionale, RC 4196 (Photo Hirmer Verlag München).*

Fig. 2.4 *Same as Fig.2.3, detail of akontist (Photo Hirmer Verlag München).*

holding the heavy discus, and by his extended left leg, his foot not touching the ground. The athlete looks alertly at his *paidotribes,* or trainer, who is seen from behind holding a forked willow branch, the trainer's usual attribute (Crowther and Frass 1998, 73). Both figures are quite youthful, with slight growth of sideburns, and both wear wreaths in added red with small leaves. On the other side of the vase (see Figs. 2.3–4) an akontist holds the raised butt end of the javelin in his left hand as he inserts his right into the *ankyle,* or throwing thong, at midpoint along the shaft. Most of his weight is on his left leg, his right foot just touching the ground. The trainer, in profile, observes from the left. Again, both figures are youthful and wear wreaths, which here have broad trilobed leaves. We note that the two athletes are literally ambidextrous; that is, their left hands are drawn quite carefully as if they were rights. I shall come back presently to this visual ambidexterity.

Both the akontist preparing to throw the javelin and the diskobolos adjusting his hold on the discus are shown in poses typical of the slightly earlier Pioneers, the group of red-figure painters with whom the young Kleophrades Painter learned his craft (Beazley 1974, 3; Robertson 1992, 56–60). The general subject of a gymnasium scene with athlete and *paidotribes* is also reminiscent of several Pioneer compositions. A notable example is Euphronios's calyx-krater in Berlin (Fig. 2.5), with its paratactic line-up of athletes, trainer, and *paides* on either side (Antikenmuseum, Staatliche Museen Preussischer Kulturbesitz, F 2180). It is as though the Kleophrades Painter has zoomed in on the

young discus thrower and trainer of side A, selecting a single pair of figures on whom he can focus more closely. In these quiet scenes of athletic instruction the Kleophrades Painter is particularly interested in the body's response to gravity, and the vivid contours and inner markings of his nude figures demonstrate his ability to represent corporeal volume. The earlier Pioneers were usually not so interested in three-

Fig. 2.5 *Red-figure krater by Euphronios, side A, athletes and trainer; Berlin, Antikenmuseum, Staatliche Museen Preussischer Kulturbesitz, F 2180 (Photo Hirmer Verlag München).*

dimensionality or the effects of weight. In this regard the Kleophrades Painter's diskobolos can be compared to the similar but earlier figure of Euphronios (see Fig. 2.5).

In Greek athletics the discus and javelin throw were contests within the composite event of the pentathlon, the other three stages of which were the foot race, wrestling, and the broad jump (Ebert 1963; Kyle 1993, 180–81). Of the five contests, only the foot race and wrestling also existed as separate events in the games. Consequently, we can be sure that the subjects on the Tarquinia krater are in training for the pentathlon. Given that individual pentathletes needed to train for all five events, we should consider whether the same competitor is shown here preparing for two of them. The Kleophrades Painter's vase recalls Euthymides's neck amphora in Malibu, where the well-known pentathlete Phaullos may be represented on both sides (New Acquisitions 1985, 84AE.63). The close resemblance of the diskobolos and akontist on the Tarquinia vase might, of course, be owed to the artist's characteristic avoidance of specificity in the depiction of individuals, and the consequent adoption of a standard figure type. In that case the depictions would constitute independent figure studies related by their athletic subjects. Yet it is noteworthy that both trainers are also youthful and, like the athletes, bear a resemblance to each other.

There are other reasons to suppose that the same figures are depicted on both sides of the vase. Both pairs of figures could be called *ageneioi*, or beardless youths, the inter-mediate category in the three age groups that competed in the games at Nemea and Isthmia as well as in the Panathenaic games (*paides* or boys, *ageneioi* or beardless youths, *andres* or men; on the age groups, see Golden 1998, 101–16). Young trainers also appear on other vases, though not so often as bearded figures; examples by the Kleophrades Painter can be seen on a neck amphora in St. Petersburg (Beazley 1916, 126–27) and a stamnos in Florence, where the figures are similar to those of the Tarquinia vase though less carefully drawn and where the athletes have anatomically correct hands (Philippaki 1967, pl. 21,2). In the early fifth century the epinician poet Pindar praises trainers in several odes (Race 1997, 14), in one case a young athlete called Pytheas who instructed his brother Phylakidas in the *pankration*, an event combining boxing and wrestling; Pytheas had won a victory as an *ageneios* in the *pankration* at Nemea (Pind., *Nem.* 5) probably in 485 or 483 BC, and his brother won later at the Isthmos as both *pais* and *aner* (Pind. *Isth.* 5.59–61, 6). The paired young men on the Tarquinia krater suggest the possibility of such a fraternal relationship. As usual the Kleophrades Painter does not offer help in identifying the figures by inscribing names (Boardman 1976, 15).

We can also consider whether the vase itself was commissioned for an event celebrating a specific athlete's victory, or victories, in the pentathlon. The social function

of late archaic sympotic vases has been emphasized by Lissarrague (1990) and Giuliani (1991, 17), and in the following article in this volume Alan Shapiro discusses the special wine cups known as *choes*. Kraters were the centerpieces of banquets and symposia, and their painted subjects have at times been interpreted as clues to the specific function of the vases they decorate. The many allusions to marriage on the François Vase have been regarded as evidence that that great black-figure volute-krater was made for a wedding banquet (Robertson 1975, 126), and it has been convincingly argued that a red-figure krater in Larisa attributed to the Painter of Munich 2335 was commissioned for a musical victory in the Panathenaia (Tiverios 1989, 133, 142); Ross Holloway (1966, 112–19) has himself proposed that an Attic red-figure amphora depicting victorious musical performances was also a commission. Euphronios depicted a musical performance on side B of the calyx-krater with Herakles and Antaios in Paris, and athletes are the only subject of his Berlin calyx-krater (see Fig. 2.5); we may wonder whether these important sympotic vases were not made to order for celebrations of musical and athletic victories, respectively. An inscription on such a vase might also refer to a commission: on his black-figure dinos in Rome, Exekias declares that it was a gift from Epainetos to Kharopos, presumably for use on some celebratory occasion (Beazley 1956, 114,20).

On the Tarquinia krater the leaves of the wreaths worn by both athlete and trainer are quite dissimilar on the two sides, as Gloria Ferrari has observed (1988, 73). The differences certainly seem intentional and must indicate separate victories in the pentathlon, but not necessarily by separate athletes. The smaller leaves suggest the olive crown of Athens (Blech 1982, 142; Valavanis 1990, 341, 352) or, less probably, of Olympia. The larger trilobed leaves could denote the wild celery of Nemea (Blech 1982, 134–37). If indeed we are dealing with the same figures on both sides of the vase, we might guess that *c.* 490 BC the Kleophrades Painter's athlete has won victories in the pentathlon at Athens and Nemea.

A further clue favoring the identity of the figures on the two sides of the vase in Tarquinia is the curious "ambi-dexterity" of the athlete in both scenes. To the extent that it has been noted at all, it has been attributed to carelessness (Gardiner 1907, 16; Ferrari 1988, 73 n. 1, where it is said that the right hand of the akontist is rendered as a left). The Kleophrades Painter is, to be sure, not always anatomically accurate in his drawing of hands. Other instances of such ambidexterity can be cited: on the fine but fragmentary calyx-krater in the Metropolitan Museum of Art, one of the warriors on side A (Fig. 2.6) smoothes back his hair with a left hand drawn as a right (Richter 1936, 34); the same mistake (if that is what it is) occurs in the drawing of the left hands of both the Minotaur and Prokrustes, the opponents of Theseus depicted on the two sides of the stamnos in the

Fig. 2.6 *Red-figure krater by the Kleophrades Painter, side A, arming scene; New York, Metropolitan Museum of Art, Rogers Fund, 1908 (08.258.58) (Photo © Metropolitan Museum of Art).*

British Museum (Beazley 1974, pl. 28,1); and, in at least one case (Hermes, on the volute-krater with the *psychostasia*, or soul-weighing, that precedes the mortal combat of Achilles and Memnon, in the Cabinet des Médailles; Beazley 1974, pl. 2), a right hand is drawn as a left. Recently it has been shown that the careful draftsman Euphronios rendered a contorted right hand holding a drinking cup as a left because he used his own left hand as a model, drawing with his right (Neer 2002, 116). Among the Kleophrades Painter's depictions of athletes, only the figures on the Tarquinia krater appear to be ambidextrous, the others having correctly drawn hands in renderings that are generally less ambitious than the two detailed pentathletes on the Tarquinia vase. While errors are always possible (Robertson 1954, 229–30), we may wonder whether the same mistake would be made twice on this unusually fine vase.

The Kleophrades Painter "clearly … was a careful draughtsman who worked hard on his designs" (Robertson 1992, 64). I therefore propose that we have here two images of the same pentathlete whose visual ambidexterity is intentional. By giving him two right hands, the Kleophrades Painter in this hypothesis praises the skill that led to victory in the multiple contests that make up the pentathlon. The athlete is περιδέξιος or ἀμφιδέξιος, figuratively ambidextrous

– or perhaps even actually so; in the modern sport of baseball an ambidextrous pitcher can be a sought-after phenomenon (*New York Times*, April 7, 2007). Both of the Greek terms have a positive charge in early literature (Humer 2006, 273–76), just as ἀμφαρίστερος (Ar., frag. 512, "ambisinistrous") can mean "clumsy" or "luckless" (*Liddell and Scott, A Greek-English Lexicon*). In the figurative sense περιδέξιος can have the meaning of "expert," as in the περιδέξιοι λόγοι (expert arguments) described by the chorus in Aristophanes's *Clouds* (line 949). Literal ambidexterity occurs in the *Iliad*, where in a fierce and protracted encounter Achilles's ambidextrous opponent Asteropaios can throw with both hands and so is especially dangerous (Hom. *Il.* 21.161–204). Asteropaios's first spear strikes Achilles's shield; his second, presumably thrown with his left hand, inflicts the only wound Achilles receives in the *Iliad* (ὅ δ᾿ ἁμαρτῇ δούρασιν ἀμφὶς / ἥρως Ἀστεροπαῖος, ἐπεὶ περιδέξιος ἦεν, [with two spears at the same time, one in either hand, the hero Asteropaios (threw), since he was ambidextrous]; Hom. *Il.* 21, 162–63). More suggestive of combat sports is the taunt of Hipponax, presumably directed against his usual enemy Boupalos: ἀμφιδέξιος γάρ εἰμι κοὐκ ἁμαρτάνω κόπτων, (for I am ambidextrous and do not miss with my punches) (West 1992, fr. 121). In his ode for the young Aiginetan pankratist Phylakidas, Pindar praises the ability of his trainer-brother Pytheas, who is χερσὶ δεξιός, (able [literally, right, dexterous] with [both] hands) (Pind. *Isthm.* 5.61).

If the visual ambidexterity of the Tarquinia pentathlete denotes such physical prowess, it may well have a similar meaning in the other cited examples – for the young warrior facing combat on the New York krater (see Fig. 2.6), and for the strong opponents of Theseus on the stamnos in London. It is, in fact, tempting to identify the ambidextrous warrior in New York as Asteropaios himself. The four warriors depicted on the vase would then consist of Trojans arming before their assault on the Greek camp, as described in book 12 of the *Iliad* (lines 88–107), and the giant bird on side B (Fig. 2.7) would then be the eagle that serves as a powerful omen when the Trojan warriors prepare their assault (Hom. *Il.* 12, 200–5). In this reading the three other figures on the vase are Sarpedon, Glaukos, and (on side B, observing the omen) either Hektor or Poulydamos (the latter, if the two surviving letters -ος belong to a name; Boardman 1976, 15, where this figure is called Glaukos). If indeed the New York warrior with two right hands is περιδέξιος Asteropaios, the likelihood increases that the ambidexterity of the Kleophrades Painter's athletes is intentional. The Hermes with two lefts in the fine Paris psychostasia could still be a mistake, although we may ask whether the god's double left-handedness could be a sign of the fateful outcome of the soul weighing, which leads in short order to the deaths of both Memnon and Achilles.

I therefore suggest that in his Tarquinia krater the Kleophrades Painter praises the skill of a young Athenian

Fig. 2.7 *Red-figure krater by the Kleophrades Painter, side B, arming scene with bird; New York, Metropolitan Museum of Art, Rogers Fund, 1908 (08.258.58) (Photo © Metropolitan Museum of Art).*

pentathlete through the visual metaphor of literal ambidexterity. In this hypothesis, the athlete will have won two contests as an *ageneios* in the early years of the fifth century BC, and the commissioned krater is to become the centerpiece of a banquet celebrating the second of the two victories. So understood, the Kleophrades Painter's vase would thus serve as a visual and functional analogue to Pindar's poems of praise. It also serves as a suitable vehicle for the purpose of this essay, which is offered in celebratory mode to the most περιδέξιος of scholars.

Works Cited

Beazley, J. D. (1916) Two vases in Harrow. *Journal of Hellenic Studies* 36, 123–33.

——— (1956) *Attic Black-Figure Vase-Painters*. Oxford, Clarendon Press.

——— (1974) *The Kleophrades Painter*. Mainz, Verlag Philipp van Zabern.

Bentz, M. (1998) *Panathenäische Preisamphoren, eine athenische Vasengattung und ihre Funktion vom 6.-4. Jahrhundert v. Chr.*, Basel, 18. Beiheft Antike Kunst.

Blech, M. (1982) *Studien zur Kranz bei den Griechen*. Berlin, W. de Gruyter.

Boardman, J. (1976) The Kleophrades Painter at Troy. *Antike Kunst* 19, 3–18.

Crowther, N. B. and Frass, M. (1998) Flogging as a punishment in the ancient games. *Nikephoros* 11, 51–82.

Ebert, J. (1963) Zum Pentathlon der Antike, Abhandlungen der Sächsischen. *Akademie der Wissenschaften zu Leipzig, Phil.-hist. Klasse* 56, Heft 1.

Ferrari, G. (1988) *I vasi attici a figure rosse del periodo arcaico*. Materiali del Museo Archeologico Nazionale di Tarquinia 11. Rome, G. Bretschneider.

Gardiner, E. (1907) Throwing the diskos. *Journal of Hellenic Studies* 27, 1–36.

Giuliani, L. (1991) Euphronios: Ein Maler im Wandel. In *Euphronios der Maler*, exh. cat., 14–24. Berlin, Staatliche Museen Preussischer Kulturbesitz.

Golden, M. (1998) *Sport and Society in Ancient Greece*. Cambridge, Cambridge University Press.

Holloway, R. R. (1966) Music at the Panathenaic Festival. *Archaeology* 19, 112–19.

Humer, E. (2006) *Linkshändigkeit im Altertum, Zur Wertigkeit von links, der linken Hand und Linkshändigkeit in der Antike*. Tönning, Lübeck, and Marburg, Der Andere Verlag.

Kyle, D. G. (1993) *Athletics in Ancient Athens*. Leiden, E. J. Brill.

Lissarrague, F. (1990) *The Aesthetics of the Greek Banquet, Images of Wine and Ritual* (Eng. Trans. A. Szegedy Maszak). Princeton, Princeton University Press.

Neer, R. T. (2002) *Style and Politics in Athenian Vase-Painting: The Craft of Democracy, ca. 530–460 B.C.E.* Cambridge, Cambridge University Press.

New Acquisitions (1985) *J. Paul Getty Museum Journal* 13, 168, no. 17.

Philippaki, B. (1967) *The Attic Stamnos*. Oxford, Clarendon Press.

Race, W. H., editor and translator, (1997) *Pindar, Olympian Odes, Pythian Odes*. Cambridge, Mass., Harvard University Press.

Richter, G. M. A. (1936) *Red-figured Athenian Vases in the Metropolitan Museum of Art*. New Haven, Yale University Press.

Robertson, M. (1954) Review of F. Eichler, *Corpus Vasorum Antiquorum, Österreich, Wien, Kunsthistorisches Museum I. Die rotfigurigen attischen Trinkgefässe und Pyxiden*, Vienna, Anton Schroll 1951. *Journal of Hellenic Studies* 74, 229–30.

——— (1975) *A History of Greek Art I*. Cambridge, Cambridge University Press.

——— (1992) *The Art of Vase-Painting in Classical Athens*. Cambridge, Cambridge University Press.

Tiverios, M. A. (1989) *Perikleia panathenaia, enas krateras tou Z. tou Monachou 2335*. Thessalonike, Andromeda Books.

Valavanis, P. (1990) La proclamation des vainqueurs aux Panathénées. *Bulletin de Correspondance Hellénique* 114, 325–59.

3

Orestes in Athens

H. A. Shapiro

In the enormous range of Ross Holloway's publications in classical art and archaeology, Greek vases have not played a leading role, but neither have they been neglected. One thinks of his exemplary publication (1966), some forty years ago, of one of the most iconographically significant vases ever found in the excavations of the Athenian agora, the red-figure krater with scenes of musical competition (Agora P 27349; Moore 1997, 135, cat. 8; Greek vases also play a modest part in Holloway 1973, primarily for the Preclassical period). The present paper was inspired in part by Ross's most recent publication devoted to a Greek vase, the remarkable *chous* in the Rhode Island School of Design Museum of Art that he rescued from obscurity with a new and ingenious interpretation (RISD 25.090; *ARV²* 1215, top, 2; Holloway 1998; originally published in *CVA* [Providence 1] 31 and pl. 23, 2) (Fig. 3.1). This in turn provoked another reading by Jenifer Neils and yet a third that I offered tentatively in the course of studying a different *chous* (Neils and Oakley 2003, 153; Shapiro 2004, 90–91). Here I do not wish to dwell on the Providence vase but rather to expand the dossier that was opened in my earlier paper, on a myth that I believe has been curiously overlooked in the repertoire of Attic vases. At the same time, I want to explore further a question that has vexed all scholars of the vases we know as *choes*, that of the relationship between their imagery and the festival of the Anthesteria.

To start with the last issue first: all modern studies of *choes* recognize a clear distinction between those that are miniature vases (under *c*. 10 cm in height) and those that are full-size (20–23 cm) (Green 1971; *cf.* Moore 1997, 41, who distinguishes three categories: full-size, small, and miniature; Schmidt 2005, 152–55, with earlier references). The miniature *choes* can all be dated between *c*. 420 and 390 BC, and the great majority feature scenes of babies and small children, suggesting that these vases were made expressly for children at the time of the festival (Van Hoorn 1951; Schmidt 2005, 201–6; *cf.* Ham 1999; Neils and Oakley 2003, 145–47). The full-size *choes* are fewer in number, often of high quality, occur over most of the fifth century

Fig. 3.1 *Attic red-figure chous. Rhode Island School of Design Museum of Art 25.090 (Courtesy Gina Borromeo, RISD Museum).*

(and, in black-figure, even earlier), and often have subjects that, while quite inventive and rare, are more difficult to connect directly with the Anthesteria (for an excellent overview of the iconography of full-size *choes*, from the mid-sixth century to the late fifth, see Schmidt 2005, 165–94). Richard Hamilton (1992, esp. 83) took the extreme position that the full-size *choes* have no connection whatever to the festival and largely excluded them from his attempt to reconstruct it by combining the written sources with the evidence of the miniature *choes*. Without debating this point, we may observe that a significant number of the full-size *choes*, whether made specifically for the Anthesteria or not, clearly revolve around two closely related themes: the worship of Dionysos and the consumption of large quantities of wine. Among the best-known examples of the shape are scenes of a drunken Dionysos propped up on a satyr attendant; women preparing a *liknon* with a mask of the god; a reveler relieving himself on the way to or from a symposium; and a drunken *komast* banging on the door of a startled woman (for these and other, related scenes of revelers traveling to or from Anthesteria parties, see Schmidt 2005, 166–71).

Mythological narratives, as van Hoorn (1951, 53) pointed out in his comprehensive study of *choes*, occur only rarely (*cf.* Schmidt 2005, 170–71). Gods and heroes outside the circle of Dionysos also occur very rarely, including Apollo, Artemis, and Demeter with Triptolemos. It was the obviously mythological but enigmatic scene on a beautifully drawn *chous* by the Eretria Painter that first drew me to investigate the possibility of an aitiological myth associated with the Anthesteria (Fig. 3.2) (Athens, Vlasto Collection; *ARV²* 1249, 20; for full references, see Shapiro 2004, 87–89). In particular, we are told in several sources that the distribution of individual drinking vessels to participants in the *choes* (the second day of the festival) was explained by Orestes's arrival in Athens as the Anthesteria was in progress. Not wanting to exclude the guest from the festivities, but wary of the contamination of his blood-guilt, the reigning king came up with the compromise solution of individual vessels for everyone (for the sources, see Parker 2005, 293; the chief one is the historian Phanodemos, *FrGH* 325 F11). One version of the story is recounted by Orestes himself, in Euripides's *Iphigenia among the Taurians* (939–60), when he tells his sister of his recent sojourn and trial in Athens. He does not, however, refer to the Anthesteria by name. The poet Kallimachos (178.2), writing about an Athenian expatriate in Alexandria in the early third century who faithfully observes the Anthesteria, refers to the "Orestean *choes*" (Parker 2005, 301).

Furthermore, in a version of Orestes's trial for the murder of his mother and her paramour that postdates the *Eumenides* of Aeschylus, it is Erigone, daughter of the two victims, who acts as the prosecutor. Chagrined at Orestes's acquittal, she hangs herself (sources in *LIMC* 1.485–86, *s.v.* "Aletes"; 3.824–25, *s.v.,* "Erigone"; Shapiro 2004, 89; add now Humphreys 2004, 242; Parker 2005, 301). This is the story I wished to recognize on the *chous* in the Vlasto Collection (see Fig. 3.2): Orestes seated between his half sister and accuser Erigone and his steady companion Pylades (the trial of Orestes is not depicted on extant monuments before the Roman period, but several scholars have tried to reconstruct a Classical painting as the source; see E. Simon in *LIMC*

Fig. 3.2 *Attic red-figure chous. Athens, Vlasto Collection (Photo: German Archaeological Institute, Athens).*

1.486, *s.v.* "Aletes"). Looking for other references to the story of Orestes's arrival in Athen, I came upon several more *choes*, all belonging to the years *c.* 430–415. These include a *chous* at Yale that had already been associated with Erigone and Orestes (Yale University Art Gallery 13.139; Shapiro 2004, 90, with earlier references, and pl. 14, 3), a well-known *chous* in the Louvre depicting the arrival of a young horseman in a sanctuary (Louvre S 1659, MNB 1033; Lezzi-Hafter 1988, pl. 141; Shapiro 2004, 90 and pl. 14, 4), and the *chous* in Providence (see Fig. 3.1). For the latter, I thought of the moment that the traveler Orestes, his horse tired from the journey, is received by the Athenian king.

I would not press this suggestion too hard, nor is it essential for my argument here. Instead, I would like to pursue the evidence for the story of Orestes in Athens and propose other candidates for depictions of this episode that indicate its central importance in the late fifth century.

There is no doubt that Orestes was an extremely popular figure with Athenian vase painters. The Murder of Aegisthus is one of the earliest mythological scenes we have on an Athenian vase, the well-known Protoattic krater in Berlin (Morris 1984, 60–61), and from the turn of the fifth century

– well before the production of Aeschylus's *Oresteia* in 458 – it is a favorite subject of Attic red-figure (Prag 1985, 13–32; *LIMC* 1.372–76, *s.v.* "Aigisthos"). In the last play of the trilogy, *Eumenides*, Aeschylus introduced the story of Orestes's trial in Athens, perhaps not for the first time but in a version that is not attested earlier than this (Sommerstein 1989, 2–5, argues against the prevailing view that the whole idea of a trial in Athens is an invention of Aeschylus). Within a few years, the vase painters responded with a half dozen examples of what may have been one of the most dramatic moments in the play: Orestes, still pursued by the Erinyes, taking refuge at a rough pile of stones, presumably representing the Areopagus in Athens (San Antonio Museum of Art 86.134.73; *ARV*² 1907, 21 *bis*; Shapiro et al. 1995, no. 88; *cf.* Prag 1985, 49–50, pls. 30–32) (Fig. 3.3). His protectors, Athena, Apollo, and even Artemis (who does not appear in the play), watch over him. This is one of the very few cases where an innovative scene on the Athenian stage seems to have inspired an almost immediate response from the painters (*cf.* Shapiro 1994, 114; Prag 1985, 50, where the problem of determining whether these scenes are set in Delphi or Athens is discussed).

Sometime in the later fifth century, new versions were introduced into the story of Orestes's trial. In Euripides's *Iphigenia among the Taurians* of *c.* 414, Orestes himself tells his sister that he has been prosecuted by the Erinyes (961–67), echoing the story told in Aeschylus's play. A few years later, however, in Euripides's *Orestes*, Apollo informs Orestes that he will be tried on the Areopagus by a jury of the gods (1648–52) – not Athenians, as in Aeschylus (*cf.* Eur. *El.* 1258–65). A third version, that his accuser was his half sister Erigone, may have been introduced by the playwright Philokles, a nephew of Aeschylus and contemporary of Euripides, in his play titled *Erigone* (Snell 1971, 139; for other tragedies titled *Erigone,* see 246–47 [Cleophon]; of the *Erigone* and the *Aletes* of Sophocles we

Fig. 3.3 *Attic red-figure column-krater, San Antonio Museum of Art 86.134.73 (Courtesy the museum).*

know almost nothing; see Radt 1999, 146, 232–33; on the confusion with other Erigones, including the daughter of Ikarios, see Johnston 1999, 219–20; Humphreys 2004, 243–44, who argues that the Ikarios-Erigone father-daughter pair is so poorly attested before the third century that there is no reason to associate it, or the swinging ritual, with the fifth-century Anthesteria). At about the same time, the historian Hellanikos of Lesbos wrote about the trial of Orestes, implying that the accusers were kinsmen of the victims who came to Athens "from Lakedaimon" (*FGrH* 323a F22). The fourth-century BC Roman tragedian Accius apparently followed this version in a play also named for Erigone (Dangel 1995, 170–71, 326–28).

Orestes's arrival in Athens may thus have been well known to late-fifth-century audiences for two reasons: its dramatization on the tragic stage and its association with one of the most popular festivals of Dionysos. Its appearance on vases need not necessarily be limited to *choes,* like that in the Vlasto Collection (see Fig. 3.2) and others I have

proposed. I suggest here one strong candidate that has so far gone unrecognized (Athens NM 1395; *ARV*² 1444, middle, 2) (Fig. 3.4). The scene on a calyx-krater in Athens of the early years of the fourth century was designated by Beazley "unexplained," but I think the visual clues lead to an unambiguous interpretation (*ARV*² 1444; the only other discussion of the vase I am able to find is that of Schefold 1934, 77 and fig. 18, who deals only with the drapery style and not the iconography). A youth sits on an elaborate stone altar covered with added white. He has draped his garment across the altar, leaving his body nude, but holds his sword in one hand and the scabbard in the other. He looks to a mature, bearded man who addresses him with a speaking gesture of his raised right hand, while a second youth, standing behind the protagonist, makes a similar gesture. The two striking motifs of sitting on an altar and ostentatiously displaying the naked sword can only signify that the youth is seeking asylum in a sanctuary for a crime committed with this weapon. No other hero fits these criteria as does Orestes

Fig. 3.4 *Attic red-figure calyx-krater. Athens National Archaeological Museum 1395 (Photo: German Archaeological Institute, Athens).*

Fig. 4.2 *Herakles, Perithoos, and Theseus in the underworld. DAI, Rome, Inst. Neg. 66.1836 (Photo © Deutsches Archäologisches Institut).*

when it is seen juxtaposed with a third relief, which shows Herakles again, Perithoos seated, and Theseus (Fig. 4.2). This meeting most likely takes place on the Isle of the Blest (Harrison 1964, 76–84) or, perhaps, in a Virgilesque glimpse of Elysium.

In the last of the four, Medea stands aside with a container (presumably of magical ingredients) in her hand, as a daughter of Pelias prepares the cauldron that rests just left of the center of the stele. Another Peliad contemplatively holds the knife that will be used in their macabre ritual.

Homer Thompson (1952) noted the stylistic similarity of the four reliefs, each known from several copies and sometimes found together with one another. He ascribed all four of these reliefs to the Altar of Pity in the agora of Athens, mostly based on their scale. Since then, it is commonly believed that the reliefs replicate a lost Classical original, but all have been hard-pressed to find a convincing iconographical relationship between the reliefs, and most of the scholarship on them has focused toward that end.

Attempts at finding a unifying theme in the four scenes include: four examples of piteous reversal of fortune from the Altar of Pity (Thompson 1952), the quest for lasting good (Harrison 1964), threshold between life and death (Beschi et al. 1959), tragic love (Mobius 1965), and the contrast between the weakness of humanity and the triumph of good (Meyer 1980, 134). It is notable that none of these admirable attempts to unite the reliefs thematically result in any conclusions that are acceptable in the case of all four

scenes, except in very general terms. Langlotz (1977) ascribes the reliefs to a four-sided sculpted funerary monument of an Attic tragedian. Although this hypothetical reconstruction is possible, it is difficult to cite contemporaneous comparanda for such a monument.

Perhaps the solution to the problem of iconographical relationships between the reliefs is simpler than previously assumed: a series of decorative reliefs in similar scale and unified more by the aesthetic appeal of their three-figured composition than by religious or political programs. A Neoattic workshop specializing in decorative sculpture for contexts such as homes, baths, and peristyles might have offered several pieces of similar scale and composition with no more unity of iconography and program than one would find in the catalogues of its modern equivalents. In reference to wall paintings depicting similar subjects, Ling (1991, 138) writes, "The chief factor which seems to have dictated the choice of pictures in a given room was the possibility of achieving a formal balance." That the clearest correspondences between all four reliefs in the group is the similarity of scale, and the three-figured composition, suggests the importance of such considerations.

However, most of the subjects chosen for the reliefs were current in the literature of the Augustan period. Theseus and Perithoos's descent into the underworld, for example, is mentioned twice in the *Aeneid* alone, once just a few lines away from Orpheus's ill-fated return with Eurydice, which Virgil discusses in more detail in *Georgics* (4:453–522; *Aen* 6.382–96, 6.122 on Theseus; 6.119 on Orpheus): Ovid deals with Medea and the Peliads in great detail, and makes some mention of Herakles and the apples of the Hesperides (Ov. *Met.* 7.297–349, on Medea; *Met.* 9.190, on Herakles). The iconographical taste of either the patron or designer of the reliefs, then, was very much in line with the literati of the day. Thompson (1952, 61–62) himself points out that the prototypes from which the reliefs were carved must have been quite accessible, considering the large number of copies preserved (five of the Orpheus scene and three each of the others), "a situation without parallel among works of this general order." Götze (1938, 239) notes that the reliefs must have been designed as part of a project by one master and subsequently executed by two sculptors (he sees Alkamenes as the master behind the compositions). What better a solution to this set of circumstances than that where the original is produced in the same workshop as the copies? The prototypes, designed by one master as a series, either as stock scenes or with the subject matter chosen by the original patron, could have remained readily available for exact copying, and Thompson's "situation without parallel" as to the number of copies could simply represent the mass production of a workshop specializing in producing such reliefs. The form of the preserved reliefs, which, according to Thompson (1952, 62), must have been freestanding stelai, perhaps with attached framing and crowning members, instead lends itself easily to the decoration of a peristyle, courtyard, garden, or other such outdoor setting. Comparison with reliefs of similar size, shape, and subject matter, such as the second-century AD Palazzo Spada reliefs, masterfully discussed by Natalie Kampen, strongly suggests that such works would be displayed in shallow wall niches:

> The framed mythological paintings of Pompeian and Roman houses, framed stuccoes, and large mythological reliefs would all have appeared to be set into walls, physically distinct from their setting, yet visually and intellectually part of it. The tastes and habits of thought and perception are, thus, inextricably connected in both art and literature of the educated Roman. (Kampen 1979, 594)

Unlike the Palazzo Spada reliefs, which show too many tendencies of Hadrianic and Antonine art to have been unanimously considered a "copy" of a Classical Greek monument, the four three-figured reliefs under discussion share no such traits. This is most likely because they are a product of a century earlier than the Spada reliefs, when Augustan classicism favored the elegant yet austere style of the late fifth century BC. Such similarity to Classical work, either in copies or new creations, is achieved mainly during the Julio-Claudian period (we see here none of the embellishment so characteristic of Hellenistic work, nor the fascination with light and shadow indicative of the Hadrianic and Antonine periods; if not Classical in date, the reliefs probably belong to the early first century AD).

Of the Orpheus relief, Bowra (1952, 121) points out that "the relief displays too little distress for so tragic a catastrophe." Such lack of facial response to trauma should be read as a stylistic trait of both Classical and Neoattic art more than as an iconographical barometer. M. Owen Lee (1962, 401), for example, quite rightly notes that, from a philological perspective, the version of the story in which Orpheus successfully recovers Eurydice from the under-world was both earlier and more popular than the "second death myth" most often cited today, which he traces to Virgil. If we should see the reliefs as original creations of a Neoattic workshop, roughly contemporaneous with Virgil, the author's version might well have influenced the sculpture. The slight restraining touch of Hermes's hand on Eurydice's wrist signifies that he is taking possession of her, to lead her back to Hades, as a groom might lead a bride to his house, hence presenting the Virgilian version (Neumann 1965, 59–66; Boegehold 1999, 18). As for the gesture of Eurydice's free hand, she reaches to Orpheus in vain, in a manner that recalls her words in *Georgics*:

> "Fata vocant, conditque natantia lumina somnus./Iamque vale: feror ingenti circumdata nocte/invalidasque tibi tendens, heu non tua, palmas!" (Verg. *Aen.* 496–98).

That such literary works may well have influenced the home decor of literate Romans is demonstrated in an impressive fashion. The Peliad relief shares its subject matter with the Casa di Giasone in Pompeii. Although different scenes in the myth of Medea and the Peliads have been chosen for the paintings, the date and extensiveness of the Peliad scenes roughly coincide with Ovid's treatment of the subject. Ling (1991, 119) describes the scene of Jason and Pelias as "a typical example of Augustan classicism," a stylistic trait that, like its date and subject matter, is shared by its Neoattic counterpart.

It is also notable that, if dated to the fifth century, as many would have it, the Orpheus relief would represent the earliest known evidence of the myth of Orpheus and Eurydice in art (Touchette 1990, 78). Parapets of altars may seem an odd place for Classical Athenians to experiment with unprecedented iconography; likewise, monumental relief sculpture in general. As Touchette (1990, 85) points out, the relief has little in common with funerary reliefs of the Classical period: "Although H. A. Thompson cites 'numerous echoes' of this relief on Attic grave stelai of the fifth and fourth centuries BC, an examination of A. Conze's *Die attischen Grabreliefs* reveals that the echoes are of the most general sort. The iconography of the Orpheus relief is in fact unparalleled." Instead, the group represented on the relief fits much more easily into the context of a later period:

> The artistic evidence from the first century BC onwards, seemingly unaffected by the tragic version of the myth narrated by some of the Latin poets, continues to point to a successful ending to Orpheus' mission. Orpheus and Eurydice are depicted amongst the inhabitants of Hades on a first-century BC fresco in the Louvre. A century later, on the stuccoes from the Basilica Sotterranea, Orpheus appears in a mirror-reverse rendering of his pose on the three-figure relief. (Touchette 1990, 84)

On the following page, Touchette (1990, 85) comes to terms with the near-absence of Hermes Psychopompos from Classical Attic red-figure, but fails to acknowledge that there are, perhaps, too many problems with dating the relief to the Classical period. Likewise, Touchette states that "[t]he gestures of Orpheus and Eurydice are echoed most closely on a relief from the Palatine. On examination, however, this piece is revealed as a Neoattic creation of the Roman period" (1990, 86–87). The evidence for the interpretation of the Orpheus relief as a Neoattic creation becomes, at this point, overwhelming.

Gadbury (1992, 483), in her reexamination of the Altar of the Twelve Gods (which Thompson considers to be synonymous with the Altar of Pity), disassociates the reliefs from the parapet by stratigraphically redating it to the third quarter of the fourth century. Moreover, Ridgway has shown that the Altar of Pity and the Altar of the Twelve Gods should be considered two separate monuments. Considering these factors, the argument for the association of the reliefs with the altar, based more on the scale of the panels than on iconographical unity, becomes very flimsy indeed.

In the reexamination of the four reliefs, especially the

Orpheus relief (upon which most of the attention has been lavished, partially due to the issues surrounding its iconography) several discrepancies between the scenes depicted herein and in the works that would be considered contemporaneous if we accept a Classical date for them become obvious. In addition, as has been noted, it is difficult to credibly unite the four scenes thematically, making it difficult to ascribe them to any one monumental program. Gadbury's redating of the Altar of the Twelve Gods parapet makes Thompson's connection between the reliefs and the monument dubious if not impossible. This conviction is strengthened by the number, exactness, and nature of the copies, which suggest that the prototype was very easily available, with copies of the reliefs being mass produced by a small number of copyists over a relatively short time, perhaps in a single workshop. Differences in copies may relate to the styles of different copyists of the same workshop, or perhaps a later series of copies, using the original Neoattic creations as its prototype. Gestures and poses of the figures in the Orpheus relief find their best comparanda in Neoattic art, and the iconography itself had no precedent in relief sculpture of the Classical period. With these factors in mind, it seems logical to interpret the reliefs as a Neoattic creation of Roman date, probably of the first century AD, mass produced as decorative elements for the gardens of wealthy houses and villas.

The marble of the reliefs and fragments are generally "said to be of Pentelic marble," (Harrison 1964, 76) often without the benefit of isotopic analysis. In spite of the material, most of the pieces with known provenances have been discovered in Central Italy (Götze 1938, 200–202), and the workshop or workshops that produced them may have been located there. F. Van Keuren (this volume) argues that certain Neoattic motifs in sarcophagi gained currency in Rome, having been employed by Greek artists working in Central Italy. The case of three-figured reliefs may be quite similar.

By necessity, analysis from the perspective of ancient viewers requires a certain degree of hypothetical speculation. This issue is compounded when the question of the original context of a work is uncertain. Considering the form of the relief panels, the number and distribution of copies, iconography, and style, it seems reasonable to conclude that the three-figured reliefs decorated elaborate houses, baths, or peristyles of the first century AD.

The subjects of the reliefs are current in contemporary literature, and the buyers or patrons of such art might also be the consumers of such poetry, or those aspiring to demonstrate their familiarity with literature upon visitors to their home or garden. In a way, these monuments, seen by scholars for decades as later copies of famous fifth-century BC works, might have been read by their intended audience as demonstrating an interest in contemporary literature as much or more than an artistic tradition from the distant past.

That Roman viewers associated works of art with specific literary compositions is amply demonstrated both artistically, in works such as the Odyssey Landscapes, and in literature, such as the decoration of Trimalchio's house in the *Satyricon*. The difference here is that subjects from literature contemporary with the artwork have been depicted, demonstrably specific in the case of Orpheus and Eurydice. Although the style of the reliefs is focused on the Classical past, the specifics of the iconography are united in their treatment in Augustan Latin literature. Would a viewer read the works as a panegyric to the accomplishments of contemporary literature? Mythological iconography is not static over the centuries but finds a different expression in the treatment of new authors, artists, readers, and viewers.

In any case, it seems that the three-figured reliefs are Neoattic creations, most likely chosen by a patron from specific literary iconography. Sculptors of the Roman period, like artists in other media, were free to copy from contemporary art or their own creations, instead of replicating the Classical Greek past. The stylistic preference for classicism was just one of many choices in the sculptor's vocabulary. Whereas some sculptures that are known from many copies made in the Roman period clearly are reproductions of famous earlier works and some are elaborations or variations on a theme, some may, in fact, be new compositions, consciously influenced by centuries of artistic tradition, rather than replicas of a specific composition.

Acknowledgments

This study benefitted greatly from discussion and comments over a number of years by, notably, R. Ross Holloway, Rolf Winkes, Derek Counts, Michael Smith, Anthony Tuck, Christopher Fletcher, and Heather Caunt-Nulton.

Works Cited

Beschi, L., Bertocchi, F. A., Pollacco, L. (1959) *Sculture greche e romane di Cirene e romane di Cirene.* Padua, Università di Padova.

Boegehold, A. L. (1999) *When a Gesture Was Expected.* Princeton, Princeton University Press.

Bowra, C. M. (1952) Orpheus and Eurydice. *Classical Quarterly* 2, 113–126.

Gadbury, Laura M. (1992) The Sanctuary of the Twelve Gods in the Agora: A revised view. *Hesperia* 61, 447–89.

Götze, H. (1938) Die Attischen Dreifigurenreliefs. *Mitteilungen des Deutschen Archäologischen Instituts, Römische Abteilung* 53, 189–280.

Harrison, E. B. (1964) Hesperides and Heroes: A note on the three-figure reliefs. *Hesperia* 33, 76–84.

Kampen, N. B. (1979) Observations on the ancient uses of the Spada reliefs. *L'Antiquité Classique* 48, 583–600.

Langlotz, E. (1977) Das Hesperiden-Relief Albani. In *Bonner Festgabe J. Straub*, 91–112. Bonn, Rheinland-Verlag.

Lee, M. O. (1964) Mystic Orpheus: another note on the three-figure reliefs. *Hesperia* 33, 401–4.

Ling, R. (1991) *Roman Painting*. Cambridge and New York, Cambridge University Press.

Meyer, H. (1980) *Medeia und die Peliaden*. Rome, G. Bretschneider.

Mobius, H. (1965) *Die Reliefs der Portlandvase und das antike Dreifigurenbild*. Munich, Verlag der Bayerischen Akademie der Wissenschaften.

Neumann, G. (1965) *Gesten und Gebärden in der griechischen Kunst*. Berlin, de Gruyter.

Thompson, H. (1952) The Altar of Pity in the Athenian Agora. *Hesperia* 21, 47–82.

Touchette, L. A. (1990) A new interpretation of the Orpheus relief. *Archäologischer Anzeiger* 1, 77–90.

5

Some Observations on the Flavian Victory Monuments of Rome

Jodi Magness

In 70 CE the First Jewish Revolt against the Romans officially ended with the fall of Jerusalem and the destruction of the Second Temple. The following year (71), Vespasian and his son Titus celebrated a joint triumph in Rome with a parade of captives and spoils. The Flavian victory was memorialized by Josephus and by the minting of coins and the erection of monuments around Rome. In this paper I examine several of the victory monuments along the parade route. It is a pleasure to dedicate this paper to R. Ross Holloway, a colleague and mentor whose own publication record includes an important article on the Arch of Titus (Holloway 1987).

The Beginning of the Parade: The Porta Triumphalis, Temple of Isis, and Theaters

Josephus gives a detailed account of the victory parade and the fullest surviving description of any imperial triumph (*BJ* 7.123–58; Eberhardt 2005, 259, including a discussion of whether Josephus was an eyewitness to the parade; Millar 2005, 101; also see Beard 2003). A briefer account of the Flavian triumph is provided by the fifth-century Christian historian Paulus Orosius (*Historiae* 7.9; see Aitken 2001, 81 n. 28). Josephus tells us that Vespasian and Titus spent the night near the temple of Isis (*BJ* 7.123), apparently at the Villa Publica in the Campus Martius (Makin 1921, 26). From there they set out at dawn the next morning to the Porticus Octaviae to meet the Senate, and then "went back" or "withdrew" (ἀνεχώρει) to the triumphal gate (Porta Triumphalis) (*BJ* 7.124–30). Before setting off from the gate Vespasian and Titus had breakfast, put on their triumphal robes, and sacrificed to the gods whose statues had been set up beside the gate (*BJ* 7.131: τοῖς τε παριδρυμένοις τῇ πύλῃ θύσαντες θεοῖς).

The identification of the beginning of the parade route depends on the location of the Porta Trimphalis, which is a subject of debate (Coarelli 1968; Schwier 1989, 318–19;

Scott 2000, 184). Josephus's use of the term ἀνεχώρει suggests that Vespasian and Titus had to double back from the Porticus Octaviae in the direction of the Villa Publica to reach the triumphal gate (Makin 1921, 29–30; Schwier 1989, 319; Millar 2005, 104; for a different suggestion, see Coarelli 1968, 69–70, fig. a).

A relief from the late Flavian or early Trajanic Tomb of the Haterii in Rome provides important evidence for some of the monuments associated with the Flavian triumph (Jensen 1978; Kleiner 1992, 196–99). The relief depicts a row of structures including the Colosseum and three arches. There is no consensus as to whether these structures are related topographically and follow the route of the funeral procession, or whether they are all Flavian building projects in Rome in which the deceased (a contractor) participated (Jensen 1978, 103–5; Kleiner 1990, 131; 1992, 197). The arch on the left side of the relief is labeled *arcus ad Isis* (arch near to [the temple] of Isis) and the arch on the right side is labeled *arcus in sacra via summa* (apparently the Arch of Titus; see below). Kleiner (1990, 134) identifies the *arcus ad Isis* as a Vespasianic monument, whereas Jensen (1978, 150) assigns it generally to the Flavian period. Haeckl (1996, 15) identifies all three arches on the Haterii relief as Domitianic.

Scholars who favor a topographical reading of the relief locate the *arcus ad Isis* in the Third Region of Rome, where a temple of Isis of unknown date stood (Kleiner 1990, 132–33; Steinby 1993, vol. 3, 110–12). Other scholars place the *arcus ad Isis* in the Campus Martius, where there was a sanctuary of Isis that is depicted on the Marble Plan and was rebuilt by Domitian after the fire of 80 (Jensen 1978, 130; Kleiner 1990, 132; Steinby 1993, vol. 3, 107–9). In this case the *arcus ad Isis* might be related to the temple of Isis mentioned by Josephus as close to the spot where Vespasian and Titus spent the night.

I believe that the *arcus ad Isis* should be located in the Campus Martius. Perhaps the statue of Minerva depicted inside the arch's central passageway refers to the temple of Minerva Chalcidia, which was adjacent to the Iseum in the Campus Martius (Jensen 1978, 90; Kleiner 1990, 131; Steinby 1993, vol. 3, 255). In this case the *arcus ad Isis* might be the arch depicted on the Marble Plan as marking the entrance to the Iseum and Serapaeum from the temple of Minerva Chalcidia. Only a single footing of the north central pier of this arch survives, which is now called the Arco di Camigliano (Richardson 1992, 212; Steinby 1993, vol. 3, 110). A temple of Isis depicted on coins of Vespasian might also refer to the area where Vespasian and Titus spent the night before their triumph (Mattingly 1930, xlix; Richardson 1992, 211).

Kleiner (1990, 131) suggests that the deities depicted inside the passageways of the arches on the Haterii relief were a device to pinpoint the locations of the monuments for viewers. According to Jensen (1978, 134–37), since statues were not set up in passageways of arches, these deities were "intended symbolically and not as a mimetic reproduction of the sculpture of the actual prototypes" (Jensen 1978, 137; he connects these depictions with triumphal symbolism). However, Josephus's reference to the Porta Triumphalis indicates that these images might allude to actual statues: "Here the princes first partook of refreshment, and then, having donned their triumphal robes and sacrificed to the gods whose statues stood beside the gates" (*BJ* 7.131).

After the parade got under way, Vespasian and Titus drove from the Porta Triumphalis through the theaters (διά τῶν θεάτρων) to give the crowds a better view (*BJ* 7.131). There has been much debate about which theaters Josephus meant, with the solution depending partly on the location of the Porta Triumphalis. The Theater of Pompey seems to be too far out of the way (Makin 1921, 33), but Josephus could have lumped the Circus Flaminius and even the Circus Maximus together with the Theater of Marcellus (Makin 1921, 33–34; Coarelli 1968, 70; Millar 2005, 104). This possibility is supported by Humphrey's observation that Josephus did not always distinguish clearly between different types of entertainment arenas, apparently reflecting the fact that Roman terminology was still in flux. At Caesarea Maritima, for example, Josephus called the Herodian hippodrome an amphitheater because it had seats for spectators on all sides (Humphrey 1996; for a passage from Plutarch that supports this interpretation of the term "theater," see Coarelli 1968, 70). So it is easy to imagine Josephus describing as *theatron* all of the spectator arenas with seats that the triumphators passed through (a suggestion also made by Millar 2005, 106, but based on other evidence).

From this point (*BJ* 7.131) Josephus provides no more information on the route of the triumph until the parade reached the temple of Capitoline Jupiter, where Simon Bar Giora was executed (*BJ* 7.153–54; see Millar 2005, 104). Titus and Domitian kept the victory alive in the eyes of the

Roman public by erecting monuments at key points along the way, including the Porticus Divorum (a colonnaded building constructed by Domitian that enclosed shrines to Vespasian and Titus, apparently in the area of the Villa Publica), the Colosseum, and triumphal arches (Scott 2000, 184; Millar 2005, 106, 125–27; for the Porticus Divorum, see Richardson 1976; D'Ambra 1993, 33–34; for three possible lost arches of Vespasian, see Kleiner 1989; 1990; for lost arches of Domitian, see de Maria 1988, 121–23). Haeckl (1996, 17) notes that the Arch of Titus and Colosseum functioned as "dynastic pendants" to the temple of the deified Vespasian at the other end of the Roman Forum (also see D'Ambra 1993, 45–46).

Schwier identifies three high points in Josephus's description of the triumph: the temple of Isis, the display of spoils from the Jerusalem temple, and the Capitolium. He suggests that these points represented the recognition and legitimization of the Flavian victory and Flavian rule by the Egyptian gods, alluding to the fact that Vespasian's campaign had been conducted in the East and he had been proclaimed emperor while in Egypt, which he later celebrated as his Accession Day (and tying in with oracles such as those reported by Josephus, Tacitus, and Suetonius that the ruler of the world would come from the East) (Schwier 1989, 327; see Suet. *Vesp.*, 4; Levick 1999, 67, 70). Let us now consider some of the Flavian monuments that were eventually erected along the parade route.

The Arch of Titus in the Circus Maximus

A lost arch of Titus was dedicated in 81 in the center of the curved end of the Circus Maximus, apparently marking the spot where Vespasian and Titus had passed during the triumph (Millar 2005, 106–7). The scanty archaeological remains and the Marble Plan indicate that it was a triple arch decorated with reliefs (Rossetto 1987, 44–46; de Maria 1988, 119 and pl. 64; Steinby 1993 vol. 1, 108–9). The arch's dedicatory inscription reads:

> The Senate and People of Rome to Imp(erator) Titus Caesar Vespasianus, son of the Deified Vespasianus, pontifex maximus, with *tribunicia potestas* for the tenth time, (hailed as) Imp(erator) for the seventeenth time, consul for the eighth time, their princeps, because on the instructions and advice of his father, and under his auspices, he subdued the race of the Jews and destroyed the city of Jerusalem (*gentem Iudaeorum domuit et urbem Hierusolymam . . . delevit*), which by all generals, kings, or races previous to himself had either been attacked in vain or not even attempted at all. (Translation from Millar 2005, 120; for a different translation see Overman 2002, 217)

Aitken (2001, 80) notes that this inscription highlights an important dimension of Flavian ideology: the establishment of a stable succession to the throne, which had been missing during the period of the civil war (for a discussion of the false claim that Vespasian and Titus were the first to subdue the Jews and destroy Jerusalem, see Schwier 1989, 291–92). The inscription from the lost arch of Titus in Rome might be paralleled by a recent find from Jerusalem. The latter consists of a fragmentary inscription on a massive limestone slab that turned up in the collection of the Islamic Museum on the Temple Mount. Grüll (2006) identifies the Jerusalem inscription as part of an honorary arch that was dedicated to Vespasian and Titus by Flavius Silva, the commander of the Tenth Legion and governor of Judea from 73/74 to 79/80. Grüll reconstructs the first extant line as part of a longer narrative text like that on the lost arch of Titus in Rome: [*ob Iudaeos devict]os e[t Hierosolymam deletam*] (for having conquered the Jews and destroying Jerusalem) (for a different reading and dating of this inscription, see Eck 2005, 160–64).

The Arch of Titus

The better-known arch of Titus (referred to here as the Arch of Titus) was apparently erected by Domitian after Titus's death (Pfanner 1983; de Maria 1988, 119–21; Steinby 1993, vol. 1, 110). It is apparently the *arcus in sacra via summa* depicted on the Haterii relief (Jensen 1978, 99–101, 117–18; Pfanner 1983, 3; Kleiner 1992, 197; Steinby 1993, vol. 1, 110). The dedication on the attic refers to the deified Titus: "Senatus populusque Romanus divo Tito divi Vespasiani f. Vespasiano Augusto" (The Senate and the Roman People to the Deified Titus Vespasianus Augustus, son of the Deified Vespasianus) (from Millar 2005, 123). Holloway (1987, 186) noted that parallels with the arch of Trajan at Benevento, which is modeled closely after the Arch of Titus, suggest that the inscription probably appeared on both sides of the attic story (see Norman fig. 6.1, this volume).

Because of its single-bay design, the brief attic inscription, and the iconography of the reliefs, Pfanner suggested that the Arch of Titus functioned mainly as a "consecration monument" to the deified Titus rather than as a triumphal arch celebrating the Jewish war, as indicated by the panel at the apex of the arch's passageway depicting Titus's apotheosis on the back of an eagle (Pfanner 1983, 98–101, 103; Steinby 1993, vol. 1, 110–11; Norman, this volume). As Aitken observes, "the apotheosis of Titus depicted on the ceiling of the Arch has already been displayed – in his lifetime – on the day of the triumph. The Arch celebrates his consecration. . . . The ceiling coffer with the apotheosis of Titus is thus the heavenly consummation of this earthly triumph, supported by the portrayal of the guarantees of this status: the personified figures of the virtue, honor, and victory of the Augusti" (Aitken 2001, 82, including n. 35; also see Pfanner 1983, 78).

However, the Arch of Titus served also – and perhaps primarily – as a triumphal monument, since the Flavians based their claims to legitimacy on the victory over the Jews. Millar (2005, 122–25) correctly emphasizes the

triumphal nature of the arch, which straddled the triumphal route and connected it with the Colosseum, another Flavian triumphal monument. The eagle (alluding to Jupiter as well as to apotheosis) and the triumphant, deified Titus at the arch's apex literally rise above the cultic vessels from the Jerusalem temple. On the Arch of Titus at Benevento the connection between Jupiter and the victorious emperor, who received his power from the highest god in the Roman pantheon, is even more explicitly depicted (Kleiner 1992, 227–28).

The famous panels on the sides of the arch's passageway depict Titus riding in a chariot and crowned by Victory (north wall) and the parade of spoils from the Jerusalem temple (south wall) (for a description and discussion see Pfanner 1983). The spoils panel mirrors Josephus's description:

> The spoils in general were borne in promiscuous heaps; but conspicuous above all stood out those captured in the temple at Jerusalem. These consisted of a golden table, many talents in weight, and a lampstand (λυχνία), likewise made of gold, but constructed on a different pattern from those which we use in ordinary life. Affixed to a pedestal was a central shaft, from which there extended slender branches, arranged trident-fashion, a wrought lamp being attached to the extremity of each branch; of these there were seven, indicating the honor paid to that number among the Jews. (*BJ* 7.148; Loeb translation)

Josephus's emphasis on the showbread table and menorah as the highlights of the spoils taken from Jerusalem corresponds with the spoils panel, where these objects provide a snapshot of the entire parade (Pfanner 1983, 76; Schwier 1989, 323; according to Eberhardt 2005 Josephus's description and the arch panels convey different "theological" messages; also see Magness 2008). As Rives (2005, 152) notes, although the Arch of Titus was dedicated after Titus's death, it "presumably provides a reliable indication of what the Flavians regarded as its key elements. It is therefore significant that the menorah and offering table are the focus of one of its two great inner reliefs, opposite to that of Titus in a triumphal chariot."

The Templum Pacis

"The triumphal ceremonies being concluded and the empire of the Romans established on the firmest foundation, Vespasian decided to erect a temple of Peace" (*BJ* 7.158). So Josephus concludes his description of the triumphal parade, despite the fact that the Templum Pacis was not dedicated until 75. The Marble Plan provides valuable information about the Templum Pacis, which supplements the scanty archaeological remains (Anderson 1984, 101–18; Richardson 1992, 286–87; Steinby 1993, vol. 5, 67–70). The complex was located to the east-southeast of the Forum of Augustus. Whereas other Imperial fora were dominated by a temple on a raised podium at one end of an elongated plaza, the Templum Pacis had a broad apsidal cella with an open colonnaded porch facing onto a large square enclosure surrounded by porticoes and exedras (Anderson 1982, 105–6; 1984, 109–11). Furthermore, whereas the apses in the temples of other Imperial fora were oriented to the north or west, the apse in the cella of the Templum Pacis faced east (Schwier 1989, 306–7, suggests that for the Flavians the Jewish war was also a victory of the West over the East).

The interior of the enclosure of the Templum Pacis apparently was planted with a garden that contained an altar and water canals or basins connected to fountains, which are depicted on the Marble Plan as six longitudinal strips (Anderson 1984, 111; Noreña 2003, 26). The layout and design of the Templum Pacis – which in addition to the cultic vessels from the Jerusalem temple housed treasures from Nero's Domus Aurea – resembled porticoes such as the Porticus Octaviae and Porticus Liviae (Anderson 1982, 106; 1984, 106, 111–12 [where he describes the Templum Pacis as an "architectural hybrid"]; Steinby 1993, vol. 5, 69). Noreña (2003, 26, 27 n. 7) notes similarities between the Templum Pacis and Hellenistic peristyles (for other parallels, see Kleiner 1992, 181), whereas Haeckl (1996, 13) points to similarities with the principia of Roman legionary fortresses.

The Templum Pacis recalls the porticoed enclosures in the area of the Circus Flaminius, which were established by victorious generals of the Late Republic for propaganda purposes. These porticoes were filled with works of Greek art that were brought to Rome as the spoils of war (Kleiner 1992, 181; Martin 1992, 160–61). The Templum Pacis belongs to this tradition, with the cultic objects from the Jerusalem temple displayed like other works of art (for the works of art in the Templum Pacis, see Steinby 1993, vol. 5, 68; Millar 2005, 111). The peculiar design of the Templum Pacis might be due to the fact that the goddess Pax did not usually receive temples (Anderson 1982, 105–6; 1984, 109).

Scholars have observed that Vespasian's dedication to Pax was a deliberate allusion to the Ara Pacis and represents his attempt to connect himself with Augustus (Levick 1999, 70; Noreña 2003, 28). The Templum Pacis was aligned with the Forum of Augustus, although a formal connection between the two was not established until Domitian built the Forum Transitorium (completed by Nerva) (Anderson 1982; 1984, 113; D'Ambra 1984, 32–33). And just as Augustus had provided public libraries on the Palatine, the Templum Pacis had public libraries (Boyle 2003, 5; Edmonson 2005, 10; for other parallels, see Levick 1999, 73). Furthermore, the Flavian Judea Capta coins consciously evoked Augustus's Aegypto Capta coins (Edmonson 2005, 10; also see Schwier 1989, 289; Barnes 2005, 129). Vespasian's restoration of the "Pax Augusta" is made explicit by appearance of this legend on his coins (Mattingly 1930,

xliii). The destruction of Jerusalem has even been described as the "Flavian Actium," since it provided the main ideological basis for the establishment of the Flavian dynasty (Picard 1957, 343–44, 359–60; Aitken 2001, 78). Vespasian apparently dedicated the temple to Pax to connect himself with Augustus and distance himself from Nero, and to portray the establishment of his new dynasty as marking the beginning of a new era just as the Pax Augusta had (Noreña 2003, 28; Edmonson 2005, 10–11). Noreña (2003, 29) has observed that "*Pax* was the core ideal in the official construction of Vespasian's public image and one of the central claims upon which the legitimacy of his principate was based."

The Colosseum

The recent decipherment of the original dedicatory inscription tells us that the Colosseum, which was begun by Vespasian and completed by Titus in 80, was paid for out of the spoils of the Jewish war: "The Emperor Titus Caesar Vespasian Augustus ordered the new amphitheater to be made from the (proceeds from the sale of the) booty [*ex manubiis*]" (from Feldman 2001, 25; see also Alföldy 1995; Boyle 2003, 61). The Colosseum is therefore a victory monument that contrasts Flavian generosity toward the Roman public with Nero's megalomania (Noreña 2003, 36). It also represents the completion of an unfulfilled Augustan project, connecting Vespasian with Augustus (Boyle 2003, 61). In this regard the Templum Pacis is similar to the Colosseum; both are victory monuments paid for out of the spoils of the Jewish war that connect Vespasian with Augustus while contrasting (and dissociating) Vespasian and Nero (Steinby 1993, vol. 5, 67).

The Flavian Peace

So in a very real (material) sense the Jewish war and the destruction of Jerusalem and the Second Temple provided the foundation for the establishment of Flavian rule. Pax – a new era of peace ushered in by the victory over the Jews – is the theme that underlies the reigns of Vespasian and Titus (Zarrow 2006, 53). As Edmonson (2005, 9–10) notes, Josephus makes this connection explicit by referring to Vespasian's construction of the Templum Pacis immediately after concluding his description of the triumph. Overman observes that "once enthroned Vespasian is portrayed as the ruler who brought *Pax* to the world by Flavian literary figures" (Overman 2002, 214; also see Noreña 2003, 25). Edmonson (2005, 11) suggests that Josephus's *Bellum Judaicum* not only celebrated the establishment of peace by the Flavians but "served as a key text for the explication" of the Templum Pacis.

Scholars disagree about the peace that was commemorated by this Pax. On the one hand, Millar notes that "The name of the Temple, 'Peace,' could not fail to be a reference to the Jewish War" (Millar 2005, 112). Noreña (2003, 34) also connects Vespasian's new era of peace to his military victory. On the other hand, Overman (2002, 214–15) believes that the peace included the restoration of order after the civil wars (also see Zarrow 2006, 55). Beard (2003, 557) suggests that the Flavian celebration of victory in a civil war was disguised as a triumph over a "proper" (non-Roman) enemy, similar to Octavian's representation of Cleopatra as a foe in the civil war with Marc Antony. Beard's observation is supported by the fact that the Flavians used barbarian types to depict the Jews on Judea Capta coins, although Judea had become a Roman province long before the Jewish war (Cody 2003, 109–10, suggests this was a device intended to portray the Jews as worthy but uncivilized opponents). Mason (2005, 98–99) suggests that in the *Bellum Judaicum* Josephus consciously drew a parallel between the end of the civil war in Rome and the end of civil war in Judea.

Although Domitian continued to exploit the Flavian victory over the Jews as a means of legitimization, he substituted the family deity Minerva for Pax – for by this time the Flavian dynasty included a line of deified emperors. As Edmonson (2005, 12) puts it, "Domitian gradually moved away from the civic-minded and populist style of his father and brother to one that was more aloof and autocratic," including the construction of a massive imperial residence on the Palatine.

Works Cited

Aitken, E. B. (2001) Portraying the temple in stone and text: The Arch of Titus and the epistle to the Hebrews. In J. Neusner and J. F. Strange (eds.), *Religious Texts and Material Contexts*, 73–88. Latham, Md., University Press of America.

Alföldy, G. (1995) Eine bauinschrift aus dem Colosseum. *Zeitschrift für Papyrologie und Epigraphie* 109, 195–226.

Anderson Jr., J. C. (1982) Domitian, the Argiletum and the Temple of Peace. *American Journal of Archaeology* 86, 101–10.

——— (1984) *The Historical Topography of the Imperial Fora*. Brussels, Latomus.

Barnes, T. D. (2005) The sack of the temple in Josephus and Tacitus. In J. Edmonson, S. Mason, and J. Rives (eds.), *Flavius Josephus and Flavian Rome*, 129–44. Oxford, Oxford University Press.

Beard, M. (2003) The triumph of Flavius Josephus. In A. J. Boyle and W. J. Dominik (eds.), *Flavian Rome: Culture, Image, Text*, 543–58. Leiden, Brill.

Boyle, A. J. (2003) Reading Flavian Rome. In A. J. Boyle and W. J. Dominik (eds.), *Flavian Rome. Culture, Image, Text*, 1–67. Leiden, Brill.

Coarelli, F. (1968) La Porta Trionfale e la Via dei Trionfi. *Dialoghi di Archeologia* 11 (1), 55–103.

Cody, J. M. (2003) Conquerors and conquered on Flavian coins. In A. J. Boyle and W. J. Dominik (eds.), *Flavian Rome: Culture, Image, Text*, 103–23. Leiden, Brill.

D'Ambra, E. (1993) *Private Lives, Imperial Virtues: The Frieze of the Forum Transitorium in Rome*. Princeton, Princeton University Press.

de Maria, S. (1988) *Gli archi onorari di Roma e dell'Italia romana*. Rome, L'Erma di Bretschneider.

Eberhardt, B. (2005) Wer Dient Wem? Die Darstellung des Flavischen Triumphzuges auf dem Titusbogen und bei Josephus. In J. Sievers and G. Lembi (eds.), *Josephus and Jewish History in Flavian Rome and Beyond*, 257–77. Leiden, Brill.

Eck, W. (2005) Bögen und Tore als Ehrenmonumente in der Provinz Iudaea. In M. Perani (ed.), *"The Words of a Wise Man's Mouth Are Gracious" (Qoh 10, 12), Festschrift for Günter Stemberger on the Occasion of His 65th Birthday*, 153–65. Berlin, Walter de Gruyter.

Edmonson (2005) Introduction, Flavius Josephus and Flavian Rome. In J. Edmonson, S. Mason, and J. Rives (eds.), *Flavius Josephus and Flavian Rome*, 1–33. Oxford, Oxford University Press.

Feldman, L. (2001) Financing the Colosseum. *Biblical Archaeology Review* 27, 20–31, 60.

Grüll, T. (2006) A Fragment of a monumental Roman inscription at the Islamic Museum of the Haram ash-Sharif, Jerusalem. *Israel Exploration Journal* 56, 183–200.

Haeckl, A. E. (1996) Dynasty, religion, topography, architecture: The Roman contexts of the Templum Gentis Flaviae. In E. K. Gazda and A. E. Haeckl (eds.), *Images of Empire, Flavian Fragments in Rome and Ann Arbor Rejoined*, 11–25. Ann Arbor, University of Michigan, Kelsey Museum of Archaeology.

Holloway, R. R. (1987) Some remarks on the Arch of Titus. *L'antiquité classique* 56, 183–91.

Humphrey, J. H. (1996) "Amphitheatrical" Hippo-Stadia. In A. Raban and K. G. Holum (eds.), *Caesarea Maritima: A Retrospective after Two Millennia*, 121–29. Leiden, Brill.

Jensen, W. M. (1978) *The sculptures from the Tomb of the Haterii, volumes 1 and 2*. Ph.D. dissertation, Ann Arbor, University of Michigan Press.

Kleiner, D. E. E. (1992) *Roman Sculpture*. New Haven, Yale University Press.

Kleiner, F. S. (1989) A Vespasianic monument to the Senate and Roman people. *Revue suisse de numismatique (Schweizerische numismatische Rundschau)* 68, 85–91.

——— (1990) The Arches of Vespasian in Rome. *Mitteilungen des Deutschen Archäologischen Instituts Römische Abteilung* 97, 127–36.

Levick, B. (1999) *Vespasian*. New York, Routledge.

Magness, J. (2008) The Arch of Titus at Rome and the fate of the God of Israel. *Journal of Jewish Studies* 59, 201–217.

Makin, E. (1921) The triumphal route, with particular reference to the Flavian triumph. *Journal of Roman Studies* 11, 25–36.

Martin, H. G. (1992) *Römische Tempelkultbilder, eine archäologische Untersuchung zur späten Republik*. Rome, L'Erma di Bretschneider.

Mason, S. (2005) Reading Josephus' *Bellum Judaicum*. In J. Sievers and G. Lembi (eds.), *Josephus and Jewish History in Flavian Rome and Beyond*, 71–100. Leiden, Brill.

Mattingly, H. (1930) *Coins of the Roman Empire in the British Museum, Volume 2: Vespasian to Domitian*. London, British Museum Press.

Millar, F. (2005) Last year in Jerusalem: Monuments of the Jewish War in Rome. In J. Edmonson, S. Mason, and J. Rives (eds.),

Flavius Josephus and Flavian Rome, 101–28. Oxford, Oxford University Press.

Noreña, C. (2003) Medium and message in Vespasian's Templum Pacis. *Memoirs of the American Academy in Rome* 48, 25–43.

Overman, J. A. (2002) The first revolt and Flavian politics. In A. M. Berlin and J. A. Overman (eds.), *The First Jewish Revolt, Archaeology, History, and Ideology*, 213–20. New York, Routledge.

Pfanner, M. (1983) *Der Titusbogen*. Mainz am Rhein, Philipp von Zabern.

Picard, G. C. (1957) *Les trophées romains. Contribution à l'histoire de la religion et de l'art triomphal de Rome*. Paris, Boccard.

Richardson, Jr., L. (1976) The Villa Publica and the Divorum. In L. Bonfante and H. von Heintze (eds.), *In Memoriam Otto J. Brendel, Essays in Archaeology and the Humanities*, 159–63. Mainz am Rhein, Philipp von Zabern.

——— (1992) *A New Topographical Dictionary of Ancient Rome*. Baltimore, Johns Hopkins University Press.

Rives, J. (2005) Flavian religious policy and the destruction of the Jerusalem Temple. In J. Edmonson, S. Mason, and J. Rives (eds.), *Flavius Josephus and Flavian Rome*, 145–66. Oxford, Oxford University Press.

Rossetto, P. C. (1987) Circo Massimo. Il circo Cesariano e l'arco di Tito. *Quaderni del centro di studio per l'archeologia Etrusco-Italica* 14, 39–46.

Schwier, H. (1989) *Tempel und Tempelzerstörung, Untersuchungen zu den theologischen und ideologischen Faktoren im ersten jüdisch-römischen Krieg (66–74 n.Chr.)*. Freiburg, Universitäts-verlag.

Scott, R. T. (2000) The triple arch of Augustus and the Roman triumph. *Journal of Roman Archaeology* 13, 183–91.

Steinby, E. M. (1993) *Lexicon Topographicum Urbis Romae, vols. 1–5*. Rome, Quasar.

Zarrow, E. M. (2006) Imposing romanisation: Flavian coins and Jewish identity. *Journal of Jewish Studies* 57, 44–55.

6

Imperial Triumph and Apotheosis: The Arch of Titus in Rome

Naomi J. Norman

Introduction

Spectacle was an important part of life at Rome, especially the life of the Roman emperor who occupied center stage in the capital city on many occasions, particularly when he celebrated a triumph and when he was buried. As Geertz (1973, 132–40) has demonstrated, spectacle has the ability both to provide a narrative of a complex city and to give groups within the city the opportunity to tell their stories; to his observation there should be added the recognition that architecture can facilitate a group narrative by serving either as a vantage point from which the narrative may be told or as a mnemonic device for that narrative. This article takes the position that the Arch of Titus serves as mnemonic device for Roman narratives about both triumph and apotheosis. On the day of an emperor's triumph, the people and the Senate of Rome commemorated his military achievements and conquests and equated him with Jupiter Optimus Maximus for one day (I leave aside the vexing issue of whether his costume and painted face were meant to equate him visually with Jupiter; *e.g.,* see Warren 1970). On the day the emperor was buried, the people and the Senate of Rome commemorated his life and rule and, in the case of some emperors, witnessed the apotheosis that marked his identity as a god. At his funeral, final judgment was passed on the emperor and his rule: "good" emperors were divinized, "bad" emperors suffered a condemnation of memory, and all the others just faded away. For Augustus, Titus, Trajan, and the other so-called "good" emperors, the funeral and apotheosis were the culmination of a process that began on the days of their triumphs when they were privileged to get a taste of the divinity that might await them at apotheosis.

In myth, Romulus was the first ruler to be divinized; in history, it was Julius Caesar. Between the time of Augustus and Constantine, thirty-six of sixty emperors were divinized

(for a complete list of the *divi*, see Beurlier 1890). Equally striking is the fact that in the Imperial period, apotheosis was not reserved for the emperor but was on twenty-seven occasions extended to members of his family. Beard and Henderson (1998) note the quickening pace of these collateral deifications in the second century CE as new and complex issues of succession arise. That collateral deification could be an important part of an emperor's public persona is suggested by the coinage of the divine Faustina, which was in wide circulation even after the reign of Antoninus Pius (Mattingly 1948; see also MacCormack 1981, 93–158; Davies 2000, ch. 4).

The funeral and apotheosis of the emperor commemorated the past and, in addition, pointed the way to the future, for the emperor's successor emerged from the funeral bearing the potent epithet *divi filius*. Augustus quickly recognized the political value of apotheosis and of this epithet (Weinstock 1971, 356–63). Apotheosis was, therefore, particularly important when the dead emperor had no biological heir and his successor was adopted, as, for example, in the cases of Trajan and Antoninus Pius.

Both the triumph and the funeral that culminated in apotheosis offered striking opportunities for imperial image making and were popular subjects in imperial art in Rome. As Künzl (1988, 9) points out, however, the subject of the triumphal parade is not as popular as its cultural importance might lead us to expect; indeed, on his list of triumphal reliefs (162–63) nearly half belong to the Flavian and Trajanic periods. More popular are images that capture a "snapshot" from the triumph, individual scenes that stand for the entire ritual, as on the silver cup from Boscoreale (Kuttner 1995, figs. 10–12.) Surprisingly, only the Arch of Titus on the Sacra Via overtly depicts both the imperial triumph and the imperial apotheosis on the same monument (I likewise read the Column of Antoninus Pius as depicting both triumph and apotheosis, but in a much more allusive manner).

The Arch of Titus commemorates both his triumph and apotheosis and creates an official visual narrative that grounds Titus's apotheosis in his triumph over Judaea. By tapping into a powerful web of ideas connecting triumph and apotheosis, the Arch deftly binds the two spectacles together (Brelich 1938 offers a full discussion of the many connections between an imperial funeral procession and a triumphal procession). This article demonstrates how the sculptural decoration, architecture, and physical location of the Arch worked together to give voice to Roman ideas about imperial triumph and apotheosis and to illustrate the fundamental link between the two spectacles; it argues that the Arch not only memorialized Titus's triumph and divinization but also gave spectators the opportunity to experience and reactivate either one of those spectacles each and every time they passed through the Arch on their way into or out of the Roman Forum.

The Imperial Triumph

The triumph is a ritual with a very long pedigree in Rome, stretching back beyond the Republic, all the way to the legendary Romulus (Plut. *Vit. Rom.* 16). Scholarship on the Roman triumph includes a variety of perspectives and interpretations (see, *e.g., RE* VIIA 493–511, *s.v.* "Triumphus" [W. Ehlers]; Künzl 1988; Barini 1952; Versnel 1970; MacCormick 1981; and Beard 2007). During the Republic, a triumph was the highest honor that a general could earn in recognition of his military achievements, growing in both complexity and splendor with each passing generation. In the Imperial period, it was the exclusive prerogative of the emperor or members of his immediate family (see Barini 1952, 201–4, for a complete list of all imperial triumphs).

Though each triumph has its own distinctive tempo and features, every celebration shares a common shape and structure with its predecessors and successors. For example, every triumph revolves around three venues, each of which is associated with a particular audience: the Campus Martius and its association with the military; the Forum Romanum with its emphasis on the people and Senate of Rome; and the Capitoline hill, home to Jupiter Optimus Maximus. The parade also has a tripartite structure: first come the spoils and prisoners of war; then the victor, public officials, and sacrificial animals; and at the end the army. Thus the ritual is inscribed onto the topography of Rome and draws within its orbit much of the population of Rome.

The Flavian Triumph

For the Flavian triumph over Judaea, celebrated in 71 CE and featured on the Arch of Titus, we are fortunate to have Josephus's rich and detailed written account (*BJ* 7.116–57;

see also Beard 2003 and Magness, this volume). As he tells the story, the Senate had originally decreed separate triumphs for Vespasian, Titus, and Domitian, but the Flavii decided to celebrate a common triumph instead. Josephus records that the entire city came out to witness the event, so filling up the route (Fig. 6.6a) that there was barely enough room for the parade to pass. The night before the triumphal parade, participants gathered in the Campus Martius; at dawn, the three Flavii emerged to receive the acclamation of the crowd at the Porticus Octaviae where Vespasian prayed to the gods. Afterward, the troops marched forth with seven hundred prisoners of war who had been specially selected by Titus for their stature and beauty, accompanied by the Judaean booty and vivid displays of the battles.

The parade exited the Campus Martius and entered the city through the Porta Triumphalis, the exact date, form, and location of which is problematic (see Magness this volume for a brief discussion of the problems). There the Flavii, each dressed in the garb of a *triumphator* (αὐτοκράτορες in Josephus [*BJ* 7.123]), sacrificed to the gods. From the Campus Martius, the participants could see in the distance their destination: the temple of Jupiter on the Capitoline (Favro 1994, fig. 6). The triumphal route took them through the markets to the Circus Maximus, around the Palatine, across the Forum Romanum, and finally up the Capitoline to the Jupiter temple.

So massive was the Flavian triumph that Josephus declares himself incapable of describing it, opting instead to call it a symbol of the greatness of Roman rule (τῆς Ῥωμαίων ἡγεμονίας … τὸ μέγεθος; *BJ* 7.133). On display were tapestries, statues, gems – so many gems, indeed, that Josephus dares anyone to continue to consider them rare – and other marvels. He likens the great masses of displayed booty to a river flowing through the city (τις ῥέοντα ποταμόν; *BJ* 7.134). The procession also included sacrificial animals and prisoners of war, all accompanied by Roman soldiers, officials, standard bearers, and others. Some participants held plaques describing the exotic booty; others held models or platforms (πήγματα) depicting the battles or the cities or the captured generals. Josephus saves his greatest praise for these platforms (some as high as three or four stories), which vividly depicted important episodes in the war and gave spectators the sense of actually "being there": ἡ τέχνη δὲ καὶ τῶν κατασκευασμάτων ἡ μεγαλουργία τοῖς οὐκ ἰδοῦσι γινόμενα τότ' ἐδείκνυεν ὡς παροῦσι (both the art and the magnificent workmanship of these structures at that time revealed the incidents to those who did not see them, as though they were actually present; *BJ* 7.146). He remarks that the craftsmanship was so accomplished and the models so awesome that spectators feared the stages would collapse and fall on top of them. This is not quite the same fear as that experienced on the field of battle, but real fear nonetheless (see Beard 2003, 34–37, who is particularly interested in the effect of the festival on its spectators and who characterizes the parade, at some moments, as teetering precariously on the edge of bathos and, at others, of evoking so much empathy for the captives as to rob the *triumphator* of the limelight). Surely one of the points of the triumph was to give the Roman people some sense of what Roman military action meant and what it was like for the Roman state to go to war. In other words, the triumph helped Roman citizens experience, albeit at one remove, some of the very real emotions of battle.

Josephus records that most of the booty was carried along in heaps (*BJ* 7.148). The exceptions were the spoils from the temple at Jerusalem (*BJ* 7.149), which stood out above all the rest: namely a golden table many talents in weight (i.e., the shewbread table), a lamp stand also made of gold (i.e., the menorah), and a copy of the Jewish Law (i.e., the Torah). These sacred relics were followed by gold and ivory statues of Victory and finally by the Flavii themselves – Vespasian and Titus, each riding in a triumphal chariot, followed by Domitian riding a magnificent white horse. The parade ended on the Capitoline, at the temple of Jupiter Capitolinus, where the emperor and his sons performed the sacrifices (see Makin 1921 for discussion of the route); afterward they and the entire city spent the rest of the day feasting, some in the palace, the rest scattered throughout the city.

This triumph was a magnificent spectacle – a loud, messy, exuberant, awe-inspiring celebration of the emperor, the empire, the army, and the Roman people. It was also a moment in time that transcended time. The triumphal route traced the history of Rome in broad strokes, from the pomerial boundary of the city to Romulus's hut on the Palatine to the wellspring of Roman religion on the Capitoline. And scattered along the route, like the footprints of earlier triumphs, were the monuments built by earlier generals and emperors to commemorate their own triumphs: here is the temple of Janus built by Duilius to commemorate his victory over Carthage; and there, the arch of Augustus lauding his victory at Actium and inscribed with the *fasti triumphales* recording the names of all *triumphatores*, beginning with Romulus (*CIL* I².1 Acta triumphorum p. 43–50).

Because the itinerary of the triumph was not static, *triumphatores* vied to locate their triumphal monuments at nodal points along the route: the southern end of the Campus Martius, the Circus Maximus, the Roman Forum, and the Capitoline. Similarly, they designed routes to suit their own purposes, passing by the triumphal monuments erected by their ancestors and bypassing those erected by their enemies. The path traced by a triumph could either recall to memory an earlier triumph or completely ignore it, assigning to it a sort of passive *damnatio memoriae*. Each triumphal route was thus both a celebration and a didactic journey; it created a three-dimensional timeline, what Favro (1994, 154) calls a kinetic history of the Roman state. Earlier triumphs were

remembered and in a sense reactivated whenever later parades passed under or alongside these earlier triumphal monuments. Thus each triumph was linked to the past and laid the groundwork for the future. Each triumph served to weave the *triumphator* into the fabric and history of the city; each triumph tapped into the distinct power of the city of Rome. So close was the identification of the triumph with Rome that Antony was roundly criticized for trying to celebrate one in Alexandria instead (Plutarch, *Vit. Ant.* 50.2).

On the day of his triumph, the *triumphator* was the center of attention, the object of all eyes (see Brilliant 1999; Beard 2003 views it quite differently). According to Josephus each of the Flavii, like all previous *triumphatores*, wore a purple cloak over a star-studded toga. According to tradition, the *triumphator* carried a scepter crowned with an eagle in one hand and a laurel branch in the other and rode in a magnificent gilded chariot drawn by four horses (the costume, the chariot, and the slave all appear on the silver cup from Boscoreale; see Kuttner 1995, figs. 10, 25). Behind him in the chariot stood a slave whose job it was to hold above the *triumphator*'s head a crown of laurel leaves known as the *corona triumphalis* and whisper in his ear, "look behind you, and remember that you are a man" (Tert. *Apol.* 33.4; also Juv. 10.41, Plin. *HN* 38.41, Beard 2007, 85–92 for different view). In the Imperial period, the *servus publicus* was replaced by various members of the imperial family – in a nod to the future of the ruling family and the stability of their rule – and, sometimes, by Victory herself.

The traditional interpretation of the whispered words of the slave is that, in response to the parts of the ritual that assimilated the *triumphator* with Jupiter, the slave was there to remind him of his mortality and to keep him from succumbing to *superbia*: "remember that you are a man." But the slave also tells him to "look behind" and thus "to the future" for in much of Roman literature, the future is conceptualized as coming from behind rather than lying ahead (Sen. *Ad Lucilium* 49.9; Suet. *Dom.* 23.1; Cic. *Div.* 1.49 *ff.*; see Bettini 1991, 151–57). On the day of triumph, then, the *triumphator* was advised to look beyond the present day and his status as "god for a day" and think about the future. In other words, he was urged to look to the future and accomplish those feats that would secure his deification for all time.

The Arch of Titus

The Arch of Titus (Fig. 6.1), located at the eastern end of the Roman Forum, at the head of the Sacra Via, commemorates the Flavian triumph but presents Titus as the sole protagonist in the event. Key images from the triumph occupy pride of place in the sculptural program of the Arch. Two large relief panels decorate the interior of the single bay of the Arch and illustrate two moments in the triumph: the display of

Fig. 6.1 *East facade of the Arch of Titus, Rome (Photo: © DAIR 79.2000).*

the spoils from Jerusalem and Titus in his triumphal chariot.

The Relief Panels in the Bay of the Arch

The spoils panel occupies the south side of the bay (Fig. 6.2). In it, two of the three most important relics mentioned by Josephus are depicted: the menorah and the shewbread table, each shown in great detail and each carried on a *ferculum*. Traditionally stored inside the Temple at Jerusalem and known only to the high priests there, they are here put on public display, subject to the gaze of the vast crowd of spectators, most of whom had no knowledge of what they were seeing or of the importance of these objects to Judaism. Attendants carrying identifying placards follow the objects, and everyone moves toward an arch on the extreme right side of the panel which Kleiner (1990, 129) identifies as the arch voted for Vespasian by the Senate in the year before the triumph (Dio 65.7.2).

On the north side of the bay is the relief depicting Titus in his triumphal chariot and accompanied by a crowd of lictors and other officials (Fig. 6.3). He wears the costume of the *triumphator* and holds in his left hand Jupiter's scepter crowned with an eagle and extends a palm branch in his right (illustrated in Pfanner 1983, especially fig. 32, pl. 52.1, 3). In the place of the slave stands Victoria Augusti, holding the *corona triumphalis* over his head. The chariot, decorated with a frieze of baetyls on its rim and an eagle standing on a thunderbolt below (illustrated in Davies 2000, figs. 56–57), is guided by Roma (or perhaps Virtus) and is accompanied by the Genius Populi Roman (or perhaps Honos), the Genius Senatus, and togate officials. The presence of the personifications in the scene and the focus on Titus to the exclusion of his fellow *triumphator*es elevate the scene from the purely historical to the symbolic.

The triumph also figures on the exterior decoration of the Arch, at the level of the cornice where a small, poorly preserved frieze depicts the procession. Plainly visible are

Fig. 6.2 *Spoils relief in the bay of the Arch of Titus, Rome (Photo: © Alinari/Art Resource, New York, AL5839).*

Fig. 6.3 Triumphator *relief in the bay of the Arch of Titus, Rome (Photo: © DAIR 79.2491).*

Fig. 6.4 *Small triumph frieze from below cornice of Arch of Titus, Rome (From Künzl 1988, fig. 10).*

a number of soldiers – some carrying placards, some carrying shields – and various officials, including a *victimarius*, and a sacrificial bull (Fig. 6.4). In addition to these explicit narratives of the triumph, the other sculptural decoration of the Arch employs more generalized victory iconography: winged Victories appear in the spandrels of the Arch, each holding a different attribute alluding to the Jewish War; and magnificent personifications of Honos (or the Genius Populi Romani) and Virtus (or Roma) grace the keystones of the Arch (note that these same personifications appear in the relief panel).

Reading the Relief Panels

The figures in the spoils panel march from left to right; those in the triumph relief, from right to left, so that the figures in each panel move toward the temple of Jupiter on the Capitoline, the goal of the triumphal procession. As many scholars have noted, the orientation of the two panels place a viewer standing in the bay of the Arch in the midst of a sculpted re-creation of the triumphal parade. This gives the viewer the opportunity to reenact the experience of "being there" (much like Josephus's use of the deictic expression τότ᾽ ἐδείκνυεν ὡς παροῦσι in his description of the event) during the parade and to retrace the route of the procession as she moves through the Arch and into the Forum. This is not, however, the only procession reenacted by the sculpture on the Arch.

Titus's Apotheosis

The Arch is not solely a triumphal monument in the strictest sense; that is to say, it was not built merely to commemorate Titus's triumph. This was accomplished, perhaps, by triumphal arches voted for Vespasian and Titus by the Senate, which included three Vespasianic arches (Kleiner 1990) and the arch erected by Titus in the Circus Maximus (Humphrey 1986, 97–100). The inscription from the arch in the Circus Maximus (*CIL* 6.944) reads:

> The Senate and the people of Rome to the emperor Titus Caesar Vespasian Augustus the son of the divine Vespasian, Pontifex Maximus, holder of the tribunician power for the tenth time, *imperator* for the seventeenth time, consul for the eighth time, father of the fatherland, the very princeps of Rome because by the example and advice of his father he overcame the people of Judaea and destroyed the city of Jerusalem which before was besieged by generals, kings and peoples in vain or left unmolested by them.

This is a typical triumphal inscription and quite different from the dedicatory inscription on the east side of the attic of the Arch of Titus. Holloway (1987, 187) provocatively suggested over twenty years ago that the Arch functioned primarily as a monumental pedestal for the inscription on its attic (a duplicate of which may have appeared on the west side as in the Arch of Trajan at Beneventum), and that its sculpture was the equivalent of a funerary *elogium*. The inscription is monumental in scale (letters range from 35 to 46 cm in height) but surprisingly terse: SENATUS / POPULUSQUE ROMANUS / DIVO TITO DIVI VESPASIANI F / VESPASIANO AUGUSTO (The Senate and the people of Rome to the divine Titus Vespasian Augustus, son of the divine Vespasian; *CIL* 6.945; restored by G. Valadier in 1822–24, see Dyson, this volume). The inscription is crystal clear: the Arch was dedicated sometime after Titus's death in 81 CE. Lehmann-Hartleben (1934) suggested that the Arch was actually Titus's tomb and suggested that Titus's ashes were placed in a small chamber in the attic. Although his argument has not found wide acceptance, scholars do acknowledge that the Arch commemorated the emperor's apotheosis and thus had funerary connotations, and Pfanner (1983, 98–103) has convincingly demonstrated that the principal programmatic theme of the Arch was Titus's apotheosis.

A small relief panel placed in the summit of the vault of the Arch provides explicit reference to Titus's death and apotheosis (Fig. 6.5). The panel is framed by thick garlands that are held at the corners by small putti. Within this garlanded frame, we see Titus perched – albeit somewhat

Fig. 6.5 *Apotheosis relief from vault of Arch of Titus, Rome (Photo: © DAIR 79.2393).*

awkwardly – on the back of an eagle and ascending to heaven to join the company of the gods. In Roman illustrations of apotheosis, the deceased generally rides to heaven in a chariot, as on the Belvedere altar, or on a winged creature, either an eagle as here or a personification, as in the apotheosis of Sabina relief or the apotheosis relief on the Antonine column base (Kleiner 1992, fig. 86, Belvedere altar; fig. 222, Sabina relief; fig. 253, Antonine column relief). The crippled Claudius seems to have been the only emperor to have walked to heaven (Sen. *Apocol.* 1) which may explain why his bid for divinization was rejected by the gods. Titus rode on an eagle, and this relief is the first monumental Roman state relief sculpture to use an eagle as the vehicle of apotheosis (for a completely different reading of Titus's eagle, see Beard and Henderson 1998).

Imperial Death, Burial, and Apotheosis

What do we know of Titus's death, burial, and apotheosis? Almost nothing. Suetonius records that Titus died of a fever at the age of forty-two, only two years, two months, and twenty days after his father's death. According to Suetonius (*Tit.* 11; *Dom.* 2.3), he was widely mourned by the people and extravagantly praised by the Senate, though Domitian "bestowed no honor on him, except for deification, and often slandered his memory in ambiguous phrases, both in his speeches and in his edicts." Although no ancient source describes Titus's funeral, it must have followed the model established by Augustus's funeral, especially since the Flavii

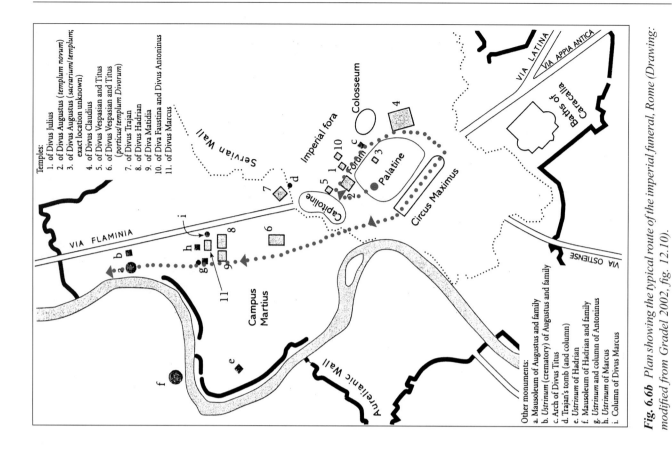

Fig. 6.6b *Plan showing the typical route of the imperial funeral, Rome (Drawing: modified from Gradel 2002, fig. 12.10).*

Fig. 6.6a *Plan showing the typical route of the imperial triumph, Rome (Drawing: modified from Gradel 2002, fig. 12.10).*

Temples:
1. of Divus Julius
2. of Divus Augustus (*templum novum*)
3. of Divus Augustus (*sacrarium/templum*; exact location unknown)
4. of Divus Claudius
5. of Divus Vespasian and Titus
6. of Divus Vespasian and Titus (*porticus/templum Divorum*)
7. of Divus Trajan
8. of Divus Hadrian
9. of Diva Matidia
10. of Diva Faustina and Divus Antoninus
11. of Divus Marcus

Other monuments:
a. Mausoleum of Augustus and family
b. *Ustrinum* (crematory) of Augustus and family
c. Arch of Divus Titus
d. Trajan's tomb (and column)
e. *Ustrinum* of Hadrian
f. Mausoleum of Hadrian and family
g. *Ustrinum* and column of Antoninus
h. *Ustrinum* of Marcus
i. Column of Divus Marcus

were fond of revitalizing Augustan precedents. Fortunately, we know quite a bit about Augustus' funeral which drew upon the earlier tradition of the aristocratic funeral of the Republic (the primary source is Polyb. 6.53–54, contextualized by Toynbee 1971, 43–64; Flower 1996, ch. 4). Augustus's funeral also borrowed from the ceremonies for Sulla (Plut. *Vit. Sull.* 38.3; App. *B Civ* 1.106.497–500) and Julius Caesar (App. *B Civ* 2.616; Dio 47.18.3–19.3). It set the precedent for all imperial funerals to come, although some variations were introduced, especially after inhumation replaced cremation as the principal funerary rite in Roman culture (see Richard 1966a–d; 1978; Price 1987; Arce 1988). According to Dio (56.34–46), Augustus's funeral began with a ceremonial procession that transported his body from his house on the Palatine down to the Forum (Fig. 6.6b). Like the aristocratic Republican funeral, the procession included images of Augustus's ancestors and deceased relatives alongside images of other prominent Romans, going all the way back to Romulus. Also present were likenesses of all the countries he had conquered (τὰ τε ἔθνη πάνθ' ὅσα προσεκτήσατο; Dio 56.34.3) and two golden images of Augustus himself: one carried in from the Curia and another that came in a triumphal chariot (ἐφ' ἅρματος πομπικοῦ; Dio 56.34.2). The actual body was kept hidden from view inside a coffin secreted within the funerary couch while a wax effigy of the emperor – dressed in triumphal garb (ἐν ἐπινικίῳ στολῇ; Dio 56.34.1) – was on public view, the recipient of public ritual. Though wax portraits of deceased ancestors were an integral part of the funeral for aristocratic Republicans, the idea of exhibiting a full-size wax effigy of the deceased seems to have originated at the funeral for Julius Caesar (App. *B Civ* 2.147.612). Another prototype could well have been the figure of Sulla that was made of frankincense and cinnamon and was burned at his funeral (App. *B Civ* 1.105–6; Plut. *Vit. Sull.* 38.3). Eulogies to Augustus were delivered once the procession reached the Forum. Consonant with the doubling of the body was a doubling in the performance of the eulogy: Drusus extolled the private virtues of Augustus, delivering his remarks from the Rostra of the Orators, while Tiberius, speaking from the Julian Rostra, spoke of his public virtues and accomplishments.

After the speeches were delivered, the funerary couch bearing both the body and the effigy was taken to the limit of the city, passed through the Porta Triumphalis, and, accompanied by senators, equites, their wives, praetorian guardsmen, and virtually anyone else who was in the city at the time, solemnly made its way northwest to the Campus Martius. There, near the mausoleum that Augustus had built earlier, the funerary couch was placed on a magnificent pyre. At that point, the priests, equites, and infantry began the *decursio* – the elaborately choreographed circling of the pyre that was designed to perpetuate the emperor's memory (see Davies 2000, 124–26 on the perpetuation of memory;

for the *decursio* itself, see Suet. *Aug.* 100.3; Dio 56.34–46 on the funeral of Augustus; App. *B Civ* 1.106, Sulla; Suet. *Claud.* 1, Drusus; Dio 59.11.2, Drusilla; 75.4–5, Pertinax; Herodian 4.2, Septimius Severus). Afterward, centurions took up torches and lit the pyre from below. As it burned, those present threw on it their own triumphal decorations and watched them burn along with the body of Augustus.

Once the pyre was completely consumed, an eagle was released from it to signify the emperor's spirit ascending to the gods. Because the eagle is missing from Suetonius's description of the funeral, Price (1987, 95) suggests that Dio anachronistically included the bird in his account, but I see no reason to discount, as Price does, the evidence from first-century gems that show eagles carrying emperors to the heavens (see Megow 1987, 199–200, inv. A80, pl. 27.1; Fraschetti 1984, 180–84). Dio reports that after five days, Livia gathered up Augustus's burnt bones and placed them in the Mausoleum in the northern Campus Martius. Sometime after that, Numerius Atticus vowed that he had personally witnessed Augustus ascending to heaven in the manner of the legendary Romulus (Dio 56.46.2); the Senate then voted him divine honors, and the apotheosis was complete. (Because Romulus did not actually ascend to heaven from the flames of his funeral [Plut. *Vit. Rom.* 27.5–28.3], it may have been Herakles who provided a model for apotheosis from the pyre [Soph. *Trach.*; Apollod. *Bibl.* 2.7.7; Diod. Sic. 4.38.3–5]. The fact that Tiberius's eulogy for Augustus likens him to Herakles [Dio 56.36.4] seems to support this).

The numerous and explicit allusions to the imperial triumph that run through the funeral are striking. For example, Augustus's effigy was clothed as a *triumphator*; another image of the emperor processed in his triumphal chariot; the procession included images of captive countries; the body and effigy exited the city via the Porta Triumphalis; the ritual took place in the Campus Martius where triumphal parades marshaled before entering the city proper; and those present dedicated their triumphal rewards to him. These individual elements, when taken together, suggest a deep, foundational connection between these two spectacles, each centered on a resplendent protagonist, each anchored in the concept of a man who becomes a god. Seneca (*ad Marciam de consolatione* 3.1) describes the procession to bring Drusus's body back from Germany to Rome for burial and likens it to a triumph: "And to these circumstances of his death . . . there was added the unbounded sorrow of his fellow-citizens, of the provinces and of all Italy, through the length of which crowds poured forth from the towns and colonies and, escorting the funeral train all the way to the city, made it seem more like a triumph."

Like a triumph, an imperial apotheosis was not a single moment in time; rather it was the theatrical climax of a process that moved through space and stretched backward and forward in time. The process moved the body horizontally out of the *urbs* and vertically up to the heavens, establishing both a horizontal human axis and a vertical divine one, not unlike the axis of the triumphal route that ran through the city and up to the Capitoline. By moving along both axes, the body of the emperor straddled the line between human space and divine space, between mortality and immortality (*c.f.* Dupont 1989; Bickerman 1972).

The pyre in the Campus Martius was the crucial setting for the funeral, both as the locus of the cremation and as the venue for apotheosis (Price 1987 discusses the importance of the pyre, though he insists that the emperor continued to be cremated long after inhumation had become the standard burial rite throughout the Roman world; but there is too much evidence, including the sarcophagus of Balbinus that suggests the opposite). Though the final act of the funerary spectacle may have occurred at the pyre, the funerary ritual as a whole cut a wide swath across much of the topography of Rome. It moved from the Palatine to the Forum to the Campus Martius, drawing participants from across the social and political spectrum of the city and creating a powerful image of unity at a time of potential disruption upon the death of the emperor. Since Augustus had not established a formal mechanism for transferring *imperium* to his successor, his death was potentially unsettling to the state and the Roman people; this sense of unease is recorded in Dio (56.45.2) as a series of bad omens that accompanied the succession of Tiberius. The difficulty of the succession was eased by Augustus's apotheosis, which bestowed on Tiberius the mantle of *divi filius*, the same role co-opted by Augustus during his own rise to power. In later years, apotheosis afforded heirs, especially those who were adopted by the emperor, considerable political leverage and significantly eased their transition to the purple. For example, when the Senate balked at giving Hadrian divine honors, Antoninus insisted and made it a condition of his becoming emperor, saying that, if the Senate so hated Hadrian, they could decide to annul all his acts, including his own adoption; the Senate, anxious for Antoninus to rule, relented and divinized Hadrian, thus ensuring the succession (Dio 70.1.2–3). The very full accounts of the funerals of Pertinax (Dio 75.4–5) and Septimius Severus (Herodian 4.2) indicate that subsequent imperial funerals followed the same general pattern established by the funeral of Augustus and drew upon many of the same themes, including the deployment of triumphal imagery.

The funeral of Trajan provides an excellent example of the interplay between triumph and apotheosis. When Trajan died on campaign far from Rome, the ritual cycle was telescoped and, according to his late biographer, his Parthian triumph and funeral were combined into one magnificent public event when his cremated remains were finally returned to Rome; for that event Hadrian placed a lifelike effigy of Trajan in the triumphal chariot and paraded it through the streets of Rome in a triumphal procession. At the culmination

of the triumph, his ashes were interred in the base of his column and he was proclaimed *divus* (SHA *Hadr.* 6.3; Eutropius, *Breviarum ab urbe condita* 8.5.2–4; according to Aurelius Victor, *Epitome de Caesaribus*, 14.12, Trajan's body was burnt at Seleucia and the ashes were later sent to Rome for interment). Thus Trajan triumphed, was buried, and became divine all on the same day. The event was commemorated by coins bearing on the obverse the head of Trajan with the legend *Divo Traiano Parth[ico] Aug[usto] Patri* and on the reverse the triumphal chariot driven by the emperor/effigy holding a scepter with the legend *triumphus Parthicus* (*BM Coins Rom. Emp.* 3, 244, no. 47, pl. 47.7; another aureus minted by Hadrian depicts the divine Trajan not in the traditional fashion with toga and mantle but as a cuirassed military figure; *BM Coins Rom. Emp.* 3, 318, no. 603, pl. 59.3; also see Richard 1966c). Triumph and deification appear quite literally as two sides of the same coin. Rhetorically this link between the triumph and apotheosis of Trajan is articulated by Pliny who, when describing the effect of gazing at Trajan during his first triumph in 99 CE, remarked that the emperor "towered above us" like a god (Plin. *Pan.* 22.2.3, 24.5). Pliny tells Trajan: "by your own renown and glory, by freedom and by your subjects' love, you are borne aloft far above . . . [other] rulers; you are lifted to the heavens by the very ground we all tread, where your imperial footsteps are mingled with our own." Panegyric demands superlatives, but this goes beyond mere praise; it is the language of divinity. Compare this to the experience of a viewer standing in the bay of the Arch of Titus who sees Titus similarly towering above her.

The Arch of Titus eloquently articulates the web of ideas and symbols that unite triumph and apotheosis. On it, as we have seen, both the triumph and the apotheosis of the emperor are illustrated; but, despite the fact that they appear in independent relief panels, they are not depicted as completely independent events but rather are united by a number of sculptural details. Not only does Titus in the apotheosis panel wear the same tunic and toga as on the triumphal relief, but the apotheosis eagle takes the same stance as the eagle carved on Titus's triumphal chariot (Davies 2000, 71, figs. 56–57; the eagle on Titus's chariot also resembles the one depicted on the pediment of the temple of Jupiter Capitolinus on the Boscoreale cup). Similarly, the garlands that frame the apotheosis panel recall the triumphal wreath of laurel that Victoria Augusti places on Titus's head in the chariot panel. These are subtle but altogether clear visual cues that encourage us to read the panels together and to acknowledge that Titus's divinization is grounded in his triumph. Titus's apotheosis at the very apex of the vault, then, serves as the climactic "text" of the Arch. The triumphal panels in the bay remind us that Titus's apotheosis is founded on his significant military achievements. To borrow Davies's (2000, 72) phrase, the triumphal

Fig. 6.7 *Interior of the Arch of Titus, Rome (Photo: courtesy Timothy N. Gantz).*

reliefs in the bay are a "visual *res gestae.*" Holloway (1987) calls the reliefs an *elogium.* Whatever term one uses, the idea is essentially the same: the reliefs create a text that narrates the achievements that earned Titus divine status after his death and serve as an exemplum for others.

That message is conveyed not only by these sculptural details but also by the orientation of the reliefs on the Arch. As mentioned above, the triumphal reliefs inside the bay of the Arch are most legible as one follows the path of the triumphal procession; the apotheosis panel, however, is most legible as one follows the path of the funerary procession (Fig. 6.7). A spectator passing through the Arch going into the Forum is moving in the direction of the triumphal parade as it heads toward the Capitoline to the temple of Jupiter, the goal of the *triumphator.* Such a spectator finds herself surrounded by the triumph and feels as if she herself is moving in the triumphal parade, with the display of the spoils on her left and the resplendent emperor in his chariot on her right. The apotheosis panel, however, is most legible when one moves in the opposite direction, going from the Forum to the Campus Martius, following the path of the funerary procession. To read the reliefs properly and to appreciate their interdependence, a spectator must first trace the triumphal route of Titus and then his funerary route, reenacting both of these moments in time and bringing to life both spectacles and the commemoration of Titus.

The architecture of the Porta Triumphalis also articulates the link between triumph and apotheosis. Coarelli identifies the Porta Triumphalis as part of the Porta Carmentalis, a double gate in the Servian Wall whose exact location is unknown. He argues that it consisted of two arches placed at right angles to one another. For anyone leaving the city, the arch to the right was called the Porta Scelerata because it was the gate through which corpses were regularly carried out of the city to pyres in the Campus Martius (Ov. *Fast.* 2.201–4); the arch to the left was the Porta Triumphalis, generally used only by those entering the city, in particular by *triumphatores* and triumphal processions (Coarelli 1968, 55–103; 1988, 363–414; Richardson 1992, 301, *s.v.* "Porta Carmentalis," accepts this reconstruction; see also Versnel 1970, 132–63, who maintains that the gate was opened only for triumphal parades; Kleiner 1989). The emperor's corpse seems to have been the only one to exit the city via the Porta Triumphalis (first documented for Augustus: Tac. *Ann.* 1.8.4; Suet. *Aug.* 100.2; Dio 56.42.1). This was not simply a mark of special honor. Rather, it marked the completion of the process of his deification that began on the day of his triumph.

Conclusion

The imperial funerary procession reversed the route of the triumph; it began at the Palatine, traversed the Forum, and ended in the Campus Martius. The imperial triumph and apotheosis together thus formed a circle, with the one completing the arc (both literal and metaphorical) begun by the other. The triumph and the funeral were conceptually two halves of the same idea. The funeral completes the circuit begun by the triumph and moves the emperor from the center of the city to the Campus Martius, both the start of the triumphal procession and the final resting place for the Roman emperors (Trajan is, of course, the great exception; he was given the honor of interpomerial burial, within his forum, which was itself a magnificent triumphal/ victory monument). The goal of the triumph was to make the emperor a god for one day; the goal of apotheosis was to make him a god forever. For the so-called "good" emperors, the triumph was but a taste of the divinity that awaited them at apotheosis.

The Arch of Titus is a complex monument. The placement of the relief panels within the architectural frame reinforces the connection between triumph and apotheosis. Furthermore, the location of the Arch at a major nodal point along the routes taken by both triumphal and funerary processions ensures that, over and over again, spectators will witness and remember the spectacles of Titus's triumph and apotheosis and will reactivate them. In this way, the Arch is a mnemonic device that is simultaneously retrospective and prospective. It both records two distinct moments in time and opens up the possibility of reliving those historical moments, as future triumphal parades and funerary processions pass through its bay and under its vault.

Acknowledgments

This paper is a kind of footnote to Ross Holloway's article on the Arch of Titus that appeared in 1987. That article is like so much of his scholarship – full of learning and the product of looking once again at ancient monuments we thought we knew and well understood. This reading of the Arch arose from my own decision to look again at that familiar monument.

Works Cited

Arce, J. (1988) *Funus Imperatorum: Los funerals et los emperadores romanos*. Madrid, Alianza Editorial.

Barini, C. (1952) *Triumphalia. Imprese ed onori militari durante l'impero romano*. Turin, Società editrice internazionale.

Beard, M. (2003) The triumph of the absurd: Roman street theatre. In C. Edwards and G. Woolfe (eds.), *Rome the Cosmopolis*, 21–43. Cambridge, Cambridge University Press.

Beard, M. (2007) *The Roman Triump*. Cambridge, Harvard University Press.

Beard, M. and Henderson, J. (1998) The emperor's new body: Ascension from Rome. In M. Wyke (ed.), *Parchments of Gender: Deciphering the Bodies of Antiquity*, 191–219. Oxford, Clarendon Press.

Bettini, M. (1991) *Anthropology and Roman Culture: Kinship, Time, Images of the Soul*. Baltimore, Johns Hopkins University Press.

Beurlier, E. (1890) *Essai sur le culte rendu aux empereurs romains*. Paris, E. Thorin.

Bickerman, E. (1972) Le culte des souverains dans l'Empire romain. *Entretiens de la fondation Hardt* 19, 7–37.

Brelich, A. (1938) Trionfo e morte. *Studi e materiali di storia delle religioni* 14, 189–93.

Brendel, O. (1980) *The Visible Idea: Interpretations of Classical Art*. Washington, D.C., Decatur House Press.

Brilliant, R. (1999) "Let the trumpets roar!": The Roman triumph. In B. Bergmann and C. Kondoleon, *The Art of Ancient Spectacle: Studies in the History of Art, 56. Symposium Papers 34*, 221–29. Washington D.C., National Gallery of Art.

Coarelli, F. (1968) La Porta Tionfale e la Via dei Trionfi. *Dialoghi di Archeologia* 2, 55–103.

——— (1988) *Il Foro Boario: Dalle origini alla fine della Repubblica*. Rome, Quasar.

Davies, P. (2000) *Death and the Emperor: Roman Imperial Funerary Monuments from Augustus to Marcus Aurelius*. Cambridge, Cambridge University Press.

Dupont, F. (1989) The emperor-god's other body. In M. Feher (ed.), *Fragments for a History of the Human Body*, 397–419. New York, Zone.

Favro, D. (1994) The street triumphant: The urban impact of Roman triumphal parades. In Zeynep Çelik, Diane Favro, Richard Ingersoll (eds.), *Streets: Critical Perspectives on Public Space*, 151–64. Berkeley, University of California Press.

Flower, H. I. (1996) *Ancestor Masks and Aristocratic Power in Roman Culture*. Oxford, Clarendon Press.

Fraschetti, A. (1984) Morte dei "principe" e "eroi" degli famiglia di Augusto. *Sezione Archeologia e Storica Antica* 6, 151–89.

Geertz, C. (1973) *The Interpretation of Cultures: Selected Essays*. New York, Basic Books.

Gradel, I. (2002) *Emperor Worship and Roman Religion*. Oxford, Clarendon Press.

Holloway, R. R. (1987) Some remarks on the Arch of Titus. *L'Antiquité classique* 56, 183–91.

Humphrey, J. H. (1986) *Roman Circuses: Arenas for Chariot Racing*. Berkeley, University of California Press.

Kleiner, D. E. E. (1992) *Roman Sculpture*. New Haven, Yale University Press.

Kleiner, F. (1989) The study of Roman triumphal and honorary arches fifty years after Kähler. *Journal of Roman Archaeology* 2, 201–4.

——— (1990) The arches of Vespasian in Rome. *Mitteilungen des Deutschen Archäologischen Instituts, Römische Abteilung* 97, 127–36.

Künzl, E. (1988) *Der römische Triumph: Siegesfeiern im antiken Rom*. Munich, Verlag C. H. Beck.

Kuttner, A. (1995) *Dynasty and Empire in the Age of Augustus: The Case of the Boscoreale Cups*. Berkeley, University of California Press.

Lehmann-Hartleben, K. (1934) L'Arco di Tito. *Bullettino della Commissione archeologica Comunale di Roma* 62, 89–122.

MacCormack, S. (1981) *Art and Ceremony in Late Antiquity*. Berkeley, University of California Press.

Makin, E. (1921) The triumphal route, with particular reference to the Flavian triumph. *Journal of Roman Studies* 11, 26–30.

Mattingly, H. (1948) The consecration of Faustina the Elder and her daughter. *Harvard Theological Review* 41, 147–51.

Megow, W.-R. (1987) *Kkameen von Augustus bis Alexander Severus*. Berlin, Walter de Gruyter and Co.

Morris, I. (1992) *Death Ritual and Social Structure in Classical Antiquity*. Cambridge, Cambridge University Press.

Pfanner, M. (1983) *Der Titusbogen. Beiträge zur Erschliessung hellenistischer und kaiserzeitlicher Skulptur und Architektur, 2*. Mainz am Rhein, Philipp von Zabern.

Pollitt, J. J. (1986) *Art in the Hellenistic Age*. Cambridge, Cambridge University Press.

Price, S. (1987) From noble funerals to divine cult: The consecration of Roman emperors. In D. Cannadine and S. Price (eds.), *Rituals of Royalty: Power and Ceremonial in Traditional Societies*, 56–105. Cambridge, Cambridge University Press.

Richard, J.-C. (1966a) Tombeaux des empereurs et temples des "Divi": Notes sur la signification religieuse des sépultures impériales à Rome. *Revue de l'histoire des religions* 170, 127–42.

———— (1966b) Les aspects militaires des funérailles imperials. *Mélanges de l'École française de Rome, Antiquité* 78, 313–35.

———— (1966c) Les funérailles de Trajan et le triomphe sur les Parthes. *Revue des études latines* 44, 351–62.

———— (1966d) Incinération et inhumation aux funérailles imperials. *Histoire du rituel de apothéose pendant le haut-empire* (Latomus 25), 784–804.

———— (1978) Recherches sur certains aspects du culte impériale: Les funérailles des empereurs romains aux deux premiers siècles de notre ère. In H. Temporini (ed.), *Aufstieg und Niedergang der römischen Welt* (1972–) 2.16.2, 1121–34.

Richardson, L. (1992) *A New Topographical Dictionary of Ancient Rome*. Baltimore, Johns Hopkins University Press.

Strong, E. (1915) *Apotheosis and After Life: Three Lectures on Certain Phases of Art and Religion in the Roman Empire*. London, Constable.

Toynbee, J. (1971) *Death and Burial in the Roman World*. Baltimore, Johns Hopkins University Press.

Versnel, H. S. (1970) *Triumphus: An Inquiry into the Origin, Development and Meaning of the Roman Triumph*. Leiden, Brill.

Warren, L. B. (1970) Roman triumphs and Etruscan kings: The changing face of the triumph. *Journal of Roman Studies* 60, 49–66.

Weinstock, S. (1971) *Divus Julius*. Oxford, Clarendon Press.

7

Heaven's Exarchs: Observations on Early Byzantine Archangels

John Kenfield

Though the propaganda advantages of imperially attired archangels have long been recognized and discussed generally (Lamy-Lasalle 1968, 189–98; Brown 1984, 155–59; Maguire 1989, 223–31; Peers 1997, 53–57; Jolviet-Lévy 1998, 121–28), Maguire (1995, 64–69), in an article that might serve as a methodological model, was the first to demonstrate the manner in which the image could be manipulated to promote a specific and potentially unpopular imperial policy, in this instance to justify and atone for murders committed by Basil I (r. 867–86) in attaining the throne (Fig. 7.1). On the frontispiece of Paris Gr. 510, folio C verso, probably produced for Basil between 880 and 883, Gabriel and Elijah, though difficult to see because of the fugitive paint, flank the emperor. Elijah hands Basil the labarum while Gabriel crowns him. All three stand side by side on the same bejeweled dais with their heads at the same level. Basil and the archangel are dressed similarly, with the *loros* and the red shoes adorned with pearls, both holding orbs of universal power. Since post-Iconoclastic archangels wear imperial regalia only when in Heaven, the image implies that the crowning of Basil is taking place there, his earthly crimes notwithstanding, and that there is a similarity between Basil and the archangel, as if both belong to the same rank in the heavenly hierarchy. The emperor is, in effect, an archangel, an agent of Christ and subordinate to Him (Maguire 1995, 67).

In pre-Iconoclastic Byzantine art, at least until the reign of Justinian II (r. 685–95, 705–11), the subordinate role of the emperor to Christ is not so explicit. Christ and the emperor are treated as parallel rulers, each in his sphere of competence. To underscore this division of power, even when angels, "those courtiers whose rank placed them nearest to the ear of God" (Brown 1973, 14), and the emperor appear in the same scene, they always inhabit separate figure fields, the angels the higher, as on the Barberini diptych (Fig. 7.2). Nikai, not angels, are the only winged figures to appear in the emperor's presence. The rare surviving pre-

Iconoclastic archangels in imperial attire appear to contradict this separation of power, but when their dates and locations are considered, it seems probable that the comparison of

Fig. 7.1 *Paris, Bibliothèque Nationale, cod. gr. 510, folio C verso (Photo: library).*

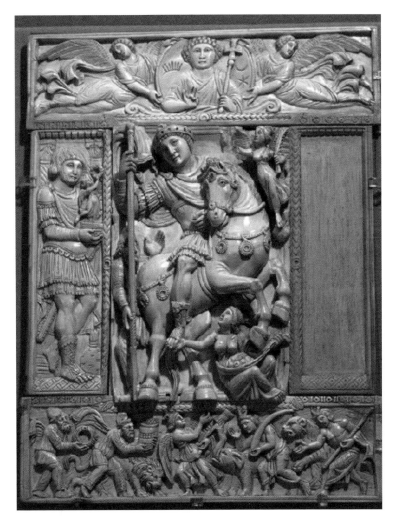

Fig. 7.2 *Paris, Musée du Louvre, Barberini diptych (Photo: University of California at San Diego).*

Fig. 7.3 *Istanbul, Archaeological Museum, Sarigüzel sarcophagus (Photo: University of California at San Diego).*

Fig. 7.4 *Madrid, Academy, detail, Missorium of Theodosius (Photo: University of California at San Diego).*

indication that in the reign of Heraclius, a sizeable percentage of the praetorian units remained ethnically German; Oman 1953, 1–13). Expensive and dangerous noncitizens, these elite troops were German, the enemy, especially after Adrianople, and hated by the Romans among whom they lived (Oman 1953, 4–5; Vasiliev 1964, 84–94; Frank 1969, 59–79). At the end of the fourth century, Synesius of Cyrene, speaking to Emperor Arcadius, refers to the latter's bodyguards as "these tall youths with curly blond hair" and criticizes their recruitment, saying that the emperor's elite guard ought to be men "whom our lands and cities have raised to be your defenders. . . . The shepherd does not guard his flock with wolves" (Synesius, *De Regno* 18, 21–22; Liebescheutz 1990, 1–48; Cameron and Long 1993, 103–42; trans. Frank 1969, 64). It would seem then that long before surviving examples assume imperial attire, the angelic image, in an ideology in which the imperial court was meant to be a terrestrial reflection of the court of Heaven, proved useful to the government in justifying policy.

Fig. 7.5 *Istanbul, Hippodrome, detail N.W. side, base of the obelisk of Theodosius (Photo: University of California at San Diego).*

imperially clad archangels is not to the emperor but to his immediate subordinates. Such a meaning would resolve a paradox that troubled Byzantine writers: that archangels, subordinates, could command the heavenly hosts, a role of the Pantokrator (Maguire 1995, 67).

Indeed, angels in Early Byzantine art (Fig. 7.3), like those holding the Christogram on the Sarigüzel sarcophagus, almost always wear civilian clothes (Maguire 1995, 65; Peers 2001, 74–76 n. 33), but their physical characteristics are those of important members of the military elite. Tall and blond, their hair style, different from that of any Roman, is also that of the emperor's personal bodyguard (Fig. 7.4), as on the Missorium of Theodosius and the base of that emperor's obelisk (Fig. 7.5). Except for their civilian clothing, these angels are meant to look like the *candidati*, an elite unit of forty men who formed the emperor's personal bodyguard (for *candidati*, see Frank 1969, 127–42; Haldon 1984, 129–30. Kitzinger [1958, 6], in discussing the "conscious and somewhat studied effort to imitate and vie with work of the Theodosian period" in the David Plates, does not mention the appearance of this German hairstyle for the bodyguards in the scene depicting the coronation of Saul, either a bit of early-seventh-century antiquarianism or an

Fig. 7.6 *Ravenna, Sant'Apollinare Nuovo, detail mosaic frieze, nave wall (Photo: University of California at San Diego).*

Long after the threat of Germanization in the eastern empire began to recede (Frank 1969, 201–18; Brown 1984, 70–77; Liebescheutz 1990, 89–146; Cameron and Long 1993, 323–33), angels attendant on Christ and the Virgin continue to have a Germanic appearance, as in the sixth-century mosaic of Christ enthroned between four archangels on the nave wall of Sant'Apollinare Nuovo at Ravenna (Fig. 7.6) (Lowden [1997, 124] sees this part of the mosaic as a remnant of the pre-Justinianic decoration). In spite of their Germanic physicality, these archangels are hybrid creatures, assuming the dress and role not of the *candidati* but of the civilian elite who in comparable imperial scenes are always closer to the emperor, separating him from the *candidati* (see Fig. 7.5), as on the base of the obelisk of Theodosius (Fig. 7.7), in comparable scenes on the base of the column of Arcadius (Fig. 7.8), and most famously in the mid-sixth-century dedicatory procession mosaic of Justinian and his imperial entourage on the choir wall of San Vitale in Ravenna. These images suggest that until military crises of the reign of Maurice (582–602), the civilian elite was still ascendant, at least in its ability to determine court precedence and its heavenly reflection in the visual arts (for the rise of the military elite, see Frank 1969, 7–45, 167–232; Brown 1984, 39–108; for the crises of Maurice's reign, see Whitby 1988, 3–24).

Fig. 7.7 *Cambridge, Trinity College, 1574 drawing, west side, base of the column of Arcadius (Photo: University of California at San Diego).*

Fig. 7.8 *Ravenna, San Vitale, choir mosaic, Justinian and entourage (Photo: University of California at San Diego).*

Nevertheless, archangels in imperial attire must have been fairly common in the early sixth century. Severus, patriarch of Antioch from 512 to 518, and others attacked them as idolatrous and of pagan derivation. In a text quoted at the Second Council of Nicaea, Severus says, "The insolent hand of painters, favoring as it does the inventions of pagans, decks out Michael and Gabriel like princes and kings, in a robe of royal purple, adorns them with a crown and places in their right hand the token of universal authority." Severus further objects to the image as overweening for a servant, a clear indication that imperial attire was not associated with subordination in the early sixth century (Severus of Antioch, *Les homiliae cathedrals*, in Brooks 1919, 82; Mango 1984, 39, 41–44; Peers 2001, 74–76; trans. Mango 1984, 44). In spite of Severus's statement, only four pre-Iconoclastic sets

of imperially clad archangels survive. Of these, two sets are presumed post-Iconoclastic restorations, and interestingly none wears the crown Severus mentions, apparently that item of imperial attire separating emperors from other archangels.

The earliest of the four surviving sets of archangels in imperial garb dates to Severus's time, appearing in illuminations on five of the extant folios from the Cotton Genesis, those on 71 verso the best preserved (Fig. 7.9) (Weitzmann and Kessler 1986, 81–82, pl. VII, 19). In this illumination, Abraham pleads with two angels who wear vermillion leggings and a purple chlamys decorated with a gold tablion and gold highlights at the hem. The only surviving imperially attired archangels to appear in a narrative context (Maguire 1995, 65–66), to modern eyes to his newly created subordinate, the exarch of Ravenna, a devolution of imperial power established by the hard-pressed Maurice to confront the Lombard conquests in Italy (Ostrogorsky 1957, 73, 87, 106–7, 110, 119, 125; Vasiliev 1964, 174–76; Brown 1979, 20–23; 1984, 46–53; Whitby 1988, 12, 16; Haldon 1997, 210–11). No images of exarchs are known, but that they should appear identical to the emperor though without the crown is logical since:

> Unlimited in his power, the exarch was given imperial honors. His palace at Ravenna was considered sacred and called Sacrum Palatium, a name usually applied only to an imperial residence. Whenever he arrived at Rome, he was accorded an imperial reception: the Senate, the clergy, and the populace met him outside the walls in a triumphant procession. All military affairs, the entire administration, judicial and financial matters all were at the full disposal of the exarch. (Vasiliev 1964, 174–75)

Fig. 7.9 *London, British Library, Cotton Genesis, folio 71 verso (Photo: Weitzmann and Kessler 1986, Pl. VII, 19).*

they seem to trivialize a normally powerful, iconic image, perhaps the reason the Cotton Genesis is "without surviving parallels in Late Antiquity or the Middle Ages, whether in the East or the West" (Lowden 1992, 40–53, esp. 50).

In short, surviving evidence, often a risky basis for assumptions about pre-Iconoclastic art, suggests official opposition to the image until the sudden appearance of the monumental archangels in imperial attire at Sant'Apollinare in Classe (Fig. 7.10). This apparent about-face in officially accepted images suggests a political motivation, and it is perhaps not accidental that these archangels are at Ravenna. Holding aloft the labarum decorated with the trisagion, the archangels are presented as members of a second elite military detachment, the *praepositi* labarum, "the bearers of the emperor's personal flag . . . in especially close relation to the sovereign, for as his standard-bearers, their place in battle was by definition close to him" (Frank 1969, 142–45). But these *praepositi* are something more. They stand on the imperial dais and wear imperial garb, the red boots decorated with pearls and the purple chlamys or *sagion* decorated with the gold tablion. These archangels, subordinates of Christ and projections of His power, refer not to the emperor but

Fig. 7.10 *Classe, Sant'Apollinare, mosaic of archangel Michael (Photo: University of California at San Diego).*

If the Classe archangels do refer to the exarch rather than the emperor, they probably date to the late sixth or early seventh centuries, when the newly created office was at the acme of its power (Brown 1984, 48–53). To assign the Classe archangels to the reign of Maurice or later requires a revision of the Justinianic date usually assigned to them, but the date of Maximian's consecration of the church on his return from Constantinople need not apply to the mosaics of the archangels (Deichman 1969, 270–71; von Simson 1976, 41), and by all requisite criteria, they are icons of the late sixth or early seventh century, when "the holy figure in statuesque isolation assumes a central position in the church" (Kitzinger 1977, 105; see also Brown 1973, 21–23; and Cameron 1979, 3–35, esp. 24). Usually sent out from the East where many had previously held high military commands, exarchs were not German (Brown 1984, 64–69; Whitby 1988, 14–17) and thus their archangelic counterparts have shed the Germanic appearance of their brethren in civilian garb.

Though post-Iconoclastic replacements, probably of the late ninth century, the archangels on the bema before the apse of Hagia Sophia in Constantinople are thought to reproduce the appearance of the presumed pre-Iconoclastic originals (Oikonomidès 1985, 111–15; Maguire 1989, 223; 1996, 70–71; Peers 2001, 52), at least in terms of their anachronistic dress, a form of imperial attire not worn by Middle Byzantine emperors (Fig. 7.11) (though the hovering immateriality of the archangels at Hagia Sophia, usually identified as a post-Iconoclastic contribution, is presaged by the later series of mosaics in Hagios Demetrios at Salonika, the Middle Byzantine changes in their iconography may include the excision of a dais on which each stood. All known pre-Iconoclastic monumental images of archangels in imperial garb, including those at Nicaea, stand on a dais). Since their attire is similar to that worn by the archangels at Sant'Apollinare in Classe, the originals at Hagia Sophia may have been more or less contemporary with them, and, like them, be images not of emperors, but of their immediate subordinates, either the exarchs or the *strategoi*, the imperial viceroys of the East who governed the *themata*, large military districts established in Anatolia and the Balkans to confront the simultaneous Arab and Slavic threats of the seventh century (Haldon 1997, 201–15).

Of these *themata*, the Opsikion, that closest to the city and home to the army's praesental regiments, was the most important. Its *strategos* was titled the count of the Opsikion, *komes tou Opsikiou*, and was at the acme of the military elite, often that military man closest to the emperor (Haldon 1984, 213–14) discusses the count of the Opsikion as accompanying Constantine IV to the sixth ecumenical council, and all of the seven exarchs and *strategoi* listed in the *iussio* of Justinian II sent to the pope in 687 in confirmation of the acts of the sixth ecumenical council; Haldon [1984, 360] cites Marinos, no. 10, in a list of counts

Fig. 7.11 *Istanbul, Hagia Sophia, mosaic of archangel Michael (Photo: University of California at San Diego).*

of the Opsikion, who, during the first part of the eighth century, is also referred to as *exarchos*). The territory of the Opsikion thema was Bithynia, though the jurisdiction of the *komes* often included Thrace, the Thrakesion thema, especially when Constantinople was threatened from the West (Haldon 1984, 164–82). Though its *komes* was usually resident in the city, the capital of the Opsikion was Nicaea, the second city of the eastern empire, the setting for two important ecumenical councils and considered by Constantine as a possible capital before settling on Byzantion. Given the apparent association of archangels and exarchs at Ravenna, that the last set of pre-Iconoclastic archangels in imperial dress was in the church of the Dormition at Nicaea suggests a similar interpretation. The architecture, sculpture, and epigraphic evidence indicate a late-seventh or early-eighth-century date for the building and presumably the mosaics originally decorating the bema and the apse. (Fig. 7.12) Altered in the Iconoclastic period, their post-

Fig. 7.12 Iznik (Nicaea), Church of the Dormition, mosaic of archangelic powers Arche and Dynamis (Photo: University of California at San Diego).

Iconoclastic restorations survive only in early-twentieth-century photographs. Most scholars believe that the post-Iconoclastic mosaics, like their brethren at Hagia Sophia, reproduce the original images with slight modifications (Kitzinger 1958, 12–16; Underwood 1959, 235–43; Barber 1991, 43–60; Mango 1993–94, 168–70; Peers 2001, 42, 81–88, figs. 9–10). Inscriptions dating to the pre-Iconclastic phase above the archangels refer to them not by their biblical names but as personifications of Christ's powers (Mango 1993–94, 170; Peers 2001, 42–43 n. 55). They are, in effect, the exarchs or *strategoi* of His *themata*. Like the archangels at Classe, those at Nicaea held the labarum inscribed with the trisagion and originally stood on daises, but the rest of their regalia are typically Middle rather than Early Byzantine, especially the long, bejeweled sash called the *loros*. A garment worn by Roman consuls until Justinian I abolished the office, the *loros* became an item worn by junior emperors (Condurachi 1935/36, 37–45; Ševčenko 1991, 1251–52; Peers 1997, 54–56) and clearly indicates subordination (Fig. 7.13). In the imperial portraits on the reverses of his gold solidi, Justinian II is the first emperor to wear the *loros*. Since Justinian is likely to have been emperor at the time of the church of the Dormition's construction, the appearance of the *loros* in his regalia suggests that the imperial garb of the restored archangels at Nicaea reproduces that worn by the originals of the late seventh or early eighth centuries (they do not, however, stand on an imperial dais but appear to hover immaterially against a golden ground, perhaps a feature introduced with their replacements. In their counterparts in the church of the Dormition at Nicaea (see Fig.

Fig. 7.13 Gold solidus, obverse (Christ) and reverse (Justinian II), Washington, Dumbarton Oaks Collection, (Photo: Breckenridge 1959, pl. I, no. 5).

7.11) the imperial daises of the originals are apparent in the suture lines but not restored, producing the same hovering, immaterial effect as the archangels in Hagia Sophia). More important, "For the first time, the earthly Autokrator cedes his traditional place on the obverse of the coin to his heavenly overlord . . . " (Kitzinger 1963, 261, figs. 5–7). "Christ and the basileus appearing together, on two sides of the whole, typifying vividly the earthly sovereign's role as deputy for the heavenly one" (Head 1972, 56). Thus, in spite of his highly authoritarian character, Justinian is now clearly Christ's exarch or *strategos*, in a manner that will become the norm in post-Iconoclastic art (see Galavaris 1958, 106–9; Breckenridge 1959, 28–62, 91–104). Justinian's motive, it would seem, was to shift responsibility for the calamities befalling the empire away from the imperial government and onto the shoulders of Him for Whom the government worked. The next move would be to shift that responsibility onto the shoulders of the idolatrous inhabitants of the empire.

Acknowledgments

The following, a foray into a field far from my norm, is the result of an idea conceived during a lecture by Kurt Weitzmann in spring 1968 and pondered sporadically for the next forty years. Any insight it might present can in no small measure be credited to R. Ross Holloway, my undergraduate professor and the first to teach me to look at art with an historian's eye. Any mistakes, however, can in no way be attributed to those who advised and assisted me and whom I would also like to thank: Archer St. Clair Harvey, Erik Thunø, and Ljubomir Milanovic of Rutgers University; Slobodan Curcic, John Haldon, and Nino Zchomelidse of Princeton University; and Shari Kenfield, Visual Resources Collection, Department of Art and Archaeology, Princeton University.

Works Cited

Barber, C. (1991) The Koimesis Church, Nicaea. The limits of representation on the eve of iconoclasm. *Jahrbuch des österreichischen Byzantinistik* 41, 43–60.

Breckenridge, J. D. (1959) *The Numismatic Iconography of Justinian II.* New York, American Numismatic Society.

Brooks, E. W. (ed. and trans.) (1919) *Patrologia Orientalis, 12/2. Severus of Antioch (ca. 465–538): Collection of Letters of Severus of Antioch from Numerous Syriac Manuscripts.* Paris, Firmin-Didot.

Brown, P. (1973) A Dark Age crisis: Aspects of the iconoclastic controversy. *English Historical Review* 87, 1–34.

Brown, T. S. (1979) The church of Ravenna and imperial administration in the seventh century. *English Historical Review* 94, 1–28.

——— (1984) *Gentlemen and Officers: Imperial Administration and Aristocratic Power in Byzantine Italy, AD 554–800.* Rome, British School at Rome.

Cameron, A. and Long, J. with a contribution by Sherry, L. (1993) *Barbarians and Politics at the Court of Arcadius.* Berkeley and Los Angeles, University of California Press.

Cameron, A. (1979) Images of authority: Elites and icons in late sixth century Constantinople. *Past and Present* 84, 3–35.

Condurachi, E. (1935/36) Sur l'origine de l'evolution du loros imperial. *Art si archeologia* 11/12, 37–45.

Deichman, W. F. (1969) *Ravenna. Hauptstadt des spätantiken Abendlandes. II/2 Kommentar.* Wiesbaden, F. Steiner.

Frank, R. I. (1969) *Scholae Palatinae: The Palace Guards of the Later Roman Empire.* Papers and Monographs of the American Academy in Rome 13. Rome, American Academy in Rome.

Galavaris, G. P. (1958) The symbolism of the imperial costume as displayed on Byzantine coins. *American Numismatic Society Museum Notes* 8, 106–9.

Haldon, J. (1984) *Byzantine Praetorians: An Administrative, Institutional and Social Survey of the Opsikion and Tagmata. c. 580–900.* ΠΟΙΚΙΛΑ BYZANTINA 3. Bonn, Rudolf Habelt GMBH.

——— (1997) *Byzantium in the Seventh Century: The Transformation of a Culture.* Cambridge and New York, Cambridge University Press.

Head, C. (1972) *Justinian II of Byzantium.* Madison, University of Wisconsin Press.

Jolivet-Lévy, C. (1998) Note sur la représentation des archanges en costume imperial dans l'iconographie Byzantine. *Cahiers archéologiques* 46, 121–28.

Kitzinger, E. (1955) On some icons of the seventh century. In K. Weitzmann (ed.), *Late Classical and Mediaeval Studies in Honor of Albert Mathias Friend, Jr.* Princeton, Princeton University Press.

——— (1958) Byzantine art in the period between Justinian and iconoclasm. *Berichte zum XI Internationalen Byzantisnischen Kongress, München 1958,* 1–50 = Kitzinger (1976) *Art of Byzantium and the Medieval West: Selected Studies by Ernst Kitzinger,* 157–206. Bloomington, University of Indiana Press.

——— (1963) Some reflections on portraiture in Byzantine Art. *Zbornik radova, 8/1.* In Mélanges G. Ostrogorsky, *Receuil des travaux de l'Institut d'Études Byzantines,* no. 8, vol. 1, 105–193.

——— (1977) *Byzantine Art in the Making.* Cambridge, Mass., and London, Faber and Faber.

Lamy-Lasalle, C. (1968) *Les archanges en costume imperial dans la peinture murale italienne. Synthronon: Art et Archéologie de la fin de l'Antiquité et du Moyen Age.* Paris, Librairie C. Klincksieck.

Liebescheutz, J. H. W. G. (1990) *Barbarians and Bishops: Army Church and State in the Age of Arcadius and Chrysostom.* Oxford, Clarendon Press.

Lowden, J. (1992) Concerning the Cotton Genesis and other illustrated manuscripts of Genesis. *Gesta* 31, 40–53, esp. 50.

——— (1997) *Early Christian and Byzantine Art.* London, Phaidon.

Maguire, H. (1989) Style and ideology in Byzantine imperial art. *Gesta* 28, 217–31.

——— (1995) A murderer among the angels: The frontispiece

miniatures of Paris Gr. 510 and the iconography of archangels in Byzantine art. In L. Brubaker and Th. Ousterhout (eds) *The Sacred Image East and West*, 64–69. Urbana and Chicago, University of Illinois Press.

———(1996) *The Icons of Their Bodies: Saints and Their Images in Byzantium*. Princeton, Princeton University Press.

Mango, C. (1984) St. Michael and Attis. *Deltion tes Christianikes Archaiologikes Hetaireias* ser. 4, 12, 39–62.

———(1993–94) The Chalkoprateia Annunciation and pre-eternal logos. *Deltion tes Christianikes Archaiologike Hetaireias* ser. 4, 17, 168–70.

Oikonomidès, N. (1985) Some remarks on the apse mosaics of St. Sophia. *Dumbarton Oaks Papers* 39, 111–15.

Oman, C. W. C. (1953) *The Art of War in the Middle Ages: AD 378–1515*. Ithaca, Cornell University Press.

Ostrogorsky, G. (1957) *History of the Byzantine State*. New Brunswick, Rutgers University Press.

Peers, G. (1997) Patriarchal politics in the Paris Gregory (B. N. gr. 510). *Jahrbuch des österreichischen Byzantinistik* 47, 53–57.

———(2001) *Subtle Bodies: Representing Angels in Byzantium*. Berkeley and Los Angeles, University of California Press.

Ševčenko, N. P. (1991) Loros. *Oxford Dictionary of Byzantium*, vol. 2. Oxford and New York, Oxford University Press.

Underwood, P. A. (1959) The evidence of restorations in the sanctuary mosaics of the church of the Dormition at Nicaea. *Dumbarton Oaks Papers* 13, 235–43.

Vasiliev, A. A. (1964) *History of the Byzantine Empire*. Madison and Milwaukee, University of Wisconsin Press.

von Simson, O. (1976) *Sacred Fortress: Byzantine Art and Statecraft in Ravenna*. Chicago, University of Chicago Press.

Weitzmann, K. and Kessler, H. L. (1986) *The Cotton Genesis: British Museum Codex Cotton Otho B. VI*. Princeton, Princeton University Press.

Whitby, M. (1988) *The Emperor Maurice and His Historian: Theophylact Simocatta on Persian and Balkan Warfare*. Oxford and New York, Clarendon Press and Oxford University Press.

SECTION II
INTRODUCTION

Crossroads of the Mediterranean: Cultural Entanglements Across the Connecting Sea

Rebecca H. Sinos

Everything that is interesting in archaeology, as in most disciplines, comes of making comparisons and connections. In the study of an individual object, or of the patterns apparent in data, the most significant discoveries come not from careful observation and description (though these are fundamental) but from the interpretations suggested by comparison to other objects or patterns, sometimes like, sometimes unlike. Here is where the archaeologist needs the most imagination and takes the greatest risks. Of course the greater one's command of evidence from various times and places, the more apt one's questions and the more successful one's comparisons will be.

Ross Holloway's adventurous and stimulating comparisons have enlivened his teaching and scholarship throughout his career. His work on the Bronze Age Mediterranean has indicated more and earlier connections between the people of the Aegean and of South Italy and Sicily than previously recognized; his excavations have pushed our understanding still further. But Ross's contributions to the field of archaeology include not only the Bronze Age findings for which he is celebrated and his other substantial work in Sicily and South Italy, but also much more. The architecture of the Athenian acropolis, the sculpture of the Temple of Zeus at Olympia, Greek vases, Roman iconography – Ross's spirited contributions have shed light on virtually every facet of Classical archaeology. And throughout his work the parallels he provides reveal an even broader interest. To illustrate the talismanic protection which may have been attributed to the bone plaques of Troy and Sicily in the Bronze Age, he points to the sacred charges of Hanseatic merchants of Novgorod in the Middle Ages. To shed light on the motives impelling Iron Age Phoenicians, he introduces the attitudes evident in the letters of their successors, the Jewish and Islamic merchants of the Middle Ages. On the problem of the archaic acropolis of Athens, and the type of building to which the smaller pedimental sculptures belonged, Ross brings to bear not only Demetrius of Phaleron and his prostitutes, but also buildings of Etruria, Latium, and especially houses in Morgantina in Sicily. Bold interpretations will never convince everyone, and to each of us some ideas are more persuasive than others. But surely no one can come away from Ross's elegant writing, or his teaching, without feeling excited by the possibilities he has shown and stimulated to think further and more imaginatively than before about the subject at hand.

Ross's achievement in seeing beyond obvious differences and superficial similarities to meaningful connections between cultures is all the more dazzling in view of the intractability of much of the available evidence. For "the connecting sea" that is the Mediterranean laps at the shores of many cultures perceived as distinct through fragmentary remains and incomplete knowledge. Ross's skill at reconstructing the disparate pieces as well as the larger puzzle is particularly evident in his work in prehistoric Sicily, but is characteristic of all of his work. His scrupulous attention to the details of all kinds of evidence, from excavation reports to the interpretation of iconography to the possible readings of an inscription or of a literary passage, gives his work a thorough grounding remarkable for work of such imagination and such great temporal and geographic range. In this Ross is the consummate classicist, conversant with every kind of evidence he can bring to bear on his subjects.

Ross became a classicist at Amherst College. In his senior year he wrote a thesis entitled "Pindar and Power," for which he was awarded a degree in Classics *summa cum laude.* The philological skills he honed at Amherst are evident throughout his work in his translations of the passages he quotes. At the same time, Ross's work as an undergraduate was equally directed towards ancient art. While he was writing his honors thesis, he was also working with Charles Morgan, writing an essay which he would publish two years later in the *American Journal of Archaeology* (vol. 62, 1958), "The Date of the Eleusis Relief"; he also brought order to an unlabelled group of casts of coins and gems that the College had acquired. Clearly he had already developed the comprehensive interest in the ancient Mediterranean that would take him in so many productive directions throughout his career. In his thesis it is evident that he had begun to think in the connective manner that makes his work so stimulating. His study of Pindar's victory odes draws not only from the range of literary passages that help to elucidate the imagery of this poetry, but also from a variety of examples of Greek sculpture that project comparable qualities. In identifying as a common thread of Ross's various endeavors his talent for noticing worthwhile connections, I follow his lead in his pursuit of Pindar's unity in this thesis.

Thanks to Ross's appreciation of his education at Amherst and his professors, John Moore, Wendell Clausen, and Charles Morgan, he has stayed in touch with his *alma mater* and the Classics Department there. He reached out to a young faculty member with interests somewhat similar to his own when I was new to Amherst, and his kind interest in the department has never flagged. I envy the students who have been able to benefit firsthand from Ross's vast knowledge and also from his energy and the generous encouragement that we at Amherst have found such a boon from a distance. It has been a great pleasure to see Ross's influence in the papers in this section of the Festschrift by his former students and other colleagues.

In these papers we see further exploration of some of the different kinds of connections that Ross's work has demonstrated. Their geographic range – from the Black Sea to the west coast of Italy and Sicily, their temporal spread – from the earliest levels of human occupation to the first century C.E., as well as the subjects treated – from the finds of survey work to the analysis of stylistic influences in architecture, sculpture, and painting, are suitable to the catholic interests of the man this volume honors.

Doonan's paper on the region of the Black Sea puts to the test the model of Mediterranean diversity and connectivity adduced by Horden and Purcell in *The Corrupting Sea.* The Black Sea area, while not as diverse ecologically as is the whole Mediterranean region, provides a distinct difference in resources and, sometimes, in climate between the north coast and the southeast area. The author's analysis of the relation of the Sinop promontory to the surrounding area concludes with a proposal for cooperation to allow a more productive comparison of field results, a reminder of the magnitude of Ross's accomplishment in knitting together the evidence of disparate sites with different terminologies and traditions of dating as well as methodologies.

In a paper on an oinochoe from Pithekoussai, Hussein constructs the "hierarchy" of objects found at a site and suggests that a prejudice in favor of objects that are imported from a colony's mother city has led to the suggestion that this vase is Euboean rather than Etruscan. The difficulty in disentangling the possibilities – that a vase is an import, that it is an import of an imitation, that it is a local imitation, that it is local ware – illustrates the intense communication of ideas and techniques that characterizes many sites throughout the Mediterranean. The author's discussion of this object's value as an indicator of local values and ties bears out Ross's insistence that we keep in mind the range of testimony that may be provided by material evidence.

Maggidis' study of the frieze of the Temple at Assos identifies the tradition reflected in this temple's figural decoration in terms of interactions between Aeolian and Ionian Greeks and local populations in Asia Minor. The author notes that temples with similar decorative schemes to the Assos temple are also found further west, and we are reminded of the blend of Doric and Ionic elements which Ross has emphasized in his studies of Greek temples in the west.

A Pompeiian plaque, in Bonfante's essay, provides an illustration of the religious power inherent in native Italian iconography as well as of the influence of Hellenistic sculpture, the same fusion of traditions evident in the *Aeneid*. In Bonfante's description of the vitality of the native images I am reminded of Ross's eloquent statement of the original power of early Greek art, the combination of awe before the magical presences evoked by the images and appreciation for the beauty and accomplishment of their execution.

A different interest in the vitality of ancient traditions comes across in McConnell's account of Paliké, a Sikel sanctuary. Incised decorations on burial chamber walls, evidence for the influence of the Greeks and black-figure vase painting, also attest to the interest in preserving traditional tales, much like the preservation of Plains Indians' tales in ledger books. The striking parallel employed here, as the author notes, is reminiscent of one of the most memorable parts of Ross's arsenal of skills.

The last essay of this section, Tsakirgis' fine discussion of Sicilian houses, demonstrates the influence of Macedonian palace architecture on house plans in Hellenistic Sicily as well as Greece. Her interest in what this form of architecture communicated, as well as the way it was transmitted, corresponds to Ross's insistence that we ask questions that go beyond the analysis of forms to penetrate their meaning to the people that created them.

All of these essays, in their variety as well as their common focus on the connections apparent in the objects or sites they examine, exemplify the lively spirit of engagement that Ross has exhibited throughout his career as a scholar and teacher. There is no better testimony to the vitality of the intellectual life that he has lived and fostered in others than this demonstration of the ongoing and exciting achievements of scholars exploring connections in the ancient Mediterranean world.

8

The Corrupting Sea and the Hospitable Sea: Some Early Thoughts Toward a Regional History of the Black Sea

Owen Doonan

Introduction

Ross Holloway was among the pioneering scholars who reexamined the long-term function of the central Mediterranean. He challenged the notion that the historical processes of Mycenaean and eighth-century Greek colonization had created the first significant and lasting interaction between South Italy, Sicily, and the Aegean (Holloway 1981). His critical reexamination of the evidence for early contact in Italy and the Aegean suggested that precolonial central and west Mediterranean communities were actively engaged participants in a maritime Mediterranean network. This hypothesis suggested that maritime interaction was part of the central Mediterranean cultural pattern long before the establishment of formal trade routes by Mycenaean and Greek colonists (Voza 1972; 1973; Vagnetti 1982).

The general approach Holloway developed in *Italy and the Aegean* was put to the test in a series of projects including the excavations at La Muculufa (Holloway *et al.* 1990; McConnell 1995) and I Faraglioni (Holloway *et al.* 1995; 2001). My dissertation on the architectural traditions of Early and Middle Bronze Age Sicily demonstrated not only the early contacts between Sicilian and Aegean populations but also the importance of native Sicilian initiative in the resulting cultural exchanges (Doonan 1993; 2001). A central problem was the analysis of cultural process at multiple scales (object, house, village, region), which led to an engagement with Braudel's tripartite model of historical process in the Mediterranean (Braudel 1972).

Italy and the Aegean and the Crossroads of the Mediterranean conference emphasized a geographical framework for interaction that was in tune with Braudel's famous model, although not derived from it. The research involved breaking down the model of a culturally closed Aegean in the third and early second millennia BC and viewing the entire Mediterranean as a linked arena of economic and cultural development. When the opportunity arose to collaborate on the Black Sea Trade Project, I became interested in pursuing a similar avenue of research in an emerging Mediterranean-related region. Although multiscalar processes were at the heart of the Black Sea Trade Project, our research design and methodology were decidedly different (Hiebert *et al.* 1997; Doonan 2004b).

Transforming Braudel's Model

Since the publication of Horden and Purcell's challenging work *The Corrupting Sea* (2000) the studies of Mediterranean societies have been turned inside out (Shaw 2003; Malkin 2003). Braudel attempted to fit the diverse components of *l'histoire evenementielle* into a top-down geographical framework based on cultural-ecological proxies (*e.g.,* extent of olive cultivation). However, Horden and Purcell constructed their bottom-up model of the Mediterranean out of the microenvironments and small-scale communities that typify the region. Three major points that Horden and Purcell (2000; Purcell 2003) emphasize in their model of the Mediterranean are of particular interest here: (1) the tremendous diversity of the Mediterranean when considered on the local scale; (2) the inherent risk in Mediterranean agriculture resulting from a variable and arid climate; and (3) the connectivity of the region that facilitates the redistribution of people and commodities through space.

According to the model, great annual variation in rainfall causes the microecological geographical units in the Mediterranean to remain in a constant state of stress. Redistribution of things and people across space is necessary because of the circumscribed potential that these microecological units possess in terms of agricultural or industrial products. Relational networks arise as a response to this stress and are maintained despite the changing political-economic systems that influence specific patterns of connectivity over the spaces of the Mediterranean (Horden and Purcell 2000, ch. 5; Algazi 2005). "Connectivity" is the infrastructure and practices that can move things (including people – traders, slaves, colonists, etc.) across space in response to uneven or unsustainable distribution of production, or political and economic power (Algazi 2005, 242–43). Risk is a particularly significant factor to be minimized through connectivity and so is an especially important aspect that drives the persistent need for connection between Mediterranean microenvironments.

Horden (2006) and Purcell (2003) avoid the temptation to define the Mediterranean, a frequent problem encountered in studies dealing with the region as a whole. The charge has been made that their model is thus too vague to be tested. Purcell asserts that one way to test their model is to apply it to a case study of another region. The analysis of the Black Sea as a geographic, economic, and cultural unit holds great potential for such a test; there are a number of critical differences between the two regions, but they were enmeshed in closely related economic, cultural, and historical systems from the early first millennium BC to the early twentieth century AD. Although Horden and Purcell include the Black Sea as a marginal zone within the greater Mediterranean area (Purcell 2005, 17), let us examine the case to be made for considering the Black Sea as a "unit of analysis" in its own right (Özveren 2001).

The Black Sea as a Unit of Analysis

Few studies have attempted to consider the Black Sea as a whole for the purpose of historical analysis. Far more common has been a tendency to view the Black Sea as the backyard of the Mediterranean (as in the cases of Braudel and Horden and Purcell). The development of geographically and ecologically informed history as a major genre coincided with the partitioning of the Black Sea by the Iron Curtain, and as a result the opportunities for collaborative research in the region have been limited to the past decade and a half (for a review, see King 2004).

Bratianu's (1969) pioneering study of the Black Sea was a contemporary of Braudel's *Mediterranean* and shares the emphasis on broad geographic themes; his introductory chapter begins with a wide-ranging account of the ports and other features of Mediterranean geography. He then proceeds to discuss the geographic setting of the Black Sea largely as it has related to the civilizations that surround it. Eyup Özveren (1997; 2001) posed the question of whether the Black Sea could be considered a unit of analysis in a pair of thoughtful articles devoted primarily to the Ottoman period. Özveren (2001) posed his question primarily in economic terms, suggesting that during the period of Ottoman domination through the early twentieth century, the Black Sea region formed a sufficiently integrated economy with a developed division of labor to warrant consideration as an integrated unit.

Neil Acherson's *Black Sea* (1995) is an evocative and wide-sweeping work of historical nonfiction that represents the first post-Soviet foray into Black Sea history. Charles King's *The Black Sea: A History* (2004) is a more comprehensive treatment of Black Sea history, with particular strengths in the early modern periods. Both of these are occupied by history *in* the Black Sea area rather than history *of* the region, in the sense of Horden and Purcell (2000, 9). King's volume is the most complete overview of Black Sea history since Bratianu's, but it does not attempt a systematic analysis of how the Black Sea regional geography structured long-term historical trends.

The increasingly collaborative spirit of research among eastern and western scholars since 1992 has catalyzed a great number of studies of the region within temporally or culturally restricted frameworks (Tsetskhladze 1998; Aybak 2001; Yanko-Hombach *et al.* 2007; Tsetskhladze and Doonan [forthcoming]). International collaboration was pioneered by the series of Vani conferences convened by Otar Lordkipanidze and expanded by his compatriot Gocha Tsetskhladze in the journal *Colloquia Pontica* (now *Ancient West and East*) and series of the same name.

Recent initiatives to create a sense of solidarity in Black Sea studies have centered on the environmental crisis and the need for economic development such as the Black Sea Economic Cooperation Organization (BSEC) and its International Center for Black Sea Studies (http://icbss.org/index.php?option=com_frontpage&Itemid=1). Efforts at the diplomatic and economic levels have spawned a variety of Black Sea studies programs in Europe, for example, the Danish National Black Sea Research Center Aarhus (http://www.pontos.dk/) and the British Academy Black Sea Initiative (http://www.biaa.ac.uk/babsi/). These programs have contributed to an increasingly transdisciplinary quality to Black Sea regional studies and offer opportunities for research transcending traditional cultural-historical boundaries (*e.g.,* Erkut and Mitchell 2007). Despite these remarkable advances in a decade and a half, there has still been no attempt to develop a comprehensive history *of* the Black Sea. Horden and Purcell, by way of contrast, may provide a kernel of just such a vision.

Returning to the question posed above, might it be possible to examine the Black Sea as a second case study to assess the validity of Horden and Purcell's model of the Mediterranean? If so, what are some of the critical differences between the two regions that would make comparison useful? Risk is one of the main drivers of a persistent tendency to interact in Horden and Purcell's model of the Mediterranean. The Black Sea has a highly diverse but basically stable continental climate in contrast to the Mediterranean that provided highly favorable conditions for agriculture (Table 8.1).

Table 8.1 *Comparison and contrast of physical and demographic features of the Mediterranean and Black Seas.*

	Mediterranean	**Black Sea**
Coastal configuration	Broken up; widely distributed islands; high proportion of sea within sight of land features	Smooth; almost no islands; majority of the sea out of sight of the coasts
Hinterland interface	Few major river systems provide extensive access	Large river systems provide access to extensive catchments; extensive coastal deltas
Topography	Coastal mountains frequent (north and east); severe desert conditions along south limit communications	Coastal mountains (south and east); steppe desert along north ties in with extensive Eurasian zone
Climate	Predominantly arid; pockets of higher rainfall in mountainous areas; marginal agriculture	North: continental climate sustains extensive grain production; south: subtropical supports fruit, nut, olive production
Risk of crop failure	Frequent (1–2/decade)	Infrequent (< 1/generation)
Nonagricultural resources	Clustered distribution of mineral and wood resources; extensive distribution of fish	Extensive distribution of mineral and wood resources; seasonal migration patterns create strong patterning in fish distribution
Demography	Coastal lowlands densely settled; highlands sparsely settled	Low population density except for Asian and European bosphoroi

Climate and Risk

A new study of annual climate patterns in Black Sea Anatolia based on tree-ring and historical data determined that over the past four hundred years there were only a handful of drought years (Akkemik *et al.* 2005). Modeling of the annual climate variation across the entire Black Sea region suggests much more stable patterns of rainfall than are typical of the Mediterranean (Ruter 2005). Overall the pattern indicates far less climate-dependent risk for agriculturalists in this region than in the Mediterranean (Fig. 8.1).

If risk and ecological fragmentation did not encourage connection in the Black Sea region, what factors did, and how might they impact long-term patterns? Highly diverse conditions along each coast yield different agricultural and natural resources (Doonan 2004b). The broad river deltas and warm dry summers of the north coast provide ideal conditions for grain production there. Warmer winters and moderate summers permit growth of olives along the south. The main mineral resources of the region are concentrated in the southeast. Despite these differences, each part of the Black Sea littoral provides resources for a largely self-sufficient subsistence economy. Other factors must have driven interaction in many periods, and we should expect a different overall pattern from that of the Mediterranean.

Few parts of the Black Sea show the extreme degree of local ecological fragmentation that, according to Horden and Purcell, is basic to the fabric of Mediterranean interaction. Black Sea ecological diversity is more coarsely grained than that of the Mediterranean, encouraging less of the persistent microinterdependence of the Mediterranean model.

One of the remarkable features of Black Sea ecology is the seasonal migrations of several fish species that circulate in a clockwise fashion. Anchovies, mackerel, and other species spawn in the shallow waters of the northern shelf and depart on an annual migration that brings them around the sea and back to the same spawning grounds each year. The Varna convention of 1959 was a cooperative international attempt to manage fish stocks and to share ports, and infrastructure in cases of emergency (Mee 2001, 138). The exploitation of fish in this region stretches back to the first millennium BC and probably earlier (Gavriljuk 2005; Doonan 2007a). Gavriljuk suggests that fish imagery is part of the iconography of early steppe nomads who developed fishing technology in the Eurasian river systems. As waves of Eurasian migrants settled on the north shores of the Black Sea, they adapted fishing and other steppe economic practices to their new environment (Hiebert 2001). The spirit of the Varna convention reflects the regional structure of the marine ecology that has encouraged contact and cooperation by fishermen for millennia (Doonan 2007b).

Repeated waves of migration by steppe nomads, imperial encroachments by Near Eastern powers, and bursts of activity by Mediterranean mercantile systems have redirected the flows of Black Sea interaction on many occasions over the past five thousand years (Doonan 2007b). Özveren (2001) emphasizes the strong impact of middle-range processes, including the rise and fall of local empires

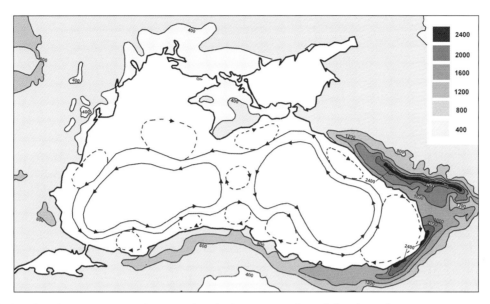

Fig. 8.1 *Rainfall and surface current circulation in the Black Sea. Annual rainfall indicated in 400 mm intervals from light (low rainfall) to dark gray (high rainfall). Primary surface currents are indicated in solid lines, secondary currents in dashed lines (Data after Steinhauser 1970).*

and trade systems, in determining the intensity of intra-regional engagement in any given historical period.

Given these various factors, we could expect a different pattern of long-term interaction in the Black Sea from that of the Mediterranean. Possible are wide swings between periods when the region exhibits a high degree of regional interdependence and others when only occasional interaction between populations sharing maritime resources is apparent (Price 1993; Hiebert 2001; Bauer 2006).

The Sinop Case Study

The Sinop Regional Archaeological Project (SRAP) is the terrestrial component of the Black Sea Trade Project. The latter was an initiative led by the author with Drs. Fred Hiebert and Robert Ballard to investigate processes of production, exchange, and consumption "from mountaintop to ocean bottom" through a coordinated program of systematic archaeological survey on land and underwater (Hiebert *et al.* 1998; Ballard *et al.* 2001). Since 1996 SRAP has coordinated systematic archaeological survey, geo-morphological research, and historical studies in the rugged Sinop promontory on the south coast of the Black Sea (Doonan 2004a; 2004b) (Fig. 8.2). The Sinop promontory, the northernmost point in Anatolia, complements the best natural port on the southern coast of the Black Sea with a fertile and well-watered hinterland. The promontory is set opposite the Crimea in a position ideally suited to control north–south and east–west shipping lanes (Doonan 2004a).

Sinop promontory, like many parts of the Black Sea littoral, is sufficiently fertile and well-watered to support an independent subsistence economy. The prehistoric ceramic record in Sinop suggests long continuity with little outside

Fig. 8.2 *Modified CORONA image of the Sinop promontory indicating survey areas in light gray. The port of Sinope is located on the isthmus connecting the headland of Boztepe to the mainland.*

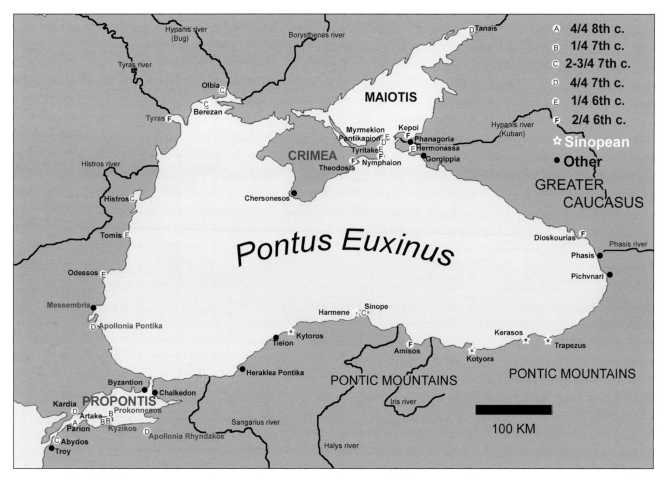

Fig. 8.3 *Greek colonies in the Black Sea.*

contact or economic integration. The numerous prehistoric mounds in the area are small in scale (typically well under 1 ha) and situated on slopes overlooking springs and fertile valley floors. We see evidence of low-intensity interaction in the third millennium based on shared ceramic technologies and styles (Bauer 2005). This does not suggest economically significant trading but occasional overseas contact, most likely incidental to patterns of maritime exploitation.

Evidence of Bronze Age coastal occupation is fleeting and appears to expand during the early first millennium BC (Doonan 2004a). In the case of one settlement at Sinop Kale, the ceramic and architectural finds suggest a small village or camp founded by visitors from the north Black Sea region (Doonan 2007b). Sinop Kale and similar sites along the coast may represent temporary or seasonal camps established by fishermen from the north harvesting the late summer and autumn catch during a season when mature fish would largely be absent from the northern shores.

Shortly after the abandonment of the Sinop Kale camp, Greeks from the city of Miletus founded the colony of Sinope. Sinope founded a string of colonies of its own along the south coast that controlled access to the metal-rich

eastern mountains (Fig. 8.3). According to the near complete absence of Greek-related material from the hinterland, no effort was made to establish extensive agricultural territories anywhere on the promontory until the second quarter of the fourth century BC. Datames's disruptions in the early fourth century disturbed Sinope's relations with its eastern colonies and encouraged reorientation of the economy toward the promontory (Doonan 2007b).

Conovici (2005) shows a distinct peak in Sinopean trade with Istros, Kallatis, Tomis, Olbia, and Pantikapaion *c.* 270–250 BC – a couple of generations after the disruptions of Datames. Ongoing research by a Ukrainian-Russian-Danish team in the Saki and Dzharylgach lakes, Crimean Peninsula, suggests a significant climatic disruption in the early third century BC (Stolba 2007). A disruption of this type may have encouraged the development of inter-dependent relationships with more ecologically stable parts of the Black Sea. Thus, the case can be made that the first significant engagement of the Sinop hinterland with the Black Sea economy resulted largely from external political disruptions followed by a significant episode of climatic stress. For nearly one thousand years, the Sinop hinterland was integrated into the regional economies of the Black Sea and Mediterranean. Further cycles of isolation and re-engagement can be observed in conjunction with the Turkic incursions into Anatolia, the Ottoman imperial system and its collapse, and the fall of the Iron Curtain. In each case, the impact of powerful neighboring political and economic systems was key to the establishment of locally and regionally integrated economies.

Discussion and Prospects for Research

This is a brief sketch of a framework for developing a long-term history of the Black Sea. The Sinop case study suggests interesting potential for an alternative history of interaction in the Black Sea that, if explored more fully, can lead to an illuminating test of Horden and Purcell's model of Mediterranean interactivity. Before such arguments and models can be advanced, it is necessary to establish a body of evidence founded on common principles of systematic research and best practices. Presently Black Sea regional research is a hodgepodge of methodologies and practices that eliminate any chance to make meaningful comparisons between regions and even within regions. This author in collaboration with colleagues at Ruhr-Universitat Bochum, has proposed the establishment of a Milesian Colonial Landscapes Initiative, a working group of archaeologists who will share methodological and theoretical ideas with the goal of generating comparable field results in different parts of the Black Sea (Doonan 2006). Such a working group could provide a platform for further collaborations that would encompass archaeological sites and landscapes beyond the initial group of Greek colonies and provide a solid foundation for the understanding of the historical processes distinctive to the Black Sea.

Works Cited

Acherson, N. (1995) *Black Sea*. New York, Hill and Wang.

Akkemik, Ü., Dagbrevedeviren, N., and Aras, A. (2005) A preliminary reconstruction (AD 1635–2000) of spring precipitation using oak tree rings in the western Black Sea region of Turkey. *International Journal of Biometeorology* 49, 297–302.

Algazi, G. (2005) Diversity rules: Perigrine Horden and Nicholas Purcell's *The Corrupting Sea*. *Mediterranean Historical Review* 20, 227–45.

Aybak, T. (ed.) (2001) *Politics of the Black Sea: Dynamics of Cooperation and Conflict*. London, Tauris.

Ballard, R., Hiebert, F. Coleman, D., Ward, C., Smith, J., Willis, K., Foley, B., Croff, K., Major, C., and Torre, F. (2001) Deepwater archaeology of the Black Sea: the 2000 season at Sinop, Turkey. *American Journal of Archaeology* 105, 607–23.

Bauer, A. (2006) Between the steppe and the sown: Prehistoric Sinop and inter-regional interaction along the Black Sea coast.

In D. L. Peterson, L. M. Popova, and A. T. Smith (eds.), *Beyond the Steppe and the Sown*, 225–46. Leiden, Brill.

Bratianu, G. (1969) *Le Mer Noire*. Acta Historia 9. Munich: Societas Academica Dacoromana.

Braudel, F. (1972) *The Mediterranean in the Age of Phillip II*. New York: Harper and Row.

Conovici, N. (2005) The dynamics of trade in transport amphoras. In Vladimir F. Stolba and Lise Hannestad (eds.), *Chronologies of the Black Sea Area in the Period c. 400–100 BC*, 97–117. Aarhus, Aarhus University Press.

Doonan, O. (1993) Domestic architecture of the Sicilian Bronze Age: a study of social transformation and architectural innovation. Ph.D. dissertation, Brown University.

—— (2001) Domestic architecture and settlement planning in early and middle Bronze Age Sicily: Thoughts on innovation and social process. *Journal of Mediterranean Archaeology* 14, 159–88.

—— (2004a) *Sinop Landscapes: Exploring Connection in the Hinterland of a Black Sea Port*. Philadelphia, University of Pennsylvania Museum Publications.

—— (2004b) Sampling Sinop: Archaeological survey in a low visibility environment. In L. Wandsnider and E. Athanassopoulou (eds.), *Recent Developments in Mediterranean Survey Archaeology*, 37–54. Philadelphia, University of Pennsylvania Museum Press.

—— (2006) Exploring community in the hinterland of a Black Sea port. In P. Guldager Bilde and V. Stolba (eds.), *Surveying the Greek Chora: The Black Sea Region in a Comparative Perspective*. Aarhus, Danish National Research Foundation Centre for Black Sea Studies.

—— (2007a) Colony and conjuncture: The early Greek colony at Sinope. In J. Cobet (ed.), *Frühes Ionien: Eine Bestandsaufnahme*, 613–20. Milesische Forschungen 5. Mainz am Rhein, Philipp von Zabern.

—— (2007b) New evidence for the emergence of a maritime Black Sea economy. In V. Yanko-Hombach, A. Gilbert, N. Panin, and P. Dolukhanov (eds.), *The Black Sea Flood Question: Changes in Coastline, Climate and Human Settlement*, 697–710. Dordrecht, Springer.

Erkut, G. and Mitchell, S. (eds.) (2007) *The Black Sea: Past, Present and Future: Proceedings of the International, Interdisciplinary Conference, Istanbul, 14–16 October 2004*. London, British Institute at Ankara.

Gavriljuk, N. A. (2005) Fishery in the life of the nomadic population of the northern Black Sea area in the Early Iron Age. In T. Bekker-Nielsen (ed.), *Ancient Fishing and Fish Processing in the Black Sea Region*, 105–13. Aarhus, Aarhus University Press.

Hiebert, F. (2001) Black Sea coastal cultures: trade and interaction. *Expedition* 43, 11–20.

Hiebert, F., Smart, D., Gantos, A., and Doonan, O. (1998) From mountaintop to ocean bottom: A holistic approach to archaeological survey along the Turkish Black Sea coast. In J. Tanacredi and J. Loret (eds.), *Ocean Pulse*, 93–108. New York, Plenum.

Holloway, R. R. (1981) *Italy and the Aegean*. Louvain-la-Neuve, Institut supérieur d'archéologie et d'histoire de l'art, Collège Erasme.

——, Joukowsky, M. S., and Lukesh, S. S. (1990) La Muculufa,

the Early Bronze Age sanctuary: The Early Bronze Age village. *Revue des archeologues et historiens d'art, Louvain* 23, 11–67.

——, Lukesh, S. S., and Cruz-Uribe, K. (1995) *Ustica I: Excavations of 1990 and 1991.* Providence and Louvain-la-Neuve, Center for Old World Archaeology and Art, Brown University and Institut supérieur d'archéologie et d'histoire de l'art, Collège Erasme.

—— and Lukesh, S. S. (2001) *Ustica II.* Providence, Center for Old World Archaeology and Art, Brown University.

Horden, P. (2006) Mediterranean excuses: Historical writing on the Mediterranean since Braudel. *History and Anthropology* 16, 25–30.

Horden, P. and Purcell, N. (2000) *The Corrupting Sea.* Oxford, Blackwell.

King, C. (2004) *The Black Sea: A History.* Oxford, Oxford University Press.

Malkin, I. (2003) Introduction. *Mediterranean Historical Review* 18, 1–8.

McConnell, B. (1995) *La Muculufa II: Excavation and Survey 1988–1991. The Castelluccian Village and Other Areas.* Providence and Louvain-la-Neuve, Center for Old World Archaeology and Art, Brown University and Institut supérieur d'archéologie et d'histoire de l'art, Collège Erasme.

Mee, L. (2001) Can the marine and coastal environment of the Black Sea be protected? In T. Aybak (ed.), *Politics of the Black Sea: Dynamics of Cooperation and Conflict,* 133–62. London, Tauris.

Özveren, E. (1997) A framework for the study of the Black Sea world, 1789–1915. *Review* 20, 77–113.

—— (2001) The Black Sea as a unit of analysis. In T. Aybak (ed.), *Politics of the Black Sea: Dynamics of Cooperation and Conflict,* 61–84. London, Tauris.

Price, R. (1993) The West Pontic maritime interaction sphere: A long-term structure in Balkan prehistory? *Oxford Journal of Archaeology* 12, 175–96.

Purcell, N. (2003) The boundless sea of unlikeness: On defining the Mediterranean. *Mediterranean Historical Review* 18, 9–29.

Ruter, A. (2005) Macrophysical modeling of climatic variability in the Pontic Basin. International roundtable seminar on "Paleoclimate and Environmental Changes in the Black Sea Area." Aarhus, Danish National Black Sea Research Foundation 16.02.2005. Abstract available at http://www.pontos.dk/research/ra_5/Ruter_pontus abstract.pdf.

Shaw, B. (2001) Challenging Braudel: A new vision of the Mediterranean. *Journal of Roman Archaeology* 14, 419–53.

Steinhauser, F. (1970) *Climatic atlas of Europe = Atlas climatique de l'Europe.* Geneva, World Meteorological Organization.

Stolba, V. (2007) *RA5: Climate changes and long-term history.* Aarhus, Danish National Research Center for Black Sea Studies. Available at http://www.pontos.dk/research/ra_5.

Tsetskhladze, G. (ed.) (1998) *Greek colonization of the Black Sea area.* Historia Einzelschriften 121. Stuttgart, Franz Steiner Verlag.

Tsetskhladze, G., and Doonan, O. (forthcoming) *Dictionary of Black Sea Antiquity.* Leiden, E.J. Brill.

Vagnetti, L. (ed.) (1982) *Magna Graecia e mondo miceneo. Atti della Convegno di studi sulla Magna Grecia, Taranto* 22. Taranto, Istituto per la Storia e l'Archeologia della Magna Grecia.

Voza, G. (1972) Thapsos: Primi resultati delle più recenti ricerche. *Atti della XIV Riunione scientifica, Istituto italiano di preistoria e protostoria,* 175–205.

—— (1973) Thapsos: resoconto sulle campagne di scavo del 1970–1971. *Atti della XV Riunione scientifica, Istituto italiano di preistoria e protostoria,* 133–57.

Yanko-Hombach, V. A., Panin, N., Gilbert, A. S., Dolukhanov, P. (eds.) (2007) *The Black Sea Flood Question.* Dordrecht, Springer.

9

Imports, Imitations, and Immigrants:
A Note on Pithekoussai

Angela Murock Hussein

...we must also avoid limiting our vision of the past only to the surviving material evidence without acknowledging that the objects are also pointers to technology – and thus to verbally transmitted knowledge – to traditions – and thus to social continuity – to both utility and display – and thus not only to the working life of a community but also to creativity and the diplomacy of men's relations with neighbors and gods at home and foreigners over the horizon. (Holloway 2000, 1)

It is with great pleasure that I present this article to Professor R. Ross Holloway as an expression of my gratitude for all of the aid and guidance he has given to me. Since my graduate school career at Brown began in 1998, a career that Holloway, more than any other person, has made possible, I have benefited greatly from the wealth of his knowledge and experience. This paper came about as a product of my doctoral dissertation, which Professor Holloway supervised. During the course of this research, he made invaluable comments and raised concerns about the subject of the relationship between the Aegean and Italy, a field in which he is a leading expert and to which his contributions are considerable (Holloway 1981; 2000).

Although scholarship in classical archaeology has long been examining how we look at processes such as acculturation and cultural fusion (Morel 1984, 124–35), there still exist certain biases when interpreting and classifying artifacts. These biases can cause us to overlook crucial evidence of just how reciprocal and fluid human interaction can be. As the quote above states, artifacts are not just objects to be classified and ordered but represent stories of the complexity of human relations within and among communities. The example cited below from the Iron Age Tyrrhenian should serve to demonstrate this fact.

In the eighth and seventh centuries BC, the wealthy south Etruscan cities imported a great deal of Greek and Near Eastern products, including pottery. The Etruscans were an important market for Greek painted pottery from the time of their initial contacts through the fifth century. This phenomenon is seen as part of the process of "orientalization" of the Etruscans. The Etruscan taste for Greek decorated vessels during the eighth century BC led not only to the importation of fine pottery from the eastern Mediterranean but also to the arrival of Greek artisans in Etruria who produced the desired items and finally to local imitations of the Greek pottery style manufactured by the Etruscans themselves. This process is well known and has led to a classification system for Greek-style pottery on Etruscan sites that was first outlined by Blakeway (1935, 173) and which is a model that still functions well not only for Etruscan Italy but also for similar cultural situations (Ridgway 1973, 29; Canciani 1987, 9–10; Coldstream 2001, 232–34).

One oinochoe (Inv. 168509 [Inv. = inventory number of the pieces at the Museo Archeologico Nazionale di Napoli, though most of the material from Pithekoussai is now housed at the Museo Archeologico di Pithecusae]), found at Tomb 652 in Pithekoussai, has been assigned a place in the story of the orientalization of Etruria based on its context from this Greek emporion, which was founded in the first half of the eighth century BC. Tomb 652 from the Late Geometric II period was the grave of an adult female, which also included a large hoard of bronze jewelry and fibulae as well as a few iron fibulae and even an Egyptianizing scarab. The oinochoe is evidently not of Pithekoussan manufacture. It was identified as imported "Euboean?" by the excavators, and has been held up as an example of a colonial intermediary between Greek originals and this Etruscan style (Buchner and Ridgway 1993, 631 n. 20, pl. 182; Tanci and Tortoioli 2002, 171 n. 35) (fig. 9.1).

I propose that this oinochoe comes instead from Etruria. The decoration of the vessel, although its dark-on-light decoration is based originally on the Greek Geometric painted pottery, is a rather standard class of Etruscan

Fig. 9.1 *Oinochoe from Pithekoussai, Tomb 652 (After Buchner and Ridgway 1993, Pl. 182.1).*

imitation known as "Metopengattung" (Åkerstrom 1943, 91–94; Canciani 1974, Tav. 18.1.–3, 19.4–6, 22.6, 29.2, 29.4–6, 31.1–5, 36.9–12, 37, 38.1–5, 42.1, 42.3–5; Tanci and Tortoioli 2002, 171–71, 177–78). This type was prevalent particularly in the Italian Geometric-style pottery made in the region of the Etruscan city of Tarquinia in the late eighth and early seventh centuries BC (Leach 1986, 305–7; Canciani 1987, 12) (figs. 9.2–3). If the piece had been found in an Etruscan cemetery in Tarquinia or Vulci, it would have easily been interpreted as local Geometric-style pottery and hardly would have received notice.

It is not surprising that pottery from Etruria should reach Pithekoussai. There were other Etruscan imports, such as two incised impasto amphorette (Inv. 166706, Tomb 159; Inv. 239079, Tomb 944; Buchner 1970, 89, figs. 22–23; Ridgway 1973, 16, fig. 2c; 1992, 65, fig. 13.3; Buchner and Ridgway 1993, 198–99, Tav. CXXIV, 61). These are characteristically Etruscan-style wares and so they were easily recognized even in their context far from Etruria. In addition, seventh-century inscriptions in the Etruscan language come from Greek tableware found in Pithekoussai, providing evidence of Etruscan inhabitants (Colonna 1995, 325–342). It has even been hypothesized that Greek settlers

of Pithekoussai commonly took Etruscan wives (Morel 1984, 134–35; Coldstream 1993, 89–108). Therefore, the community at Pithekoussai was one with close Etruscan connections.

Yet, the cause of the misidentification of the piece from Tomb 652 is the apparent disbelief that imitations of Greek pottery could show up in a predominantly Greek setting, where consumers could get the "real thing" so to speak. The concept of orientalization, which implies an exclusively westward motion for artistic styles and technology, has imposed a hierarchy for contexts of eastern-style artifacts. In the case of Geometric-style pottery, the top of this hierarchy would be the origin of that pottery style, that is, native Greek cities. Next would be western emporia and colonies overseas, presumed intermediaries between the East and West. There, the pottery we might expect to find would be imports from the East, pottery made by the inhabitants similar to that made in their homeland, and occasional imports from neighboring regions. It is believed that these latter imports should look very foreign and that they were imported for their novelty. Finally, there are foreign contexts, such as Etruscan settlements. According to expectations, the pottery here should include the local styles, desirable imports from the East, and local imitations thereof. Consequently, imitations of Greek pottery are conventionally viewed as being only for a non-Greek clientele. According to this hierarchy in the process of orientalization, orientalia should not be flowing back upstream.

Nevertheless, human beings have always been extremely mobile, and where they move, so move their possessions. It should not be too hard to believe that an oinochoe made in Etruria was carried to Pithekoussai, since Etruscan people and objects apparently reached that settlement. The problem, however, lies with us and how we view and classify the artifacts. The context of the oinochoe from Tomb 652 at

Figs. 9.2–3 *Metopengattung Style Oinochoe from Tarquinia (After Åkerstrom 1943, Pl. 24.7).*

Pithekoussai provides a glimpse into just how easy it can be to classify and structure artifacts based on expectations. As we see from this example, an assumption was made that the oinochoe could fit into only one of two classes based on its Greek-style decoration. The emphasis on looking at the process of orientalization of the Etruscans has caused the piece to be interpreted as evidence for an intermediary between Greece and Etruria rather than evidence that this item, and possibly the individual interred with it, moved "east" from Etruria to Pithekoussai. The oinochoe from Tomb 652 cannot be the only piece of its kind to ever reach Greek settlements; no doubt parallels remain to be discovered.

Works Cited

Åkerstrom, A. (1943) *Der Geometrische Stil in Italien*. Lund, C. W. K. Gleerup.

Blakeway, A. (1935) Prolegomena to the study of Greek commerce with Italy, Sicily and France in the eighth and seventh centuries BC. *Annual of the British School at Athens* 33, 170–208.

Buchner, G. (1970) Mostra degli scavi di Pithecusa. *Dialoghi di Archeologia* 3, 85–101.

Buchner, G. and Ridgway, D. (1993) *Pithekoussai I*. Rome, G. Bretschneider.

Canciani, F. (1974) *Corpus Vasorum Antiquorum: Italia, Museo Archeologico Nazionale Tarquinia*. Rome, G. Bretschneider.

Canciani, F. (1987) La ceramica geometrica. In M. Martelli (ed.) *La Ceramica degli Etruschi, La Pittura Vascolare*, 9–15. Novara, Instituto Geografico de Agostini.

Coldstream, J. N. (1993) Mixed marriages on the frontiers of the Greek world. *Oxford Journal of Archaeology* 12, 89–108.

Coldstream, J. N. (2001) Greek Geometric pottery in Italy and Cyprus: Contrasts and comparisons. In L. Bonfante and V. Karageorghis (eds.) *Italy and Cyprus in Antiquity 1500–450 BC*, 227–38. Nicosia, The Costakis and Leto Severis Foundation.

Colonna, G. (1995) Etruschi a Pitecusa nell'Orientalizzante Antico. In E. Lepore and A. Storchi Marino, *L'Incidenza dell'Antico: Studi in Memoria di Ettore Lepore, 1*, 325–42. Naples, Luciano.

Holloway, R. R. (1981) *Italy and the Aegean: 3000–700 BC*. Louvain-la-Neuve, Institut supérieur d'archéologie et d'histoire de l'art, Collège Erasme.

Holloway, R. R. (2000) The classical Mediterranean, its prehistoric past and the formation of Europe. *Joukowsky Institute for Archaeology and the Ancient World: Online Publications: Italian Prehistory*. http://www.brown.edu/Departments/Joukowsky_Institute/resources/papers/classicalmed/report.html.

Leach, S. S. (1986) Subgeometric "Heron" pottery: Caere and Campania. In J. Swaddling (ed.) *Italian Iron Age Artefacts in the British Museum*, 305–8. London, British Museum Publications.

Morel, J-P. (1984) Greek colonization of Italy and the West (problems of evidence and interpretation). In T. Hackens, N. Holloway, and R. R. Holloway (eds.) *Crossroads of the Mediterranean*, 123–61. Providence, Center for Old World Archaeology and Art.

Ridgway, D. (1973) The first Western Greeks: Campanian coasts and southern Etruria. In C. and S. Hawkes (eds.) *Greeks, Celts and Roman: Studies in Venture and Resistance*, 5–38. London, J. M. Dent.

Ridgway, D. (1992) *The First Western Greeks*. Cambridge, Cambridge University Press.

Tanci, S. and Tortoioli, C. (2002) *La Ceramic Italo-Geometrica*. Rome, G. Bretschneider.

10

Between East and West: A New Reconstruction of the Decorated Architrave Frieze of the Athena Temple at Assos and the Regional Tradition of Unconventional Architectural Decoration in East Greece

Christofilis Maggidis

Introduction

The temple of Athena at Assos (Clarke 1882; 1898; Clarke *et al*. 1902; Sartiaux 1915; Wescoat 1983; 1987; 1995; Finster-Hotz 1984; FHW at http://fhw.gr/fhw/en/projects/3dvr/assos) is the only known Archaic Doric temple in Asia Minor and certainly one of the most unusual Doric temples anywhere on account of three diagnostic features that set it apart from its counterparts: the unique combination of decorated metopes and a sculptured architrave frieze in a conscious effort to integrate the two architectural styles, Doric and Ionic; an idiosyncratic amalgam of select iconographic traditions; and a stylistic eclecticism that draws from several different sources.

The temple of Athena at Assos has yielded thus far fifteen complete or fragmentary sculptured architrave blocks and at least eleven undecorated ones (Figs. 10.1–2), all made of the local volcanic andesite (trachite); this nondurable, coarse, and porous stone bears the blame for the poor preservation of the eroded slabs, many of which deteriorated even further as they were later embedded in medieval and Turkish walls. The sculptured blocks are now located in three different museums (the Museum of Fine Arts, Boston, the Louvre, and the Constantinople Museum), while three recently found fragments are kept in the excavation depot at Assos (see Fig. 10.1).

The architrave frieze includes scenes that fall into two

#	Museum Cat. #	Iconography	Length of block Pres.	Length of block Total/(est)	Length of regulae L	Length of regulae Center	Length of regulae R	Anathyrosis (underside) L	Anathyrosis (underside) R	Corner Block	Height of Block	Thickness of Block top	Thickness of Block bottom
I	Boston 84.67	Herakles & Pholos	2.48m	(2.88m)	(0.5m)	0.565m	(0.27m)	(0.9m)	?	Yes (L)	0.818m	?	0.294m
II	Const 245	Galloping Centaurs		2.605m	0.25m	0.54m	0.33m	?	?		0.812m	0.331m	0.276m
III	Louvre 2830 + new fragment	Galloping Centaurs	2.505m	(2.70m)	0.32m	0.575m	(0.30m)	?	?		0.820m	0.41m	0.277m
IV	Louvre 2831	Galloping Centaurs	1.935m	(2.60m)	?	0.48m	0.25m	?	?		0.812m	?	?
V	Louvre 2828	Herakles vs Triton		2.941m	0.345m	0.574m	?	0.68m	0.58m	Yes? (L)	0.818m	?	?
VI	Louvre 2829	Symposium		2.884m	0.354m	0.555m	0.385m	0.66m	0.695m	Yes? (R)	0.819m	?	?
VII	Boston 84.68 + Const 779	Heraldic sphinxes		2.554m	0.232m	0.56m	?	0.36m	?		0.820m	0.35m	0.305m
VIII	Const 246 + Louvre 2837	Heraldic sphinxes		2.580m	0.27m	?	0.205m	0.30m	0.495m		0.820m	0.325m	0.288m
IX	Louvre 2832	Battling bulls		2.510m	0.312m	0.523m	0.372m	?	?		0.814m	?	?
X	Louvre 2833	Battling bulls	1.41m	(2.5m)	?	0.522m	?	0.54m	?		0.817m	?	?
XI	Louvre 2836	Lioness vs bull	1.185m	(2.85m)	?	?	0.295m	?	0.70m	Yes? (L)	0.820m	?	?
XII	Louvre 2834	Lion vs deer	1.545m	(2.68m)	0.195m	0.473m	?	0.44m	?		0.817m	?	?
XIII	Const 244 + new fragment	Lion & lioness vs deer		2.68m	0.33m	0.573m	0.20m	0.47m	0.377m?		0.820m	0.304m	0.271m
XIV	Const 243 + new fragment	Lions vs boar	2.41m	(2.68m)	0.32m	0.575m	?	0.66m	?		0.813m	0.330m	0.277m
XV	Louvre 2835	Lion(ess?) vs stag	0.75m	(2.85m)	?	?	0.522m	?	?	Yes (R)	0.815m	?	?

ATHENA TEMPLE AT ASSOS: Decorated Architrave Blocks

Fig. 10.1 *The decorated architrave blocks from the temple of Athena at Assos, list of technical details and measurements.*

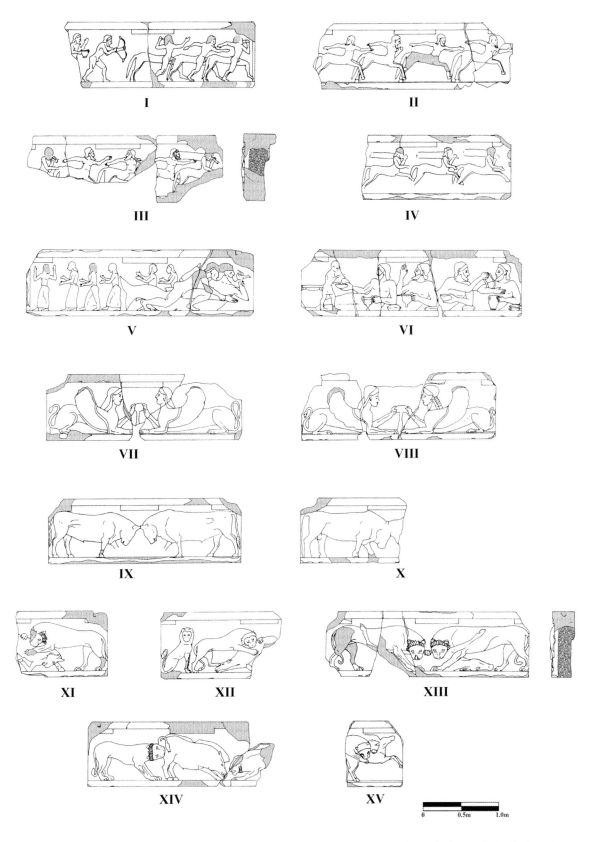

Fig. 10.2 *The decorated architrave blocks from the temple of Athena at Assos (Based on Clarke et al. 1902, 151; Finster-Hotz 1984, pls. 1–32; Wescoat 1995, figs. 11.2–12, 11.15–17, 12.13).*

major categories: mythological scenes with heroes and/or mythical monsters, and apotropaic animal battles. More specifically, the depicted scenes can be classified into five distinct groups (see Figs. 10.1–2): the Herakles and Pholos theme (I–IV); the Herakles and Triton theme (V); a banquet scene (VI); heraldic sphinxes (VII–VIII); and animal battles (IX–XV). Furthermore, four of the surviving carved metopes echo some of the frieze themes (boar, pair of heraldic sphinxes, and, twice, centaur fleeing to the right), whereas the remaining metopes depict other mythological themes, easily identifiable (Europa on the bull) or rather ambiguous (duels of men, pair of men running to the right). It is interesting to note (Finster-Hotz 1984, 99–106) that some of these metopes find almost exact parallels in West Greece (Foce del Sele, Selinus) and on mainland Greece (Sikyonian and Athenian treasuries at Delphi) in the Archaic period. The Assos metopes are the only carved metopes known from Asia Minor in the sixth century BC.

Theoretical Reconstruction of the Architrave Frieze

A coherent and comprehensive interpretation of the iconographic program at Assos necessitates a synthesis of several variables, including iconographic, semiotic, architectural, and archaeological evidence, and consequently a theoretical reconstruction of the architrave frieze as a whole. The iconographic program of the architrave frieze must be read collectively and in its entirety, beyond and above the multiple allegoric connotations of individual scenes or the diverse symbolic nuances of isolated motifs and polysemic key themes; seemingly disparate or unrelated scenes often acquire a different meaning when correlated with other scenes by spatial association of their original physical location on the monument. A comparative examination of the iconography, size, shape, and morphology of the surviving decorated architrave blocks, combined with the study of their architectural setting, may suggest a new theoretical reconstruction of the architrave frieze. Early reconstructions were based more on conjectural iconographic sequences without fully engaging the architectural and archaeological evidence (Clarke *et al.* 1902; Sartiaux 1915). Ambiguities about the architectural plan of the temple, however, complicate the theoretical reconstruction of the architrave frieze: the precise intercolumniations on the facades and the flanks are unknown; it is not certain whether there was angle contraction or not, or if the problem was solved only by means of a longer architrave corner block and a wider end metope; there is no evidence of an inward inclination of the corner columns (no curvature in the stylobate has been detected). Gaps in the archaeological record and the poor preservation of the architrave blocks further impede the reconstruction of the frieze: many architrave blocks were not found in situ or lying around the temple, but in secondary use (embedded in Turkish and medieval walls in the wider area) which makes their findspots or their spatial distribution practically irrelevant for the purpose of the architrave reconstruction; most architrave blocks are partially preserved, and their original total length is often hard to estimate due to irregularities and deviations from axial symmetry; furthermore, the rear parts of all the architrave blocks in the Museum of Fine Arts, Boston, and the Louvre unfortunately have been cut off to flatten the "awkward" Γ-shaped rear side and to facilitate their exhibit on the museum wall, thus resulting in the loss of invaluable technical data (size of anathyrosis, contact surfaces, dowel sockets, tool traces).

The temple of Athena at Assos (Figs. 10.4–5) is Doric hexastyle peripteral (14.03 × 29.60 m at stylobate level) with six columns on the front and thirteen columns on the flank; the temple has a long and narrow cella with a rather shallow pronaos, distyle in antis, but no opisthodomos. The peristyle stands on a two-step *krepidoma* (stylobate and stereobate) and forms a deeper east pteron; the columns of the peristyle are set at the edge of the stylobate, thus producing front intercolumniations (2.6 m on average) greater than flank ones (*c.* 2.4–2.5 m); the central intercolumniation of the east peristyle is, however, slightly wider (by *c.* 0.10 m) in alignment with the wider spacing of the two pronaos columns and the cella doorway. This Doric temple incorporates several Ionic architectural features (Dinsmoor 1950, 88), such as a continuous Ionic frieze (albeit on the architrave), the alignment of the third-flank columns with the pronaos antae, Ionic cyma on the anta capitals, and the absence of anta returns and of pediment sculpture. Other interesting architectural details are the omission of guttae on the cornice and the architrave, the projecting taenia at the bottom of the architrave framing the relief sculptures, the use of mutules of equal width above triglyphs and metopes, and the carving of sixteen flutes on the peristyle columns (eighteen on the pronaos columns) with an arris at the front (Dinsmoor 1950, 88). The integration of elements of both architectural orders became highly fashionable in Classical Athens (*e.g.,* the temple of Poseidon at Sounion, the Hephaisteion, and especially the Parthenon), while a similar blend is attested in the Heraion at Foce del Sele (Doric entablature with carved metopes, Ionic porch and moldings), which stands very close to Assos iconographically as well (Ridgway 1977, 266–67; for recent theories on the date of the Heraion and the reuse of the early Archaic metopes in the fully realized temple [*c.* 510 BC] alongside metopes carved in the current style, *cf.* De la Geniere *et al.* 1997). The dimensions and proportions of the temple at Assos, combined with the alignment of the successive wider central openings on the east side, the lack of opisthodomos, and the deeper east pteron that is further outlined and enframed by the architrave friezes of the pronaos and the decorated flank returns of the east peristyle emphasize the frontality of the temple and further accentuate its east façade. A similar spatial design is attested in the Early Archaic second temple of Aphaia at Aegina, where the interior of the prostyle porch was decorated with a smaller triglyph-metope frieze running on the back of the exterior Doric frieze and with another frieze running across the wall over the doorway (*cf.* Schwandner 1985). These spatial elements may be early manifestations and forerunners of a favorite design in Attica in the fifth century BC that emphasized the east front of the temple (*e.g.*, the Hephaisteion, the temple of Poseidon at Sounion, possibly the temple of Ares, and the temple of Nemesis at Rhamnous – all of which were previously attributed to the so-called Theseion Architect, but have been arguably dissociated in recent studies, *cf.* Miles 1989, 242). This spatial concept involved designing a deeper east pteron and pronaos, aligning the third-flank columns with the pronaos antae, thus creating an intimate connection between exterior and interior structural elements, and setting off the deep east pteron as an enframed front compartment, surrounded by carved metopes on the outside (east front and flank returns) and/or a frieze over the pronaos columns, often extending over the north and south pteron to the north and south peristyles (Hephaisteion), or running along all four interior walls of the east pteron (Sounion) (Dinsmoor 1950, 179–82; Coulton 1977, 117, fig. 48; Ridgway 1981, 84–87, 102).

The discovery of fifteen decorated architrave blocks and of at least eleven undecorated ones suggests that only select parts of the architrave were decorated, most likely those on the east and west facade, leaving the greater part of the flank architrave blank (see Fig. 10.4). The number of decorated architrave blocks is far greater, though, than the number of intercolumniations on the short sides (total of ten), which indicates that the rest of the decorated blocks must have been placed over the columns in-antis of the pronaos (three intercolumniations) and either at the eastern and western ends of the flanks as decorated returns of the friezes of both short sides (minimum of four intercolumniations), or most probably over the first two easternmost intercolumniations of the flanks as decorated returns of the east frieze, thus framing and emphasizing the east facade of the temple (maximum of four intercolumniations). The discovery of both blank and sculptured metopes (at least eight) suggests a similar pattern of spatial distribution of the decorated metopes on the entablature, directly above the decorated architrave friezes, which they often echo iconographically. The architrave blocks have a height of 0.812–0.820 m and a peculiar Γ-shaped profile of varied thickness (top: 0.304–0.410 m; bottom: 0.25 m). This distinct profile of the architrave blocks in correlation with the reverse profile of the L-shaped metopes, the existence of antithema (backers) indicated by the roughly worked (thus not visible) back surface of the architrave blocks and the size of the abacus (1.2 × 1.2 m), the absence of clamp sockets for the antithema on the top surface of the architrave blocks, and the location of dowel sockets suggest a construction of the type shown in Figure 10.3. Two decorated architrave blocks can be securely identified as corner blocks (see Figs. 10.1–2: I, XV) and three more (see Figs. 10.1–2: V, VI, XI) tentatively so on account of several key technical details, including their greater length (by 0.20–0.30 m) required to span the longer space of the corner intercolumniation extending to the edge of the abacus of the corner column (2.850–2.941 m); a longer anathyrosis on their underside (0.68–0.90 m instead of average 0.4–0.6 m) corresponding to the contact surface on the top of the abacus of the corner column; and a near full-size left or right regula (*c.* 0.4–0.5 m) corresponding to a corner triglyph above.

Assuming that the Herakles and Pholos theme that unrolls to the right on at least four surviving architrave blocks (originally five?) may have been prominently placed on the east facade (the length of Blocks II, III, IV [2.6–2.7 m] indicates front intercolumniations), the composition of the theme and the arrangement of these blocks must have been as follows (see Figs. 10.4–5): the main narrative scene, which features the core dramatic action between the key protagonists and three manlike centaurs, is depicted on a left corner block (Block I) set at the southern end of the east architrave frieze. Block III must have been placed over the wider central intercolumniation of the east peristyle, as indicated by its greater length (*c.* 2.7 m) compared to that of Blocks II and IV (2.6 m), which must have been originally placed on either side of it. Block III was probably preceded by Block II and followed by Block IV, a tentative sequence based on firm iconographic criteria: Block II must have been closer to the main scene, since the first centaur turns back his head, and the fleeing centaurs (except one?) carry no tree trunks yet; Block IV must have been placed farther away and most likely beyond Block III, given the faster galloping of the fleeing centaurs, none of whom turns back his head toward the main scene (unlike the preceding blocks), and because all four centaurs carry tree trunks, a marked change from the rhythmic alternation of galloping centaurs and those carrying tree trunks on the adjacent Block III. Given the lack of an appropriate right corner block among the discovered pieces, we must assume that a corner block decorated with galloping centaurs carrying tree trunks (like those on Block IV) must have been placed over the northernmost intercolumniation at the right (northern) end of the east peristyle. According to this proposed reconstruction (I–IV), the composition of the theme is characterized by a gradual transition from narrative to more decorative scenes (centaurs resisting in action, running, and fleeing), rhythmic alternation, and gradual escalation of iconographic patterns and motifs.

The established or tentative iconographic association of the remaining two mythological themes with Herakles (Blocks V, VI), the size and morphology of these corner blocks, and the distinct possibility that the west architrave

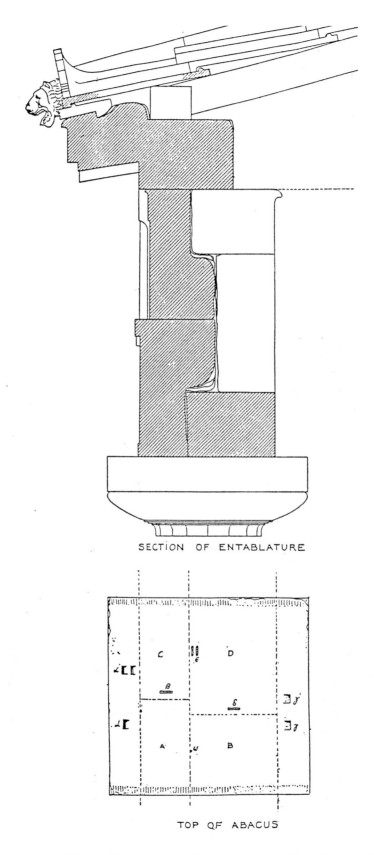

SECTION OF ENTABLATURE

TOP OF ABACUS

Fig. 10.3 *Cross-section of the entablature, temple of Athena at Assos (After Clarke et al. 1902, figs. 1–2).*

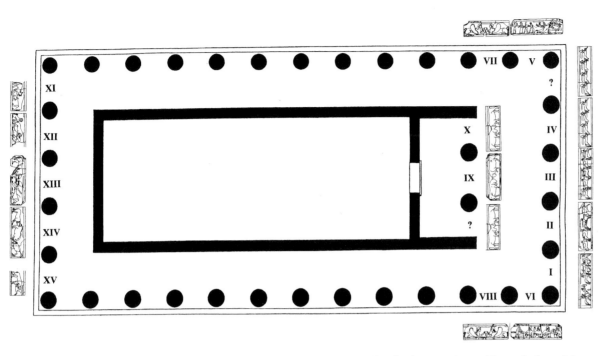

Fig. 10.4 *Theoretical reconstruction of the decorated architrave friezes, temple of Athena at Assos (Ground plan of the temple after Clarke et al. 1902, fig. 3).*

Fig. 10.5 *Drawing reconstruction of the east facade of the temple of Athena at Assos (Modified version of the digital reconstruction at www.fhw.gr/fhw/en/projects/3dvr/assos, Foundation for the Hellenic World).*

frieze contained solely animal battle scenes suggest that these two corner blocks could have only been placed over the easternmost flank intercolumniations as decorated returns of the east centauromachy frieze, thus complementing the mythological iconography of Herakles (see Figs. 10.4–5): the left corner block featuring the Herakles and Triton theme (Block V) was probably set at the eastern end of the north flank, and the right corner block portraying the symposion scene (Block VI) was placed at the eastern end of the south flank. The deep east pteron and the alignment of the third flank columns with the antae indicate that the second easternmost flank intercolumniations may have also been spanned by decorated architrave blocks, most likely Blocks VII and VIII featuring heraldic sphinxes (length 2.554–2.580 m), set on the north and south flank, respectively; these mythological creatures, which appear frequently as border decoration on altar antae and temple anta walls in Asia Minor or as pediment akroteria, are quite befitting as borders of the decorated returns of the east frieze, thus appropriately framing the mythological scenes and the east pteron, and further accentuating the east facade and frontality of the temple.

The architrave frieze on the west facade must have included all the lion-and-prey scenes, as indicated by the length of Blocks XII–XIV (2.68 m), which assigns them on a short side, and the tentative identification of Blocks XI and XV as left and right corner blocks set on the northern and southern end of the west side, respectively (see Fig. 10.4); the latter is based on the estimated length of Block XI (2.85 m), which is required to span the longer space of the corner intercolumniation extending to the edge of the abacus of the corner column, and the full-size right regula of Block XV (0.522 m) corresponding to a corner triglyph above. The central intercolumniation of the west peristyle must have been spanned by Block XIII featuring the symmetrical heraldic composition of two lions devouring dead prey, which recalls similar central groups of contemporary pediment sculpture from Athens and mainland Greece; this central symmetrical scene was probably framed on either side by the lion-and-prey scenes of Blocks XII and XIV. According to this proposed arrangement (XI–XV), the composition of the theme is characterized by rhythmic alternation and gradual transition of iconographic motifs (kneeling prey, dead prey, resisting or fleeing prey).

Finally, the remaining two architrave blocks, decorated with heraldic battling bulls (Blocks IX, X) must have been placed over the columns in-antis of the pronaos, as indicated also by their length (2.50–2.51 m); the central intercolumniation of the pronaos was probably spanned by Block IX, which was bordered by the adjoining Block X set over the northern opening between the north anta and the pronaos column (Block X could be an end block, since its right end is not preserved and, therefore, the possibility of a right-end regula remains), and, hypothetically, another identical block

placed over the southern opening extending to the south anta (see Figs. 10.4–5).

Stylistic and Iconographic Analysis

The sculptured architrave blocks were carved in the orientalizing "flat-relief" technique which finds the closest parallels in Assyrian, North Syrian, and Phoenician reliefs (Ridgway 1977, 253): the contours of figures were cut straight back to the background with vertical sides, whereas their fronts were plastically modeled, thus resulting in a flat and low relief (average height: 0.04–0.05 m; min. 0.02 m; max. 0.08 m) with sharp, clear outlines and a linear rendering of the figures on an empty background, which produces clarity and visibility. Other diagnostic stylistic features of the Assos reliefs (Finster-Hotz 1984, 107–19), where more than one hand and manner can be detected, include a marked preference for painted rather than carved details or metal attachments: only the most essential anatomical details are plastically rendered and summarily modeled (e.g., parallel groves for muscles) on otherwise soft and smooth surfaces; the background and many of the details, now lost, must have been rendered in paint (e.g., minor anatomical details, hair, beards, animal skin folds, manes, clothes, objects and attributes such as bows, quivers, weapons, and vases), whereas no metal attachments were used, as indicated by the complete absence of any type of dowel sockets. Human figures are very slim and animal bodies are slender and elongated (therefore space filling). The figures have a distinct "archaic" appearance, and their posture, movement, and gestures are generally stiff, awkward, or exaggerated (cf. the awkward movement of the fleeing Nereids in Figure 10.2: V; the gesture of the banqueter, second from left, in fig. 10.2: VI; the stiff posture of the attacking lion in fig. 10.2: XIV); occasionally, however, they are quite convincing or even dramatic and full of vigorous action (cf. the banqueters' gestures in fig x.2: VI; Herakles shooting at centaurs who turn back their heads while fleeing in Figure 10.2: I; Herakles and Triton wrestling like athletes in Figure 10.2: V; violent animal battles in Figure 10.2: XI, XII, XV). The figures are lined up in a paratactic composition with sporadic minimal overlapping which allows for clarity but lacks the sense of depth (cf. Herakles, Triton, and two of the fleeing Nereids overlapping on three successive planes in Figure 10.2: V; the servant boy, the banqueters' legs and torsos in Figure 10.2: VI; and the overlapping centaurs' legs in Figure 10.2: I–IV). The depicted scenes are of a mixed decorative and narrative character; even scenes of narrative or mythological content employ strong decorative elements to fill as much space as possible – repetition of scenes, figures, and forms, heraldic animals, elongated animal bodies – which is typical of the Ionic "monotonous" repetitive friezes (Ridgway 1977, 259–60; on the development of Greek architectural friezes in general, see Demangel 1933; Ridgway 1966, 188–204; 1977, 253–76, esp. 260–65; 1981, 73–99; 1999, 53–55; Bookidis 1967, 269–403; Felten 1984). The composition focuses mainly on the horizontal axis (*cf.* the horizontal axis of the high-swinging arms, the tree trunks, and the horse bodies of the centaurs in Figure 10.2: I–IV; the wrestling pair of Herakles and Triton in Figure 10.2: V; and the elongated animal bodies), therefore accentuating the structural role of the architrave frieze as a supporting horizontal member of the post-and-lintel system, whereas the vertical axis is hardly emphasized (*cf.* the vertical axis of the fleeing Nereids in Figure 10.2: V).

The iconographic and stylistic analysis of the Assos architrave frieze reveals an idiosyncratic amalgam of select iconographic traditions fused together by a distinct stylistic eclecticism. The architrave frieze partakes of both the Hellenic and Oriental world by embedding Oriental archetypes and integrating diverse Greek regional traditions: much as the temple itself combines Doric order with distinct Ionic elements, its sculptural decoration blends together local and regional (Ionic and Aeolic) elements of an established iconographic style in East Greece with distinct mainland features under an identifiable Attic influence. Some of the "foreign" or extra-regional elements, nevertheless, might have been originally Ionic or Aeolic in origin, but merely known to us only from their peripheral diffusion in other regions, or from their reappearance at Assos after having been transformed in Attica or elsewhere on mainland Greece.

The Herakles and Pholos Theme

The Herakles and Pholos theme unrolls on at least four architrave blocks and follows the common version in vase painting (on the Herakles and Pholos theme, see Schauenburg 1971, 43–54; Finster-Hotz 1984, 12–34; Wescoat 1995, 296, 302 nn. 22–27). In the main scene (see Figs. 10.1–2: I) Herakles shoots arrows at three manlike centaurs fleeing to the right, whereas Pholos, behind him, holds a *kotyle* and makes a gesture of despair; Herakles is portrayed in heroic nudity and holds no attribute other than his bow. The other three related architrave blocks (see Figs. 10.1–2: II–IV) are decorated with a rhythmic but monotonous repetition of horselike centaurs galloping to the right with sporadic minor variations, such as heads occasionally turning back, some hands holding stones or branches, or arms carrying tree trunks instead of swinging intensely (echoed also as an isolated image on two of the surviving metopes; Finster-Hotz 1984, 104), which add some variety to this rhythmic procession across the architrave and highlight the narrative elements of the composition (frightened or reacting centaurs); no falling or dying centaurs, however, are allowed to disrupt the rhythm of repetition and destroy the decorative character of the scene. The imagery of sporadic, frail reaction (*e.g.,*

the first and the third centaur on slab I attempt to throw a stone at Herakles while fleeing, see Figure 10.2) classifies this scene as the Athenian rather than the Corinthian iconographic version.

This scene is the only attested architectural relief, apart from the metopes of the Heraion at Foce Del Sele (Zancani Montuoro and Zanotti-Bianco 1951; 1954, esp. 121, pls. LIV *ff*; Van Keuren 1989; Ridgway 1999, 150–56, esp. 151–53; De la Geniere *et al.* 1997), to employ both types of centaurs (Schiffler 1976; Finster-Hotz 1984, 28–34). The earlier version of a manlike centaur (human body from which springs the rear part of a horse), attested on mainland Greece and in East Greece already by the seventh century BC, is employed in the central scene to distinguish Pholos, the "civilized" centaur, and the leaders of the centaurs from the rest of the flock. The later version of a horselike centaur (horse body from which springs a human torso), which is first attested in Attica during the last quarter of the seventh century BC and introduced in East Greece under Attic influence in vase painting after 550 BC (alongside a mixed transitional version, the North Ionic type – human body with hooves instead of feet and the rear part of a horse – which was gradually replacing the earlier well-established type) is employed on the other three related slabs, where the required fast action and motion were obtainable only by means of galloping, for which the horse body is much more suitable; indeed, the intensive swinging of the arms and the contrast between the back legs on the ground and the front ones in the air suggest fast motion quite successfully, in spite of the motionless tails. It appears, therefore, that the coexistence of both centaur types in the same scene was symbolic as well as practical, dictated by the need to denote the distinction between "civilized" and brutish centaurs, and to convey fast and repetitive motion for part of the composition. Unlike the image of centaur with long and untidy hair and beard, typical of mainland and West Greece, the heads of the centaurs at Assos are almost totally human. The centaurs carry either tree trunks with triangular roots or branches with flower-shaped roots, thus complying with their iconography of the seventh and sixth centuries BC, or hold small stones, therefore following a new fashion in their iconography, introduced already in the sixth century BC (*cf.* the François Vase and the metopes from the Heraion at Foce del Sele).

There are several iconographic parallels in vase painting and architectural stone/terracotta relief decoration in the seventh and sixth centuries BC (for a complete list, *cf.* Finster-Hotz 1984, 16–24; Wescoat 1995, 302 n. 23). The architectural comparanda (some of which are still rather ambiguous) include a painted terracotta metope from the Apollo Lyseios temple at Thermon (*cf. Archaiologikon Deltion* 1915, 47; 1916, 187), six stone metopes from the Heraion at Foce del Sele (Zancani Montuoro and Zanotti-Bianco 1951; 1954, esp. 121, pls. LIV *ff*.; Van Keuren 1989), architectural terracotta revetments from Akalan (Åkerström 1966, pl. 64/65), Larisa at Hermos (Kjellberg 1940, pl. 20/21; Åkerström 1966, pl. 26/27; also Finster-Hotz 1984, 22 n. 44), Neandria(?) (Åkerström 1966, pl. 4), a terracotta plaque from Pazarli(?) (Åkerström 1966, pl. 94.1), a terracotta antefix from Mytilene(?) (Åkerström 1966, pl. 12.1), a stone relief and terracotta parapet-sima fragments from Thasos(?) (Åkerström 1966, 56), even part of the decoration of the Amyclaean throne and the Kypselos chest, according to Pausanias (3.18.11 and 5.19.9, respectively) The large number of iconographic parallels suggests that the Herakles and Pholos theme was very popular during the Archaic period: the physical struggle of the great hero against the half-human/half-beast monsters exemplified the meta-physical clash between the forces of good and evil, intellect and animal instinct, civilization and chaos, Greeks and barbarians, often at a high price (the two good and wise centaurs, Pholos and Cheiron, were accidentally wounded and killed during the struggle, and even Herakles himself, after several confrontations with centaurs ultimately falls to the dying Nessos's devious revenge). Much as the Classical versions of the centauromachy theme acquire political and historical symbolisms and allude on the analogy of giantomachy, amazonomachy, and Trojan war to the Persian wars and the struggle between Greeks and barbarians (Pollitt 1972, 35–36, 80–82; Ridgway 1999, 150–66), the Archaic versions may echo the conflicts of Greek colonists with barbaric native populations (Van Keuren 1989, 157). This theme was favored in East Greece, where it may have also been intended to allude to the Thessalian origin of the Aeolians (Holtzmann 1979, 6). Another interpretation views the popularity of the Pholoe myth among peoples in peripheral, well-forested regions in the Archaic period in light of an alleged allegoric connection with hunting, which was later replaced by different centauromachy versions (*e.g.,* Lapiths vs. centaurs) in the more urbanized centers in the Classical period (Szeliga 1977, as cited by Ridgway 1999, 150–56; for the changing meaning and semantic nuances of the centauromachy theme in its different versions, *cf.* Ridgway 1999, 150–56). The regional popularity of cen-tauromachy in Archaic East Greece, which carried strong allegorical symbolism for the Greeks of the diaspora, the association of Herakles with Athena (his great patron), and the suitability of its repetitive composition for space filling (unlike other versions of centauromachy, *e.g.,* Herakles vs. Nessos, which are isolated episodes and, therefore, icono-graphically self-contained and unsuitable for filling long, continuous spaces) justify the inclusion and prominence of the Herakles and Pholos theme, extending on at least four architrave blocks, in the iconographic program of the Athena temple at Assos.

The Herakles and Triton Theme

The Herakles and Triton theme is depicted on a single architrave block (see Figs. 10.1–2: V). The struggle of Herakles with the half-fish/half-human sea demon, an Oriental mythical monster, was introduced already in the seventh century BC and soon became a favorite subject in the Archaic art of East Greece (Finster-Hotz 1984, 35–45, with bibliography; Wescoat 1995, 298–99 n. 57). In the first half of the sixth century BC the struggle involved Herakles and Nereus, the wise old man of the sea, as attested in early iconography (for a list of early gems, metalwork, and vase painting from Melos, Samos, Boeotia, Olympia, Attica, and elsewhere, see Finster-Hotz 1984, 36 n. 80), and in several later literary sources (Scholion to Apollodoros Rhodios, 4.396; Pherekydes, *FGrH*, F16; Ap. Rhod. 2.114–15; for the Herakles and the sea monster theme in literature, see Finster-Hotz 1984, 41–44). Just before the middle of that century, though, a variation of this subject involving Herakles and Triton emerged in Athens, prominently featuring in the east poros pediment (550–540 BC) of the Hekatompedon and in a small poros pediment (Red Triton pediment, *c.* 570–560 BC) from the Athenian Acropolis with recognizable Oriental elements in their iconography and style (Ridgway 1977, 199–202, 220–21; 1999, 110–11, with bibliography). This new variation apparently lacks any literary basis, having survived only in art; therefore, only speculation can be made about the replacement of Nereus (whose complicated iconography with various transforma-tions was quite unsuitable for Greek iconography) with Triton in the myth. Kourouniotes (1893) suggested that this fight was a substitute for the famous contest between Athena and Poseidon, a theory later elaborated by Howe (1955, 287–301). In the literary sources Triton is called "δεινός θεός" (Hes. *Theog.* 931) and is always related with water (sea or river), either as a Libyan deity, connected with the Argonauts myth and the foundation of Thera and Cyrene (Pind. *Pyth.* 4; Hdt. 4.179–88; Ap. Rhod. 4.1551), or as a Greek god in the local myths of Tanagra (birth of Athena near his river, Paus. 9.204.4) and Arcadia (small river at Aliphera). Brize (1980, 66–105, esp. 103–5) convincingly argues for a mythological syncretism, an amalgamation of the two myths caused by their mutual association with Libya: the Herakles and Nereus myth is connected with the Hesperides deed, which was located either generally in the West (Hespera) or specifically in Libya (Eur. *Hipp.* 741 *ff.*), and Triton appears as a Libyan deity connected with the Argonauts myth; in the subsequent replacement of Nereus with Triton, Brize views the change of Herakles's opponent, the downscaling of his antagonist in size and status (god to sea demon), and the transformation of the episode's character and parameters ("life-or-death" battle to athletic contest of wrestling) as a reflection of the developing self-perception of a rising aristocratic society in Archaic Athens. Other theories interpret it as an allegory with political implications (possibly Peisistratos's propaganda) and allusions to Athenian naval victories (sea victory over Megara, see Boardman 1972, 57–60; 1975, 10; occupation of Sigeion, see Glynn 1981, 121–32, esp. 130–32). The Herakles and Triton theme soon developed and established itself in Athenian vase painting, until the end of the sixth century BC, when interest in this subject suddenly declined (for the chronological development, geographical distribution, and allegorical symbolisms of this theme variation, see Glynn 1981, 121–32; Ahlberg-Cornell 1984; Brommer 1984, 90–92; Finster-Hotz 1984, 35–45; Schefold 1992, 138–41, fig. 164). It is the Herakles and Triton version that is depicted at Assos, as indicated by certain iconographic elements and details that distinguish it from the earlier version of Herakles and Nereus: Herakles here is not smaller than his opponent but of the same size (hence forecasting the successful outcome of the struggle), nor does he ride the sea monster in an attempt to strangle him but swims or runs alongside in an effort to wrestle with him and immobilize him with a characteristic pankration grip (no longer a fight for life or death). Triton holds a fish in his hand as an attribute and hallmark of the environment in which the fight takes place, while spectators emerge in the scene (fleeing Nereids at Assos, dancing Nereids, even Nereus himself or the triple-bodied monster elsewhere). Although earlier interpretations either preferred the Herakles and Nereus version or opted for a theme connected with the Troad (*e.g.,* Menelaos vs. Proteus with Helen and companions attending, *cf.* Texier 1882, 50; Menelaos or Aristaios against Proteus, *cf.* Clarac 1841, 1157; liberation of Hesione from the sea monster by Herakles, with Trojan women applauding in joy, *cf.* Clarke 1898, 209; Sartiaux 1915, 50), the correlation of diagnostic iconographic elements of Triton with the secure identification of the hero as Herakles on the basis of his quiver, make the interpretation of the scene indisputable. The inclusion of the Herakles and Triton theme in the iconographic program of the Athena temple at Assos is certainly explained by the association of Herakles with Athena and the suitability of its repetitive composition for space filling; it may also be interpreted as a result of Athenian influence and a conscious attempt to affiliate Athena Polias at Assos with the Athenian Acropolis, where at least two Archaic pediments featured this subject that echoed the famous contest between Athena and Poseidon; furthermore, the depiction of a sea victory of Herakles at faraway places is quite befitting for the temple of a nautical Greek coastal city on foreign lands (Finster-Hotz 1984, 45).

The Banquet Scene

The banquet scene, which at Assos is depicted on a single architrave block (see Figs. 10.1–2: VI), is a rather unusual image for a Greek temple. The banquet theme is of Oriental origin, and the first attested example is the famous relief from the palace of Assurbanipal in Nineveh (*c.* 635–600 BC) (on the banquet and symposion iconography in Greek art, see Dentzer 1971; 1982; Fehr 1971; Finster-Hotz 1984, 46–74; Lissarrague 1990; Wescoat 1995, 295–98). Banquet scenes appear very rarely in early Greek sacred architecture, and almost exclusively in East and West Greece, such as the Dionysos pediment from Corfu (Dentzer 1982, R331, 248–51, fig. 573), the North Building frieze from the Heraion of Samos (Furtwängler and Kienast 1989, 156, nos. 29–32), the parapet frieze(?) from the Artemision of Ephesos (Muss 1983, 149, 154–57), a relief from Paros (Felten 1984, pl. 8.1), terracotta friezes from Larisa at Hermos (Åkerström 1966, pls. 28–29; Dentzer 1982, R64, 230–34, figs. 320–28) and Kebren (Åkerström 1966, 3, fig. 2; Dentzer 1982, R67, 234–35, fig. 331), and a terracotta relief from Sicily(?) (Dentzer 1982, R501, 251–52, fig. 721; Finster-Hotz 1984, 46–50 with bibliography). On the contrary, isolated images of banqueters appear more frequently in freestanding votive sculptures in East Greece (*e.g.,* the reclining statue of the Geneleos group from Samos, *cf.* Freyer-Schauenburg 1974, 116–23, no. 63, pls. 51–53; the reclining statue dedicated by Hermonax and his wife from Myus, *cf.* Blümel 1963, 63, no. 66, pls. 213–14; two reclined torsos from Samos and Didyma, *cf.* Freyer-Schauenburg 1974, 148–49, no. 70, pl. 58, and Tuchelt 1976, 55–66, figs. 1–3), while banquet scenes are rather familiar imagery in Archaic funerary architecture and a favorite subject in Archaic vase painting (Finster-Hotz 1984, 46–54, with bibliography). Four different types of banquets are depicted in Greek art, including mythological banquets, mainly involving Herakles or Achilles; religious or cult banquets, such as Dionysian feasts or cult banquets for Demeter and Kore; everyday-life symposia; and funerary banquets or "Totenmahl." The Assos banquet scene, which is the only noncompetitive narrative scene on the architrave frieze, contains an eclectic amalgamation of iconographic elements: the scene involves four symposiasts whose dress – himation covering only the lower body and the legs while leaving the torso naked – complies with the mainland and West Greek iconography (in East Greek art banqueters customarily wear a chiton and a mantle; see Finster-Hotz 1984, 54–61, with bibliography), whereas their pose with legs joined, parallel and superimposed follows the East Greek tradition (in the banquet iconography of mainland and West Greece the symposiasts' right leg is raised and bent, *e.g.,* the Dionysos pediment from Corfu; see Finster-Hotz 1984, 54–61, with bibliography); the scene also includes a small servant boy dressed in a short chiton, in accordance with the East Greek established tradition, whereas the type of the naked *pais* was introduced into Attic black-figure and red-figure vase painting in the late sixth century BC. The symposiasts lie on the projecting lower taenia of the architrave; the absence of klinai, unparalleled among the few comparanda of banquet scenes in early Greek architectural sculpture, may have been an artistic convention under the influence of contemporary Ionic votive sculptures in the round, or merely a concession dictated by practical necessity to fit awkward space and maintain proportions: if klinai were to be included in the scene, the symposiasts would have been smaller in size compared to the standing young servant, and the whole scene would have suffered in terms of clarity and visibility (in Greek vase painting klinai are occasionally omitted when the shape of the surface is unsuitable for their depiction, *e.g.,* the tondo of phialae or cups). The images, however, of symposiasts reclining on the ground or on mattresses in Archaic Greek vase painting and freestanding sculpture usually indicate an outdoor and often sacred setting, such as a cult feast (Wescoat 1995, 297), or occasionally a mythological banquet involving Herakles or Dionysos and taking place outdoors or in a cave. The drinking vases depicted on the Assos scene point also to the same direction. The scene includes a column-krater, an oinochoe, two kantharoi, two phialae, and an amphora of types generally common in the second half of the sixth century BC or paralleled in the local Bucchero Ware in Asia Minor (*e.g.,* the amphora), with the notable exception of the oinochoe (resembling a type depicted on a phiale by Oltos, see Simon 1976, pl. 94) and the goblet-shaped kantharos held by the second symposiast (see *CVA* 28, München 6, pl. 295), both of which are extraordinary and almost unparalleled. The use of kantharoi (once painted, perhaps, as golden or silver, as suggested by their metallic, carinated or rounded shapes) – a form associated with Dionysos and Herakles in Attic vase painting (Boardman 1979, 149–51; Carpenter 1986, 118–22) – signifies a heroic context and an extraordinary banquet, while the absence of the usual kotylai, kylikes, skyphoi, or the traditional East Greek drinking horn dissociates the scene from the daily-life aristocratic symposion (*e.g.,* Åkerström 1966, pls. 28–29; Fehr 1971, 122–23; Dentzer 1982, R64, 230–34, figs. 320–28; *cf.* Wescoat 1995, 297). There are no identifying attributes of heroes or gods, or at least not rendered in relief; the fourth symposiast, however, is singled out by several diagnostic iconographic details indicating that he is the guest of honor: he leans his elbow on two pillows, he is offered a ribbon or a wreath and makes a gesture of gratitude, and, finally, he oddly uses an amphora as drinking vessel, a clear implication of his exceptional wine consumption ability. The first symposiast is the only participant that holds two vases. He sets down a kantharos while extending a phiale to be filled by the servant boy, possibly in preparation for a libation; this gesture, combined with the passing of a wreath, the prominent position of the krater, the exclusive use of drinking cups, and the complete absence of tables with food may indeed suggest that this is not vaguely a banquet but more specifically a symposion scene (Wescoat 1995, 297). The krater that holds the wine mixed with water, a custom that distinguishes civilized men from barbarians,

is the source and communal vase of the symposium, thus symbolizing communal sharing, social bonding and integration, hospitality and friendship (Wescoat 1995, 297).

The iconographic idiosyncrasies of the Assos banquet scene have allowed various readings that attempt to contextualize the scene in its sacred setting, to establish an association with Athena, to correlate it with at least some of the other scenes of the frieze, and, potentially, to trace some connection with the Troad region (for a discussion of different interpretations of the scene, see Finster-Hotz 1984, 74–78; Wescoat 1995, 296–98). The banquet scene has been interpreted as an everyday-life aristocratic symposion (Mendel 1914, 7, claiming that mixing mythological and everyday-life scenes is an Aeolic feature; Demangel 1933, 437; Fehr 1971, 117; Dentzer 1982, 237); this, however, seems rather improper for temple decoration and incongruous amid the iconographic program of the building. Conversely, it has been suggested that the scene may portray a religious or cult feast, which presumes, though, an early depiction of the "theoxenia" ritual and involves certain iconographic anachronisms (*e.g.,* emergence of the theme of gods in banquet and lack of attributes before the Classical period), or even a funerary feast, which is certainly out of place thematically and presents fundamental iconographic differences. Finally, the scene has been interpreted as a mythological banquet and several alternatives have been suggested with various protagonists, most of which are either unparalleled elsewhere or unrelated with the rest of the frieze (Finster-Hotz 1984, 74–77): banquet of Menelaos and Proteus (Clarac 1841, 1158) which, however, requires a filmlike scene – depiction of two different moments on the same slab – and a direction from right to left, both foreign to Greek art, and depends on Clarac's mistaken identification of the Herakles and Triton scene as the fight of Menelaos against Proteus; wedding banquet of Peirithous (Texier 1849, 204) which would be part of a different centauromachy version – Thessalian episode involving Lapiths, Peirithous and Deidameia – but has no attested parallels; and banquet of a local hero (Finster-Hotz 1984, 77–78). More plausible appears the connection of the banquet scene with Herakles, given the secure identification of two other minor deeds of his in the iconographic program of the temple. Various identifications have been proposed, such as the apotheosis of Herakles (Sartiaux 1915, 53; Perrot and Chipiez 1903, 260; disputed by Jacobsthal 1911, 15), the banquet of Eurystheus and Herakles (Clarke 1898, 225, 242), or of Eurytos and Herakles (Robert 1919, 241; Hölscher 1972, 94; *cf.* Finster-Hotz 1984, 77–78). The apotheosis of Herakles, attractive though it may be, is rather unsatisfactory for a number of good reasons: gods are never depicted without attributes before the fifth century BC (Finster-Hotz 1984, 77), the theme of the Olympic gods in banquet (with the notable exception of Dionysos) does not appear before mid-fifth century BC (Jacobsthal 1911, 15, London phiale of Kodros P., *c.* 440 BC), and there is also the diagnostic absence of Athena, who is always the one introducing Herakles to Olympus. The banquet offered by Eurystheus in honor of Herakles for bringing the belt of Hippolyte to the king is partly connected with Clarke's mistaken identification of the Herakles and Triton theme as the myth of the liberation of Hesione. The banquet offered by Eurytos, king of Oichalia, in honor of Herakles for winning the archery competition to claim the prize, the king's daughter Iole (Hom. *Od.* 21.13, 21.22 *ff.*; Apollod. 2.127; Diod. Sic. 4.31.2) fits in better with the rest of the frieze as it further illustrates the hero's archery skills; furthermore, this mythological theme appears in Archaic vase painting and shares several iconographic elements with the Assos banquet scene (*e.g.,* the Early Corinthian Eurytos Krater, Louvre E 635, *cf.* Simon 1976, 52, XI; Finster-Hotz 1984, 77–78). According to another interpretive approach (Wescoat 1995, 294–96, 298–99), the banquet scene, whether heroic or not, is assigned a pivotal role for the interpretation of the Assos iconographic program as a whole: the congenial symposion defines civility and humanity by embodying communal sharing and fostering social cohesion, piety, hospitality, and friendship; as such, it represents the civilized counterpart of the natural order that is exemplified by the imagery of wild lions savaging prey, whereas the failed symposion of Pholos and the ensuing centauromachy balances between these two polar opposites as the conflict of civilized and barbaric, half-human behavior. If read collectively, therefore, the intertwined themes of the frieze may reveal the key concept that pervades the iconographic program of the temple, allegedly that of eating and drinking, the two primary actions that sustain life, form identity, forge solidarity in both the natural and the civilized world. Though this coherent interpretation is quite intriguing, it forces a rather far-fetched reading of the Herakles and Triton scene in an attempt to connect it with the theme of food (Wescoat 1995, 299), and presumes a central, prominent position of the banquet scene, which may not be the case after all, according to the proposed theoretical reconstruction of the architrave frieze.

Heraldic Sphinxes

Two architrave blocks (see Figs. 10.1–2: VII–VIII) depict a pair of antithetic heraldic sphinxes framing a central motif, the Oriental Tree-of-Life or possibly a column (Ridgway, personal communication) symbolizing in abbreviated form the entire temple they guard (much like the entablature-bearing column on the Lion Gate relief at Mycenae). The sphinxes present the typical iconographic features of the sixth century BC in the hair style (ribbon or diadem on the forehead, two long tresses behind the ears framing the long wavy hair), their elongated space-filling bodies, and their curved wings with an S-shaped band separating their feathers, once rendered in paint, from the breast. The

sphinxes lean one of their front paws on the central motif, unlike the heraldic sphinxes on a metope from the Assos temple, which lacks the central motif. The sphinx, a mythological creature of Oriental origin, is the favorite subject of Orientalizing and early Archaic vase painting in East Greece and on the Greek mainland. Sphinxes appear often as votive freestanding sculptures and in funerary reliefs (*e.g.,* the Naxian dedication sphinx at Delphi, *cf. FD* 2:4, 1953, 1–32, pls. 1–15, sphinxes in the round recently found at Didyma, and sphinxes crowning Attic grave stelai, *cf.* Ridgway 1977, 156–60; Richter 1961), but very rarely as sculptural decoration of temples on mainland Greece, other than stone or terracotta akroteria. On the contrary, there is a regional preference for sphinxes in East Greek architectural sculpture (on friezes and anta walls), which is already well-established in the sixth century BC (*cf.* Ridgway 1977, 156–60, esp. 157, 179, with bibliography): relief sphinxes on the antae of altars from Samos (Rhoikos altar, Freyer-Schauenburg 1974, no. 128), Didyma (*Jahrbuch des Deutschen Archäologischen Instituts* 79, 1964, 202–29), Myus (Blümel 1963, no. 64, figs. 186–92), and Erythrai (architectural terracottas with confronted sphinxes); relief sphinxes from Halikarnassos (Tuchelt 1970, L65), sphinxes carved on the anta walls of the archaic temples of Hermes and Aphrodite (Freyer-Schauenburg 1974, nos. 129–32) and of Heraion IV on Samos (Freyer-Schauenburg 1974, nos. 133–34); an architectural(?) limestone slab from Sicily depicting two antithetic sphinxes turning their backs to each other and framing a palmette (Langlotz 1963, pl. 13). The Assos sphinxes belong to this regional iconographic tradition, acting as guardians of the temple with their divine strength and apotropaic power, while functioning as a repetitive, space-filling decorative motif on different parts of the temple (architrave frieze and metopes).

Animal Battle Scenes

Animal battles are depicted on seven architrave blocks (see Figs. 10.1–2: IX–XV) and may be classified into two distinct groups: pairs of battling bulls (IX–X) and lions attacking or savaging prey (XI–XV) (for animal battles, see Finster-Hotz 1984, 80–89, 94–99). The bulls have identical elongated, space-filling bodies with light and slender proportions, unlike the mainland iconography of the animal, which emphasizes physical size and strength; occasional relief details like twirled tails indicate that finer details, such as the favorite Archaic skin folds of the neck, must have been rendered in paint. The confronted bulls are almost motionless, butting their heads in a moment of a head-on fight, which is an extremely rare composition in architectural sculpture where bulls are usually portrayed as prey to lions or in sacrificial procession (*e.g.,* relief bulls in procession on the antae(?) of the Archaic Artemision at Ephesos, *cf.* Lethaby 1917, 1–2; fragments of a bull frieze from Larisa in Thessaly, *cf.* Biesantz 1965, pl. 46; or, later on, the sacrificial procession of bulls on the Parthenon frieze, *cf.* Ridgway 1977, 199, 220, 263–64). The repetitive scenes of battling bulls have been regarded as merely decorative (Sartiaux 1915, 57–58), which is only partially true; other interpretations, though, recognize the special symbolism of the bull as an expression of apotropaic power and primal force of procreation (Wescoat 1995, 295; *cf.* Holloway 1986 on apotropaic power of bull images at Tarquinia), the image of the bull as the ultimate sacrificial animal and precious votive offering, the association of the animal with the cult of Athena Polias and Tauropolos (Clarke 1898, 283, on the local cult of Asian/Trojan Athena; Finster-Hotz 1984, 89, on local traditional connection of Athena with bulls; Hölscher 1972, 93–94, on Tauropolos Athena and bulls; Shapiro 1989, 29–32, on Athena and bulls in art), and the symbolic overtones conveyed by the image of a duel between two equals, whose semiotics (balance of opposite forces) differ fundamentally from the typical imagery of animal battles involving predator and prey (primal instinct and survival of the strongest) (Wescoat 1995, 295).

Such non-narrative animal battle scenes of lions and lionesses attacking or devouring prey (bull, stag, doe, boar) are vividly portrayed on five more architrave blocks (see Figs. 10.1–2: XI–XV), each involving at least three animals, and echoed in the isolated image of a boar (Calydonian?) on one of the surviving metopes (Finster-Hotz 1984, 105–6). The lions belong to the Assyrian type, and their crude heads (short and wide head, deep-set eyes, sharp muzzle, leaf-shaped ears, wild short mane framing the head, once continued on the neck in paint) bring them much closer to the mainland iconography of the animal rather than the Ionic version with globular head; all but one (XIV) of their faces are rendered in frontal view, which increases the effect of their facial wildness. Their elongated (hence space-filling), slender, flexible, and elegant bodies comply, however, with the Ionic iconographic type rather than the strong and muscular lion type of mainland Greece with thick neck and strong legs; in fact, the Assos lions would appear more like panthers (frontal face and slender, flexible body) had it not been for their mane (for the lion image in early Greek art, see Gabelmann 1965). Lions and prey are portrayed in various positions, which adds some rhythmic variety to the frieze: the lions attack from behind (XIV, XV), from the front (XI, XII, XIV), or from both sides (XIII, XIV); the prey resists (XIV), gallops to escape (XV), kneels down while collapsing under the attack (XI, XII), or is already dead, turned over and lying on the ground (XIII); the lions always grasp the prey with their front paws and bite it on the back (or the belly), with a single exception (XIV) where the bristles along the spine of the boar make such an attacking position quite impossible and unnatural; quite rare is the sphinxlike pose of a lion (Block XII), possibly reflecting a close physical proximity to a sphinx on the frieze

or on a metope above. The kneeling prey motif (XI, XII), well known in Oriental art, is attested in East Greece and the Greek mainland in the first half of the sixth century BC, while the imagery of dead prey being devoured by lions recalls the Archaic animal battle pediments on mainland Greece. Indeed, most of the parallels of animal battles in architectural sculpture involve lions and bulls as their prey – the power and strength of the lion is emphasized when it is depicted prevailing over the powerful bull (Hölscher 1972, 14) – and come from Archaic Doric pediments of Athenian monuments on mainland Greece (*cf.* Ridgway 1977, 196–206, 220–21; 1999, 110–11): *e.g.*, the poros pediments of the Hekatompedon, the "Lion and Boar" small poros pediment, and the Late Archaic marble pediment from the Old Temple of Athena on the Athenian Acropolis (Hölscher 1972, G1–G4, 69–73); part of a marble pediment found near the Athenian Olympieion and fragment of a poros pediment from the Athenian Agora (Hölscher 1972, G5–G6, 73); the east marble pediment of the Alkmeonid temple of Apollo and fragment of a pediment from the temple of Athena Pronaia at Delphi (Hölscher 1972, G8–G9, 74–75); fragments of pediments from Karystos in Euboea and Tanagra in Boeotia (Hölscher 1972, G10, 75). Such monumental heraldic compositions of animal fights were the popular central motif of pediment sculpture in the sixth century BC and were characterized by sudden changes of scale (to adapt to the difficult space at both corners of the pediment's tympanum) and abrupt theme transitions (mixture of non-narrative animal imagery in the center and mythological scenes at both ends) (*cf.* the pediment of the Artemis Gorgo on Corfu; Rodenwaldt 1939/40; Robertson 1945, fig. 26; and the Hekatompedon on the Athenian Acropolis; Dinsmoor 1947, 145–47). Animal battle scenes were soon displaced by mythological themes in Late Archaic pediments and altogether abandoned by 500/490 BC in favor of narrative mythological scenes composed with unity of theme and scale. The appearance, therefore, of such lion-and-prey imagery on the Assos architrave frieze may indicate strong mainland influence and a possible connection with Athens. The lions are generally regarded as apotropaic symbols and powerful guardians of the temple (Hölscher 1972, 68, 82–94, 100–4; Ridgway 1977, 199–200), especially connected with Athena Polias and Herakles, who assumed the qualities of the wild beast, allegorically symbolized by the lionskin attribute, after killing the Nemea lion. The lion is a manifestation of supernatural strength, valor, and cunning, a symbol of dominance and survival in the natural world, a wild beast to which heroes are constantly compared in art and literature as human counterparts embodying the same qualities in the mythical world (Hölscher 1972, 59–60, 103–4; *cf.* the Homeric lion similes in *Il.* 3.23–26; 5.161–62; 11.113–16, 172–76; 12.298–307; 15.630–36; 16.485–90, 751–54, 756–58, 823–28), Herakles more than anyone else. The lion-and-prey imagery, therefore, is highly befitting for the iconographical program of the Assos temple on so many different symbolic and ideological levels.

Chronology

The iconographic and stylistic analysis of the frieze may further establish its chronology: with the extreme datings safely dismissed, both the high date suggested by Perrot and Chipiez (*c*. 700 BC; 1903, 268) and the low date proposed by Clarke (fifth century BC; 1898, 292), most scholars agree on a dating *c*. 550–530 BC for the architrave frieze (570/560 BC: Robertson 1945, 84–85, 325; 1975, 82; Fuchs 1969, 425; 550 BC: Richter 1949, 117; after 540 BC: Dinsmoor 1950, 88; *c*. 530 BC: Åkerström 1966, 13–14, 18–19; Finster-Hotz 1984, 120; Barletta 2001, 117; late sixth century BC: Lawrence and Tomlinson 1996, 81). A comparative study of the Assos frieze and contemporary architectural terracotta reliefs from Asia Minor (Åkerström 1966, 13–14, 18–19), the coexistence of several Early and Late Archaic elements in the frieze, and certain architectural details and proportions (Dinsmoor 1950, 88) further support a dating to the third quarter of the sixth century BC, which is strengthened considerably by the viable hypothesis that the Hekatompedon and other monuments on the Athenian Acropolis (*c*. 570–540 BC) may have exerted some influence on the Assos iconographic program, and therefore must have preceded it by a decade or so.

Interpretation of the Architrave Frieze

The proposed theoretical reconstruction of the Assos architrave frieze allows a collective reading of the iconographic program of the temple toward a coherent and comprehensive interpretation, beyond the symbolic nuances of isolated themes and above the allegoric connotations of individual scenes. Explicit messages with a primary and clearly intelligible content or firm programmatic unity with a crystallized definite context are probably not to be expected on a Greek temple, all the more so on a Preclassical one; apart from the inherent difficulties posed by external factors (fragmentary state of monuments and their sculptural decoration, limited ancient literary sources, modifications or interruptions of iconographic programs in antiquity), our interpretative abilities are further hindered by internal variables and parameters (limited or distorted modern perception of ancient semiotics, remoteness from the time of their execution, constant changing of original meaning, inherent polysemy of ancient iconography) (Wescoat 1995, 293, 299; Ridgway 1999, 87–88, 143–66, 184–207, esp. 165–66, 184–87). Preclassical temple iconography involves a loose nexus of paratactic assemblages of animal or mythological imagery with multivariate polysemy, which includes an idiosyncratic amalgam of religious, allegoric, or historico-political symbolisms and regional or ethnic

associations; these symbolic nuances were neither hermetically tight nor mutually exclusive but often complementary and interconnected, diffused on multiple layers in an endless variety of patterns on the most important building of the polis, its temple, which, too, functioned on many different levels, embodying religious practices, moral ideology, ethnic and civic identity, sovereignty as territorial marker, social bonding, artistic virtuosity, financial capacity (Wescoat 1995, 293, 299). Yet, if read collectively and evaluated in their cumulative effect, these intertwined themes and the nexus of their direct or implicit associations may reveal one or more key concepts that pervade the iconographic program of the temple. The decorated architrave friezes at Assos present an Archaic vision of the polar opposite, but complementary and intertwined prime forces that sustain and govern the world: wild forces of the chaotic natural world, which is ruled and dominated by wild beasts and monsters fighting for survival (west facade), counterbalanced by the civilized forces of the human and mythical world, best exemplified by Herakles, the favorite mortal of Athena and panhellenic hero (east front). Herakles embodies the apotropaic power, courage, and superb qualities of the guardian lions but is distinguished from them by his virtue and sense of justice, wisdom, and civility; he is portrayed facing all types of opponents (just like his patron goddess), wrestling down supernatural sea demons, killing sacrilegious and barbaric half-beasts, and sharing a feast with mortals after victoriously competing with their king; he is shown fighting in the sea and on land, in faraway places and in Greece, both wrestling and in archery, in action or in triumphant relaxation. This encompassing iconographic variety of prototypical actions elevates Herakles to the sphere of superhuman, the archetypal symbol of human and Greek superiority over beasts and uncivilized barbarians respectively. The hero, paradoxically, also connects and embraces both worlds and conflicting prime forces by action and through his persona, with his mythical unsurpassed deeds and unmatched qualities. These two equal forces are perhaps embodied in the battling bulls over the pronaos entrance, the most favorite sacrificial animal, whose presence there alludes also to animal sacrifice rituals in honor of Athena.

Conclusion: Contextualization of the Assos Architrave Frieze within the East Greek Tradition of Unconventional Architectural Decoration

The proposed theoretical reconstruction of the Assos architrave frieze may shed new light onto the perplexing problem of its surprising position on the temple. Many theories have been advanced in an effort to explain away this "peculiar" decorated architrave frieze, which is generally viewed as an isolated, atypical phenomenon and odd anomaly. The Assos architrave frieze has been regarded as a late translation of another medium into stone, the epilogue of an old regional tradition in Asia Minor of terracotta or metallic crowning figural friezes and decorative revetments converted into stone relief in the delayed "provincial" region of Aeolia (Demangel 1933, 205); conversely, the Assos frieze has been viewed as the start of a new trend incorporating an old tradition in stone, which would further develop later on (*e.g.,* the Nereid Monument at Xanthos, the Limyra and Halikarnassos Heroon; see Weickert 1929, 157, 211; Gruben 1963, 335). This hypothetical petrification process is allegedly echoed in the low relief and the decorative repetitive character of the Assos frieze, both recalling molded mechanical repetition. Friezes in stone, terracotta, or metal, however, are arguably more or less contemporary, and no fixed limits can be securely set between narrative stone friezes and decorative metallic or terracotta ones (Ridgway 1966, 189–93; 1977, 253–60, 277, with bibliography): stone friezes appear occasionally earlier than terracotta or metallic revetments, such as the warriors frieze, relief decoration or carved guidelines for painted decoration(?) on the cella walls of Heraion II on Samos, *c.* 700–650 BC (for a different reconstruction of the Samian Heraion I–II without the peristasis and dating of its different phases, see Kienast 1992; 1993; 1996). The Assos architrave frieze has also been viewed as a result of Ionic influence from the Archaic temple of Apollo at Didyma (Dinsmoor 1950, 88, 133) The Archaic Didymaion, however, has no frieze within its Ionic entablature but only dentils immediately over the architrave – customary in Asia Minor – and its architrave is not decorated with a continuous narrative frieze but with relief Gorgons at the corners and possibly lions and other figures placed in between. The Assos architrave frieze has even been seen as early Doric experimentation on an archetype of the Ionic frieze in Asia Minor (Robertson 1975, 81); this theory, however, presumes a dating of the Assos temple in the early sixth century BC and overlooks the fact that the Ionic frieze was ultimately placed over the architrave, not on it. The extant corpus of evidence suggests a rather different development of the Ionic frieze (Gruben 1963, 142; 1972, 7–36; Ridgway 1977, 253–76, esp. 274–76; 1999, 54; Barletta 2001, 117–20). The concept of the continuous decorative frieze, which was initially placed on various temple parts and members – column drums and pedestals, cella walls, anta walls, the architrave, parapets and simas – without securing a fixed or exclusive position on the entablature (*cf.* Ridgway 1977, 275; 1999, 54), originated in East Greece under Oriental influence and diffused in Magna Graecia in the form of terracotta figured friezes; the frieze, however, as a blank entablature member occurred first in the Cyclades, whereas in Asia Minor the Ionic temples have dentils immediately over the architrave; ultimately, concept and field were combined in the Late Archaic period on mainland Greece (*e.g.,* Ionic frieze on Cycladic Treasuries at Delphi, and over the porches of the Old Temple of Athena on the Athenian Acropolis) where the continuous frieze eventually acquired a fixed position on the Ionic entablature and highly narrative content, primarily in Classical Athens.

Many of the proposed theories, evidently, focus on isolating the Assos architrave frieze to explain it away, rather than integrating and contextualizing it. Contrary to popular belief and the established view that the ancient Greeks did not decorate the structural parts of their buildings, it appears that architectural decorative principles in the sixth century BC varied considerably in terms of content, compositional structure, and position on the building, and particularly in Asia Minor where a decorated architrave may have been the rule rather than the exception (Gruben 1963, 176; Ridgway 1977, 274–76). The distinction between structural and nonstructural members for decorative purposes was arguably emphasized primarily on mainland Greece in an attempt to standardize the architectural orders by imposing conventions and establishing fixed and exclusive positions for architectural decoration. Relief figural friezes, whether decorative or narrative, were employed at various "unconventional" places on East Greek temples and monuments in the sixth century BC (for bibliographical references to the listed monuments, see Ridgway 1977, 259–65, 274–79; 1999, 42–43, 50–60, 173 n. 19; Gruben 1963, 176): around column drums (*columnae caelatae*) of the Archaic Artemision at Ephesos (550–460 BC) and the Didymaion at Miletos (550–525 BC), and possibly from Kyzikos (*c.* 540 BC); on column pedestals of the Archaic Artemision at Ephesos (550–460 BC); on the corner architrave blocks and perhaps on a narrow frieze course above the architrave of the Archaic Didymaion at Miletos (525–500 BC) (see Schattner 1996, 1–23, figs. 19a–b), or across the architrave of later monuments (*e.g.,* the Ionic Nereid Monument at Xanthos, *c.* 380 BC, and the Doric temple of Apollo Bresaeus or Dionysos on Lesbos, second/first century BC, carried also a decorated architrave following the same regional tradition; see Dinsmoor 1950, 256–57, 271; Webb 1996, 152); along or around the cella walls of Heraion II (*c.* 700–650 BC) and possibly of Heraion IV and the North Building (500–470 BC) on Samos, of the Dionysos temple at Myus (550–540 BC), and possibly from Karaköy near Didyma (540–530 BC), Kyzikos (530–520 BC), and Iasos (570–550 BC); on the pronaos anta walls of the Aphrodite and Hermes temple (530–525 BC) and of Heraion IV on Samos (after 510–500 BC); on the parapet sima (or balustrade) of the Archaic Artemision at Ephesos (520–460 BC), and on several terracotta revetments from Larisa at Hermos, Ephesos, Neandria, Thasos, Lesbos, even in non-Greek areas such as Akalan, Pazarli, Sardis, and Gordion in the sixth century BC; quasi-narrative scenes, such as Bellerophon and Chimaira or Herakles archer, appear even on antefixes (Lesbos, Thasos), and occasionally decorate city gates (Thasos), echoing a Neo-Hittite and Assyrian practice.

The decorated architrave frieze of the Athena temple at

Assos is not an isolated anomaly in conventional Greek architectural sculpture but an integral part and manifestation of a very strong Archaic regional tradition in Asia Minor favoring figural decoration anywhere on the building, on either structural or nonstructural parts, a tradition that continued well into the Classical period (*e.g.,* the Nereid Monument at Xanthos, the Mausoleum at Halikarnassos) and the Hellenistic age (*e.g.,* Hellenistic temple of Apollo at Didyma, temple of Apollo Bresaeus or Dionysos on Lesbos, the Great Altar at Pergamon; see Dinsmoor 1950, 229–33, 256–61, 271). This regional tradition originated in the cultural interaction between the Aeolian and Ionian Greeks and local populations in Asia Minor, and eventually generated an idiosyncratic and eclectic amalgam of Oriental and Hellenic stylistic and iconographic elements, diagnostic of the region that bridged East and West.

Acknowledgments

This paper is dedicated to Professor Ross Holloway, distinguished colleague and good friend, in celebration of a lifetime of recognized scholarship, field research, and inspiring teaching. I take this opportunity to express my gratitude to Ross for his unfailing support, advice, and guidance during my years at Brown and beyond. This paper originated in one of the inspiring graduate seminars of Professor B. S. Ridgway at Bryn Mawr College; I am indebted to Bruni, to whom I owe my passion for Greek sculpture, for our fruitful discussions, her insightful remarks and comments, her advice and constant support. I also wish to thank my research assistant, Jenn Danis, who prepared the drawings of the surviving decorated blocks and the drawing reconstruction of the temple.

Works Cited

Ahlberg-Cornell, G. (1984) *Herakles and the Sea Monster in Attic Black Figure Vase Painting.* Acta Instituti Atheniensis Regni Sueciae 4, 33. Stockholm, Svenska institutet i Athen.

Åkerström, A. (1966) *Die architektonischen Terrakotten Kleinasiens.* Acta Instituti Atheniensis Regni Sueciae 4, 11. Lund, Gleerup.

Barletta, B. (2001) *The Origins of the Greek Architectural Orders.* Cambridge and New York, Cambridge University Press.

Biesantz, H. (1965) *Die thessalischen Grabreliefs.* Mainz am Rhein, Philipp von Zabern.

Blümel, C. (1963) *Die archäisch griechischen Skulpturen der Staatlichen Museen zu Berlin.* Berlin, Akademie-Verlag.

Boardman, J. (1972) Heracles, Peisistratos and sons. *Revue Archéologique,* 57–72.

——— (1975) Herakles, Peisistratos and Eleusis. *Journal of Hellenic Studies* 95, 1–12.

——— (1979) The Karchesion of Herakles. *Journal of Hellenic Studies* 99, 149–51.

Bookidis, N. (1967) A study of the use and geographic distribution of architectural sculpture in the Archaic period. Ph.D. dissertation, Bryn Mawr College.

Brize, P. (1980) *Die Geryoneis des Stesichoros und die frühe griechische Kunst.* Beiträge zur Archäologie 12. Würzburg, Triltsch.

Brommer, F. (1984) *Herakles II: Die unkanonische Taten des Helden.* Darmstadt, Wissenschaftliche Buchgesellschaft.

Carpenter, T. (1986) *Dionysian Imagery in Archaic Greek Art: Its Development in Black-Figure Vase Painting.* Oxford, Clarendon Press.

Clarac, F. (1841) *Musée de sculpture antique et moderne ou description historique du Louvre* II. Paris, Imprimerie Royale.

Clarke, J. Th. (1882) *Report on the Investigations at Assos 1881.* Papers of the Archaeological Institute of America, Classical Series I. Boston, Williams & Co.

——— (1898) *Report on the Investigations at Assos 1882/83.* Papers of the Archaeological Institute of America, Classical Series II. New York, The Macmillan Co.

Clarke, J. Th., Bacon, F., and Koldewey, R. (1902) *Expedition of the Archaeological Institute of America: Investigations at Assos 1881–83.* Leipzig.

Coulton, J. J. (1977) *Ancient Greek Architects at Work: Problems of Structure and Design.* Ithaca, Cornell University Press.

De la Geniere, J., Greco, G., and Donnarumna, R. (1997) L'Heraion de Foce del Sele. Decouvertes recentes. *Comptes rendus des séances de l'Académie des inscriptions et belles-lettres.* 333–49.

Demangel, R. (1933) *La frise ionique.* Paris, De Boccard.

Dentzer, J. M. (1971) Aux origines de l'iconographie du banquet couché. *Revue Archéologique,* 215–59.

——— (1982) *Le motif du banquet couché dans le Proche-Orient et la monde grec du VIIe au IVe siècle avant J.C.* Rome, Ecole française de Rome.

Dinsmoor, W. B. (1947) The Hekatompedon on the Athenian Acropolis. *American Journal of Archaeology* 51, 109–51.

——— (1950) *The Architecture of Ancient Greece.* New York, Norton.

Fehr, B. (1971) *Orientalische und griechische Gelage.* Bonn, Bouvier.

Felten, F. (1984) *Griechische tektonische Friese archaischer und klassischer Zeit.* Waldsassen-Bayern, Stiftland-Verlag.

Finster-Hotz, U. (1984) *Der Bauschmuck des Athenatemples von Assos.* Rome, Giorgio Bretschneider.

Freyer-Schauenburg, B. (1974) *Bildwerke der archaischen Zeit und des strengen Stils. Samos* XI. Bonn, R. Habelt.

Fuchs, W. (1969) *Die Skulptur der Griechen.* Munich, Hirmer Verlag.

Furtwängler, A. E. and Kienast, H. J. (1989) *Der Nordbau im Heraion von Samos. Samos* III. Bonn, R. Habelt.

Gabelmann, H. (1965) *Studien zum frühgriechischen Löwenbild.* Berlin, Mann.

Glynn, R. (1981) Herakles, Nereus and Triton. A study of iconography in sixth century Athens. *American Journal of Archaeology* 85, 121–32.

Gruben, G. (1963) Das archaische Didymaion. *Jahrbuch des Deutschen Archäologischen Instituts* 78, 78–182.

——— (1972) Kykladische Architektur. *Münchener Jahrbuch der bildenden Kunst* 23, 6–36.

Holloway, R. R. (1986) The bulls in the "Tomb of the Bulls" at Tarquinia. *American Journal of Archaeology* 90, 447–52.

Hölscher, F. (1972) *Die Bedeutung archaischer Tierkampfbilder.* Beiträge zur Archäologie 5. Würzburg, Triltsch.

Holtzmann, B. (1979) *Thasiaca. Bulletin de Correspondance Hellénique, Supplément V.* Athens and Paris, École française d'Athènes.

Howe, T. P. (1955) Zeus Herkeios: thematic unity in the Hekatompedon sculptures. *American Journal of Archaeology* 59, 287–301.

Jacobsthal, P. (1911) *Theseus auf dem Meeresgrunde.* Leipzig, E. A. Seeman.

Kienast, H. J. (1992) Topographische Studien im Heraion von Samos. *Archäologischer Anzeiger,* 171–213.

——— (1993) Zur Baugeschichte der beiden Dipteroi im Heraion von Samos. In J. Des Courtils and J.-C. Moretti (eds.), *Les Grands ateliers d'architecture dans le monde égéen du Vi siècle av. J.-C.: Actes du colloque d'Istanbul, 23–25 mai 1991,* 69–75. Istanbul, Institut français d'études anatoliennes.

——— (1996) Die rechteckigen Peristasenastützen am samischen Hekatompedos. In E.-L. Schwandner (ed.), *Säule und Gebälk,* 16–24. Mainz am Rhein, Philipp von Zabern.

Kirk, G. S. (1970) *Myth: Its Meaning and Function in Ancient and Other Cultures.* Berkeley, University of California Press.

Kjellberg, L. (1940) *Larisa am Hermos 2: Die Architektonischen Terrakotten.* Stockholm, Kungl. Vitterhets historie och antikivits akademien.

Kourouniotes, K. (1893) *Herakles mit Halios Geron und Triton auf Werken der älteren griechischen Kunst.* Munich, Druck von C. Wolf & Sohn.

Langlotz, E. (1963) *Die Kunst der Westgriechen in Sizilien und Unteritalien.* Munich, Hirmer Verlag.

Lawrence, A. W. and Tomlinson R. A. (1996) *Greek Architecture.* New Haven and London, Yale University Press.

Lethaby, W. R. (1917) The earlier temple of Artemis at Ephesus. *Journal of Hellenic Studies* 37, 1–16.

Lissarrague, F. (1990) *The Aesthetics of the Greek Banquet: Images of Wine and Ritual.* Princeton, Princeton University Press.

Mendel, G. (1914) *Catalogue des sculptures grecques, romaines et byzantines des Musées Ottomans* 2. Constantinople, En vente au.

Miles, M. M. (1989) A reconstruction of the temple of Nemesis at Rhamnous. *Hesperia* 58, 133–249.

Muss, U. (1983) *Studien zur Bauplastik des archaischen Artemisions von Ephesos.* Ph.D. dissertation, Rheinische Friedrich-Wilhelms-Universität, Bonn.

Perrot, G. and Chipiez, Ch. (1903) *Histoire de l'art dans l'antiquité 8: La Grèce archaique: La sculpture.* Paris, Hachette.

Pollitt, J. J. (1972) *Art and Experience in Classical Greece.* Cambridge, Cambridge University Press.

Richter, G. (1949) *Archaic Greek Art against Its Historical Background: A Survey.* New York, Oxford University Press.

——— (1961) *The Archaic Gravestones of Attica.* New York, Phaidon Publishers.

Ridgway, B. S. (1966) Notes on the development of the Greek frieze. *Hesperia* 35, 188–204.

——— (1977) *The Archaic Style in Greek Sculpture.* Princeton, Princeton University Press.

——— (1981) *Fifth Century Styles in Greek Sculpture.* Princeton, Princeton University Press.

——— (1999) *Prayers in Stone: Greek Architectural Sculpture ca. 600–100 BCE.* Berkeley and Los Angeles, University of California Press.

Robert, C. (1919) *Archäologische Hermeneutik: Anleitung zur Deutung klassischer Bildwerke.* Berlin.

Robertson, D. S. (1945) *A Handbook of Greek and Roman Architecture.* Cambridge, Cambridge University Press.

Robertson, M. (1975) *A History of Greek Art.* London, Cambridge University Press.

Rodenwaldt, G. (1939/40) *Korkyra: Archäische Bauten und Bildwerke* 2. Berlin, Gebr. Mann.

Sartiaux, F. (1915) *Les sculptures et la restauration du temple d' Assos en Troade.* Paris, E. Leroux.

Schattner, T. (1996) Architrav und Fries des archaischen Apollontempels von Didyma. *Jahrbuch des Deutschen Archäologischen Instituts* 111, 1–23.

Schauenburg, K. (1971) Herakles bei Pholos. *Mitteilungen des Deutschen Archäologischen Instituts, Athenische Abteilung* 86, 43–54.

Schefold, K. (1992) *Gods and Heroes in Late Archaic Greek Art.* Cambridge and New York, Cambridge University Press.

Schiffler, B. (1976) *Die Typologie des Kentauren in der antiken Kunst vom 10. bis zum Ende des 4.Jhs.v.C.* Ph.D. dissertation, Franfurt, Lang.

Schwandner, E.-L. (1985) *Der ältere Porostempel der Aphaia auf Aegina.* Denkmäler Antiker Architektur 16. Berlin, Walter de Gruyter.

Shapiro, H. A. (1989) *Art and Cult under the Tyrants.* Mainz am Rhein, Philipp von Zabern.

Simon, E. (1976) *Die griechischen Vasen.* Munich, Hirmer Verlag.

Szeliga, G. N. (1977) The centauromachy at Pholoe in architecture of the Archaic period. M.A. thesis, Bryn Mawr College.

Texier, Ch. (1849) *Description de l'Asie Mineure.* Paris, Firmin Didot frères.

——— (1882) *Asie Mineure; description géographique, historique et archéologique des provinces et des villes de la Chersonnése d'Asie.* Paris, Firmin-Didot et cie.

Tuchelt, K. (1970) *Die archaischen Skulpturen von Didyma. Beiträge zur frügriechischen Plastik in Kleinasien.* Instabuler Forschungen 27. Berlin, Gebr. Mann.

——— (1976) Zwei gelagerte Gewandfiguren aus Didyma. *Revue Archéologique,* 55–66.

Van Keuren, F. (1989) *The Frieze from the Hera I Temple at Foce del Sele.* Archaeologica 82. Rome, G. Bretschneider.

Webb, P. (1996) *Hellenistic Architectural Sculpture: Figural Motifs in Western Anatolia and the Aegean Islands.* Madison, University of Wisconsin Press.

Weickert, C. (1929) *Typen der archaischen Architektur in Griechenland und Kleinasien.* Augsburg, B. Filser.

Wescoat, B. D. (1983) The architecture and iconography of the Temple of Athena at Assos. Ph.D. dissertation, Oxford University.

——— (1987) Designing the temple of Athena at Assos: Some evidence for the capitals. *American Journal of Archaeology* 91, 553–68.

———— (1995) Wining and dining on the Temple of Athena at Assos. In C. S. Scott (ed.), *The Art of Interpreting*. Papers in Art History from the Pennsylvania State University 9, 293–320. University Park, Pennsylvania State University Press.

Zancani Montuoro, P. and Zanotti-Bianco, U. (1951) *Heraion alla Foce del Sele* I. Rome, Libreria dello Stato.

———— (1954) *Heraion alla Foce del Sele* II. Rome, Libreria dello Stato.

11

An Etruscan Demon in Pompeii

Larissa Bonfante

For Ross Holloway, who has shown us things that were not visible.

In 1993, at an exhibition on new material from Pompeii at the Palazzo dei Conservatori in Rome, which had previously been displayed in New York in 1990, a beautiful terracotta plaque caught my eye (Fig. 11.1) (*Rediscovering Pompeii* 1994, cat. no. 233, inv. P 40633). It showed two standing female figures, with a dog between them. The two female figures, executed in such high relief that they appeared to be freestanding, had a strikingly statuesque, monumental appearance. Their heads were missing, but the terracotta plaque was otherwise in excellent condition. It was part of a set of the same size, similar in style, many sections and fragments of which were found in 1983 in the *Insula Occidentalis* of Pompeii, where they had been reused in a wall. The nail holes show that when they were made, between the second half of the second century and the beginning of the first century BC, they had been nailed to a support as the decoration of an earlier building. The plaque, 60.3 × 61.5 cm, belongs to Type A (they are all *c.* 60 cm. square, but they were cut before firing, so the measurements after firing vary slightly; see De Lucia 1990, 191, 196, 204, 207, pl. 26.1). The iconography of the plaques that have been preserved makes it clear that they represented a group of mythological figures; the original frieze is not complete, however, and we do not know how they were organized. The plaques may have decorated a suburban cult building and have had a religious significance.

Four plaques are almost complete. One shows a kneeling youth facing right with arms outstretched toward a seated male figure; both are almost entirely nude. They could represent the seated Apollo and the Phrygian Olympos. The composition recalls that used for Priam before Achilles, but the youthful appearance of the kneeling figure precludes this interpretation (De Lucia 1990, 196). In the background stands a third figure, bare-chested, draped from the waist down. On a second plaque, a figure with a kithara is recognizable as Apollo, and the woman standing next to him as one of the Muses. Another, narrower plaque shows

a standing female figure holding a rectangular box. Finally, the one we examine here: a winged female, nude down to the hips, stands next to another frontal female figure dressed in a short, knee-length chiton and high-topped boots. Between them stands a dog.

All the plaques have some traces of color, and though very little of it survives, there is enough to suggest that they were once brightly painted. Missing are almost all the heads, including that of the dog. Their deliberate destruction, consistently carried out, was perhaps due to a *damnatio memoriae* for religious reasons (De Lucia 1990, 246).

Fig. 11.1 *Nike and Artemis. Terracotta plaque from Pompeii, Insula Occidentalis, 150–100 BC (From Rediscovering Pompeii 1994, 308).*

The idea that the group represented the myth of Apollo and Marsyas (*Rediscovering Pompeii* 1994, 308) would agree with the iconography of three of the plaques, one of which could be interpreted as Apollo and the personification of Olympos, the place where the contest took place, another as Apollo with a Muse. Our plaque would then represent Apollo's twin sister, Artemis, with her hunting dog, next to the winged Nike, or Victoria, signifying the victory of the god. Nike and Artemis are regular bystanders in representations of the myth of Apollo's musical contest with Marsyas, which illustrates the danger of defying the will and power of the gods.

This was evidently the significance of these figures in the artist's intention. I would like to trace some of the influences on the iconography of these two figures, which in the eyes of the viewers were identified as Nike and Artemis, as an example of the way the geographical and cultural position of Pompeii in the art of the period between Rome and Magna Graecia allowed artists to draw from a rich and varied mix of influences, Greek and Italic traditions, and on ancient religious and ritual connotations.

The winged female on the left is nude down to below the smoothly modeled belly, revealing her pubes. Around her hips is tied a heavy, richly draped mantle, a himation, reaching down to her bare feet. Part of the mantle is wrapped on her left forearm and hangs down at her side. Her left hand holds up a fold of it, her right arm is raised to her head as if to arrange her hair. Her nudity is set off by her jewelry: she wears bracelets on her upper arms and a necklace with pendants on her neck. The most remarkable feature of her appearance is the set of wings spread out behind her, their crisply modeled feathers exceptionally well preserved. The dog turns toward her, lifting its paw to her drapery.

The figure is a descendant of the well-known Venus of Capua, a type that was extremely popular in Roman art for both nude images of the goddess and more modestly draped figures, such as the Victory of Brescia and the related figure of Victoria inscribing names on a shield on the Column of Trajan (Delivorrias 1981, 71–73, *s.v.,* Aphrodite, 7a, nos. 627–42; Hölscher 1979, 67–79, pls. 54–58). The huge wings, typical of Nike and of the Roman Victoria (Kousser 2006, 218–43), are also reminiscent of the wings on the demons so frequent in representations of the underworld in Italic and Etruscan art (De Lucia 1990, 196), a connection that has been suggested for the winged figure of Nemesis (or Vanth?) in the Pompeian painting of the Villa of the Mysteries, and a highly relevant connotation in view of the iconography of the figure next to her.

This frontal figure is sturdier in build and stance than her graceful nude companion. Her arms are bent, hands (now missing) once held firmly on hips. She too wears bracelets on her upper arms and a necklace with pendants on her neck. The hunting dog standing next to her is a frequent attribute of Artemis, as is the quiver, the top of

which is visible above her right shoulder. Her costume, appropriate for an active figure, includes a short chiton belted below the breasts, in the Hellenistic fashion. The crossed straps between her breasts are no doubt meant to fasten the quiver. Her tightly rolled mantle is tied over the chiton to get it out of her way; its ends hang down along her left side (some traces of a greenish color remain on the folds).

This is the dress of Artemis the huntress. It is the disguise adopted by Venus when she appears to Aeneas (*Aen.* 1.314–20), looking like a young Spartan or Thracian woman out hunting: "For from her shoulder in huntress fashion she had slung the ready bow and had given her hair to the winds to scatter; her knee bare, and her flowing robes gathered in a knot." When Aeneas wonders at her appearance, she explains that he is in Punic country, and that young Tyrian women normally wear the quiver and lace their ankles high with purple boots. A drawing by Claude Lorrain in the British Museum illustrates the formal meeting between Aeneas and his mother, who is dressed as a huntress (Fig. 11.2) (Gardner 1993, 22; Boyer 2001, 102, fig. 1). They talk, and it is only when she turns to leave her son that she reveals herself to him. He witnesses the epiphany as it takes place: the folds of her linen chiton fall down to her feet (*pedes vestis defluxit ad imos*), a perfumed aura envelops her, and she walks away like a goddess. Too late, her son recognizes his mother, the goddess of love and beauty (*Aen.* 1.402–405).

On this terracotta plaque we see the two images conjured up by the poet, Artemis the huntress and Venus, the most feminine of the goddesses. But in the *Aeneid* Venus appears as the Roman Venus Genetrix, Venus the Mother, fully dressed, rather than as the erotically nude Aphrodite of the Hellenistic tradition (for Venus Genetrix, see Vermeule 1977, 30–31, pls. 23–27).

Fig. 11.2 *Venus, disguised as a huntress, meets Aeneas near Carthage, Drawing by Claude Lorrain, 1678, London, British Museum (From Gardner 1993, 22).*

The high relief, the Classical style, and some of the figures, such as Apollo, have been compared to the late Hellenistic architectural sculpture of the temple of Hekate at Lagina (Caria), in Asia Minor (Stewart 1990, 226, 229, figs. 828–30). It has even been suggested that the right-hand figure represents Hecate. But the iconography is wholly Italian, and inspiration for the figure comes from the north and from the south of Pompeii, from Etruscan images of Vanth and South Italian Furies.

Artemis's crossed straps, or baldric, serve to attach the quiver, visible on her back. Crossed straps can serve a practical purpose in Etruscan art, for example, to fasten Daedalus's wings. But here they appear between her bare breasts. On this figure we can clearly see that instead of being fastened on her shoulders, the upper part of her chiton has dropped down and hangs below the belt as a long overfold, or *apoptygma,* leaving the breasts bare. Artemis is not normally shown with bare breasts. (It is odd that the dog, which is her attribute, is more interested in the other female figure than in his mistress. For a statue of Bendis with bare breast from Gela, see Gicheva 1999, 20–25.) Bare breasts with crosses between them were instead part of the costume of the West Greek type of Erinyes, or Furies, who were normally shown in hunting attire, with short chiton that sometimes left the breasts bare and with boots (for crossed straps worn over a chiton, with a ritual connotation, see Gicheva 1999, 20–25). Crossed straps are regularly worn over the short chitons of South Italian images of the Erinyes or Furies, while bare-breasted Furies are rarer (see a late-fourth-century Apulian red-figure crater with Theseus and Peirithoos, from Ruvo, Jatta Coll. 1094; Trendall 1978–82, 397.14; Carpenter 1991, fig. 128), examples of which appear on Hellenistic Etruscan funerary urns from Chiusi (Haynes 2000, 342, fig. 269; de Grummond 2006, 176, fig. VIII.3). Naked breasts and crossed straps were also adopted as a feature of the iconography of the Etruscan female demon, Vanth. She was shown in a variety of ways, with short skirt or long dress, with or without wings, wholly or partly nude – with bare breasts, like this figure, or pulling her dress aside to show her sex (Weber Lehmann 1997, 2000).

A handsome terracotta ash urn in Worcester shows her in a typical pose and costume, standing before an arched gate, the door of death or of the underworld, wings outspread. Her upper body is nude, except for the crossed straps or baldric with central ornament worn between the breasts. She wears a bloused chiton, boots, bracelets on her upper arms and wrists, and twisted around her neck a necklace in the form of a snake (Fig. 11.3) (found near Chiusi in 1858; Richardson 1964, 164–65, pl. XLV). Almost as ubiquitous in the Hellenistic funerary art of the Etruscans as her male counterpart, the death demon Charu, Vanth often has the costume but not the character of the Greek Fury. For she is a kind guide, like Hermes Psychopompos, helping the dead

Fig. 11.3 *Vanth before the door to the Underworld, Terracotta ash urn from Chiusi, Worcester Art Museum (Courtesy Worcester Art Museum, Acc. No. 1926.19).*

on their journey to the underworld and carrying a torch to light their way (Simon 2006, 61).

That the South Italian Fury and the Etruscan Vanth are related, and that the iconography of the Etruscan figure was adopted from South Italian images of the Erinyes, has long been recognized (Beazley 1947, 144; Brendel 1966, 230–34, esp. 232, referring to the Villa of the Mysteries [Lyssa]; Krauskopf 2006, 73, 81 n. 47). They could easily be fused in the popular imagination. They were fused in the literary imagination, as part of that blend of Hellenistic Greek art and traditional Italian imagery that was assimilated in Augustan art. In an article on Vergil's *Dirae*, Mackie (1992, 352–61, *e.g., Aen.* 12.845–52) finds reflections of the iconography of the South Italian Fury and the Etruscan Vanth in symbols and imagery of the *Aeneid*, especially in respect to Turnus, whose fate is willed by the gods, and whose doom is foreshadowed: "It may be important . . . given the more frequent occurrence of female demons in South Italy and Etruria than is found in Attic vase-painting, that Aeneas encounters the full force of the female demon figures only after he reaches Italy." In the *Aeneid*, figures of Vanth and the Furies announce impending doom, a connotation that is also appropriate for the story of Marsyas.

Of the Etruscan funerary monuments where the image of Vanth accompanies the representation of Greek myths, Brendel (1995, 380) says, "Their images pass by, almost as one; in all their apparent variety they each evoke the same memory, pronounce the same sentence: death is a rover, man his victim" (Mackie 1992, 354). The connotation of the two figures on the terracotta plaque from Pompeii, identified as Nike and Artemis in their Roman context, must have been similar to that of the iconography of such images of doom and of divinely fated destiny that lies behind them and gives them so much of their power.

It is not surprising to find such a rich artistic native Italian tradition together with the more familiarly Classical, Hellenistic figures so close to Rome, the center of art and power. In these figures, we still feel the vitality of the old religion and some of the potency of its images, which Vergil called upon to foretell the beginning of a new era.

Works Cited

Beazley, J. D. (1947) *Etruscan Vase Painting*. Oxford, Clarendon Press.

Boyer J.-C. (2001) *Claude le Lorrain et le monde des dieux*, exh. cat, Épinal, Musée Départmental d'Art Ancien et Contemporain.

Brendel, O. J. (1966) Der Grosse Fries in der Villa dei Misteri, *Jahrbuch des Deutschen Archäologischen Instituts* 81, 230–234.

———— (1995) *Etruscan Art*. New Haven, Yale University Press.

Carpenter, T. H. (1991) *Art and Myth in Ancient Greece*. London, Thames and Hudson.

Delivorrias, A. (1981) *Lexicon Iconographicum Mythologiae Classicae* 2, s.v. Aphrodite, 7a, 71–73, nos. 627–642.

de Grummond, N. T. (2006) *Etruscan Myth, Sacred History, and Legend*. Philadelphia, University of Pennsylvania Museum of Archaeology and Anthropology.

De Lucia, E. M. M. (1990) Le terrecotte dell' "Insula Occidentalis." Nuovi elementi per la problematica relativa alla produzione artistica di Pompei del II secolo a.C. In Maria Bonghi Jovino (ed.), *Artigiani e Botteghe nell'Italia Preromana: Studi sulla Coroplastica di Area Etrusco-Laziale-Campana.* 179–246. Rome, L'Erma di Bretschneider.

Gardner, J. (1993) *Roman Myths*. London, British Museum Press.

Gicheva, R. (1999) Die Gekreutzen Gürtel in der Kunst von Magna Graecia und die Thrakische Mitho-Rituelle Tradition. *Art Studies Quarterly* [Sofia, Bulgaria] 4, 20–25. In Bulgarian, with abstract and captions in German.

Haynes, S. (2000) *Etruscan Civilization. A Cultural History*. Los Angeles, The J. Paul Getty Museum.

Hölscher, T. (1979) Die Victoria von Brescia. *Antike Plastik* 10, 67–79, pls. 54–58.

Kousser, R. (2006) Conquest and Desire: Roman Victoria in Public and Provincial Sculpture. In S. Dillon, K. E. Welch (eds.), *Representations of War in Ancient Rome*, 218–243. Cambridge, Cambridge University Press.

Krauskopf, I. (2006) The Grave and Beyond in Etruscan Religion. In N. T. de Grummond and E. Simon (eds.), *The Religion of the Etruscans,* 66–89. Austin, TX, The University of Texas Press.

Mackie, C. J. (1992) "Vergil's Dirae, South Italy, and Etruria." *Phoenix* 46, 352–361.

Rediscovering Pompeii (1990) Exhibition by IBM-ITALIA, New York City. "L'Erma" di Bretschneider.

Richardson, E. (1964) *The Etruscans*. Chicago, The University of Chicago Press.

Simon, E. (2006) Gods in Harmony: The Etruscan Pantheon. In N. T. de Grummond and E. Simon (eds.), *The Religion of the Etruscans,* 61–65. Austin, TX, The University of Texas Press.

Stewart, A. (1990) Greek *Sculpture*. New Haven, Yale University Press.

Trendall (1978–82) = Trendall, A.D., and A. Cambitoglou, *The Red-Figured Vases of Apulia*. Oxford University Press.

Vermeule, C. C. (1977) Greek Sculpture and Roman Taste. Ann Arbor, University of Michigan Press.

Weber Lehmann, C. (1997) Die sogenannte Vanth von Tuscania, Seirene Anasyromene, *Jahrbuch des Deutschen Archäologischen Instituts* 112, 191–246.

Weber Lehmann, C. (2000) Anasyrma und Götterheit. In F. Prayon and W. Röllig (eds.), *Der Orient und Etrurien, Zum Phänomen des "Orientalisierens" im westlichen Mittelmeerraum (10–6 Jh. V. Chr)*, 263–274. Pisa, Istituti editoriali e poligrafici internazionali.

12

Reflections on an Interesting Historical Parallel: The Sikels of Fifth-Century BC Sicily and the Cherokee in Nineteenth-Century North America

Brian E. McConnell

This festschrift offers the occasion to reflect on methods of teaching and the impact that they have on both the thinking of one's students and the directions in which they point future research. As a graduate student in Ross Holloway's numismatic seminar in the 1980s, I remember his showing us a favorite film, *Disappearing World: Ongka's Big Moka, the Kawelka of Papua, New Guinea*. The film documented the last performance of a wealth-distribution ceremony called *moka* that was practiced in Papua New Guinea by a cinematogenic tribal leader named Ongka. ("Ongka, an endearing and charismatic tribal leader of the Kawelka tribe of New Guinea, has spent five years as an orator and negotiator to amass the 600 pigs and assorted valuables which he will give away in a festive ceremony, a *moka*. Unforeseen events threaten his largesse, stirring up rumors of sorcery and a threat of war"; Facets Multimedia film catalogue entry [www.facets.org/asticat]).The point of showing the film was to underscore that relations of wealth and power could exist in a nonmonetary economy and, therefore, that the creation of coinage, a refined system for measuring wealth, was a remarkable innovation that had a major impact on the way we live today. Ross never asserted that one could see the star of the documentary as a Phaidon of Argos or as a precursor of Croesus of Lydia or even that Greeks of the Archaic period acted out anything like Ongka's big *moka*; nevertheless, the parallel did set a tone for the study of antiquity in that it put humanity into the somewhat dry, lifeless objects we were studying, and it gave us a way to understand them in other contexts. The ethnographic parallel also gave us the notion that people can interact and use objects in similar ways over time, and that by seeing sometimes more complete pictures that are available in modern times we may have a sense for understanding the less complete pictures of antiquity and therefore be able at least to tell good stories about them. Ross once made the

memorable assertion: "I am Herodotus – I tell a good story." The point was that what we can know of antiquity is only a partial picture, at best, and what makes antiquity worth studying is a coherent picture that uses all of the information to the best extent possible, in the tradition of the early Greek historian.

There is nothing new about the use of ethnographic parallels in archaeological explanation, and the dangers of misapplying historical or contemporary sociopolitical or economic relations to ancient ones is well known in archaeological theory and cultural anthropology. It is worth considering whether or not the stories of mythology, legend, or ethnography offer an intellectual explanation for archaeological phenomena and historical events or a kind of allegory for other purposes. Modern interest in the classical world to some degree has been motivated by a desire to maintain a particular form of social order, and the impact that classics and classical archaeology have had on the phenomenon of nationalism and the political geography of the Mediterranean is considerable (see Stoneman 1987; McConnell 1989; Silberman 1989; Kohl and Fawcett 1996). Trying to understand antiquity in the first person, by looking at presumably analogous and accessible situations, has been a modus operandi in archaeological studies for a long time, and it has led to important stages in our understanding of the past, which are eventually tempered by time. Ancient Greek historians tend to present both myth and plausible historical narrative distinguished by the credible, human qualities of the protagonists. Thucydides, in his famous description of the early, "barbarous" (non-Greek) peoples of Sicily (6.2–6), passes politely and quickly from the one-eyed Cyclopes and the Laestrygonians of Homer to the legends of Sicans, Sicels, and Elymians, which must have described geographical, as well as geneto-ethnic, divisions among the indigenous peoples of Sicily by his time in the fifth century BC. Just over four centuries later, the historian Diodorus Siculus compiled his "universal" history with much attention given to his Sicilian homeland, and in it he tells detailed stories that intertwine legend and geographical fact. His story of the flight of Daidalos from Crete to the territory of King Kokalos in western Sicily (4.78) stands as the motivation for archaeological parallels drawn between Bronze Age chamber tombs with certain architectural features found in Sicily and built and rock-cut tholos tombs in Mycenaean Greece (see discussion in Leighton 1999, 184–86; there is an extensive bibliography on Sicilian rock-cut tombs, such as those at Monte Campanella [Milena] and other locations, which have a roughly circular plan, raised bench along the chamber wall, and cupola carved at the apex of a roughly conical chamber, as well as some grave goods with affinities to materials in thirteenth-century BC Cyprus and Greece; see Tomasello 1995–96). While the similarities are quite striking, an equal number of parallels can be seen in contemporary Sicilian domestic architecture (see McConnell 1987), but the scales of interpretation seem to be tipped in favor of the foreign origin precisely for the weight of the mythological narrative, which conveniently anticipates the later arrival of Greek colonists.

Greek historians tend to describe the history of art in terms of individual artists and architects, who either learn specific skills elsewhere or make innovations on their own, in order to make a linear story and one that is understandable in human terms. Was bronze sculpture not brought to the Greeks from Egypt by Theodorus, who together with Roikos also built one of the major iterations of the Temple of Hera on Samos? The later composition of Vasari's *Lives of the Artists*, for all its simple, linear progression and simplification, makes the development of art in Renaissance Italy a digestible narrative, and no one challenges the historicity of the protagonists. More recently, ethnographic parallels have been offered to explain the fundamental nature of Paleolithic art, the longest period in art history, first by Henri Breuil, and more recently by Jean Clottes and David Lewis-Williams (an extremely readable and thoughtful account of the development of Paleolithic art studies with an up-to-date bibliography may be found in Curtis 2006; for a discussion of methodology and the use of analogy, see especially Lewis-Williams 1991). Ross Holloway himself enjoyed using the parallel of the Kula trading ring in the seas of Polynesia as a convenient parallel, or model, to explain the presence of bossed bone plaques at sites from Troy to many locations in Early Bronze Age Sicily (Holloway 1981, 20; 1991, 12).

The issue of using ethnographic parallels appears once again in trying to flesh out what we know about the indigenous peoples of Sicily in the age when the Greek colonies had already been well established. A fair number of literary sources have enabled scholars to compose histories of the island's Greek cities and considerable archaeological remains that provide actual spaces in which visitors can experience the scale of their cities and sanctuaries; less information has been available for the lands of the indigenous Sikels and Sikans, although several archaeological sites, such as the monumental Late Bronze Age necropoleis of Pantalica, have been famous for over a century. Holloway was actually a pioneer in identifying the spaces of the Sikels – using literary sources, he identified the territory of the southern Sikels by plotting the paths of travelers across it on a map (Holloway 1990) – and subsequent field research has confirmed just how accurate his initial positioning was. In particular, archaeological research in and around the Margi River valley since the mid-1990s has brought to light extensive remains at ancient Paliké, the Sikels' most important sanctuary that was described extensively by Diodorus Siculus and other ancient authors, as well as other sites that relate to its lengthy occupation (research at ancient Paliké and other nearby sites has been promoted by the Soprintendenza per i Beni Culturali ed Ambientali di Catania under the supervision of Dr. Laura Maniscalco; a basic survey of the Paliké site and its background can be found in Maniscalco and McConnell 2003 and *Il santuario dei Palici* 2008).

Paliké in the Southern Sikel Heartland

The true core of the Paliké sanctuary was a series of so-called boiling lakes that were formed partially due to volcanic activity but mostly for the chemical interaction of water and limestone rock beneath the surface of the Margi River valley plain. Until recent industrial activity captured the significant quantity of natural carbon dioxide gas that was produced at this location, the lakes were known to boil, sometimes violently, in an area just south of a natural outcrop of volcanic rock that predates Mount Etna, Europe's largest active volcano, and that is known locally as Rocchicella di Mineo. Along the southeastern slope of this outcrop, set against the backdrop of a large grotto, a series of terraces preserve the remains of monumental structures that once served the Sikels and others who frequented the sanctuary (Fig. 12.1). While the area had been occupied since Middle Paleolithic times, the first monumental structures seem to have been erected in the Archaic period, roughly in coincidence with a literary reference that says the site had been "built up" in the seventh century BC. Large buildings with all the hallmarks of Greek architecture, including two stoas, a *hestiaterion*, and a monumental platform that extended the space covered by the dining facility, were erected in a later, second phase of building in the subsequent Hellenistic period, and the site seems to have been used as a sanctuary through at least the first century of the Roman empire (for discussion of the Paliké site in the context of fourth century BC and later population movements, see Pope, this volume) (Fig. 12.2).

Figure 12.1 *Rocchicella di Mineo. View from Stoa B (foreground) up towards Complex P, the hestiaterion and the natural grotto (Photo: B. E. McConnell).*

The long life of the Paliké sanctuary stands in contrast to the burst of historical information that is available about its relations to the indigenous Sikels. Diodorus Siculus (11.88.2–90.2) tells us that for a brief period in the mid-fifth century BC, an enterprising leader from nearby Menae (modern Mineo) named Douketios seems to have been able to form a league of Sikel communities that rose up in rebellion against the powerful Greek cities of Syracuse and Akragas. He moved a portion of the population from his hometown to Paliké, and it would seem that the sanctuary served as the seat of the Sikel league (although Diodorus Siculus never states so explicitly).

Although Douketios's time in power did not last long, his impact seems to have been great, not the least in the realm of archaeological explanation. While it is tempting and dangerous to associate everything that is Sikel with this prominent period in Sikel history, the remains themselves at Paliké and other sites seem to fit the picture of an indigenous community that quickly learned the ways of the colonists and over the centuries, and particularly in the fifth century BC, when there seems to have been a spate of building at both coastal and inland centers (the phenomenon is noted, also, by Tsakirgis, this volume). Not only is there evidence for major buildings at Paliké but also the social roots that nurtured Douketios (he appears as a kind of Sikel tyrant) seem to come forth in a series of Greek-inspired images of horses, deer, dogs, and warriors carved into the walls of two monumental chambers that lie roughly eight kilometers from Paliké at the site of Caratabia, which is discussed below (Fig. 12.3).

While structures and images do much to draw our attention to the importance of the Sikel communities in the strategies and drama of life in fifth-century BC Sicily, we still lack much information about the character of these communities, or even that of their most famous protagonist. We have no sense for the ethnic composition of these communities, although it seems increasingly clear that there was neither a great social or economic divide between the Greek cities of the coast and inland centers nor a Sikel identity that existed independently of the Greek presence. We cannot even be certain if Douketios was his true name or if was a term for an office or a role (the name "Douketios" may be little more than a title; the Sikel language, even though what we have of it is written in a Greek script, was part of the Italic language family, and *douketios*, like the Latin *dux* and its Oscan etymological cousins, may simply mean "leader"). In and of themselves, the available literary and archaeological sources leave the curious observer in a state of frustration, and for this reason it is tempting to look elsewhere for instructive parallels, even those that are distanced greatly in space and time.

Figure 12.2 *Rocchicella di Mineo. View of the hestiaterion (foreground), Complex P, and portions of Stoa B from atop the grotto (Photo: B. E. McConnell).*

Figure 12.3 *Mineo. Panorama of the Caratabia chambers with Mount Etna (Photo: B. E. McConnell).*

Native American Analogies

The story of Paliké is strikingly similar to one we can find in North America – that of New Echota, the Cherokee capital in northwest Georgia. New Echota was an experiment in urbanism of the Cherokee who had moved from the Appalachian regions of North Carolina and Georgia to found a national capital in the piedmont region of northern Georgia, near the modern city Dalton (a useful summary treatment of the site is found in Woodward 1963, 151–56, *passim*). At New Echota, from 1825 to 1838, the Cherokee founded a town with streets, public buildings, and one hundred one-acre property lots, many with private homes. The city had a newspaper, the *Cherokee Phoenix,* published bilingually in English and in Cherokee language by Elias Boudinot, a Cherokee who had attended school in Connecticut and returned to Georgia with his Connecticut-born wife, Harriet Gold. In town there was also a Christian missionary named Samuel Austin Worcester, who served as a teacher, helped to found the newspaper, served as federal postmaster, and lived in a New England-style home that still stands on the site today (New Echota is maintained as a State Historic Site of the state of Georgia and it has a manned interpretive center with extensive displays on local history and Cherokee culture).

The Cherokee created a government and a judicial system modeled on those of the U.S. federal government. For virtually all of New Echota's existence, the Cherokee were guided by their elected president, John Ross. Although Ross was only one-eighth Cherokee by blood, he counted himself and was recognized as a Cherokee 100 percent. New Echota seems to have been like many other southeastern towns in the first half of the nineteenth century, although it was subject to constant harassment by non-Cherokee homesteaders and gold diggers. The conflict reached a point where the Cherokee filed suit in U.S. Supreme Court against the State of Georgia's laws, which discriminated against them, and although the Cherokee actually won their legal battle, they lost ultimately to the voracious and racist ambitions of the new settlers, who were championed by then President Andrew Jackson. The subsequent removal of the Cherokee nation to Oklahoma in 1838 is known as the infamous "Trail of Tears."

Parallels between New Echota and Paliké are numerous. First of all, the name of each city is derived from an important religious site. Second, the leader is a charismatic figure. Third, the physical form of the center is modeled on that of the colonizers in a sort of architectural "globalization." Fourth, writing is developed as an important element of modern life – Sikel was written for both public monuments and odd dedications, which suggests that there were people who could read it. Finally, the presence of an indigenous world parallel to that of the colonizers was vexing to the latter who felt threatened by it, were desirous of its land,

and in the end were quick to eliminate it. Although we do not have a Sikel Trail of Tears per se, the population movements ordered by Dionysius I (which include movements of Greeks and Sikels from the territory of Lentini to new foundations such as Adrano) may be seen in somewhat similar light. Much like the Cherokee, who adopted foreign building forms and techniques, writing, and even a democratic governmental structure, the Sikels also seem to have adopted Greek building practices, a Greek script, and possibly even Greek-style political institutions, all for their own purposes. Clearly, there was no overarching Sikel state, like the developing United States led by Andrew Jackson of which the Cherokee nation was supposedly a part – and the Sikels were not citizens of Syracuse – but there was a Sikel frontier that stood in the way of Syracusan territorial expansion, and that presented a potential political and military threat as much as it presented the possibilities of alliance, markets, and a ready source of labor (with regard to indigenous labor on projects at Greek coastal centers, see Maniscalco and McConnell 2003, 175 n. 176; whether or not there was a Greek Samuel Austin Worcester we can only guess, but certainly the buildings and the material culture at Paliké suggest without a doubt that Greeks or Sikels quite familiar with Greek craftsmanship were present doing things).

At a deeper level, the figure of Douketios is somewhat similar to that of John Ross. Could the Sikel Douketios, like Ross, have really been a figure with family roots in both the indigenous Sikel and Greek worlds? Certainly, Greek-indigenous intermarriage has been discussed at length, and intercommunal rights were even part of the dispute between Selinus and Segesta that led to the famous Athenian Expedition that anticipated the Peloponnesian War at the end of the fifth century BC (Marconi 1997, 1094–95). Ross spent considerable time in Washington arguing the cause of his people to the various branches of the U.S. federal government. Perhaps Douketios, too, was not unfamiliar with the streets and the places of power at Syracuse; it is hard to believe that the treatment that he received, following a military defeat near Akragas, when he supposedly abandoned "his people" and fled to Syracuse – where, as Diodorus tells it (11, 92), he asked for and received not only clemency but even an exile's pension to Corinth – was not based on some fairly strong, possibly familial ties with important elements of the Syracusan citizenry. All of this remains supposition, but at this point I like to think of Douketios as a John Ross–style figure, firmly rooted in the world of his Sikel people but with an awareness and contacts well beyond the limits of Sikel territory.

But the Cherokee parallel is useful also in another way. The introduction to the rich history *The Cherokee,* published by Grace Steele Woodward in 1963, expresses a very clear ideology with regard to the adoption of colonial ways by indigenous peoples. In the very first sentences of the first chapter she writes:

> The emergence of any primitive Indian tribe or nation from dark savagery into the sunlight of civilization is a significant event. But in the case of the Cherokees, the event is both significant and phenomenal. Between 1540 and 1906 the Cherokee tribe of Indians reached a higher peak of civilization than any other North American Indian tribe. (Woodward 1963, 3)

This statement was written at a time when civilization was still equated with progress – a time when the western world, just as the Sikels, looked to the Greeks as standard-bearers of an advanced way of life. I don't know whether, in this day and age of the Global Village, we can or even should congratulate the Sikels in the way that Woodward congratulated the Cherokee. What did they gain by "going Greek"? What did they lose of their own?

Woodward makes another statement about the site of New Echota that we, too, could make about Paliké:

> New Echota's three public buildings, when finished, resembled those of near-by white settlements. But to the nineteenth-century Cherokee they must have seemed totally unlike those of the whites; New Echota's public building represented to them their nation's progress and its ability to carry out a well-planned educational, cultural, and governmental program. (Woodward 1963, 152)

And she goes on to write: "But to unprogressive Cherokees like Whitepath, all of the New Echota buildings were as ugly and depressing as the white man's customs." Such sentiments and tensions as these may well have been present among the Sikels from their various communities who frequented Paliké.

A single, simple model of acculturation, such as the over-used term "hellenization," certainly does not account for all the processes of change that were going on, nor the perceptions of those who were the protagonists. Irad Malkin, in a recent article on the colonial experience in Campania, employs the notion of Middle Ground Theory first developed by Richard White in regard to the Great Lakes region of North America (Malkin 2002). Instead of explaining the transmission of elements of Greek culture during the Archaic period as a matter of, as he puts it, pouring from a full cup into a waiting indigenous one, the notion of a Middle Ground involves creative misperceptions and accommodation on each side of the cultural divide. The popularity of Greek goods and particularly Greek mythologies among the indigenous peoples of Italy in this context would have been facilitated by the fact that the Greeks, in an ethnocentric yet strangely evangelistic way, considered their own worldview the norm: "What made it possible for Greeks to ascribe their heroic genealogies to others was precisely the quality that made them attractive to others. Greeks did not regard the heroic genealogies as Greek: they were simply heroic" (Malkin 2002, 157).

Perhaps we can see a Middle Ground at Paliké. The very name of the divinities, the divine Palikoi, has opposing etymologies that may be reconciled in this manner. The well-known story in Macrobius's *Saturnalia* (19.15–17) of the nymph Thalia, who bore twin sons to Zeus and who hid them in the earth to avoid Hera's wrath, seems to have a Greek origin that conveniently relates the boiling lakes to the Greek words παλιν ʼικεσθαι – the boys return again from the earth in the bubbles of the lakes. Yet the equally, if not more, attractive theory of J. Croon (1952) that derives the παλ- in "Palikoi" from Latin words for gray or clayey (Sikel is an Italic language) and relates the divinities in a direct manner to the quality and properties of the lakes themselves may be equally valid to the extent that it holds the first Sikel or at least pre-Greek notion of the nature of these divinities.

Whether the name "Palikoi" was adapted by Greeks to provide a hellenic explanation for everything they found in Sicily and/or whether the Sikels themselves adopted such a hellenic framework thereby, as Malkin put it in another context, appropriating another's myths in order to transform one's own status we shall never really know. Clearly, however, from the remains that have been unearthed at Paliké we are drawn to think of the sanctuary as a place where people, goods, and ideas mingled and were transformed. Perhaps the stoas, *hestiaterion*, and other buildings that remain to be revealed served not only the material needs of sustenance and commerce but also other spiritual and educational activities that may have taken place at this important center.

A sense for the sophisticated and at the same time eclectic character of Sikel education may, in fact, be gleaned from another parallel that can be established between the world of the Sikels and that of Native Americans a continent away. Already, we have mentioned the incised decorations in artificial chambers at Caratabia, near Mineo (ancient Menae) in the hills just to the east of ancient Paliké. (The documentation of the incised decoration and the protection of the site have been the prerogative of the Soprintendenza per i Beni Culturali ed Ambientali di Catania under the direction of Laura Maniscalco. The site is administered by the Comune di Mineo. A complete publication of the chambers and their incised decoration is in an advanced state of preparation by the author.) Despite their poor state of preservation, the quality of their execution and the importance that these illustrations give to the location are still quite evident. They consist in an array of horses, some with riders and one led by a standing figure, and at least two canines that are shown moving in a clockwise direction around the interior of the western chamber (Fig. 12.4). A larger, standing human figure holds a shield to the right of a door to a smaller, rear chamber. In the eastern chamber, at least three deer are shown in the same clockwise motion, while they turn their heads toward the doorway from the outside into the chamber (Fig. 12.5).

Figure 12.4 *Mineo. Caratabia western chamber, rear wall. Incised figures of horses, riders, and small, standing figure holding a shield (Photo: B. E. McConnell).*

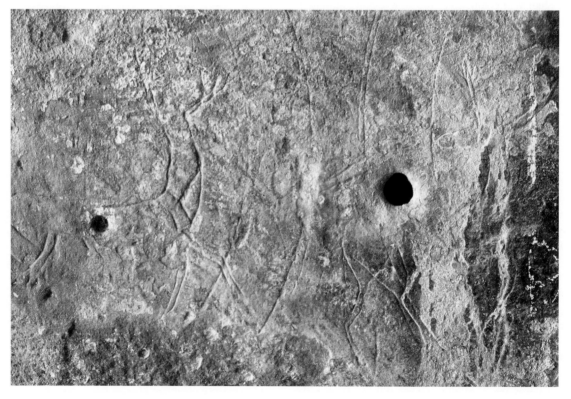

Figure 12.5 *Mineo. Caratabia eastern chamber, western wall. Figures of deer with heads turned toward the chamber entrance incised over other incised geometric decoration (Photo: B. E. McConnell).*

There are also circles and other motifs set in a kind of layering of incisions beneath these animal and human figures, and several smaller incisions may indicate the presence of inscriptions, which nonetheless are difficult, if not impossible, to decipher. Initial comparisons with motifs and compositions in Greek art, and in particular with Archaic ceramics, would seem to date these illustrations to the late seventh or sixth century BC. The technique of incising the outline and details of figures, in particular, would seem to be derived from that used in black-figure ceramics.

It appears likely that these chambers stand as *heroa* for distinguished burials of the Sikel elite, who did not have qualms about employing techniques, motifs, and compositions derived ultimately from Greek art. Nevertheless, it would be an error to read these illustrations as simply another aspect of hellenization. Such discussion inevitably results in a view of the Sikels, by virtue of the peripheral position attributed to their culture, as being at best only partially capable of grasping the subtlety and multiplicity of meaning that was achieved by good Greek artists. Instead, comparative research into at least superficial artistic similarities elsewhere may afford more useful interpretive schemes. One parallel that seems particularly relevant may be found in the art of the Plains Indians cultures of the United States and Canada. A recent study by James D. Keyser (2000) of biographic warrior art committed to ledger books in the nineteenth-century Flathead Indians of western Montana reveals a medium of illustration with striking parallels in formal terms.

The illustrations, copied on leaf-ledger books while Flathead Indians were in the company of Jesuit missionaries or other circumstances, are shown primarily by outline with relatively little attention to internal detail – the point was not to engage in figure study but to place significantly recognizable representations of people, horses, and other elements, such as guns, spears, shields, and items indicating rank (but rarely anything to indicate landscape or other setting) in compositions that told a specific plotline. The apparent simplicity of the scenes belies the specific narratives that could be told by a person familiar with the events and/or the protagonists. Keyser recounts the considerable degree of competition among prominent warriors in Flathead Indian society and the way in which one felt compelled to compete with the other, even on the field of commemorative art.

While we are not looking for similarity of hand, layout, or figural perception, the choice to use art as a means of immortalizing and communicating personal achievements and the eagerness to adopt such a medium alongside or in place of writing as a means of storytelling is quite comparable. In the context of indigenous Sicily, art itself was in many ways a product of the colonial-native Middle Ground, and the incised decoration at Caratabia was intentional visual communication on a monumental scale (the fact is that monumental art is lacking for the most part among the cultures of pre- and protohistoric Sicily; see Palermo 2005). It preserved memory through the image, and it probably served as a means of maintaining family prestige and social standing in the presence of those who visited the burial site. It would seem likely, also, that such an environment shaped the figure of Douketios, who, at least 150 years and several generations after the illustrations had been created at Caratabia, found the impetus to manifest the pride and independence of his people at Paliké. Certainly, the understanding that he would have had of his own people's past would have been shaped by his present situation, and he could only have been connected with the true past through "good stories" – stories that might have been told in the presence of ancient pictures on the Caratabia chamber walls.

Works Cited

Croon, J. H. (1952) The Palici: An autochthonous cult in ancient Sicily. *Mnemosyne* 5, 116–29.

Curtis, G. (2006) *The Cave Painters: Probing the Mysteries of the World's First Artists*. New York, Knopf.

Holloway, R. R. (1981) *Italy and the Aegean 3000–700 BC*. Louvain-la-Neuve, Institut supérieur d'archéologie et d'histoire de l'art, Collège Erasme.

——— (1990) The geography of the southern Sicels. In J. Descoeudres (ed.), ΕΥΜΟΥΣΙΑ: *Ceramic and Iconographic Studies in Honour of Alexander Cambitoglou, Mediterranean Archaeology*, Suppl. 1, 147–53.

——— (1991) *The Archaeology of Ancient Sicily*. London, Routledge.

Keyser, J. (2000) *The Five Crows Ledger: Biographic Warrior Art of the Flathead Indians*. Salt Lake City, The University of Utah Press.

Kohl, P. L. and Fawcett, C. (1996) *Nationalism, Politics and the Practice of Archaeology: On the Constructions of Nations and the Reconstructions of the Remote Past*. Cambridge, Cambridge University Press.

Leighton, R. (1999) *Sicily before History: An Archaeological Survey from the Paleolithic to the Iron Age*. Ithaca, Cornell University Press.

Lewis-Williams, D. (1991) Wrestling with analogy: A methodological dilemma in Upper Paleolithic art research. *Proceedings of the Prehistoric Society* 57, 149–62.

Malkin, I. (2002) A colonial Middle Ground: Greek, Etruscan, and local elites in the Bay of Naples. In C. L. Lyons and J. K. Papadopoulos (eds.), *The Archaeology of Colonialism*, 151–81. Los Angeles, Getty Research Institute.

Maniscalco, L. and McConnell, B. E. (2003) The sanctuary of the divine Palikoi (Rocchicella di Mineo, Sicily): Fieldwork from 1995 to 2001. *American Journal of Archaeology* 107, 145–80.

Marconi, C. (1997) Storie di Caccia in Sicilia Occidentale. *Seconde Giornate Internazionali di Studi Sull'Area Elima, Gibellina, 22–26 ottobre 1994, Atti 2*, 1071–120. Pisa-Gibellina, Centro Studi e Documentazione sull'Area Elima.

McConnell, B. E. (1987) Architettura domestica e funeraria nel Bronzo Medio. In *Atti del Convegno Storia e Archeologia della Media e Bassa Valle dell'Himera (3 giornata di studi sull'archeologia licatese, I convegno sull'archeologia nissena,* a cura di Pietro Meli e Giuseppe Cavaleri, Licata-Caltanissetta 30–31 maggio 1987.

———— (1989) Mediterranean archaeology and modern nationalism: a preface. *Revues des Archeologues et Historiens d'Art de Louvain* 22, 107–13.

Palermo, D. (2005) Le manifestazioni artistiche. In *SIKANIA: Tesori archeologici dalla Sicilia centro-meridionale (secoli XIII–VI a.C.). Catalogo della mostra Wolfsburg-Hamburg, ottobre 2005–marzo 2006*, a cura di Carla Buzzone con la collaborazione di Marina Congiu, 109–13 (German trans. 115–18). Palermo, Giuseppe Maimone Editore.

Il santuario dei Palici (2008) *Il santuario dei Palici: un centro di culto nella valle del Margi*, a cura di Laura Maniscalco, Regione Siciliana, Assessorato dei beni culturali, ambientali e della pubblica istruzione, Collana d'Area, n. 11, Area – Soprintendenza per I beni culturali e ambientali di Catania, Servizio per I beni archeologici, Unita` Operativa XII, Palermo.

Silberman, N. A. (1989) *Between Past and Present: Archaeology, Ideology, and Nationalism in the Modern Middle East*. New York, Henry Holt and Company.

Stoneman, R. (1987) *Land of Lost Gods: The Search for Classical Greece*. Norman, University of Oklahoma Press.

Tomasello, F. (1995–96) *Le tombe a tholos della Sicilia centro-meridionale*. Catania, Cronache di Archeologia, 34–35.

Woodward, G. S. (1963) *The Cherokees*. Norman, University of Oklahoma Press.

13

The Greek House in Sicily: Influence and Innovation in the Hellenistic Period

Barbara Tsakirgis

Introduction

The public world of sanctuary and agora has long been the preferred focus of most books and articles on the ancient Greek world, whether those dedicated to the archaeology of the mainland or those looking at Magna Graecia. In 1991 our honoree R. Ross Holloway published *The Archaeology of Ancient Sicily*, an important introduction for student and scholar alike to the culturally rich and varied antiquities of Sicily, the island dubbed "that America of antiquity" by Giuseppe de Lampedusa for its ancient multicultural heritage. In his book, Holloway surveyed the archaeology of ancient Sicily by period, and while he justly paid attention to the public architecture in the island's Greek centers, he turned a special spotlight on the Classical and Hellenistic houses of Sicily; I return to the subject of Greek houses in Sicily in the present paper to consider some of the varied influences that came together to create the forms and features of domestic architecture on the island in the Hellenistic period.

While many aspects of the Greek house on Sicily are intrinsic to Greek domestic architecture in general, there are several features of Hellenistic Sicilian houses that can be seen as evidence for possible influence from several sources, including the Carthaginian residents of western Sicily and North Africa. Numerous elements of the Sicilian houses can be traced to Macedonian palace architecture, which had a profound impact on much of Greek domestic architecture in the Hellenistic period. I am not the first to point out this link to Macedonian palatial forms; Hans Peter Isler (1996) first raised the question of it some years ago in a paper for a conference on Hellenistic palace architecture. In this chapter I review domestic architecture in Hellenistic Sicily and attempt to understand the varied cultural forces that were at work in the creation of houses on the island in the third, second, and first centuries BC; in some ways this paper is an expansion of Isler's initial idea to suggest means

by which Macedonian forms were transmitted to Sicily in the early Hellenistic period and superimposed on the Greek domestic architecture there. A focus of this chapter is the Hellenistic houses at Morgantina, a site where both Ross Holloway and this author worked as graduate students, but I also consider houses elsewhere on the island, especially at Iaitas (modern Monte Iato) and Megara Hyblaia.

The Greek houses of ancient Sicily follow many of the trends of domestic architecture established on the Greek mainland. This mirroring of the forms of the motherland should come as no surprise, as the island was Hellenized from an early date, with Greek colonists on the eastern shore in the late eighth and early seventh centuries BC and acculturation of the interior at least as early as the sixth century BC. What is remarkable is the alacrity with which both the Sicilian Greeks and Hellenized indigenous population of the island picked up changes in domestic architecture and interior decoration as they occurred in the motherland and in the Greek east. Buildings do not travel as do pottery, sculpture, and many other objects of material culture; nonetheless, the houses of the Hellenistic period in Sicily model forms soon after they were established on the mainland. The means of transmission of these innovations in private art and architecture have previously been touched on in the scholarly literature, but it is time to revisit the question to understand better how the Sicilian Greeks kept up-to-date in their domestic design.

Current scholarship on the Greek house takes a holistic view of the *oikos* by considering not only the architecture of the house but also the material found within, as well as the people who lived in the domestic space and used the objects recovered there (*e.g.*, Cahill 2002; Ault 2005). Given the circumstances of abandonment and destruction of many Sicilian houses, including those at Morgantina, there is very little material evidence for household activity left in situ for the scholar to consider the Sicilian house and household together. Household equipment is found where it was once used but only where there was a destruction and neither subsequent rebuilding on the site nor opportunity for rehabitation. At sites such as Olynthos in northeastern Greece and to a certain extent Pompeii, houses and their attendant domestic assemblages have been found in such a state, but similar finds of household material in context are quite rare. In many more sites the residents had ample opportunity to collect their most valuable and treasured possessions and to take them away; none of the Sicilian towns and cities where Hellenistic houses were excavated fits the model seen at Olynthos or Pompeii. This is not to overstate the case for Pompeii, as Penelope Allison (2004) has voiced appropriate caution about regarding Pompeii as an undisturbed site and has successfully debunked the "Pompeii premise." A serious impediment to using the small finds from most of the Sicilian houses for any spatial analysis is that the small amount of domestic material left in the houses is not in a primary or even secondary deposit (for discussion of the deposition of material in houses, see LaMotta and Schiffer 1999). Ample evidence exists that Morgantina, for one, was finally abandoned, possibly after a period when its population had already begun to decline, and just a few houses were used for both residence and the collection of salvageable material. After their abandonment, several houses were further sifted through by looters who not only took portable objects but also lifted some of the floors, as can be seen in both the House of Ganymede and the House of the Doric Capital. Because of the scarcity of undisturbed domestic assemblages in the Sicilian Hellenistic houses, this chapter focuses on the architecture and architectural embellishment of the houses and leaves aside consideration of the small finds. This is not to say that the artifacts are irrelevant, rather that the focus here is on architecture.

Before the Third Century BC

Greek cultural influence began in earnest on Sicily at the time of the colonization of its eastern shores in the late eighth and seventh centuries BC; certain remains of material from the Greek Bronze Age have been found on the island, but no Mycenaean influence is detectable in Sicily's early domestic architecture. This absence may be due to the fact that the Bronze Age Greek contact with the island was exclusively motivated by trade rather than by the need to accommodate a larger Greek population in colonies. This does not mean that trade was not a factor in the colonization of Sicily in the eighth and seventh centuries BC; in fact, it was likely the major motivator for the establishment of many of the first colonies on the island. But other factors were probably at work, including the desire to find more arable land than mainland Greece could provide to a burgeoning population. The first Greek colonists on Sicily brought their cults and customs from the mainland to their new island

home, but from the outset the newcomers were innovators. The regularly planned street grids in the settlements of Megara Hyblaia and Naxos would not have good parallels in mainland Greece until centuries after the first orthogonally planned settlements were laid out on Sicily (Megara: Gras *et al.* 2004; Naxos: Lentini 1984). The early houses found nestled in the grid of streets in the island colonies were small and architecturally unimpressive in the early colonial period, as were their counterparts in mainland Greece. One or two rooms opening to the south were the usual extent of these early western Greek homes. Courtyards were not built as part of the interior of the houses; rather, open areas to the south of the small houses probably served as domestic courtyards (Vallet *et al.* 1983).

The sixth- and fifth-century domestic architecture of Sicily, both in the Greek colonies and in Hellenized sites in the hinterland, reveals awareness of building trends that developed in the motherland. At settlements such as Monte San Mauro (Spigo 1979; 1986) and Akragas (De Miro 1979; 1996), Archaic houses were larger than those of the previous century and included interior courtyards as part of the built architecture of the dwelling; these changes may signal some of the same cultural and political trends that were at work in Greece itself, where house types are seen as reflecting the development of the polis and the changing social needs of the emerging democracies (Nevett 1999). The emphasis on building larger rooms on the northern side of the house was a tendency that existed from the first both in mainland Greece and in Sicily, as we can see in the early colonial houses at Megara Hyblaia, and it became more recognizable as the Sicilian Greek houses increased in size over the course of the late Archaic and into the Classical period. The placement of the more important rooms on the northern side of the house is a feature of Greek domestic architecture attested both in the archaeological record and in the written sources (*e.g.,* Xen. *Mem.* 3.8.8; Arist. *Oec.* 1.6.7).

In the accepted typology of Greek houses, most Sicilian domestic architecture falls into the category of the *pastas* house, with a broad corridor on the northern side of the court; the *pastas* both provided access to the parts of the house behind it and alternately served as a buffer to those rooms and the activities and inhabitants contained within them (Cordsen 1995). The *pastas* contributed to the flexibility of the use of space in the house, a fundamental principle that allowed the buildings to serve as the location for male symposia or the private daily living space for the family. *Pastas* houses have been recognized at Naxos in the fifth century BC and Centuripae in the fourth (De Miro 1979; 1996; Lentini 1984; Patané 2002). The *prostas* house, with a columned porch in front of the main living, was not a feature of Sicilian Greek houses.

The preceding discussion should not be taken to say that all Sicilian houses of the Archaic and Classical periods modeled the forms prevalent on the mainland. Native Sikel huts continued to be in use in many indigenous settlements long after Greek architectural forms were included in both the public and domestic buildings at many sites, including Morgantina (Leighton 1999). If houses both reflect cultural ideals and also direct social behavior, as has been theorized and accepted by many (Rapoport 1969; Hillier and Hanson 1984; Blanton 1994), then the coexistence of native trends in domestic architecture with those known better in the Greek world represents the fact that both indigenous people and newly arrived Greeks lived together at many of these sites. The decline and disappearance of domestic structures of Sikel type from many of the settlements represent not a disappearance of the Sikel people but rather an acceptance of Greek domestic forms that pushed out the earlier native types. The Hellenization of the Sikels is a far more complex issue than can be discussed in the present paper, but by the third century BC it was a process all but complete (for a more detailed discussion of the Sikels and Greek colonization, see Antonaccio 2001). It is not certain the manner of the Hellenization of the native peoples affected the way and extent to which they embraced Greek domestic architecture and the forms that those houses would take several hundred years after the influx of Greek culture.

The Third Century BC and Beyond

It was during the time of Hieron II, over much of the third century BC, that Sicilian houses reached their most impressive size and form, a period when eastern Sicily enjoyed the prosperity that resulted from the long and peaceful reign of the Syracusan monarch. Hieron II and his subjects benefited greatly from his wise pact of friendship (lit. φιλία; Polyb. 1.16.5–8) with newly powerful Rome, and by emulating the rulers in the eastern Mediterranean, Hieron established a true Hellenistic kingdom in Sicily (de Sensi Sestito 1977). While some have seen Syracuse during Hieron's kingdom as little more than a client state of Rome, my interest here is to determine not the political status of Syracuse but rather its place in the culture of the Mediterranean world in the third century BC. Hieron II's great wealth allowed him to model himself and his kingdom after the Hellenistic rulers and their realms in the eastern Mediterranean, but we must remember that Hieron was following in large part the trend established by his predecessor Agathokles. The great altar at Syracuse is but one example of Hieron's attempts to copy the munificence and grand architectural forms of the eastern kings (Karlsson 1996).

The houses built in the third century in eastern Sicily were likely also influenced in their plans and ornament by the contemporaneous homes built in the Hellenistic mainland and Greek east, and it was likely in the major city of Syracuse that the Hellenistic housing forms could best be seen on the island; the layout and decor of the palaces of Agathokles

and Hieron II must have had significant impact on the building of houses in Hellenistic Sicily. Unfortunately, the domestic architecture of Hellenistic Syracuse presents one of the greatest lacunae in our knowledge of Sicilian houses. With the supposition that some monuments in third-century Sicilian cities resulted from royal benefaction, it can follow that the houses of the elite in Hellenistic Sicily also showed influence, both direct and indirect, from the houses and palaces built on Ortygia and the expanded Hellenistic residential districts of Syracuse. Bell (1993, 332) has proposed that an example of this euergetism can be seen in the agora of Morgantina that was not only laid out in the time of Hieron II but perhaps also planned by Syracusan architects at the behest of the king and his wife Philistis. Unfortunately, with the exception of the area around the Piazza Vittoria in Syracuse, the Hellenistic domestic architecture of the city is largely unknown (Pelagatti and Voza 1976–77, 551–60; for other excavations that revealed domestic architecture, see Gentili 1951a, 156–59; 1951b, 261–334; 1956, 66–94). The excavated houses are limited enough in their extent to provide little confirmation of the idea that Syracusan houses provided some of the models for the domestic architecture of Hellenistic Sicily.

Third-century houses have been excavated at several Sicilian sites, notably Megara Hyblaia, Morgantina, and Iaitas. Each of these three towns had a different history of contact with Greeks and thus they present varied permutations of purely Greek housing styles mixed with both other imported forms as well as indigenous architectural and decorative features. The original grid plans of streets at Megara Hyblaia, which had been one of the first Sicilian colonies, survived into the early Hellenistic period and continued to serve as the framework into which were set the houses. There were two street grids at the site and they were not oriented in precisely the same direction. The result was that near the agora a series of trapezoidal blocks and spaces were created where the two grids meet; the trapezoidal plan of the agora of Megara Hyblaia also stems from the nonparallel orientation of the streets. The trapezoidal blocks have acute angles at one corner, but despite this irregular configuration of the residential areas, the Megaran houses adhere to many of the plans and elements found in Hellenistic houses elsewhere on Sicily.

Morgantina, however, began life as a Sikel site, inhabited by the indigenous people of eastern Sicily who lived in long narrow huts on the Cittadella hill east of Serra Orlando, the ridge where the Hellenistic city was later located. Hellenization took place at Morgantina over the course of the sixth century BC and into the fifth, through a process as yet not fully understood or agreed upon by scholars. Some, such as Erik Sjöqvist (1973), have proposed that Morgantina was a secondary Greek foundation, while others such as Claire Lyons (1991) have seen a less formal contact with the Greeks of the coast gradually intensifying and resulting in a largely

Hellenized population. More recently Jenifer Neils (2003) has suggested that Morgantina was an *emporion*, a commercial outpost established to aid Greek trading relations with the native population. Whatever were the initial processes of the acquisition of Greek cultural forms, by the third century BC, Morgantina was firmly in the political and cultural sphere of Syracuse, and displaying Greek architectural forms and artifactual assemblages. In the third century BC Morgantina probably paid substantial tax to Hieron, a levy based on the output of her fertile fields located below the ridge on which the town sits; two large granaries in the southern part of the Hellenistic agora attest to the quantities of grain raised by local farmers (Deussen 1994). Bell (1988, 338–40) has proposed that Morgantina was a Syracusan possession in the third century BC, a supposition that is followed in this paper.

A somewhat similar history of Greek acculturation may have existed at Iaitas, although the indigenous population was of a different stock: Elymian rather than Sikel. Hellenization of the northwestern quadrant of Sicily occurred later than it did in eastern Sicily in general and at Morgantina in particular. The fourth century BC was a particularly formative period during which the Greek battles against the Carthaginians and the activities of Timoleon eventually brought the western part of the island into the Greek cultural sphere, although evidence of the forms of Greek material culture in this part of the island exists before that date; the Doric temple at Segesta is clear evidence of that fact. Regardless of the process of Hellenization, by the third century BC all three sites shared a level of Greek culture significant enough to be seen in both the public and private architecture.

Many of the third-century houses at Morgantina, Iaitas, and Megara Hyblaia were large, well-appointed buildings with spacious rooms decorated with attention to the contemporaneous trends in domestic decor that can be seen in mainland Greece. While it is not the rule in third-century Sicilian houses, two courtyards were a common feature of the larger dwellings. These appear in the House of the Arched Cistern (Fig. 13.1) and the House of the Official (Fig. 13.2) at Morgantina (Tsakirgis forthcoming), House 49,19 at Megara Hyblaia (Vallet *et al.* 1983); in the later Hellenistic period a house at Akragas was built with two courts (Jones and Gardner 1906) and a second courtyard was added to Peristyle House I at Iaitas (Dalcher 1994, 19–20, 40–42). Almost without exception, there are architectural and artifactual differences between the two courts in the Sicilian houses. The southern courts in the houses at Morgantina and Megara Hyblaia and the eastern court at Iaitas were grander in scale and decor than their northern and western counterparts, with porticoes around at least three sides of the central open space; the eastern court of Peristyle House I at Iaitas (Fig. 13.3) boasted a complete peristyle on two stories. The supports for the porticoes in the better-decorated courts were often stone columns, as the preserved remains in the House of the Arched Cistern and Peristyle House I at Monte Iaitas prove, or pillars as seen in the House of the Official. As in mainland Greek houses, the Doric order was most favored on the ground story, while Ionic columns were used in the upper gallery at Iaitas. In contrast, less impressive materials and forms were used in the northern porticoes at Morgantina and Megara Hyblaia and the western court at Iaitas; columns made of annular bricks stood in the northern portico of the House of the Arched Cistern and only two

HOUSE OF THE ARCHED CISTERN
HIERONIAN PERIOD

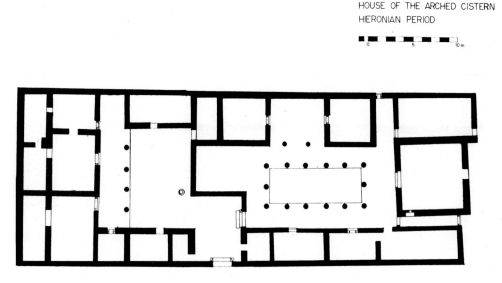

Fig. 13.1 *Morgantina, House of the Arched Cistern, plan.*

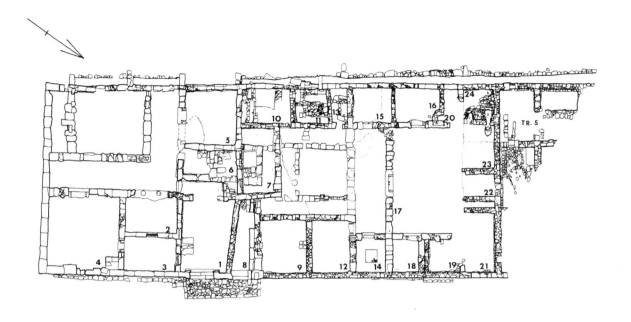

MORGANTINA

HOUSE OF THE OFFICIAL

Fig. 13.2 *Morgantina, House of the Official, plan.*

Fig. 13.3 *Iaitas, Peristyle House 1, larger courtyard (Photo: author).*

columns created a shed roof in the western portico of Peristyle House I at Iaitas. In both the House of the Arched Cistern and the House of the Official at Morgantina, the earliest forms of the northern courts had a single portico on the northern side, while the northern court of the house at Megara Hyblaia had no portico at all.

The doubling of domestic courtyards appeared first in mainland Greece in the fourth century BC, at sites such as Eretria (Reber 1988; Ducrey *et al.* 1993) and Pella (Makaronas and Gioure 1989); in the Industrial District of Athens two dwellings of originally fifth-century construction were joined and became a house with two courts at just the same date (Young 1951, 213–14). The Macedonian palaces of the fourth century BC also shared this feature (Hoepfner 1996), although the palace at Pella would eventually be enlarged by even more courtyards (Siganidou 1987; 1996; Chrysostomou 1997). As in Sicily, the houses in Greece with two courts displayed a marked difference in the size and decoration of the two open yards and in the use of the surrounding rooms; one court clearly served as the focus for public activities in the house while the other was the locus for domestic activities that were not generally displayed to an outside guest. This difference is seen clearly in the House of the Mosaics at Eretria and the palace at Vergina (Hoepfner 1996). In the former, one courtyard is distinguished by a complete peristyle, and the rooms around it include three with pebble mosaic floors. The second courtyard in the House of the Mosaics possesses neither feature. The western courtyard in the palace at Vergina is considerably smaller than the eastern, and none of the large *andrones* that characterize the southern part of the house are found here. Scholars have noted that the tendency to distinguish between areas for entertaining and those for domestic work appears in earlier Greek houses, but it is in the fourth century BC that it begins to have a distinct and recognizable mark on the architectural form of the dwellings.

Eastern Greek houses of the Hellenistic period were not immune to the multiplication of rooms and courtyards. House 33 at Priene was enlarged in the later Hellenistic period by the addition of a peristyle court, a change undoubtedly influenced by the trend already established on the mainland (Wiegand and Schrader 1904). The house was provided with a second courtyard in the Hellenistic period by a combination of the preexiting *prostas* house with its neighbor, an expansion much like that made to Houses C and D in Athens in the fourth century BC. The Hellenistic house at Erythrai has a similar duplication of courtyard space to serve as separate foci for private domestic activities and the entertainment of guests (Hoepfner 1999, 450–51).

Double courtyards appear in at least one Sicilian sacred structure, the agora sanctuary at Morgantina (Edlund-Berry 1990), and I once suspected that the double courtyard was an indigenous Sikel form that was used in various architectural monuments, both sacred and secular. The plan of

the shrine, which combined reverence for both the imported Greek Demeter and Persephone and indigenous deities, suggests that doubled courtyards might be a feature native to the island. However, given the appearance of two courts in houses in Greece earlier in date than the Morgantina shrine, it is more likely that the double courts appear in Sicilian houses as a result of Greek domestic tradition rather than Sikel cultural tradition. The doubling of courtyards is not widespread in Sicilian sanctuaries and is probably an anomaly at the Morgantina shrine rather than the norm.

In *The Archaeology of Sicily* Ross Holloway (1991, 148–51) notes the similarity between the plans of the houses at Morgantina with their two courtyards and the account of the Greek house by Vitruvius in *De architectura* (6.7.1). The first-century BC architect and architectural historian describes the Greek residence as having a peristyle court with a *pastas* or *prostas* on its north as well as courtyards with grander architectural form and associated rooms for entertaining guests separate from the quarters for women. Holloway's view is that Vitruvius based his description of the Greek house on houses in nearby Sicily, such as those at Morgantina and the other sites noted above.

While Holloway was on the right track with this observation, other features of the written text must be kept in mind. Some scholars have faulted Vitruvius for the differences that appear in his account and the preserved remains of ancient houses (Reber 1988), but more recently, Vitruvius has been recognized as being something other than a purely documentary source for the Roman, Greek, and Etruscan buildings he describes and discusses. Shelley Hales (2003, 25–29) has noted that, in writing about architecture, Vitruvius had in mind both the cultural context of the buildings as well as the social mores of the people creating and occupying those structures. By describing a Greek house that provided separate quarters for the men and the women, Vitruvius was recognizing the tendency in Classical Greece, especially Athens, to keep the sexes separate rather than necessarily detailing an actual Greek house. As many scholars have noted, actual Classical Greek houses effected this separation by having men and women sometimes use the same part of the house but at different times of the day. The Hellenistic houses with two courtyards do to a degree mirror this practice, but the separation is more one of public versus private life rather than strictly male versus female centers of activity.

In addition to the two courtyards, third-century houses at Morgantina, Iaitas, and Megara Hyblaia share another common feature: a three-room suite of rooms including a central exedra flanked by dining rooms, often of identical or nearly equal size. This type of suite is found in houses at many sites, not just the three mentioned above. A particularly fine example appears in the Southwest House at Morgantina ms. 1–3 (Fig. 13.4), and the suite in the House of the Doric Capital ms. 7–9 (Fig. 13.5) at the same site

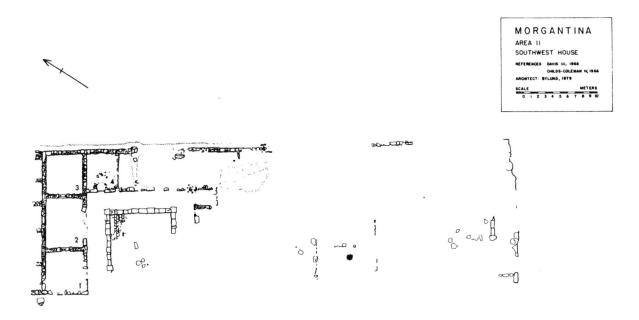

Fig. 13.4 *Morgantina, Southwest House, plan.*

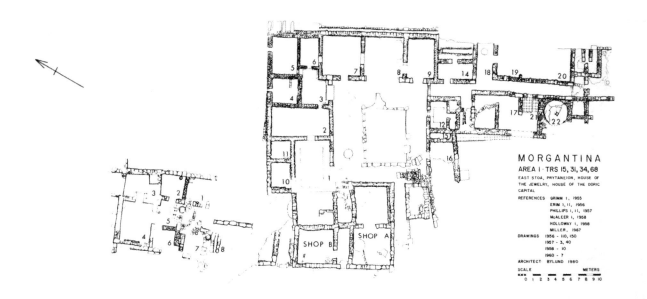

Fig. 13.5 *Morgantina, House of the Doric Capital and House of the Silver Hoard.*

was probably once equally impressive; the latter is now almost entirely stripped of its original *opus signinum* pavement. The planners of the Southwest House laid out the suite in such a way that the intercolumniation between two columns on the southern facade of the exedra aligned with the spacing between the columns in the north portico of the courtyard. The unobstructed view from the exedra into the court and vice versa from the court into the exedra is the Hellenistic precedent for the lines of sight from entertainment rooms that have been identified and studied in Roman houses and also for the houses on late Hellenistic Delos (Kreeb 1988). In Peristyle House I at Iaitas the spacing of the columns of the exedra is slightly less than that of the intercolumniation of the columns in the north portico of the courtyard, but are aligned for optimal view nonetheless. The line of sight must have worked in both directions; someone approaching the exedra from the southern and eastern porticoes could see into the exedra, and someone looking out from the exedra would have a good view of the carved stone columns and their capitals. If the three-room suite in the House of the Doric Capital at Morgantina once had evenly spaced columns in antis on its western side, the spacing of these too would have provided a view into the exedra by anyone approaching it from the entrance of the house.

This emphasis on the exedrae and their flanking rooms as the focus of display is further reinforced by the decorative program of the rooms. The central exedra of the suite in the Southwest House at Morgantina has a unique pavement of *opus signinum* with an allover net of swastika meanders (Fig. 13.6), in which occur six-petalled rosettes fashioned from specially cut lozenges of alternating white and green stone (Tsakirgis 1990, 432). Its two flanking dining rooms have only slightly less elaborate *signinum* floors with a simple border pattern surrounding a central panel of more elaborate design. The flanking dining rooms of the three-room suite in Peristyle House I at Iaitas have windows located on either side of the entrance to each room (Dalcher 1994, 30–32). The windows are distinguished by fictive frames fashioned from the wall stucco, a decoration that serves to draw attention to the windows rather than disguising them in the overall appearance of the rooms. The incomplete remains of the decorative program in the exedra in the House of the Doric Capital suggest that it may have been the most lavishly decorated suite at the site, with an *opus signinum* floor enlivened with poised squares fashioned from two white and two blue tesserae (Fig. 13.7) (Tsakirgis 1990, 428), multicolored plastered walls, and a molded stucco cornice that included both dentils and a bead and reel (Fig. 13.8).

The central exedra in these suites had multiple functions; it provided access, light, and air to the flanking rooms and served as both entrance and buffer to the spaces within. Its precedent can be seen in the anterooms of the *andrones* in houses of the Classical period, such as those in the houses at Olynthos (Graham and Robinson 1938, 176–77) and Athens (Graham 1974). Like many of those anterooms, the entrance from the courtyard into the exedra was at right angles to the approach to the entrance of the dining rooms, thus limiting if not totally obstructing any direct view from the courtyard into the flanking rooms or vice versa. The three-room suite in Peristyle House I at Iaitas provides information about the elevation of the rooms not surviving in the other houses. Windows in the wall between the exedra and the flanking rooms provide more light and air to be admitted to the dining rooms. There is no evidence for shutters that would have closed these windows, but they would not have been necessary to make the rooms more private, as the placement of the windows in the side walls would have limited any direct view into them. Similar

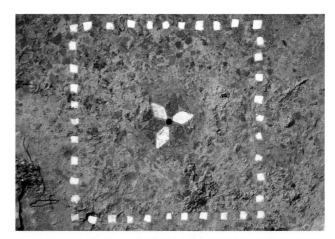

Fig. 13.6 *Morgantina, Southwest House, exedra, detail of pavement (Photo: author).*

Fig. 13.7 *Morgantina, House of the Doric Capital, Room 8 (exedra), detail of pavement (Photo: author).*

Fig. 13.8 *Morgantina, House of the Doric Capital, stucco cornice (Photo: author).*

provision for additional light and air can be seen at Eretria in the House of the Mosaics, where colonnettes were used to frame a transom space (Reber 1989; corrected reconstruction Reber 2007).

Like the double courtyards, three-room suites have parallels in the mainland and specifically Macedonian domestic architecture; V. Heermann (1980) was the first to identify the three-room suite as a specially Macedonian form. Several of the large houses at Pella, including the House of Dionysos and the palace contain three-room suites, as does the palace at Vergina (Makaronas and Gioure 1989; Hoepfner 1996). At both sites, the rooms of the suites are among the more richly decorated in the houses and palace and are located in the building with attention to the view that an approaching guest would have of the suite and that a departing guest would have of the courtyard and its adornment. In a study of the *basileia* at Alexandria, Wolfram Hoepfner has included a similar suite of rooms, restored with the flanking rooms serving as *andrones* that would accommodate seven klinai. An early Hellenistic anta capital of the Corinthian order is assumed to have served in the exedra and would have been an added element of decoration.

The decorative aspects of the courtyards and suites in Sicilian houses detailed above are examples of a greater trend toward *tryphe* (luxury) in Hellenistic houses that has been noted before. Elena Walter-Karydi (1994; 1996) has written extensively on the topic and she attributes the increase in domestic displays of luxury in domestic architecture to the dissolution of the power of the polis in the later fourth century and Hellenistic period and the consequent rise of the private house as the arena for the wealthy and powerful to advertise their wealth and taste to others. Her conclusions are applicable to Sicily in the third century BC, where the power of King Hieron II eclipsed that of the any elected official in Syracuse or another town. While public architecture as the setting for public life did exist in third-century Sicily, witness the monumentalized agora at Morgantina, it was in the houses of this period that dinner parties and luxury displays announced private wealth.

That Macedonian influence made its way to Sicily can be seen in a monument, not a house but rather a tomb. In the first years of excavation at Morgantina, Nekropolis I outside of the western city gate was briefly explored (Sjöqvist and Stillwell 1957). A shaft grave with a vaulted chamber receives brief mention in the preliminary report; regrettably no drawing or photograph of the tomb exists (thanks go to Malcolm Bell for reminding me of this tomb, which Bell hopes to explore more in the future). The architectural form of the tomb, as briefly described in the preliminary report, is reminiscent of that of many vaulted chamber tombs now known from the Macedonian world, such as the so-called Phillip's tomb at Vergina.

Parallels with Hellenistic Houses in Albania

Changing political circumstances in Albania in the past two decades have allowed that country and its archaeological remains to become a better part of our body of knowledge about the ancient world in general and the Greek house in particular. The houses at the important sites of Antigoneia, Apollonia, and Byllis in the ancient regions of Epiros and Illyria have been excavated and, more important, reported in accessible publications (Baçe and Bushati 1989, 5–48). Many of these houses display several of the features noted above in Sicilian domestic architecture. The three-room suite appears in a third-century house in Antigoneia (Budina 1972, 286–89; 1976, 327–46; 1988, 558; Ceka 1988, 227); the rooms are placed on the north side of the peristyle court as they are in many of the Sicilian houses. The square central courts with full peristyles, which were found in houses at Antigoneia, Apollonia, and Byllis (Ceka 1992), are very reminiscent of courts of the Sicilian Hellenistic examples. While the excavated and published examples of Hellenistic houses in Epiros are few in number, the limited parallels may stem in part to both limited excavations at the sites as well as scanty publications of those explored remains. The sharing of these features between the Epirote and the Macedonia houses suggests that, while the forms may have originated in Macedonian, the means of transmission of the forms to Sicily may have been Epirote.

But Wait, There's More: Possible Punic Influence on Hellenistic Sicilian Houses?

Evidence for Punic influence in the Hellenistic houses on Sicily appears to be less significant than the Greek, except for some indirect influence in the choice of paving type. Punic houses possessed some of the same general features of houses that were built throughout Mediterranean regions in antiquity, including a central open court and an entrance room, usually having the form of a corridor; see the fourth- and third-century houses at Kerkouane on Cape Bon that have these characteristics (Fantar 1985). It would be a mistake to see Punic influence in the courtyards of Sicilian houses, as the larger courtyards with colonnades in these homes more closely resemble Greek rather than Punic models. There are some vestibules in Greek houses that are corridor-like in form, but their configuration is attributable to limited available space rather than an emulation of Punic models. In her study of the late Hellenistic house at Tel Anafa, Israel, Sharon Herbert (1994, 17) has speculated that bathrooms were a feature of Phoenician homes, included within the house to serve cultural needs. Bathing rooms of a different type appear regularly in the Punic houses of North Africa and seem to carry on this tradition of including such a room within the confines of the house. Bathrooms are, in fact, found in some Hellenistic houses on Sicily. The

Fig. 13.9 *Morgantina, House of the Arched Cistern, Room 3, bath (Photo: author).*

House of the Doric Capital and the House of the Arched Cistern at Morgantina (Fig. 13.9) and Peristyle House I at Iaitas both have bathrooms in their later phases. It is striking that the bathrooms in both houses do not date to the earlier third-century phases of the houses, at a time closer to any possible Punic influence. Rather the bathing facilities are later additions that speak more of luxury accommodation. Monika Trümper (forthcoming) has recently examined the bathing facilities in Greek houses, and she too sees them as a manifestation of the luxury also displayed in the decorated pavements and spacious floor plans of the houses.

It is in the flooring of Hellenistic Sicilian houses that we can recognize Punic influence, albeit indirect influence. *Opus signinum* is commonly used in Sicily, mostly in houses but sometimes in public buildings. All of the houses at Morgantina (*e.g.,* the House of the Arched Cistern, the House of the Official, the Southwest House, and the House of the Doric Capital, all mentioned above) have many floors covered with the mix of crushed terracotta and inset stone tesserae

in a matrix of cement, as do the houses at Monte Iato and Megara Hyblaia (Tsakirgis 1990). The paving technique probably began in North Africa a century before it appeared in Sicily and was likely a response to the absence of locally quarried marbles for decorative flooring. The decorative patterns found in the *signinum* floors are derived directly from the Greek artistic repertoire and contrast with the randomly scattered tesserae most commonly seen in true Punic *signinum*. While the paving technique is Punic in origin, its use in Sicily should not be seen as proof of Punic influence in the Hellenistic houses.

Macedonian Influence on Sicilian Houses and Its Route to Sicily

That Hellenistic Sicilian houses display unmistakable influence from Macedonia has earlier been suggested by Hans Peter Isler; Inge Neilsen (1999, 79–80) in her study of Hellenistic palaces had also noted the similarity in forms, but she posited a transmission of form in the opposite direction. Both houses and palaces in Macedonia contain multiple courtyards and three-room suites; the partially excavated and incompletely published palace at Pella had five courtyards, although admittedly not all were built at the same time. The palace at Aegae/Vergina had two courtyards, and the two differ markedly in both size and architectural adornment as well as access to major rooms and suites. As in the Sicilian houses, one courtyard dominates in both size and decoration. The houses at Pella, as noted above, are huge in scale relative to both their southern Greek counterparts and Sicilian examples of domestic architecture, although the division and treatment of space in the houses at Pella is paralleled in Hellenistic Sicilian homes.

A crucial question here is the means of transmission of these architectural and decorative forms from Macedonia to the western Greek world. As I noted in the discussion of Syracuse, the two kings Agathokles and Hieron II were probably the impetus for the transmission of the forms. Agathokles's connection to northern Greece, both Epiros and Macedonian, can be seen in the marriage between his daughter and Pyrrhos of Epiros; Agathokles himself was wed to Theoxena, a Ptolemaic princess (Consolo Langher 2000, 191). Hieron's connection to the Hellenistic kings may have been a bit less direct but nonetheless a strong one. His aspirations to be seen as a king in the Hellenistic mold can be recognized in the building of the great altar to Zeus (Diod. Sic. 16.83.2), a western counterpart to the later Great Altar at Pergamon. Diodorus says that the Syracusan altar was a stade long, a size sufficient to accommodate a hekatomb, a kingly sacrifice of Homeric proportions. Hieron's silver litrae depicting the head of his wife Philistis bear a striking resemblance to Ptolemaic coins that depict queens such as Arsinoe. Hieron's euergitism has already been noted in the case of the agora at Morgantina. In another act of generosity he sent a shipload of supplies to Rhodes after it suffered an earthquake in 227 BC.

More telling for this discussion is Agathokles's and Hieron's love of private display. Agathokles constructed a banqueting hall large enough to accommodate sixty couches (Diod. Sic. 16.83.2). The building was clearly an attempt to emulate the tent of Alexander the Great that could play host to one hundred couches. In a passage much discussed because of its possibly serving as evidence of the invention of tessellated mosaic on the island of Sicily (Ath. bk. 5, 206d–9d), Hieron's private ship is described in great detail. While the vessel was ultimately used for another act of kingly generosity, to deliver wheat to Egypt to alleviate suffering during a famine, it was outfitted with luxury quarters; the officers' cabin could hold fifteen couches, and its floor seems to have been of mosaic and depicted scenes from the *Iliad*. Diodorus places emphasis on the wooden features of the ship, the doors, floors, and ceilings, probably because wood was so costly in many parts of the Mediterranean world, although parts of Sicily were well forested. The ship also held a gymnasium and gardens, a shrine of Aphrodite, a library, and a bath. Decorative fittings included colossal figures that appear to have been like the telamones on the Temple of Zeus at Akragas, and many paintings. The overall effect must have been much like that of the Liburnian galleys of Caligula, or of a modern-day ship in the Carnival cruise line. Many of the features of the ship mimic the elements of Hellenistic housing at its most luxurious. As noted above, baths, mosaic floors, and other expensive adornment are features of the Hellenistic houses in Sicily

Conclusion

The houses of Hellenistic Sicily were built in the Greek mold, following the forms developed on the mainland and in the Greek east. The similarity between the Sicilian houses and those of the motherland no doubt stem from similar cultural and social conditions at play on the island and in Greece itself. While some local innovation was at work in the choice to use *opus signinum*, the terracotta pavement developed in North Africa, the strongest influence flowed in from the east, both in the early history of housing on the island and later in the Hellenistic period. During the third century BC, elements of Macedonian palatial architecture made their way to Sicily, probably first to the palaces of Agathokles and Hieron and later to the homes of the Sicilian elite. These features, including double courtyards, three-room suites, and an emphasis on luxury decoration and amenities, highlight the need to recognize more fully how the Syracusan kings emulated the eastern monarchs of the Hellenistic period and produced art and architecture worthy to be considered with the palaces and houses of the eastern Mediterranean.

Acknowledgments

This paper brings together material from the final chapter of my publication of the Hellenistic houses at Morgantina and a paper that I delivered at a conference on ancient Sicily at Columbia University in New York; one of the other speakers at the conference was R. Ross Holloway. I would like to thank Clemente Marconi for the invitation to speak at the conference and for his encouragement to publish these thoughts on Hellenistic Sicilian houses.

Works Cited

Allison, P. M. (2004) *Pompeian Households: An Analysis of the Material Culture.* Los Angeles, Cotsen Institute of Archaeology.

Antonaccio, C. M. (2001) Ethnicity and colonization. In I. Malkin (ed.), *Ancient Perceptions of Greek Ethnicity,* 113–57. Cambridge, Mass., and London, Harvard University Press.

Ault, B. A. (2005) *The Excavations at Halieis: Vol. 2: The Houses: The Organization and Use of Domestic Space.* Bloomington, Indiana University Press.

Baçe, A. and Bushati, V. (1989) Aperçu sur l'habitation prehistorique et antique en Illyrie et en Epire. *Monumentet* 37, 5–48.

Bell, M. (1988) Excavations at Morgantina, 1980–1985: Preliminary report 12. *American Journal of Archaeology* 92, 313–42.

——— (1993) Observations on western Greek stoas. In *Eius virtutis studiosi: Classical and Post-Classical Studies in Memory of Frank E. Brown,* 327–41. Hanover and London, University Press of New England.

Blanton, R. E. (1994) *Houses and Households: A Comparative Study.* New York and London, Plenum Press.

Brem, H. (2000) *Das Peristylhaus 1 von Iaitas: Wand-und Bodendekorationen.* Lausanne, Editions Payot.

Budina, D. (1972) Antigonée (French summary of Albanian). *Iliria* 2, 269–378.

——— (1976) Antigonée d'Epire (French summary of Albanian). *Iliria* 4, 327–46.

——— (1988) Antigoneia, Eine Stadt der hellenistischen Periode. *Akten des 13 Internationalen Kongresses für klassische Archäologie,* 558–59. Mainz am Rhein, Philipp von Zabern.

Cahill, N. D. (2002) *Household and City Organization at Olynthus.* New Haven, Yale University Press.

Ceka, N. (1988) Städtebau in der vorrömischen Periode in Südillyrien. *Akten des 13 Internationalen Kongresses für klassische Archäologie,* 215–29. Mainz am Rhein, Philipp von Zabern.

——— (1992) L'urbanistique et les habitations a Byllis. *Iliria* 22, 73–96.

Chrysostomou, P. (1997) Το Ανακτορο της Πελλας. *ΑΕΜΘ* 10A (1996), 105–42.

Consolo Langher, S. N. (2000) *Agatocle. Da capoparte fondatore di un regno tra Cartagine e I Diadochi.* Messina, University of Messina.

Cordsen, A. (1995) The pastas house in Archaic Greek Sicily. In T. Fischer-Hansen (ed.), *Ancient Sicily (Acta Hyperborea 6),* 103–21. Copenhagen, Museum Tusculum Press.

Dalcher, K. (1994) *Studia Ietina VI: Das Peristylhaus 1 von Iaitas: Architektur und Baugeschichte.* Zurich, Archaeological Institute of the University of Zurich.

De Miro, E. (1979) La casa greca in Sicilia: Testimonianze nella Sicilia centrale dal VI al III sec. a.C. In *Φιλιας Χαριν: Miscellanea di studi classici in onore di Eugenio Manni,* 707–37. Rome, G. Bretschneider.

———— (1996) La casa greca in Sicilia. In F. D'Andria and K. Mannino (eds.), *Ricerche sulla casa in Magna Grecia in Sicilia,* 17–40. Archeologia e Storia 5. Galatina, Congedo editore.

de Sensi Sestito, G. (1977) *Gerone II, un monarca ellenistico in Sicilia.* Palermo, Editrice Sophia.

Deussen, P. W. (1994) The granaries of Morgantina and the *lex hieronica.* In *Le ravitaillement en blé de Rome at des centres urbains des débuts de la république jusqu'au haut empire,* 231–35. Naples and Rome, Centre Jean Bérard and École française de Rome.

Ducrey, P., Metzger I. R., and Reber, K. (1993) *Eretria: Fouilles et Recherches, vol. 8. Le Quartier de la Maison aux Mosaïques.* Lausanne, Editions Payot.

Edlund-Berry, I. (1990) The central sanctuary at Morgantina (Sicily). Problems of interpretation and chronology. *Scienze dell'Antichità: Storia, archeologia, antropologia* 3–4, 327–38.

Fantar, M. (1985) *Kerkouane, Cité punique du Cap Bon.* Tunis, Institut national d'archéologie et d'art.

Gentili, G. V. (1951a) Siracusa (Piazza della Vittoria). Resti di abitazioni sotto l'edificio occidentale delle Case Popolari. *Notizie degli scavi di antichità* ser. 8, 5, 156–59.

———— (1951b) Siracusa. Scoperte nelle due nuove Circonvallazione, ora Viale P. Orsi, e la Via Archeologica, o Viale F. S. Cavallari. *Notizie degli scavi di antichità* ser. 8, 5, 261–334.

———— (1956) Siracusa. Contributo alla topografia dell'antica città. *Notizie degli scavi di antichità* ser. 8, 10, 94–194.

Graham, J. W. (1974) Houses of Classical Athens. *Phoenix* 28, 45–54.

Graham, J. W. and Robinson, D. M. (1938) *Excavations at Olynthus, Part 8: The Hellenic House.* Baltimore, Johns Hopkins University.

Gras, M., Tréziny, H., and Broise, H. (2004) *Mégara Hyblaea 5: La ville archaïque. L'espace urbain d'une cité grecque de Sicile orientale.* Rome, École française de Rome.

Hales, S. (2003) *The Roman House and Social Identity.* Cambridge, Cambridge University Press.

Heermann, V. (1980) Studien zur Makedonische Profanarchitektur. Ph.D. dissertation, University of Erlangen.

Herbert, S. (1994) *Tel Anafa I: Final Report on Ten Years of Excavation at a Hellenistic and Roman Settlement in Northern Israel.* Ann Arbor, Kelsey Museum.

Hillier, B. and Hanson, J. (1984) *The Social Logic of Space.* Cambridge and New York, Cambridge University Press.

Hoepfner, W. (1996) Zum Typus der Basileia und der königlichen Andrones. In W. Hoepfner and G. Brands (eds.), *Basileia. Die Paläste der hellenistischen Könige,* 1–43. Mainz am Rhein, Philipp von Zabern.

———— (ed.) (1999) *Geschichte des Wohnens, Band 1. 5000 v. Chr.–500 n. Chr. Vorgeschichte, Frühgeschichte, Antike.* Stuttgart, Deutsche Verlags-Anstalt.

Holloway, R. R. (1991) *The Archaeology of Ancient Sicily.* London and New York, Routledge.

Isler, H.-P. (1996) Einflusse der makedonischen Palastarchitektur in Sizilien? In W. Hoepfner and G. Brands (eds.), *Basileia: Die Paläste der hellenistischen Könige,* 252–57. Mainz am Rhein, Philipp von Zabern.

Jones, R. P. and Gardner, E. A. (1906) Notes on a recently excavated house at Girgenti. *Journal of Hellenic Studies* 26, 207–12.

Kreeb, M. (1988) *Untersuchungen zur figürlichen Ausstattung delischer Privathäuser.* Chicago, Ares Publishers.

LaMotta, V. M. and Schiffer, M. B. (1999) Formation processes of house floor assemblages. In P. M. Allison (ed.), *The Archaeology of Household Activities,* 19–29. London, Routledge.

Leighton, R. (1999) *Sicily before History: An Archeological Survey from the Palaeolithic to the Iron Age.* Ithaca, Cornell University Press.

Lentini, M. C. (1984) Naxos: Esplorazione nell'abitato proto-arcaico orientale—casa a pastas n. 1. *Kokalos* 30–31, 809–38.

Lyons, C. L. (1991) Modalità di acculturazione a Morgantina. *Bollettino di Archeologia* 11–12, 1–10.

Karlsson, L. (1996) The altar of Hieron at Syracuse: A discussion of its function. *Opuscula romana* 21, 83–87.

Makaronas, Ch. and Gioure, E. (1989) *Οι οικίες Αρπαγής τνης Ελένης και Διόνυσου της Πέλλας.* Athens, Athenais Archaiologiki Hetaireias.

Neils, J. (2003) City versus cemetery: The imported pottery of Archaic Morgantina. In B. Schmaltz and M. Söldner (eds.), *Griechische Keramik im kulturellen Kontext,* 46–48. Münster, Scriptorum.

Nevett, L. (1999) *House and Society in the Ancient Greek World.* Cambridge, Cambridge University Press.

Nielsen, I. (1999) *Hellenistic Palaces: Tradition and Renewal.* 2nd ed. Studies in Hellenistic Civilization 5. Aarhus, Aarhus University Press.

Patané, R. P. A. (2002) Una casa del IV sec. a.C. a Centuripae. In Giovanni Rizza (ed.), *Scavi e ricerche a Centuripe,* 105–14. Catania, Consiglio Nazionale delle Ricerche I.B.A.M. – Sezione di Catania.

Pelagatti, P. and Voza, G. (1976–77) L'attività della Soprintendenza alla antichità della Sicilia orientale. *Kokalos* 22–23, 519–85

Rapoport, A. (1969) *House Form and Culture.* Englewood Cliffs, N.J., Prentice-Hall.

Reber, K. (1988) *Aedificia graecorum*: Zu Vitruvs Beschreibung des griechischen Hauses. *Archäologischer Anzeiger* 103, 653–66.

———— (1989) Zur architektonischen Gestaltung der Andrones in den Häusern von Eretria. *Antike Kunst* 32, 3–7.

———— (1998) *Eretria: Ausgrabungen und Forschungen X. Die klassischen und hellenistischen Wohnhäuser im Westquartier.* Lausanne, Editions Payot.

———— (2007) Living and housing in Classical and Hellenistic Eretria. In R. Westgate, N. Fisher, J. Whitley (eds.), *Building Communities: House, Settlement and Society in the Aegean and Beyond,* 281–88. London, British School at Athens.

Siganidou, M. (1987) Το ανακτορικό συγκρότημα της Πέλλας. *ΑΕΜΘ* 1, 119–24.

———— (1996) Die Basileia von Pella. In W. Hoepfner and G.

Brands (eds.), *Basileia. Die Paläste der hellenistischen Königen,* 144–47. Mainz am Rhein, Philipp von Zabern.

Sjöqvist, E. (1973) *Sicily and the Greeks.* Ann Arbor, University of Michigan Press.

Sjöqvist, E. and Stillwell, R. (1957) Excavations at Serra Orlando: Preliminary report 1. *American Journal of Archaeology* 61, 151–59.

Spigo, U. (1979) Monte San Mauro, scavi 1978: Aspetti di un centro greco della Sicilia Interna. *Bollettino d'arte* 64, 21–42.

——— (1986) L'anonimo centro greco di Monte San Mauro di Caltagirone nel quadro dell'arcaismo siceliota: Prospettive di ricerca. *Miscellanea greca e romana* 10, 1–32.

Trümper, M. (Forthcoming) Bathing culture in late Hellenistic housing. In C. Lang-Auinger *et al.* (eds.), *Urban Living in the Eastern Mediterranean, 4th Century BC–1st Century AD.*

Tsakirgis, B. (1990) The decorated pavements of Morgantina: The *opus signinum. American Journal of Archaeology* 94, 425–43.

——— (Forthcoming) *Morgantina Studies 7: The Domestic Architecture of Morgantina in the Hellenistic and Roman Periods.* Princeton, Princeton University Press.

Vallet, G., Villard, F., Auberson, P. (1983) *Megara Hyblaea 3: Guida agli scavi.* Rome, École française de Rome.

Walter-Karydi, E. (1994) Die Nobilitierung des Wohnhauses. Lebensform und Architektur im spätklassischen Griechenland. *Xenia* 35, 5–81.

——— (1996) Die Noblitierung des griechischen Wohnhauses in der spätklassischen Zeit. In W. Hoepfner and G. Brands (eds.), *Basileia: Die Paläste der Hellenistischen Könige,* 56–61. Mainz am Rhein, Philipp von Zabern.

Wiegand, T. and Schrader, H. (1904) *Priene: Ergebnisse der Ausgrabungen und Untersuchungen in den Jahren 1895–1898.* Berlin, G. Reimer.

Young, R. S. (1951) An industrial district of ancient Athens. *Hesperia* 20, 135–288.

among scholars, Koss, however, is never dogmatic but always open to new ideas

SECTION III
INTRODUCTION

Coins as Culture: Art and Coinage from Sicily

Carmen Arnold-Biucchi

The Table of Contents and R. Ross Holloway's bibliography (see Cova, this volume) will already have alerted the reader – if needed – to the extraordinary breadth of Ross's work, his impact on his students and colleagues in the United States and abroad. This section is dedicated to coins and this brief essay will try to do justice to the numismatic achievements of the honoree.

R. Ross Holloway's numismatic career spans over half a century: Ross went around the world of coins in fifty years, from the turtles of Aigina (1960) to the griffins and horses of Syracuse (2007, since he convincingly demonstrated that this is where the KAINON coinage must have been minted) with numerous side trips into the Roman world, in particular in the introduction of the denarius and in Constantinian history. He has lost none of his contagious enthusiasm nor his powerful momentum, almost like an Homeric hero. As with Alexander the Great, one can wonder whether he purposely set out to conquer the world [of numismatics] or whether he was brought there by the serendipity of his own strength, and it doesn't really matter; what matters are the results.

Holloway's first numismatic work is a "traditional" mint study of the early coinage of Aigina, based mainly on the die analysis and classification of the reverse punches as well as on hoard evidence. After all he took the ANS Graduate Seminar in 1957 and was duly indoctrinated in numismatic methodology by Sydney P. Noe and Margaret Thompson. One of the aims of his study was to establish a chronology and a historical context for one of the three first major mints that started issuing coins in mainland Greece in the 6th century BC. Ross never lost his interest in the beginning of coinage as his articles show: for Greek coinage "La ricerca attuale sull'origine della moneta" (1978), "The Date of the Earliest Coins" (1984) "The Early Owls of Athens and the Persians" (1999), "Why Coins in Greece?" (2004), and for Roman coinage: "Early Roman Coinage" (1990), "The Romano-Campanian Coinage" (1992). These are "big questions" for numismatists and they have generated long and sometimes bitter debates among scholars. Ross, however, is never dogmatic but always open to new suggestions and respectful of other points of view. I may not agree that the *Wappenmünzen* were not struck in Athens but in rural Attica and that the owl tetradrachms started under Peisistratos, but I find his approach and his readiness to compromise and revise his opinions refreshing and stimulating. No doubt his students have learned a lot from his way of thinking.

Holloway has written on many topics but his major numismatic contribution is to the coinages of Sicily and in particular of Syracuse, his great love. He published a die study of the last Greek king: *The Thirteen-Months Coinage of Hieronymos of Syracuse,* Antike Münzen und Geschnittene Steine III, Walter De Gruyter (Berlin, 1969). Perhaps more importantly, Holloway was from the beginning attracted to and intrigued by an area of Sicilian numismatics that had previously been less studied: bronze coinage and the "lesser" coinages of smaller denominations and smaller mints. In 1962 he published his "Eagle and Fulmen on the Coins of Syracuse" a critical review of P. R. Franke, *Die antiken Münzen von Epirus* (Wiesbaden 1961) arguing, on hoard evidence and on excavation coins found in context, that the ΔΙΟΣ ΕΛΛΑΝΙΟΥ issues did not belong to Pyrrhus but to Hiketas. It was already clear then that Ross would not be satisfied just working along traditional paths, publishing new material and die studies, though he produced his share of service to the discipline in the form of catalogues, among others *The Frederick M. Watkins Collection* (1973), *The Wheaton College Collection,* (ACNAC 1981), a revision of *The Coinage of Terina* with G. K. Jenkins, Edizioni Arte e Moneta (Bellinzona 1982). Ross is interested in coins as integral works of art within the broader context of Greek art and culture.

Everybody's favorite article, I believe, and perhaps the most influential to this day (see K. Rutter's contribution to this volume) is: "La stuttura delle emissioni di Siracusa nel periodo dei "signierende Künstler" (1977). Here Holloway re-examined L. O. Th. Tudeer's 1913 corpus *Die Tetradrachmenprägung von Syrakus in der Periode der signierenden Künstler* and determined on the basis of the symbols in the exergue of the coins, that the mint of Syracuse was organized into different workshops operated perhaps by private individuals under state contract; the major engravers were in charge: Kimon of the ear of grain workshop and Euainetos of that of the dolphin. His new arrangement has opened the way for a sounder and more precise chronology.

Holloway's interest in the bronze coinages of Syracuse and other Sicilian cities was equally ground breaking. Perhaps it originated from his experience in the excavation campaigns at Morgantina with Princeton University (see *Morgantina Studies II: The Coins* (Princeton 1989). It led to important publications on the beginning of bronze coinage at Syracuse (*CISN* 1979, *Italiam Fato Profugi* 1996), on the bronze coinage of Agathokles (*Essays Thompson* 1979) and of the earlier 4th century BC, the period between Dion and Timoleon (*Quaderni Ticinesi Numismatica e Antichitá Classiche* 1991). By publishing numerous hoards (*Ripostigli del Museo Archeologico di Siracusa,* Naples 1989) Holloway has also helped clarify the presence of Corinthian Pegasi in Sicily and date it before the arrival of Timoleon.

Holloway came to numismatics through archaeology, I think, and his approach to material culture in general has always been broad and comparative: he can do the die study but never forgets to relate it to style and art. Numismatics is not a discipline in and of itself but a way to better understand the art and culture of the Ancient Mediterranean. Like his great friend Tony Hackens, Holloway has a talent for languages and succeeded in establishing enduring international contacts, especially with Italy. He was the President of the Centro Internazionale di Studi Numismatici in Naples from 1980 to 1986 and he has represented American numismatics abroad for more than fifty years.

Of the three contributions in this numismatic section, one is written by a student of Holloway (Pope) and the other two by longtime collaborators. M. B. Borba Florenzano's article illustrates the international ramifications and ties just mentioned. Ross's teaching has helped foster interest in Sicilian coinage as far as Brazil. Spencer Pope's essay on the type of the butting bull in Sicily and the coinage of Piakos reflects Holloway's interest in the interpretation of coin types and in the smaller but important local mints in Sicily. Keith Rutter's thorough and careful discussion of the dating of the signed coins of Sicily at the end of the fifth century BC in many ways can be seen as a continuation of Holloway's 1977 article on the structure of Syracusan coin issues mentioned above.

The number of numismatic papers in *KOINE* is indirectly proportional to the importance and role of numismatics in Holloway's career, as well as to the number of friends and fellow numismatists Ross has all over the world. I have tried to highlight some of Ross's great contributions to numismatics. In conclusion I would like to add that even more important than the scholar is the man, the teacher, the supporting enthusiastic colleague.

14

Dating the Period of the "Signing Artists" of Sicilian Coinage

Keith Rutter

The end of the fifth century BC in Sicily was a period when, to an extent unparalleled in Greek coinage elsewhere, the engravers of dies for coins of Syracuse and other cities frequently signed their work. These are the famous "signing artists." Ross Holloway has enriched our understanding of this complex phenomenon from several points of view, both the technically numismatic (*e.g.*, 1974–75) and with regard to broader themes such as the artistic achievements and role of the engravers themselves (*e.g.*, 1978). In fact, with his usual perspicacity, Holloway (1998, 11) anticipated the conclusions of this paper when he wrote "the signing master coins probably were issued over a short period of time, possibly between the defeat of the Athenian invasion of Sicily in 413 BC and the coup d'état that brought Dionysius to power in 405 BC, although a longer chronology reaching back to the 420's is generally favored." This contribution is offered to him in gratitude for friendship, intellectual stimulus, and support over many years.

The length of the bibliography on the Sicilian signing artists reflects interest in the topic, but there is as yet no consensus on fundamental matters such as chronology. Everyone agrees that the outburst of die signing occurred in the last quarter of the fifth century, but within that time span precise chronologies are disputed, and if the historical context and purpose of the coins are insecure, so of course are interpretations of the types and symbols depicted on the coins. On the one hand, we have an extraordinarily creative period of die engraving; on the other, an eventful background of historical detail, but fitting the two together in ways that make mutual sense has turned out to be difficult and full of pitfalls.

This paper has the limited but necessary objective of establishing the chronological parameters for the beginning and the end of the period of the signing artists. It focuses on the series of Syracusan tetradrachms studied by Tudeer (1913), and the even more famous decadrachms of Euainetos (Gallatin 1930; Liegle 1941) and Kimon (Jongkees 1941).

Attempts to date the period of the signing artists have tended to start from its beginning. Head's date of 412 (1874, 18–19) did not survive the thorough die study of Tudeer (1913). The starting date proposed by the latter (425) has been followed by some (*e.g.*, Jenkins 1970, 66–77, 92; Westermark and Jenkins 1980, 41–42), while others (*e.g.*, Headlam 1908; Kraay 1976; Caccamo Caltabiano 1987) have been prepared to bring down that date by a few years to take into account evidence from the coinage of Leontini. In 422 Leontini was incorporated into Syracuse (Thuc. 5.4), the change of status serving as a terminus ante quem for its own silver coinage (Fig. 14.1). Since the latest tetradrachms of

Fig. 14.1 *Leontini, tetr., 420s. Gemini 5 (2009), 335.*

Leontini bear no signatures and are not influenced stylistically by the signed dies of Syracuse, the date of 422 provides a plausible terminus post quem for the Tudeer tetradrachms. That was the approach suggested by Headlam (1908) and adopted by, among others, Kraay (1976) and Caccamo Caltabiano (1987). However, it must be insisted that the terminus post quem of 422 that is derived from the coinage of Leontini is just that, a terminus post quem; it is not the fixed beginning date it is sometimes assumed to be.

If we stay for a moment with the notion of the tetradrachms starting in the late 1920s, it is tempting to look for allusions to contemporary events in the typology or in the symbolism of the coins. The defeat by the Syracusans in 413 of the Athenian expedition that had laid siege to their city has attracted particular attention, because it is described in so much detail by the contemporary historian Thucydides.

Thus a reference to the Syracusan victory over the Athenian fleet has been found in the supposed "double marine allusion" on a die (Tudeer 1913, V15) showing the flying Victory carrying "not only a wreath but also the stern of a ship," while in the exergue Scylla chases a fish (Kraay 1976, 222) (Fig. 14.2). Alternatively, the dies showing a facing head of Athena wearing a triple-crested helmet and signed

Fig. 14.2 *Syracuse, tetr. (Tudeer 46; V15 + R28). NAC 48 (2008), 47.*

Fig. 14.3 *Syracuse, tetr. (Tudeer 59; V21 + R37). Leu 81 (2001), 18. (Photo courtesy of Leu Numismatik, Zurich).*

by Eukleidas (Tudeer 1913, R36, R37) may reflect homage to the goddess at a time (post-410) of threatened invasion by the Carthaginians (Kraay 1976, 222) (Fig. 14.3). Such attempts to identify historical allusions are not confined to the tetradrachm dies but embrace the decadrachms too. Thus, the Kimonian decadrachms (and other gold issues) have been put in the same context of the triumph of the Syracusans over the Athenians referred to above (Cahn 2001, 412). Furthermore, the set of armor in the exergue of the first decadrachms of Euainetos is labelled "athla," and the arms have been interpreted (first by Evans 1891, 213) as referring to the "prizes" awarded in the Asinarian festival that was inaugurated at Syracuse in September 412, on the first anniversary of the victory over the Athenians (Plut. *Vit. Nic.* 28) (Fig. 14.4).

Fig. 14.4 *Syracuse, decadr. by Kimon (Jongkees 12). NAC 27 (2004), 121.*

However, such a dating of the decadrachms (and of the issues of tetradrachms held to be completed by 400 BC) left little if any silver coinage for the fourth century, and in particular for the reign of the tyrant Dionysius I (405–367 BC), who is known for his vast exactions and expenditures (Diod. Sic. 14.18; 41.3–43.4). A reconsideration of the problem, based in particular on hoard evidence, was begun by G. K. Jenkins (1961) and subsequently followed up by others; in particular, the decadrachms signed by Kimon and Euainetos were indeed part of the coinage issued by Dionysius to support his general program of military works and campaigns (Alföldi 1976; Boehringer 1979; Tusa Cutroni, 1980). However, in 1987 a contribution by M. Caccamo Caltabiano privileged typological and stylistic arguments to argue for a return to an earlier dating of the decadrachms, and in addition proposed a new historical context for their issue. The Syracusan tetradrachms with the name of Euainetos (EVAINETO) on a tablet held aloft by Nike (Tudeer 1913, V14) were dated *c.* 415 or 413 (Fig. 14.5). On grounds

Fig. 14.5 *Syracuse, tetr. (Tudeer 44; V14 + R26). NAC 27 (2004), 117.*

of elements in the style and composition of the quadrigae, the decadrachms of Kimon and Euainetos followed, between the tetradrachms just mentioned and those with obverse facing head of Kimon (Tudeer 1913, V28, V29). Then followed the Euarchidas-Phrygillos group of tetradrachms (Tudeer 1913, T49–T56, R30–R34). On the basis of this arrangement the decadrachms were restored to the period 412–409. Furthermore, they were associated not with the commemoration of the defeat of the Athenian invasion but with expenditure on a Syracusan naval expedition led by Hermocrates and dispatched in 412 to continue the campaign against the Athenians in the Aegean.

Both the elements of this reconstruction – the numismatic element and the historical interpretation – are open to question. Let us take the historical point first. Although the literary sources for Hermocrates's career (chiefly Thucydides, Xenophon, and Diodorus) treat him overall as a model leader, the security of his position at Syracuse can be overrated (Gomme *et al.* 1981, 284). He was replaced as general at a crucial juncture in the defense against the Athenians (Thuc. 6.103.4), and although he was apparently still able to advise the Syracusans (Thuc. 7.21.3), at a later stage, when his advice was not acted upon, he took matters into his own hands (Thuc. 7.73). During the winter after the defeat of the Athenians, he took the lead in urging his fellow

Syracusans to complete the destruction of the Athenians, and in the summer of 412 a flotilla commanded by him arrived at Miletus. It was of modest size by any account: twenty-two ships according to Thucydides (8.26.1), thirty-five according to Diodorus (13.34.4, 63.1); the discrepancy in numbers might be explained in ways other than that of finding one source in error (cf. Gomme *et al.* 1981, 61).

Given his record, Hermocrates was not perhaps the man with whom the Syracusans would have wished to entrust the family silver, and subsequent references to his expedition show that they did not. Two themes run through the accounts of the initial activities of the Peloponnesian fleet in the Aegean: first, that from the start it was beset by financial problems; second, that it was the Syracusans led by Hermocrates who were the most vociferous in their protests to the paymaster Tissaphernes (winter 412/411: Thuc. 8.29.2). Hermocrates honorably refused to take money for himself, in the interests of the whole Peloponnesian force, but it was the Syracusans who were most insistent in criticizing Tissaphernes for not producing ships and regular maintenance for the crews (Thuc. 8.45.3; 78). In the following summer it was again the Syracusan (and Thurian) sailors who were the "most bold" in demanding their pay (Thuc. 8.84.2). In connection with the subsequent banishment of Hermocrates from Syracuse and his replacement by a set of three generals, Thucydides writes (8.85.3, apparently referring to the summer of 411; cf. Gomme *et al.* 1981, 281–85): "There had always been hostility between Tissaphernes and Hermocrates concerning the payment of wages, and more recently ... Tissaphernes set upon Hermocrates, now an exile, much more violently than ever, accusing him, among other things, of once asking him for money and because he did not get it, of showing him enmity." Thus the association of the decadrachms of Kimon and Euainetos with the expedition of Hermocrates has to be discarded, like their earlier association with the aftermath of the Athenian expedition.

From the numismatic point of view, arguments for dating coins based on style alone are unreliable. Although there are some cases where it is possible to point to and even to identify a precise model for a particular die or series of dies (Fischer-Bossert 1998), arguments for stylistic or chronological contiguity cannot rest on a selection of elements in a particular design. Furthermore, in the arrangement proposed by Caccamo Caltabiano the group with the signatures of Phrygillus and Euarchidas (Tudeer 1913, 49–56) (Fig. 14.6) comes after the group with obverse showing Kimon's facing head (Tudeer 1913, 78–81) (Fig. 14.7), although the ethnic Syrakosion on the former ends with -ON rather than the later -ΩN. The problems here are undoubtedly complex, but the first task is to try to establish at least the beginning and the end of the series of signed tetradrachms. To do that, rather than proceeding forward from 422 or thereabouts, let us begin by rehearsing briefly

Fig. 14.6 *Syracuse, tetr. (Tudeer 54; V18 + R33). CNG 79 (2008), 110. (Photo courtesy of the Classical Numismatic Group, www.cngcoins.com).*

Fig. 14.7 *Syracuse, tetr. (Tudeer 80; V29 + R53). NAC 27 (2004), 118.*

the arguments for attributing the decadrachms signed by Kimon and Euainetos to the period of Dionysius I, and then consider the position of the tetradrachms.

First, the decadrachms. The general results of the discussions of the hoard and other evidence for the dating of the decadrachms cited by Caccamo Caltabiano (1987, 119 n. 3) have subsequently been confirmed (Mildenberg 1989; Boehringer 1993). Although many specimens survive, the Kimonian decadrachms were not a large issue: only three obverse dies are known. They were issued before 397, because one of the dies was closely imitated on a tetradrachm of Motya (*SNG* Lloyd 1138), which was destroyed by Dionysius in that year. To assess the date of the beginning of the series, the hoard evidence must be taken into consideration. Analysis of the contents of the Naro hoard speaks positively against an early dating of the Syracusan decadrachms and for their attribution to the reign of Dionysius I (Mildenberg 1989): decadrachms of the Euainetos type are less worn than those of Kimonian type, and both in turn less than the two decadrachms of Akragas, which must be dated before late 406 when the city fell to the Carthaginians. The contents of the Ognina hoard support such a conclusion. It was buried shortly before 402 and clearly represented an impressive treasure containing silver coins (tetradrachms and didrachms) worth more than 1,116 drachmas. Yet no decadrachms were included, an indication that at the time of the hoard's burial they could barely have been issued or even had not been issued at all.

After the decadrachms, the tetradrachms with artists' signatures. I begin with some remarks about the general character of the issues, focusing in particular on the numismatic arguments for suggesting that they were minted over a comparatively short period. Tudeer's thorough study identified 106 die combinations comprising thirty-seven obverse and seventy-three reverse dies, and very few more have been identified since. With few exceptions these die combinations are accounted for in nine die-linked groups. One of these groups is composed of thirty-nine linked-die combinations, a second of nineteen, a third of sixteen, so that three die-linked groups account for not far short of 75 percent of the just over 100 die combinations. The tight die linking by itself suggests a relatively constricted period of minting. That suggestion is strengthened by Holloway's demonstration (1974–75) that the minting of these tetradrachms was organized in part in two parallel ateliers, one starting out on its own and identified by the symbol of one or two dolphins or other sea creatures, the other joining in shortly after and identified by the symbol of an ear of barley.

What are the beginning and ending dates of these tetradrachms? Again, it is most helpful to start at or near the end of the series, with the evidence of the Ognina hoard (Boehringer 1978, 137–41). An indication of the closing date of the hoard is provided by issues of Catana contained in it, in particular the final issues, Ognina nos. 94–98. Although Boehringer (2008) has suggested a reordering of these issues, the fundamental chronological point is not affected: the tetradrachm with obverse facing head of Apollo signed by Choirion (no. 98) was struck at Catana not long before its destruction in 402 (Fig. 14.8). The dies of the coin are in fresh condition, and it must have been struck only a short time before the closure of the hoard. Other tetradrachms of Catana in the hoard were signed by the engraver Herakleidas (nos. 94–96; no. 96 has his facing head) (Fig. 14.9). They too show little wear from circulation;

no. 96 is die-linked to the Choirion issue no. 98. The latest Syracusan tetradrachms in the hoard were two (nos. 297, 298) struck with the same obverse facing head of Arethusa signed by Kimon, both in fresh condition (Tudeer 1913, 80–81, V29). Kimon's facing heads of Arethusa are part of a self-contained die sequence of two obverse and two reverse dies in four die combinations. The head in the Ognina hoard is the earlier of the two, as identified by Mildenberg (1976, 114–15). These coins were approximately contemporary with the frontal Apollo heads of Heracleidas and Choirion at Catana, and they must have been issued about 405 or shortly before (for the suggestion that the tetradrachm of Catana with obverse facing head of Apollo signed by Heracleidas in the Naxos 1985 hoard might be dated a few years earlier than that proposed in Boehringer 1978, see Garraffo in Lentini and Garraffo 1995, 44–45). Since Kimon's facing Arethusas constitute (as just mentioned) a self-contained die sequence, it is in theory possible to move them to a position earlier in the overall sequence. Such a rearrangement was proposed by Holloway (1974–75, 44) in order to place Kimon's facing Arethusas closer to the facing Athenas of Eukleidas (Tudeer 1913, R36, R37). However, as also mentioned above, the presence of an omega in the final syllable of the ethnic on R53 and R54 seems to rule out such an arrangement. The last Syracusan tetradrachm die combination in the Ognina hoard is Tudeer 81, and it is reasonable to suppose that the remaining die combinations, for the most part closely die-linked, were struck for another five years or so and came to an end about 400.

From the latest issues of tetradrachms of the "signing artists" let us turn now to the earliest. These are associated with two die engravers, Sosion and Eumenes, and are noteworthy in particular for a transformation in the composition of the obverse quadriga (Fig. 14.10). The horses

Fig. 14.8 *Catana, tetr. Ognina hoard 98. (Photo courtesy of Schweizerische Numismatische Rundschau).*

14.10 *Syracuse, tetr. (Tudeer 1; V1 + R2). NAC 48 (2008), 46.*

Fig. 14.9 *Catana, tetr. Ognina hoard 96. (Photo courtesy of Schweizerische Numismatische Rundschau).*

are no longer slow moving but are shown at a gallop, all four of them. The design is still somewhat rigid, with all the horses' legs shown parallel to each other in a fanlike formation. Three of the horses' heads are shown at the same height while the fourth (at the left) is lowered, and the single visible chariot wheel is shown in profile, part of it hidden by the hindquarters of the nearest horse. The composition is completed by a Victory flying above to crown the charioteer. A precisely similar overall design occurs on the obverses (O1–O4) of the first tetradrachms of Period 3 of Camarina, though with one noteworthy difference: the charioteer is Athena (Fig. 14.11). Westermark and Jenkins

Fig. 14.11 *Camarina tetr. (Westermark-Jenkins, Plate 12, O1 (132.3) + R1 (130.1). (Photo courtesy of the Royal Numismatic Society).*

(1980, 42) rightly noted that the close stylistic relationship between the Syracusan and Camarinaean tetradrachms implies a nearly similar dating. They suggested a date of *c.* 425, which "would coincide with the period when Camarina reached her strongest political position."

However, it is the close relationship between Syracuse and Camarina evidenced by these coins that is of crucial significance for their chronology, not simply the position of Camarina alone. And the important question is, When is such a relationship most likely to have developed within the last quarter of the fifth century? My answer to that question is: not until Camarina finally came off the fence in the summer of 413 by sending five hundred hoplites, three hundred javelin men, and three hundred bowmen to help Syracuse in her efforts against the Athenians (Thuc. 7.33.1). Let us look further at the evidence for Camarina's political alignment.

For the tetradrachms of the signing artists at Syracuse, I noted above a preliminary terminus post quem of 422. Although events in the mid-420s are not therefore strictly relevant, they do reveal the essentials of the political relationships of the Camarinaeans, caught between the devil they knew, their next-door neighbor Syracuse, and the devil they were coming to know, the most powerful naval state of the age. In the early stages of the Peloponnesian war, Camarina stood aside from other Dorian cities in Sicily and was allied with Leontini and Athens against Syracuse (Thuc. 3.86.2). In 425 the city was on the point of being betrayed to Syracuse (Thuc. 4.25.7). In 424 Gela approached Camarina with proposals for peace (Thuc. 4.58; Timaeus, *FGrH* 566), and in the subsequent settlement Camarina received Morgantina from Syracuse in return for an agreed sum of money (Thuc. 4.65.1). In 422 the Camarinaeans

responded positively to the overtures of the Athenian envoy Phaeax (Thuc. 5.4.6), though nothing came of his mission, and in 415 a further Athenian attempt to win them over failed (Thuc. 6.52). In the winter of 415/414 about twenty Camarinaean cavalry and fifty archers assisted the Syracusan defense (Thuc. 6.67.2), but this was hardly an enthusiastic show of support, and when they were approached by both the Athenians and the Syracusans they decided to stay neutral as far as possible (Thuc. 6.88.1–2; Thucydides here describes them as "always at variance with" the Syracusans). It was only after the Syracusan capture of Plemmyrium in the spring/summer of 413 ("the greatest and most serious blow to the Athenian army"; Thuc. 7.24.3) that the Camarinaeans supported the now likely winners with the forces described in the previous paragraph.

Putting together the numismatic evidence, therefore, for a relatively short period of minting for the tetradrachms of the signing artists at Syracuse (shorter than most of those previously proposed; the exception is Head 1874), and the historical evidence for the relationship between Camarina and Syracuse, I propose that the summer of 413 is the terminus post quem for the start of both the Syracusan tetradrachms and the closely similar ones that open Period 3 at Camarina. As discussed above, the issue of tetradrachms at Syracuse ceased about 400, and so 413 and 400 are the chronological parameters within which the details of the issues of the signing artists and their links with, and influence on, other Sicilian coinages must be discussed. Once again in Sicily, as so often in Greek history in general, it seems that the acquisition of large quantities of silver and other booty such as captives provided the means for creating coinage. There is evidence that Syracuse was short of cash during the period of the Athenian attack. Nicias is said by Thucydides (7.48.5) to have claimed in the summer of 413 that the Syracusans "had already spent 2,000 talents and were in debt for many more." Relief came with the defeat of the Athenians. Thucydides emphasizes (6.31) the large amounts of coined money taken to Sicily by the Athenian fleet and the individuals who served in it. We hear what happened to some of that cash toward the end of Thucydides's account, when he tells us that 6,000 Athenians who had surrendered to the Syracusans threw all the money they had into upturned shields; four shields, says Thucydides, were filled (7.82.3). Much of the silver obtained in this and other ways was no doubt subsequently used to make coins in Sicily, though the import of Athenian coins is reflected in some hoards from Sicily and southern Calabria dating from the later fifth century and the early part of the fourth (*IGCH*: 1910, Vito Superiore; 1911, Reggio 1913; 2092, Selinunte; 2095, Scornavacche; 2096, Schisò; 2103, Falconara; 2114, Campobello di Licata; 2117, Lentini; 2120, Ognina; 2121, Manfria; 2123, S. Maria di Licodia; 2130, Licata; and the Naxos 1985 hoard [Lentini and Garraffo 1995]).

Works Cited

Alföldi, M. R. (1976) *Dekadrachmon. Ein forschungsgeschicht-liches Phänomen.* Wiesbaden, Franz Steiner Verlag.

Boehringer, C. (1978) Rekonstruktion des Schatzfundes von Ognina 1923. *Schweizerische Numismatische Rundschau* 57, 102–43.

———— (1979) Zu Finanzpolitik und Münzprägung des Dionysios von Syrakus. In Otto Mørkholm, Nancy M. Waggoner (eds), *Greek Numismatics and Archaeology: Essays in Honor of Margaret Thompson,* 9–32. Wetteren, Editions NR.

———— (1993) Die Münzprägungen von Syrakus unter Dionysios: Geschichte und Stand der numismatischen Forschung. In *La monetazione dell'età dionigiana. Atti dell'VIII Convegno del Centro Internazionale di Studi Numismatici, Napoli, 29 Maggio–1 Giugno 1983,* 65–89. Rome, Istituto Italiano di Numismatica.

———— (2008) Über die Münzen von Katane im letzten Jahrzehnt des V. Jahrhunderts v.Chr. *Schweizerische Numismatische Rundschau* 87, 5–22.

Caccamo Caltabiano, M. (1987) I decadrammi di Evainetos e Kimon per una spedizione navale in oriente. In *Studi per Laura Breglia, Supplemento al Bollettino di Numismatica* no. 4, 119–37. Rome, Ministero per i Beni Culturali e Ambientali.

Cahn, H. A. (2001) Kimon. In R. Vollkommer and D. Vollkommer-Glökler (eds), *Künstlerlexikon der Antike,* vol. 1, A–K. Munich and Leipzig, K. G. Sauer.

Evans, A. J. (1891) Syracusan "medallions" and their engravers. *The Numismatic Chronicle,* 205–376, at 213 and 337–47.

Fischer-Bossert, W. (1998) Nachahmungen und Umbildungen in der sizilischen Münzprägung. *Schweizerische Numismatische Rundschau* 77, 25–39.

Gallatin, A. (1930) *Syracusan Dekadrachms of the Euainetos Type.* Cambridge, Mass., Harvard University Press.

Gomme, A. W., Andrewes, A., Dover, K. J. (1981) *A Historical Commentary on Thucydides,* vol. 5. Oxford, Clarendon Press.

Head, B. V. (1874) *On the Chronological Sequence of the Coins of Syracuse.* London and Paris, John Russell Smith and MM. Rollin et Feuardent.

Headlam, A. C. (1908) Some notes on Sicilian coins, II: The date of the signed tetradrachms. *The Numismatic Chronicle,* 4th series, vol. 8, 4–9.

Holloway, R. R. (1974–75) La struttura delle emissioni di Siracusa nel periodo dei "signierende Künstler". *Annali, Istituto Italiano di Numismatica* 21–2, 41–48.

———— (1978) *Art and Coinage in Magna Graecia.* Bellinzona, Ed. Arte e Moneta

———— (1998) *Catalogue of the Classical Collection, Museum of Art, Rhode Island School of Design: Ancient Greek Coins.* Providence, Rhode Island, Center for Old World Archaeology and Art, Brown University.

Jenkins, G. K. (1961) Dionysios I of Syracuse and his coinage. *Bulletin of the Institute of Classical Studies* 8, 86.

———— (1970) *The Coinage of Gela.* Berlin, Walter de Gruyter.

Jongkees, J. H. (1941) *The Kimonian Dekadrachms.* Utrecht, Kemink en zoon.

Kraay, C. M. (1976) *Archaic and Classical Greek Coinage.* London, Methuen.

Lentini, M. C. and Garraffo, S. (1995) *Il tesoretto di Naxos.* Rome, Istituto Italiano di Numismatica, Studi e Materiali 4.

Liegle, J. (1941) *Euainetos: Eine Werkfolge nach Originalen des Staatlichen Münzkabinetts zu Berlin. 101 Winckelmanns-program.* Berlin, W. De Gruyter.

Mildenberg, L. (1976) Kimon in the manner of Segesta. In *Actes du 8ème Congrès Internationale de Numismatique. New York–Washington 1973,* 113–21. Paris and Bâle, Association Internationale des Numismates Professionels.

———— (1989) Über Kimon und Euainetos im Funde von Naro. In G. Le Rider et al. (eds.), *Kraay-Mørkholm Essays: Numis-matic Studies in Memory of C. M. Kraay and O. Mørkholm,* 182–85. Louvain-la-Neuve: Institut supérieur d'archéologie et de l'histoire de l'art, séminaire de numismatique Marcel Hoc.

Tudeer, L. O. Th. (1913) *Die Tetradrachmenprägung von Syrakus in der Periode der signierenden Künstler.* Berlin, W. Pormetter.

Tusa Cutroni, A. (1980) La monetazione di Siracusa sotto Dionisio I. In M. José Fontana, M. T. Piraino, F. P. Rizzo (eds.), *Miscellanea di studi classici in onore di Eugenio Manni,* vol. 2, 631–47. Rome, G. Bretschneider.

Westermark, U. and Jenkins, K. (1980) *The Coinage of Kamarina.* London, The Royal Numismatic Society.

15

New Coin Types in Late Fifth-Century Sicily

Spencer Pope

Sicilian numismatics represents the intersection of two of Ross Holloway's particular areas of interest. His numerous contributions to this field include examinations of the mint at Syracuse, issues under the Sicilian tyrants, and the numismatic output from smaller, inland sites. Ross Holloway's work in this area astutely evaluated the numismatic evidence in light of historical circumstances, and has in this way pinpointed the origin and raison d'etre for many of the sporadic and limited issues of the island. The present work examines the mints of marginalized indigenous cities and mercenary groups in Sicily at the end of the fifth century BC in the context of Syracuse's rise to domination.

The period between the Athenian invasion and the fall of Agathocles can be considered the "long" fourth century BC in Sicily. This interval saw the fall of the democratic government in Syracuse and subsequent domination of tyrants. Greeks were engaged in nearly constant territorial warfare with the Carthaginians, who advanced from the western part of the island as far as the Ionian Sea. This period also saw radical changes in the political composition of the island; independent city-states were swallowed by larger powers that placed Greek, native, and Carthaginian cities alike into consolidated spheres of influence by Syracuse on one side and Carthage on the other. However, the Corinthian colony's rise and establishment of hegemony over Greek Sicily were neither immediate nor did they come about in one single step. Dionysius relied heavily upon mercenary labor in campaigns against Greek and indigenous cities and for battles against the Carthaginians between 398 and 392 BC (on mercenaries in Southern Italy and Sicily, see generally Tagliamonte 1994; on the role of mercenaries in the Greek world, see Trundle 2004). Archaeological, literary, and especially numismatic evidence attests to a drawn-out period of conflict, in which control was amassed not by military means alone but also through the careful orchestration of numerous population relocations that resulted in the loss of territory of Greeks and Sikels alike at the expense of the Syracusans and their mercenaries.

The Carthaginian invasion did much to change the demographics of Sicily. Carthaginians destroyed Selinus in 409 BC and then moved east, sacking Himera, Agrigento, Gela, and Kamarina in 406–405 BC (on the destruction of Agrigento, see Diod. Sic. 13.89–91; on the assault on Gela, see Diod. Sic. 13.108–10; on the destruction of Gela and Kamarina, see Diod. Sic. 14.60.4). Syracuse absorbed the population of the colonial cities of the south coast, a move that greatly expanded the city. Dionysius was elected *strategos autokrator* in Syracuse in 405 BC and soon thereafter struck a treaty with the Carthaginians (Diod. Sic.13.94–96; Arist. *Pol.* 5, 1305a). The agreement stipulated that the sacked Greek cities were to pay tribute to Carthage and were to remain without fortification wall, the territory of the Sikans – the indigenous inhabitants of central Sicily – was to be turned over to Carthage, and the Sikel cities were to be autonomous. With this agreement, the Carthaginians controlled more than half of Sicily, including inland areas heretofore possessed by the native population. The border between Greek and Carthaginian territory was set as a line drawn between Himera and Gela. The establishment of these precise boundaries changed the relationship between the two powers in Sicily; the defeat had ended a struggle for influence and trade but initiated competition for territory itself.

As preparations were made for war against the Carthaginians at Syracuse, Dionysius began a campaign to consolidate his power in eastern Sicily. The first objective was to bring the Sikels under his control, and to this end he enacted a siege of Herbessos, now identified with Montagna di Marzo, near modern Piazza Armerina (Diod. Sic. 14.7.6). Diodorus reports that the immediate motive for moving first against the Sikels was because of their previous alliance with the Carthaginians. This alliance, presumably during the years 409–406 BC, is however not otherwise attested (Herbessos identified with Montagna di Marzo, see Manganaro 1999, with preceding bibliography). Dionysius continued military action the following year. His first action was a siege of Aitna, which won him the fortress; from there he attacked Leontini, but, lacking adequate siege engines, he instead plundered the territory (Diod. Sic. 14.14.2–4). In an attempt to delude the Naxians and Catanians, Dionysius engaged in affairs of the Sikels, first installing Aeimnestus as tyrant of Henna and then assisting in overthrowing him, in an effort to gain confidence of the citizens of Henna. He then set out to sack Herbita, but was unsuccessful and instead struck a treaty with the city (Diod. Sic. 14.15.1). Diodorus's narrative has Dionysius passing from Enna to Herbita before turning to Katane, suggesting Herbita lies on the road between the two cities. The precise identification of Herbita remains unresolved but must be located in the area north of Enna and west of Etna, in the Nebrodi Mountains. Possible locations include Nicosia, Gangi Vecchia/Monte Alburchia, or closer to the coast at Mistretta or S. Stefano di Camastra (on the identification of the site, see G. Bejor, BTCGI, 1985).

Next to fall to Syracuse were Katane and Naxos, both of which were betrayed to Dionysius in 403 BC. The former, once in the hands of Dionysius, was turned over to and settled by a group of mercenaries. The latter was surrendered by Prokles, the commander of the Naxians, in exchange for gifts and kinship. Dionysius razed the city, sold its inhabitants into slavery, and handed the territory over to the Sikels (Diod. Sic. 14.15.2–4). Treaties with the prominent Sikel cities Agyrion, Kentoripe, and Assoros were made, while Kephaloidion (modern Cefalù) and Solunto were obtained through treachery, and the settlements at Menai and Morgantina were taken by force (Diod. Sic. 14.78.7). With the relocation of the population of Leontinoi to Syracuse and the capture of Messana, Syracuse remained the only independent city – Sikel or Greek – of the Ionian coast in the opening years of the fourth century BC. Mercenaries were eventually settled at Leontinoi to remove them from the city of Syracuse itself (Diod. Sic. 14.78.2). After an aborted march against Syracuse by Rhegions and Messenians. Dionysius feared that the cities of the straits would align themselves with Carthage and sought to win favor with the city by presenting them with a "large piece of territory" (πολλὴν τῆς ὁμόρου χώραν) (Diod. Sic. 14.44.4). This indicates that Syracusan territory was contiguous with that of Messana.

Syracuse further consolidated its territorial acquisitions with the foundation of new cities in the hinterland of the island. The colonies had a twofold purpose: first, to ensure a Greek presence in areas traditionally held by the indigenous population, and second, to provide a home and territory for exmercenaries, who were settled in large numbers. Tyndaris, located on the north coast of Sicily on territory subtracted from the *chora* of the Sikel city Abakainon (near modern Tripi), was founded with refugees from Peloponnesian Messana and enjoyed a rapid growth, undoubtedly receiving exmercenaries (Diod. Sic. 14.78.5–6. It is worthwhile to note that Carthaginian Magon used Abakainon as a base for attacks on Messene in 393 BC; Diod. Sic. 14.90.4).

Taormenion, modern Taormina, was refounded as a colony by Dionysius following a second peace treaty with the Carthaginians in 392 BC. Although previously inhabited by Sikels, the Syracusan tyrant settled mercenaries at the site, while a more formal foundation came in 358 BC with oikist Andromachos and the removal of the last inhabitants of Naxos to the city (on the foundation with mercenaries, Diod. Sic. 14.96.4; later under Andromachus, Diod. Sic. 16.6.7, 16.7.1). Adranon, founded *c.* 401 BC and identified with modern Adrano, located just beyond the slopes of Mt. Etna, served as an advanced outpost against the Carthaginians along the upper Simeto River, bordering the territory of the Sikel cities of Agyrion, Assoros, and Kentoripe. The foundation itself may have replaced the Sikel cities at Contrada Mendolito and Paternò-Civita as a population center (on the foundations of Adranon, see Diod. Sic. 14.37.5). G. Lamagna (1994, 173 n. 3; 1997–98, 75) astutely indicates that Centuripe had sided with the Athenians in 414 BC. The latest material from Mendolito dates to the mid-fifth century BC (Lamagna 1992; 1993–94; on Mendolito, Franco 1999, on Paternò- Civita, Lamagna 1994). One additional colonial foundation occurring in these years should be noted: the indigenous city Herbita founded a colony, Halaesa Archonidion, named for Archonides, the tyrant of the metropolis. This colony, located on the north coast of the island near modern Tusa, was established in reaction to population pressure at Herbita, caused in part by a multitude of mercenaries (Diod. Sic. 14.16.1; De Vido, 1997).

Dionysius's policy of centralization is reflected in the coinage circulating in eastern Sicily. The Carthaginian invasion caused a cessation in the production of coins at nearly all of the principal cities of Greek Sicily apart from Syracuse. At this point, the well-known bronze Athena Head/Hippocamp type begins to be issued; these coins would serve as the primary currency for the duration of the tyrant's reign. Although heavily overstruck by smaller poleis and ethnic groups in Sicily, this coin remained in circulation until the introduction of the Kainon type under Dionysius II (on the overstriking and countermarking of the Syracusan bronzes, see Garraffo 1993; on the Kainon coinage, Holloway 2007). However, outside of Syracuse there appeared a limited number of issues with small outputs, most often litra and hemilitra, occurring both in silver and in bronze. These issues not only brought new types into the island but also often displayed dual legends representative of displaced, relocated, changing, or fluid population groups that bring into the question the relationship between the issuing body and the named polis. The most notable of these issues appear with a butting-bull reverse, a type that appears in limited contexts in Sicily.

The introduction and distribution of the butting-bull type in Sicily merits a brief discussion. The type initially appears in Sicily at Gela, on bronze issues dating to the last two decades of the fifth century BC (Fig. 15.1) (Jenkins 1970,

Fig. 15.1. Bronze Tetras *from Gela, Jenkins Group 8 (SNG ANS 4, 106).*

Fig. 15.2 Silver Stater *from Thurii (SNG ANS 2, 878).*

group 8). In these issues, a left-facing bull appears on the obverse of the coin below the legend ΓΕΛΑΣ. Its appearance here is certainly derived from the most characteristic type in Geloan coinage, the man-faced bull, which is identified as the eponymous river god. Distinct from the man-faced bull, a case can be made that the ordinary bull was also used to represent a river god (Jenkins 1970, 170, *cf.* Head 1911, 87). The legend accompanying the butting bull is unchanged from the man-faced bull issues, ΓΕΛΑΣ, and would identify the figure rather than indicate a citizen body (ΓΕΛΩΙΩΝ, the ethnic, appears below the exergue of the quadriga obverse; Jenkins group 9). The butting bull from Thurii, interpreted as the representation of the eponymous river Thurios, is accompanied by a fish in the exergue, a symbol that has been associated with river gods (Fig. 15.2) (appearing also at Gela, Jenkins group 7); however, the reverse legend ΘΥΡΙΩΝ provides the ethnic rather than an identity for the image.

Following its initial appearance at Gela, the butting-bull coin type is next seen at Katane. The relevant issues of Katane (Figs. 15.3–4) (Manganaro 1996, 311, table VII, 68–71):

Two-litra (Ag) =
Obverse: head of Silenus, l.
Reverse: Butting bull, r., ΚΑΤΑΝΑΙΩΝ

Litra (Ag) =
Obverse: head of female divinity, l.
Reverse: Butting bull, r., shrimp in ex., ΚΑΤΑΝΑΙΩΝ

Hemidrachm (Ag) =
Obverse: head of Apollo, l.
Reverse: Butting bull, r., fish in ex., ΚΑΤΑΝΑΙΩΝ

Hemidrachm (Ag) =
Obverse: head of Apollo, l., ΛΕΟΝ (Katane/Leontinoi)
Reverse: Butting bull, r., fish in ex., ΚΑΤΑΝΑΙΩΝ

The issues date to the last decade of the fifth century and demonstrate a departure from the Amenanos/quadriga type that had directly preceded it. While the obverse types for this series are all familiar to the coinage of Katane, the butting-bull reverse, accompanied by a fish or shrimp in the exergue, makes its first appearance. The right-facing bull,

Fig. 15.3 Silver two-litra coin from Katane (After Antikenmuseum Basel und Sammlung Ludwig, Griech. Munzen aus Griechenland und Sizilien, 1988, 340).

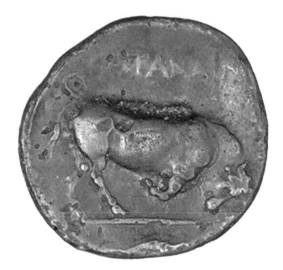

Fig. 15.4 Silver litra from Katane (SNG ANS 1270).

with head lowered to the ground, both sets of legs crossed, and its tail looping in the air, so closely emulates the style of the Thurii issues that their inspiration need not be sought elsewhere. The motion indicated in the piece contrasts with the static bull of the Geloan issues. In this case, the legend does not correspond with the type presented: ΚΑΤΑΝΑΙΩΝ is the ethnic and is not to be confused with the river god Amenanos, personified on earlier types. The historical circumstances suggest that the new type was adopted after the destruction and repopulation of Katane in 403 BC, when the city had been given over to mercenaries of Dionysius. A logical terminus ante quem for the issues is 396 BC, when the mercenaries were removed to Aitna, giving the production a window of nearly ten years (Diod. Sic. 14.58.2). The similarity with the Thurii bulls may confirm the southern Italian origin of the mercenary group.

The appearance of the new type at Katane may perhaps be paralleled by issues at Naxos. Although Diodorus Siculus indicates that the city was destroyed and the population sold into slavery, there is archaeological evidence for continued occupation at the site (Lentini 2002). It is to this period that a small output of Naxian silver litrai with the legend ΝΕΑΠΟΛΙ[ΤΑΝ] may be attributed (Cahn 1944, 86–88). The coin features the well-known obverse/head of Apollo and reverse/Silenus types, but the single legend suggests a new beginning and political discontinuity at the Chalcidian colony. Political reorganization is also is cited as the motive behind a single silver hemidrachm containing the obverse legend ΛΕΟΝ (obverse type head of Apollo facing left) and reverse legend ΚΑΤΑΝΑΙΩΝ. The coin has been interpreted as an indicator of *sympoliteia* between the two poleis (Kraay 1976, 229; Manganaro 1996, 311). However, any formal association between the two Chalcidian cities must have been extremely short-lived, as Leontinoi was presumably uninhabited in the period between the removal of the population to Syracuse and the placement of mercenaries at the site, a period of time that roughly corresponds to the mercenary presence at Katane prior to their relocation to Aitna. An alliance between the Chalcidian cities of Sicily in the years prior to the Carthaginian invasion has been proposed based on a collective reference in Diodorus Siculus (13.56). If the coin is representative of a political union of the two colonies, such an alliance ultimately carried little weight in the face of Syracusan machinations, given the eventual depopulation of both cities.

The butting-bull type appears at Kephaloidion at the same time with the following issues (Jenkins 1975, 97–99):

litra =
Obverse: head of Herakles with lionskin, r., EK
 ΚΕΦΑΛΟΙΔΙΟΥ
Reverse: Butting bull, r., fish in ex., ΗΡΑΚΛΕΙΩΤΑΝ

The silver litrai were struck shortly after 400 BC. The obverse and reverse legends together appear to make two statements: the obverse, EK ΚΕΦΑΛΟΙΔΙΟΥ, reverse ΗΡΑΚΛΕΙΩΤΑΝ. S. N. Consolo-Langher (1961) argued that the legend should be read as "Herakleans living at Kephaloidion." The reference is likely to mercenaries from Herakleia in Lucania settled at Kephaloidion. Rather than a political union as theorized for Katane and Leontinoi, it appears that the dual legend refers to a new people taking over a preexisting city; Kephaloidion was taken by Dionysius c. 400 BC (Diod. Sic. 14.78.7) and likely settled exmercenaries there. The adoption of the same reverse type for the short-lived coinage of the city (butting bull, fish in ex.) may have the same inspiration as the Katane types, if not the work of the same die engraver. The relationship between the legend and the image on the reverse is the same as at Katane: ΗΡΑΚΛΕΙΩΤΑΝ unambiguously refers to the issuing body – Herakleans – and is unrelated to the coin type. The dual ethnic on the coin finds many parallels in western Sicily. Campanian mercenaries, immediately following their service to Dionysius, moved to Entella, modern Rocca di Entella, and were absorbed into the city until they possessed it (Diod. Sic. 14.9.9). The Campanian presence is seen in the numismatic record with silver drachma and hemidrachma issues overstruck on Sicilian coins and containing the obverse legend ΕΝΤΕΛΛΑΣ and reverse inscribed ΚΑΜΠΑΝΩΝ (Garraffo 1978, 29, nos. 1, 2; cf. Garaffo 1987, 218; the practice of overstriking these coins demonstrates the provisionary nature of the issues). Corresponding issues may also be found at Nakone (legends ΚΑΜΠΑΝΩΝ/ΝΑΚΟΝΑΙΩΝ and ΚΑΜΠΑΝΩΝ/ΝΑΚΩΝΕΣ) (Tusa Cutroni 1970; on Nakone, see Facella 2002). In the case of Kephaloidion, it appears that the Heraklean mercenaries were in control of the city, and it is with them, rather than the polis of Kephaloidion, that the minting authority should be found.

A third example of the butting-bull reverse is found in the enigmatic issues of Piakos (Jenkins 1962; 1975, 92):

Litra =
Obverse: head of female divinity, r., ΠΙΑΚΙΝΟΣ
 (two examples) or ΠΙΑΚΙΝΩΝ (one example)
Reverse: Butting bull, r., fish in ex., ΑΔΡΑΝΟΣ

Hemilitra =
Obverse: head of female divinity, r., ΠΙΑΚΙ
Reverse: forepart of butting bull, r., ΠΙΑΚΙ
 (one example only)

The identification of the site is uncertain. The toponym ΠΙΑΚΟΣ is mentioned only by Stephanus of Byzantium, although a reference to the city in the index to book 12, chapter 29, by Diodorus Siculus included "ὡς Συρακόσιοι στρατεύσαντες ἐπί Πικηνούς τὴν πόλιν κατέσκαψαν" (How the Syracusans campaigned against the Pikenians and razed their city) (Steph. Byz., *s.v.* Πίακος, πόλις Σικελίας. οἱ πολῖται Πιακίνοι; Diod. Sic., index to bk. 12, ch. 29, Loeb translation with modifications). The chapter in discussion does not, however, mention Piakos but a city named Trinakie that was destroyed in 440 BC. This city is also not otherwise attested, so the text has been emended to read Paliké (Π[αλ]ικηνούς), the city founded by Ducetius and the ostensible center of the Sikel Federation (see Maniscalco-McConnell 2003, 153 n. 42; McConnell, this volume). The emendation is convincing, since Diodorus notes that Paliké was destroyed shortly after its foundation in 453 BC. The archaeological record reveals no evidence for either the foundation or destruction of the city in the mid-fifth century BC (Pope 2006, 162–226, esp. 225–26). Otherwise, Piakos has been identified with the anonymous settlement at Contrada Mendolito, Paternò-Civita, or modern Adrano, ancient Adranon (Jenkins 1962; Franco 1999, 198–202).

Silver coinage at Piakos is attested by six extant examples, three litrai and three hemilitra. Although the legends vary among the extant examples, both the obverse and reverse types are copied directly from the Katane issues discussed above (see Figs. 15.3, 15.4). The fractional ethnic ΠΙΑΚΙ on the hemilitra (three extant specimens) introduces a more complete reading found on the litra, which is also known in only three examples: the legend appears as ΠΙΑΚΙΝΟΣ on two of the specimens, and ΠΙΑΚΙΝΩΝ on the other (the first specimen was published by Jenkins 1962; a second by Manganaro 1984, 34, table 6, no. 89, who also references the third specimen, now in the collection of the American Numismatic Society [ANS 1999.31.1]). The appearance of the proper noun in the genitive plural clearly establishes the term as the ethnic. The appearance of the name in the nominative singular, ΠΙΑΚΙΝΟΣ, is unusual in Sicilian numismatics, and among indigenous cities is paralleled at

only Morgantina (ΜΟΡΓΑΝΤΙΝΑ retrograde) (Erim 1975; 1989, 5–6).

The reverse of the litra contains the legend ΑΔΡΑΝΟΣ, fully legible only on the example now in collection of the American Numismatic Society (Fig. 15.5) (ANS 1999.31.1). G. K. Jenkins published the first example with obverse ΠΙΑΚΙΝΟΣ and the legend ΑΔΡΑΝ[. . .] on the reverse, which he restored as ΑΔΡΑΝΟΝ, a reference to the Greek city. The seemingly double ethic on the coin was taken to be evidence for a *syntelia* between Piakos and Adranon (Jenkins 1962, 17). The full reading clearly indicates a noun in the masculine singular, and not "Adranon," the common name for the Dionysian colony. The reference may still be to the new foundation, however, since the city's name alternatively appears in the masculine (*Adranos* rather than *Adranon*) in Aelian, writing in the second century AD: Ἐν Σικελίᾳ Ἀδρανός ἐστι πόλις; but the reference is late and cannot be taken as conclusive (Ael. *NA* 11.20; cf. Morawiecki 1995, 40–41, who also proposes a reading of ΑΔΡΑΝΙΤΩΝ for the silver litra, although this reconstruction may be precluded on the basis of available space). The appearance of the two names together has even been taken as an indication that Adranon was constructed on the site of Piakos, thus an indigenous site would have been refounded as a Greek colony, with its first numismatic issues reflecting the names of both civic organizations (the attribution is based on the presence of archaic pottery uncovered at the site. Constructions dating to the period have not been uncovered, making the possibility less likely; Franco 1999, 203).

While the possibility that the inhabitants of Piakos were transferred to the new foundation and constituted, along

Fig. 15.5 *Silver litra from Piakos (ANS, 1999.31.1).*

with vast numbers of exmercenaries, a segment of the population of Adranon cannot be excluded, the civic reference is unlikely. In Sicily in the Classical age it was customary to place the ethnic in the genitive case, so the legend AΔPANITΩN would be expected, rather than Adranon or even Adranos. In fact, the only other issues from the city, dating to the time of Timoleon, contain the legend in the genitive (a bronze litra with the head of Apollo on the obverse and a seven-string lyre on the revere bore the legend AΔPANITAN). Important to note, there is little archaeological evidence for activity at Adranon at this point; the earliest remains of the urban settlement date to the late fourth/early third century BC, so it is unlikely that the reverse legend refers to the foundation of the city (Lamagna 1997–98, 78).

To interpret the legend, one must keep in mind that the coin type is a reproduction of the issues of Katane, and for this reason the iconography of both the bull and river nymph has limited resonance for the city of Piakos. Therefore, the legend on the reverse, AΔPANOΣ, cannot be controlled by the device. The reference most likely brought to mind by the legend is the Sikel god whose sanctuary was located in the vicinity of Mendolito and Adranon, and not a local river god. Examining the hemilitrai, Manganaro reconstructs the obverse legend as the ethnic ΠΙΑΚΙ [NΩN] and the reverse legend ΠΙΑΚΙ [NOΣ], identifying the river god personified in the forepart of a bull with the reverse legend. An eponymous Piakinos River could easily be hypothesized as one of the many tributaries of the upper Simeto at the base of Mt. Etna (contrary to Manganaro, Morawiecki 1995, 39–42).

The connection to both the god and the dependence on coinage of Katane are already observed at Piakos in the last quarter of the fifth century BC with bronze issues. The bronze issues of Piakos (Jenkins 1975, 91–92):

Hemilitra and Tetrans =
Obverse: head of a river god wreathed, with horns, l;
                Π •I•A•K•I•N•
Reverse: dog attacking stag

Uncia =
Obverse: head of river god, Π •I•A•K•
Reverse: dog

G. E. Rizzo (1946, pl. VII A) identified the bronze coinage of Piakos as the work of the "Maestro della foglia" who was responsible for the head of Apollo on the coinage of Katane in the last quarter of the fifth century BC. The bronze issues, therefore, create a precedent for the copying of the types used for the silver issues. One further note on the bronze issues is warranted. The reverse contains a unique composition: a dog attacking a stag. The type has been interpreted as a reference to the shrine of Adranos, protected by guard dogs (Ael. *NA* 11.20). In this way, too, the

appearance of Adranos as the reverse legend on the silver issues is forecasted in bronze issues. A representation of the deity also appears in the third century BC on coins produced by the Mamertines: obverse/head of Adranos, AΔPANOΣ; reverse/dog, MAMEPTINΩN.

While the appearance of the new type at Katane and Kephaloidion may be interpreted as signs of political upheaval and the appearance of a new population, the reverse legend at Piakos emphasized the city's connection with a venerable Sikel establishment at a time in which discrete indigenous identity begins to wane. The political subjugation caused by Dionysius left few differentiating characteristics of the Sikel population (Holloway 1990). Perhaps the most important element of a discrete ethnic identity was religion; indeed, the most sacred Sikel site, the Sanctuary of the Divine Palikoi located on the edge of the Plain of Catania, flourished at this time. Indigenous religion was intimately tied to Ducetius's Sikel Federation of the mid fifth-century BC, which revolved around the Sanctuary of the Palikoi (McConnell, this volume; Maniscalco and McConnell 2003; Pope 2006). In this late fifth-century example of coinage from Piakos, Sikel religion is again brought out as an important indicator of identity.

Works Cited

Bejor, G. (1985) Herbita. *Bibliografia Topografica della Colonizzazione greca in Italia e nelle Isole tirreniche*. Rome, École française de Rome.

Berger, E. (1991) Great and Small Poleis in Sicily: Syracuse and Leontinoi. *Historia* 40, 129–142.

Bernabò Brea, L. (1975) Che cosa conosciamo dei centri indigeni della Sicilia che hanno coinato monete prima dell'eta di Timoleonte. In *Le emissioni dei centri siculi finoall'epoca di Timoleonte e i loro rapporti con la monetazione delle colonie greche di Sicilia. Atti del 4 Convegno del Centro internazionale di studi numismatici, Napoli 9–14 aprile 1973*, 3–51. Rome, Istituto italiano di numismatica.

Boehringer, C. (1968) Hieron's Aitna und das Hieroneion. *Jahrbuch für Numismatik und Geldgeschichte* 18, 67–98.

——— (1981) Herbita. *Numismatica e Antichità Classiche* 10, 95–114.

Cahn, H. A. (1944) *Die Münzen der Sicilischen Stadt Naxos. Ein Beitrag zur Kunstgeschichte des Griechiscen Westens*. Basil, Birkhäuser.

Calciati, R. (1983–1987) *Corpus Nummorum Siculuorm: La Monetazione di Bronzo*. Milan, Ennerre.

——— (1991) La monetazione di Kainon. Problemi tipologici, metrologici e cronologici. In R. Martini and N. Vismara, (eds.), *Ermanno A. Arslan Studia Dicata: Parte I: Montezione Greco e Greco-Imperiale*. 35–86. Milan, Ennerre.

Castrizio, D. (1999) Le serie a leggenda "Kainon" e la monetazione mercenariale in bronzo nella Brettìa tra Dionisio II e Timoleonte. *Annali dell'Instituto Italiano di Numismatica* 46, 155–178.

——— (2000) *La Monetazione mercenariale in Sicilia. Stratigie economiche e territoriali fra Dione e Timoleonte*. Catanzaro, Rubbettino.

Consolo Langher, S. N. (1961) Gli Herakleiotai ek Kephaloidiou. *Kokalos* 7,166–198.

Cusmano, N. (1992) I Culti di Adrano e di Efesto: Religione, Politica e Acculturazione in Sicilia tra V e IV Secolo. *Kokalos* 38, 151–189.

De Vido, S. (1997) I Dinasti Dei Siculi: Il Caso di Archonides. *Acme* 50, 7–37.

Erim, K. (1975) La zecca di Morgantina. In *Le emissioni dei centri siculi fino all'epoca di Timoleonte e i loro rapporti con la monetazione delle colonie greche di Sicilia. Atti del 4. Convegno del Centro internazionale di studi numismatici, Napoli 9–14 aprile 1973*, 67–76. Rome, Istituto italiano di numismatica.

——— (1989) The mint of Morgantina. In T.V. Buttrey, K.T. Erim, T. D. Grovers and R. R. Holloway, *Morgantina Studies II: The Coins*. Princeton, Princeton University Press.

Facella, A. (2001) Nakone: la Città. In *Da un'antica città di Sicilia: I decreti di Entella e Nakone: Catalogo della Mostra, Scuola Normale Superiore di Pisa*, 197–202. Pisa, Scuola Normale Superiore di Pisa.

Franco, A. (1999) La città del Mendolito: Τρινακίη? *Sicilia Archeologica* 32, 199–210.

Garraffo S. (1978) Storia e monetazione di Entella nel IV secolo a.C. Cronologia e significato delle emissioni dei Kampanoi. *Annali dell' Instituto Italiano di Numismatica* 25, 23–43.

——— (1987) Note sulle monetazione siracusana dal 344 al 318 a.C. *Numismatica e Antichità Classiche* 16, 119–130.

——— (1993) La monetazione dell' età diogiana: contromarche e riconiazioni. In *La monetazione dell'età dionigiana: Atti del VIII Convegno del Centro internazionale di studi numismatici (8th, 1983, Naples)*, 191–242. Rome, Instituto Italiano di Numismatica.

Head, B. V. (1911) *Historia Numorum, a Manual of Greek Numismatics*, 2nd Edition, Oxford, Clarendon.

Holloway, R. R. (1990) The Geography of the Southern Sicels. In J. Descoeudres (ed.), *ΕΥΜΟΥΣΙΑ: Ceramic and Iconographic Studies in Honour of Alexander Cambitoglu*, Mediterranean Archaeology Supplement 1, 147–153. Sydney, Meditarch.

——— (2007) The Kainon Coinage. In G. Mocharete and M. Florenzano, (eds.), *Liber Amicorum Tony Hackens*, Numismatica Lovaniensia 20, 223–27. Louvain-la-Neuve, Université Catholique de Louvain.

Jenkins, G. K. (1962) Piakos. *Schweizer Münzblätter* 46, 17–20.

——— (1970) *The Coinage of Gela*. Berlin, W. De Gruyter.

——— (1975) The coinages of Enna, Galaria, Piakos, Imachara, Kephalsidion, and Longane. In *Le emissione dei centri Siculi fino all'epoca di Timoleonte e i loro rapporti con la monetazione delle colonie greche di Sicilia, atti del IV convegno del Centro internazionale di studi numismatici, Napoli 9–14 Aprile 1973* (Supplement. to *Annali dell' Instituto Italiano di Numismatica* 20, 1973), 77–103. Rome,

Kraay, C. (1976) *Archaic and Classical Greek Coins*. London, Methuen.

Lamagna, G. (1992) Adrano (Catania) Contrada Mendolito. *Bollettino d'Arte* 16–18, 255–264.

——— (1993–94) Le ultime ricerche archeologiche nei territori di Adrano e Caltagione, *Kokalos* 39–40, 873–879.

——— (1994) Adrano (Catania). Contrada Difesa, Giobbe, Zaccani. *Bollettino d'Arte* 28–30, 173–184.

——— (1997–98) Alcuni dati sulle ultime campagne di scavo ad Adranon. *Kokalos* 43–44, 71–81.

Lentini, M.C. (2002) Testimonianze della prima metà del IV secolo A.C. a Naxos. In N. Bonacasa, (ed.), *La Sicilia dei due Dionisî: atti della Settimana di Studio, Agrigento, 24–28 febbraio 1999*, 223–241. Rome, Erma di Bretschneider.

Manganaro, G. (1984) Dai *mikrà kermata* di argento al *chalkokratos kassiteros* in Sicilia nel V. Sec. a.C. *Jahrbuch für Numismatik und Geldgeschichte* 34, 11–39.

——— (1996) La monetazione di Katane dal V al I sec. a.C. *Catania Antica: Atti del Convegno della Società Italiana per lo Studio dell'Antichità Classica, Catania 23–24 Maggio 1992*, 303–329. Pisa, Istituti editoriali e poligrafici internazionali.

——— (1999) Montagna di Marzo – Herbessos. In *Sikelika: Studi di Antichità e di Epigrafia della Sicilia Greca*. 7–33. Pisa, Istituti editoriali e poligrafici internazionali.

Maniscalco, L. and McConnell, B. E. (2003) The Sanctuary of the Divine Palikoi (Rocchicella di Mineo, Sicily): Fieldwork from 1995 to 2001. *American Journal of Archaeology* 107, 145–80.

Morawiecki, L. (1995) Adranos. Una Divinità Dai Molteplici Volti. *Kokalos* 41, 29–50.

Pope, S. (2006) The fourth-century city of Paliké in Sicily, Ph. D. dissertation, Brown University.

Rizzo, G. E. (1946) *Monete greche della Sicilia*. Rome, La Libreria dello stato.

Tagliamonte, G. (1994) *I Figli di Marte: Mobilità, Mercenari e Mercenariato Italici in Magna Grecia e Sicilia*. Roma, Erma di Bretschneider.

Trundle, M. (2004) Greek *Mercenaries: From the Late Archaic Period to Alexander*. London, Routledge.

Tusa Cutroni, A. (1970) I ΚΑΜΠΑΝΟΙ e ΤΥΡΡΗΝΟΙ in Sicilia attraverso ladocumentazione numismatica, *Kokalos* 16, 250–67.

16

Ancient Sicilian Coins in a Brazilian Private Collection

M. B. B. Florenzano

Born in Paris in 1931, Alain J. Costilhes started collecting coins when he was twelve. The son of a wealthy French family, he inherited not only a small collection of Greek, Roman, and medieval French coins from his grandfather but also the taste for beautiful coins. After he established himself in Brazil during the 1950s, he decided to enlarge his collection, acquiring Brazilian coins from the colonial and modern periods. Alain was also a great reader of numismatic books, and his library included rarities such as original seventeenth-century treatises on coinage, nineteenth-century catalogues of ancient and Brazilian coins, and so forth. He published a few articles on Brazilian coinage, participated in several meetings of the International Numismatic Congress, was associated with several numismatic societies, and was contributing editor to the American Numismatic Society's *Numismatic Literature* (Florenzano 2004).

Whenever a foreign numismatist came to Brazil, Costilhes was most anxious to receive him and to proudly show his collection and discuss iconographical and historical problems concerning different coins. Ross Holloway was one of these visitors in 1992 when we had the privilege of having him among us for a series of wonderful lectures. I hope he will be glad to see these nice Sicilian coins now published in this volume (Figs. 16.1–4).

The Coins

1. Syracuse, silver tetradrachm, 17.22 g, axis: 7
466–406 BC
Obv.: Quadriga to the right; above Nike crowning the charioteer; in the exergue, *ketos*.
Rev.: ΣΥΡΑΚΟΣ–ΙΟ–Ν Head of Arethusa to the right with double pearl necklace, earrings, and hair fastened with a string of pearls. Around, four dolphins swimming to the right.
SNGANS 5, no. 128 and ff
Boehringer, no. 444

Fig. 16.1 *Syracuse, silver tetradrachm (Photos by the Author, courtesy of Vavy Pacheco Borges).*

2. Syracuse, silver tetradrachm, 17.02 g, axis: 7
310–305 BC
Obv.: Head of Arethusa to the left with necklace, earrings, and hair fastened with stalks of grain; below ΦΙ. Around, three dolphins, two swimming to the left and one to the right.
Rev.: Quadriga to the left; above triskeles; in the exergue, ΣΥΡΑΚΟΣΙΩΝ, and below monogram, ΑΙ; double exergue line.
SNGANS 5, no. 640–43

Fig. 16.2 *Syracuse, silver tetradrachm (Photos by the Author, courtesy of Vavy Pacheco Borges).*

3. Syracuse, bronze drachm, 32.22 g, axis: 6
Beginning of the fourth century BC
Obv.: ΣΥΡΑ Head of Athena to the left, wearing Corinthian helmet with laurel wreath.
Rev.: Sea star between two dolphins.
SNGANS 5, no. 454–69
SNGMorcom, no. 697–703
Calciati, II: 131, no. 66

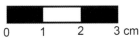

Fig. 16.3 *Syracuse, bronze drachm (Photos by the Author, courtesy of Vavy Pacheco Borges).*

4. Aetna, bronze, 16.20 g, axis: 11
400–350 BC (probably issued by the Campanian garrison established by Dionysios I)
Obv.: [ΑΙΤΝΑΙΩΝ- out of flan] Head of Athena to the right wearing plain Corinthian helmet.
Rev.: Free horse prancing to the right, free reins. Above, M.
SNGANS 5, no. 1301
Calciati, III:141–43, no. 1

Fig. 16.4 *Aetna, bronze (Photos by the Author, courtesy of Vavy Pacheco Borges).*

A Brief Iconographical Commentary

All these coins have been widely studied by numismatists and historians since at least the nineteenth century. Historical contexts for their issue, artistic style of their engravings, classification, weight standards, and chronology of the different series were and still are subjects broadly treated in articles, books, and scientific meetings. Moreover, poets, artists, and collectors have for many years been interested in the images of Siceliot coins placed – since antiquity – among the most beautiful of all Greek coins.

We all are well aware that Greek coin types can be very clear and allow, in many instances, a straightforward interpretation. We also know that they can be very puzzling, which is why it is now irresistible to put forward some ideas concerning details of the imagery on these four coins, even though the main goal of this modest paper is to make the specimens known to the scientific public.

Let us start with the quadriga, a characteristic coin type in Siceliot coinages and not at all limited to Syracusan series. The quadriga has been, at least since the nineteenth century, associated with the first generations of Greek colonists in Sicily. Related to agonistic competitions and to legendary wars, the cars pulled by horses have always been interpreted as a privilege of the aristocratic classes who were the only ones able to keep that kind of equipment. If, when these coins were issued, war was no longer fought with quadrigas or bigas, car races in the pan-Hellenic games were common and were specially sponsored by rulers or by a polis community. Very little need be added to these lines of interpretation of quadrigas in Siceliot coins. Maybe, in light of recent studies on Hellenic identity, we could point out that Greek colonists established in the Western Mediterranean might have used the representation of typical, legendary Greek war equipment to reaffirm their Hellenic ancestry (Hall 2002). However, we cannot forget the role of pan-Hellenic games in the construction of Greek character, and it is only natural that the special position of the western poleis in the Greek world led them to take advantage of these pan-Hellenic meetings to prove how Greek they were (Morgan 1994; Hall 2002).

Arethusa's representation is perhaps more problematic. Sometimes this female head is identified with Arethusa as on Figure 16.1. Other times, especially when the female head is crowned by ears of grains or just by grains, as we see on Figure 16.2 minted by Agathocles, she may appear in catalogues, articles, and books identified with Demeter or Kore/Persephone. This deity's attribute – the grains – would be definite proof that we are faced with a representation of an agricultural entity. I try in other publications to show that there are several subtleties in this representation and that the comparison with coin types from other Siceliot towns can cast some light upon the meaning of nymphs with grain crowns (Florenzano 2005). I believe that several nymphs on Siceliot coinage who appear crowned by ears of grains are still nymphs, and the use of Demeter's or Kore/Persephone's attributes only mark a relationship to these deities of agriculture and of civilization. This is the case of the nymph Pelorias, for instance, the personification of the Peloritan promontory of Messana. This nymph's head is depicted on the coinage of Messana from the end of the fifth century on crowned with grain ears, and we can be certain the female head is that of Pelorias because she is depicted with the inscription ΠΕΛΟΡΙΑΣ (*SNGANS* 4, no. 394). So here too we may affirm that in both Figure 16.1 and Figure 16.2 the female head is Arethusa's, even if in Figure 16.2 she is crowned by a stalk of grain.

I also offer some brief commentaries on the representation of the dolphins swimming around Arethusa's head, especially on Figure 16.1. Dolphins are, as a matter of course, related to aquatic environments, and we all know the importance of water in a civilization that depends on agriculture to survive, as did the ancient Greek colonies in Sicily. Moreover, the relationship between water, fish, fertility, and survival is more than well established nowadays. On Syracusan coins dolphins make their first appearance associated with Arethusa's head. As Arethusa is a fluvial and/or fountain nymph, her relationship to dolphins is nothing but normal. Nevertheless, I call attention to some aesthetic aspects of the iconographical composition of the head of Arethusa and the four dolphins. The head of Arethusa first appears on incuse reverses in the center of a swastika (see *SNGANS* 5, no. 1–5); the design then develops into a bigger head, the swastika disappears, and the four dolphins take the place of the swastika's legs in a secondary position. Is this just an aesthetic development or does it have special meaning? What does the swastika mean, and why at a certain point does it give way to the representation of the four dolphins? Do the swastika and the four dolphins have the same meaning?

The composition of this device, the swastika, is very close to that of the triskeles – seen on the reverse of Figure 16.2 – especially if we consider that (in the long history of this design) the triskeles did not always have a little foot at the end of each leg. As a matter of fact, it is clear that the notion of movement and speed is the main concept that informs both devices, the swastika and the triskeles.

Much has already been said about the triskeles in Greek art and especially as Agathocles' personal badge (Bruneau 1987; Wilson 2000; Florenzano 2007). This is not the place to repeat all the interpretative arguments concerning the use of the emblem by this ruler. Even so, I recuperate some of Agnes Baldwin's provocative ideas on the symbolism of the swastika and of the triskeles. I believe that her Jungian interpretation will help us better understand part of the meaning of these designs and clarify or enrich their articulation with the head of Arethusa. For Baldwin swastika and triskeles were "more reasonably interpreted as an expression for the sun in motion, sun's limbs, like the other 'turning' symbols. All these figures taken by themselves might be held in theory to represent the abstract concept 'speed' but their use on the monuments leads to the conclusion that that they are pictorial images of a concrete

thing in nature, the ever moving sun. . . . The sun's daily course in the heavens is conceived as a birth and a rebirth. The sun sails above the sea into which it dips every evening and every day it once more arises and is born again. . . . Light, fire, flame, the sun, sun's rays, etc., are in turn equated with life. . . . The swastika, the triskeles became potent and magic signs because they are expressions of the vital thing in human life" (Baldwin 1977, 192–93). In the case of these two strong emblematic designs, the swastika and the triskeles, I propose that they had a general meaning in antiquity, which was perceived by those who looked at them: sun, movement, energy, fertility, and so forth. According to the specific use made by the community or by a ruler, the symbol would be charged with other subsidiary meanings, some stronger and lasting and others bound to disappear. On one hand, Arethusa as the fluvial patroness of Syracuse was related to dolphins, her aquatic companions, as much as she was related to the swastika, a life and fertility symbol. On the other hand, Agathocles may have taken advantage of the more general meaning of the triskeles as a fertility or an energy symbol when he chose the it as his badge.

The representation of the head of Athena on the bronze coins (Fig. 16.3 and Fig. 16.4) deserves a few words. Even though the influence of Athenian coin typology in Western Greece – and that means Athena's head depicted with an Attic helmet – is very strong during the fifth and first half of the fourth century (AA VV 1969) what we see on these two coins is Athena with a Corinthian helmet, not an Attic helmet. The presence of Corinthian and Attic helmets on Western Greek coins have been explained mainly by the alternation of political and/or commercial influence of Corinth and Athens (AA VV 1993a; 1993b). Even if this could be a strong reason for the choice of the model of this deity's head, I believe that we have to consider other variables. For instance, why did the Campanian mercenaries of Aetna (as in Figure 16.4) choose Athena on a Corinthian helmet? For whom were these coins intended? What influences were brought from Campania? What was the role of Syracuse in the choice of this type? I believe that the representation of Athena's head in Western Greek coinage is not completely explained and would gain considerable sense if analyzed in the light of comparative studies of the several mints that adopted them.

Acknowledgments

I thank Vavy Pacheco Borges, widow of Mr. A. Costilhes, for placing this collection at my disposal for photographs and study. After completion of this article, the collection of Alain Costilhes was sold to a Brazilian Private University, Univesidade de Santo Amaro (UNISA), where it is kept and may be seen at the Library.

Works Cited

AA VV (1969) *La circolazione della moneta ateniese in Sicilia e in Magna Grecia.* Atti del Convegno del Centro Internazionale di Studi Numismatici, Naples, 5–8 April 1967. Rome, Istituto Italiano di Numismatica.

———— (1993a) *La monetazione della età dionigiana.* Atti del Convegno del Centro Internazionale di Studi Numismatici, Naples, 29 May–1 June 1983. Rome, Istituto Italiano di Numismatica.

———— (1993b) *La monetazione corinzia in Occidente.* Atti del Convegno del Centro Internazionale di Studi Numismatici, Naples, 27–28 October 1986. Rome, Istituto Italiano di Numismatica.

Baldwin, A. (1977) *Symbolism on Greek Coins.* Numismatic Publications, Sanford J. Durst, New York. (Reprinted from *American Journal of Numismatics*, ANS 1915, 49, 89–194).

Boehringer, E. (1929) *Die Munzen von Syrakus.* Berlin and Leipzig, Walter de Gruyter & Co.

Bruneau, Ph. (1987) Le "triskèle" dans l'art grec. In J. Bousquet and P. Naster (eds.) *Mélanges offerts au Docteur J.-B. Colbert de Beaulieu,* 145–56. Paris, Le Léopard d'Or.

Calciati, R. (1983–1987) *Corpus Nummorum Siculorum. La monetazione di bronzo.* Vol I–III, Edizione GM, Milan.

Florenzano, M. B. B. (2004) Obituaire. Alain Costilhes (1931–2003). *Revue Belge de Numismatique* CL, 277.

———— (2005) Coins and religion. Representations of Demeter and of Kore/Persephone on Sicilian Greek coins. *Revue Belge de Numismatique,* CLI, 1–28.

———— (2007) A note on the "triskeles" as the badge of Sicily: Territorial identity in Ancient Greek Sicily. In G. Moucharte, M. B. B. Florenzano, F. De Callataÿ, P. Marchetti, L. Smolderen and P. Yannopoulos (eds.), *Liber Amicorum Tony Hackens,* 153–157. Louvain-la-Neuve, Association de numismatique professeur Marcel Hoc.

Hall, J. M. (2002) *Hellenicity: Between Ethnicity and Culture.* Chicago and London, The University of Chicago Press.

SNGANS 4 (1977) *Sylloge Nummorum Graecorum. The Collection of the American Numismatic Society,* part 4, Sicily II: Galaria to Styella. (Prepared by E. Jaunzems *et alii*) The American Numismatic Society, New York.

SNGANS 5 (1988) *Sylloge Nummorum Graecorum. The Collection of the American Numismatic Society,* part 5, Sicily III: Syracuse-Siceliotes. (Prepared by D. Berend *et alii*) The American Numismatic Society, New York.

SNGMorcom (1995) *Sylloge Nummorum Graecorum. Volume X. The John Morcom Collection of Western Greek Bronze Coins.* (Prepared by J. Morcom) The British Academy, Oxford University Press and Spink and Son Limited, Oxford and London.

Morgan, C. (1990) *Athletes and Oracles: The Transformation of Olympia and Delphi in the Eighth Century BC.* Cambridge and New York, Cambridge University Press.

Wilson, R. J. A. (2000) On the trail of the "Triskeles": From the McDonald Institute to Archaic Greek Sicily. *Cambridge Archaeological Journal* 10, 35–61.

SECTION IV
INTRODUCTION

Discovery and Discourse: Archaeology and Interpretation

Derek B. Counts and Anthony S. Tuck

Two graduate students busied themselves clearing an area at the base of a massive Bronze Age wall in preparation for an architect's rendering. From high atop a hill to the east, Holloway's words rolled forth in a deep baritone, narrating a story of pirates, heroes, and epic battles that breathed life into those very walls his graduate students sought to render in sterile ink. From a commanding place within the island fortress of Ustica, Ross Holloway was performing the duty of many field archaeologists as he presented the archaeological discoveries of the site to students visiting from the local grade school. But unlike those for whom these tasks are tiresome distractions from the rigors of daily life in the field, Holloway had captivated these children in wide-eyed, rapt attention. A fieldtrip that began in the bored minds of twelve-year-olds ended with a true sense of the grandeur of the past.

It many respects, it is fitting that a section entitled, *Discovery and Discourse: Archaeology and Interpretation* should be the final one of this volume. As laid out in this volume's introduction, questions of the physical history of the past begin with the processes of excavation, lead us down the pathways of analysis, interrogation, discussion, and eventually, return to the field to test our conclusions and beliefs against the inevitability of new discovery. So much of Holloway's career has followed this cycle. Within the context of five decades of academic production, Holloway's contributions to field archaeology (most notably the elucidation of southern Italian and Sicilian material culture) stand at the forefront. His bibliography (Cova, this volume) is packed with interim reports from the field, synthetic discussions of finds and context, and comprehensive and prompt publications of final results. Indeed, these contributions were recognized by the Archaeological Institute of America when, in 1995, it awarded Holloway its most prestigious award, the Gold Medal for Distinguished Archaeological Achievement. In conferring this honor, the AIA directly acknowledged the significance of Holloway's research, his breadth of scope, and his unwavering dedication to archaeological fieldwork and discourse. The following is an excerpt from the citation:

> Through [his] excavations, Prof. Holloway has revolutionized the study of Italian prehistory. Carbon 14 dates obtained by him at Buccino (1967–1974) and La Muculufa (1982–1987) have pushed back the beginning of the Early Bronze Age in Italy and Sicily at least 500 years, from the late third/early second millennium to the early or mid-third millennium. His work at Buccino revealed the earliest dated bronze weapons from the Italian peninsula. That at La Muculufa discovered the earliest clearly identified regional sanctuary of Bronze Age Sicily. His book, *Italy and the Aegean: 3000–700 B.C.*, published in 1981, has proven to be a prophetic guide to the rethinking of this field. His current

excavations at Ustica have uncovered what may be the best-preserved Middle Bronze Age town of the region and have found the first stone sculpture of the area, attributed to the second millennium B.C. (published in R. R. Holloway and S. Lukesh, *Ustica I: Excavations of 1990 and 1991*). Ross Holloway has also examined later periods in Italy through his excavations at Satrianum (1966–1967). This work marked the first concerted effort to study a native Lucanian center and provided evidence for the relationship of this area to the coastal Greek cities of both the sixth and fourth centuries B.C. Several complete and prompt publications have resulted from these excavations, including *Satrianum: The Archaeological Investigations Conducted by Brown University in 1966 and 1967* (1970), *Buccino: The Eneolithic Necropolis of San Antonio. Discoveries Made in 1968 and 1969* (1973), and *La Muculufa: The Early Bronze Age Sanctuary. Excavations of 1982 and 1983* (1990) (*American Journal of Archaeology* 100, 1996, 338).

While Holloway's excavations and publications have garnered him an international reputation, his dedication to the field (which he himself traces back to an early stage in life, see Allen in this volume) has extended beyond his own research and scholarly output. As co-founder of the Association for Field Archaeology (AFFA) and long-time editorial board member of its prestigious *Journal of Field Archaeology*, Holloway was actively involved in the early efforts to establish *classical* archaeology as an academic discipline in the United States (see especially, Holloway 1983b), necessarily independent from its traditional 'parent' disciplines of classics and art history. Moreover, his ardent belief that classical archaeology demanded specialized, unique training at the undergraduate and subsequent graduate levels led to the creation of Brown University's Center for Old World Archaeology and Art (and recently rededicated as the Joukowsky Institute for Archaeology and the Ancient World). Founded in 1978, roughly a decade after the establishment of similar programs at the University of Michigan and the University of California at Berkeley, the Center was among the early pioneers of independent, degree-granting, interdisciplinary programs in classical archaeology and art in the United States.

An insistence on the artifact, its context, and the elucidation of its place in a wider history have always punctuated Holloway's research. His recognition of archaeological scholarship as a constant interplay or dialogue between the excavator, the scientist, the historian, the philosopher and even the prophet has resulted in a body of research that transforms the objects of the past into history. The papers in this section encapsulate the processes of discovery and discourse that mark the career of a field archaeologist.

The six contributions to this volume's final section each reflect different facets of a career of exploration, discovery, consideration and discussion. Lukesh's article overviews the history of Holloway's excavations at the Bronze Age Sicilian site of Ustica and highlights Holloway's role in bringing this critical body of material to the attention of audiences often unaware of the remarkable complexity of social and commercial interaction between the Eastern and Central Mediterranean during this dynamic period. Joukowsky's comprehensive presentation of her fascinating excavations at the Nabataean site of Petra begins, like Lukesh, where all archaeological inquiry must, in the field. Not only does her detailed account of the discoveries at the site reflect Brown University's longstanding commitment to the sponsorship of field projects, it also reminds us that well known sites can still yield startling revelations when re-examined with new techniques of excavation and documentation.

The spirit of rigorous reinterpretation of our academic assumptions is on display in two additional contributions to this section. Barletta expands her groundbreaking work on the origins of the Greek architectural orders by drawing on comparisons that reach far beyond the Greek world. In so doing, she not only adds considerable strength and nuance to her previous arguments, but also reminds us that evidence in support of our ideas need not always come from predictable sources. Van Keuren and Gromet's article examines Roman marble sarcophagi, which have been documented and studied by antiquarians and scholars for centuries. Nevertheless, through a careful application of isotopic and iconographic analysis, the authors provide essential commentary for both the material production and economic marketing of such sarcophagi, a process that yields some surprising results. This willingness to employ a range of archaeometric techniques in the service of traditional archaeological and art historical questions echoes Holloway's own longstanding willingness to reach out to other fields and employ new analytical techniques to advance our knowledge of the field.

Finally, the contributions of Kampen and Dyson remind us that discovery inspires and directs discourse, which in turn often yields new discoveries. Turning to one of the most famous statues of the Classical world, the Aphrodite of Knidos, Kampen's article draws upon feminist theory to consider the gendered perspective of women in ancient sanctuaries as fundamentally different from that of men. Dyson's contribution, fitting in its position at the end of this volume, considers not merely the ancient monumentality of the Ara Pacis, but also the political implications of the modern architectural framing of a pivotal element of Augustan propaganda. Both Kampen and Dyson apply approaches that shed light on the motivations of the past, as well as reveal to us how our view of antiquity shapes the ways we understand the world today.

While each of these essays offers intriguing new evidence and fresh ideas for consideration and debate, they also reflect the fact that the questions that frame the discipline of archaeology begin in the field and must always return to it. Holloway's work continues, not only though his own scholarship, but through the myriad of students, friends, and colleagues whose own thinking is continually ignited through the example of his passion for the field and his remarkable curiosity of intellect. Holloway's work will continue for generations yet to come, inspired by his vision of and commitment to the principle that the field archaeologist stands as an indispensable partner in the inquiries of history.

17

Infinite Attention to Detail: A Slice of Sicily in the Third and Second Millennia BCE

Susan S. Lukesh

More than four thousand year ago, a master craftsman surveyed the painted cups and vessels produced by a workshop and community of artisans in the river valley. This was a workshop less of a specific physical space, although that was certainly required, and more of shared design information across the community of potters and painters. Many of the objects were uniquely painted, others echoed patterns painted on similar pots, and still others attempted to replicate the master's own work; none could achieve the originality and technique his pots displayed. Many of the painted motifs reflected the glorious woven baskets and woven cup holders hanging from hut roofs and common rooms. The pots from the workshop and others like them would find their way to the regular gathering of communities at the head of the salty river, upland from the sea, below the limestone cliffs where the ancestors rested their bones; others were used to hold unguents and other precious materials. Some of the vessels might well have come from another community closer to the setting sun where minerals used for lustral practices were harvested and traded. In the same community the production of pots was organized among a number of painters for each pot. The master potter might know that his vessels would eventually be broken but could not know that one of them would be painstakingly reconstructed from hundreds of fragments during long winter nights four thousand years later to serve as proof of the talents, capabilities, and achievements of these people. With knowledge of the related pots, people millennia later would begin to appreciate the complexity and sophistication of this federation of communities in southern Sicily and would turn to study artisan colleagues farther west on the island.

West toward Agrigento and north to Caltanissetta there were other groups of people related to the master and his fellow craftsmen. In this area families joined other families in small communities, and the relationships grew into federations. They built and lived in villages of huts with stone foundations; used everyday pottery of cups, jars, and mixing craters and bowls; created and used intricately decorated painted pottery, cups, large storage vessels, and the ubiquitous footed pot; and traded among themselves. They had bone tools, loom weights, and spindle whorls that argue for weaving and manufacture of clothing. Their periodic gatherings, apparently for religious ceremonies, were quite possibly tinged with commercial purposes. When travelling long distances toward the breaking sun some wore a bone-carved amulet suspended from a cord around their necks as a token of identification in a world where people were bound by ties of guest-friendship even if thousands of mile away.

At the site of La Muculufa, the probable home of our master potter and vase painter, the gathering place faced east. Behind it were towering limestone bluffs in whose rock-cut chamber tombs the people and their ancestors were interred. These chamber tombs were prepared well before death by a small group of people whose job it was to cut tombs, and, in a climate in which the body was reduced to a skeleton in a short period of time, they allowed easy reuse of the space for a new body as old bones and grave goods were swept aside. Bronze was known to them although precious enough that it was closely guarded and little of it left behind. Their remains are largely some whole pots and broken pottery, chipped stone tools and a burned bone plaque, the latter clear testimony of travels far beyond Sicily. At La Muculufa the high craftsmanship of the master artist and other artists attempting to replicate his work and the evidence of multiple hands on pots from the group in the Agrigento areas, along with the evidence of sulphur extraction and refining, speak of complex organizations more suggestive of later times or more eastern Mediterranean peoples. West of La Muculufa, Monte Grande, Grotta Ticchiara, Piano Vento, and Ciavolaro in the Agrigento area are some of the recently excavated sites from which we can begin to reconstruct the way of life representative of this group of sites belonging to the Castelluccian culture, which takes its name from a site southwest of Syracuse excavated by the great Paolo Orsi before 1900.

Centuries later descendents of these people had an elaborate nexus of trading relationships and warehouses specifically designed for commercial purpose. Experience with sulphur mining and the commerce associated with it had propelled them to far more elaborate and long-range trading opportunities such as manufacture, sale, and transport of copper ingots. One community (I Faraglioni di Ustica) on another Bronze Age site, though of slightly later date off the northern coast, developed a fortified citadel complete with dressed stone – evocative of eastern neighbors – on the seaward side. The citadel and the group of houses and shrines located within it show clear evidence of successive destruction and rebuilding; some of the destruction occurred during rebuilding, offering argument of attack or sack. A few standard pieces of pottery served for food storage, cooking, serving, and drinking. A coarse sack-shaped vessel burnt on the inside was probably a stove, with another vessel resting on the rim, its contents heated or reheated by the coals beneath. Pedestalled bowls permitted diners seated on the ground or on the low benches to have their food at a convenient level. The inhabitants in these early days of sea commerce chose the long-standing occupation of pirate, luring vessels sailing north of the island to crash on the shore. Fires lit on the natural stone tower of I Faraglioni suggested at night that the Sicilian coast was quite close; instead shallow rocks off the island captured the vessel and its occupants, allowing the pirates to remove the goods on board, reason enough for future sacking of the site. Counters or jetons speak of a need for "bookkeeping" perhaps dictated by their commerce. Offerings to spirits or gods were made before meals through a hollow ceramic goddess stand-in (alare), a very local development whose origins are found on the Sicilian mainland; a miniature alare worn on a cord around the neck sufficed for offerings when travelling on a boat. These people evaporated salt from sea water to use medicinally, to tan animal skins, and for dietary purposes. A sculptor fashioned from local stone the only known surviving piece of stone sculpture of the second millennium BCE (Italy, Sicily, and neighboring islands), a standing clothed goddess with upraised arms. She speaks directly of the monumental handles on footed vessels from southeast Sicily. And these folks cast small bronze objects and left other remains showing additional rare but clear examples of contact with the eastern Mediterranean. This was a sophisticated settlement of the late second millennium BCE.

"Historians tell stories. That is their profession. And the goal of storytelling is to impose order on a disorderly array of facts" (Grimes 2007, E9). It is part of the archaeologist's job to acquire or reveal facts and then to tell a story. The great Scotsman Thomas Carlyle is purported to have said,

"Genius is the capacity for infinite attention to detail." If there is any single hallmark of a successful archaeologist, whether genius or not, it is attention to detail and the subsequent ability to move from detail or microscopic view to the wide lens in which fragments of history are seen in the context of the whole. Closely identified with an archaeologist's tasks is the identification and scrutiny of excavation strata, the fall of rocks, and the construction traces left in building foundations and remains, activities that are closely identified with archaeologists' abilities to interpret events thousands of years ago as well as the relationships within a site and possible relationships to other sites. In addition to analysis of the strata and buildings, close study of other remains yields enormous insight into activities and relationships of the site. The detailed study of these materials and the understanding of them in the context of their times directly develop our understandings of how prehistoric peoples lived, the social organizations they formed, the material goods that display significant levels of achievement, and even some events and activities that shaped their lives. How can we take the often meager remains from prehistoric sites and turn them into a story, an explanation of the past, not a simple catalogue of objects? Some of the material studies discussed here help us do just that, demonstrating how we can reconstruct the lives of people many millennia dead with no written records, how we "impose order on a disorderly array of facts."

Attempts to understand prehistoric times have existed as long as there has been a curiosity about the events and activities preceding the availability of written records. From the Greek side, prior to the works of Herodotus and Thucydides, Homer's songs constitute a record, albeit an oral one later transcribed. Homer also has provided us with some remarkable descriptions of daily life and objects, enormously useful in helping interpret remains found from comparable periods. And his work presents strong support for the concept of families becoming villages becoming federations. Homer's world also knows the process of families.

> And this is the village-state of Italy and Sicily, as it was remembered in the Homeric tradition, the Phaeacia of Nausithoos or the town of the Laestrygonians. This is a community where leadership is unstable because leadership belongs to the most dynamic leader in a body of citizen peers. This is a community that is never so large that the every citizen peer cannot participate directly in government. This situation gave vitality first to the village and then to the ancient city-state, and to endure as a city-state, the city-state could never grow past the limits of citizen participation in government. The ancient city-state remained a village. (Holloway 1997, 5)

If we consider later Sicilian prehistory, we see also that our understandings may be based on ancient legend, as in many other fields of later prehistory. In this instance, and from more contemporary times, we have the various fantasies

distribution networks in general and parallels early-twentieth-century studies of classical vase painters. Sir John Davidson Beazley (1885–1970), an archaeologist and art historian, concentrated his studies on Attic vase painting and, with an eye for style and a strong visual memory, succeeded in his goal of isolating individual styles and tying painters and potters to one another. Philippe Rouet offers an analysis of Beazley's development of the concepts of schools, workshops, and circles directly applicable to these concepts in Castelluccian pottery. He quotes Beazley's predecessor Hartwig, "Even if the name of the master who painted the cups . . . is not undisputed, nonetheless, as we shall see, his individual personality will become clearly apparent to us from his works" (Rouet 2001, 96), and acknowledges the handicap faced in understanding the actual production: "even today we are very short of precise information about the conditions in which vases were produced in the workshops of the Kerameikos" (Rouet 2001, 98). That in the twenty-first century we are still somewhat in the dark about fifth-century BCE ceramic production underscores why we are not close to understanding the pottery production in the late third millennium. Yet, with the vase paintings of the Salso River Valley Castelluccians, at least one individual personality comes through, one who impressed some other artisans to emulate his works.

While we may remain in the dark about the actual production of pottery, we can firmly place the geometric design patterns of many Castelluccian vases in context. Rather than argue as Sluga Messina (1983) does for parallel motifs drawn from the eastern Mediterranean, whose very expanse of the area and the lack of precise chronological connections mitigate against drawing any significant conclusions, I have argued previously (Lukesh 1999) that to account for apparently spontaneous appearances of geometric motifs one must turn to common, nonornamental inspiration, such as textiles, basketry, and wickerwork. Clear connections between long-standing traditional basketry and woven patterns not only provides a source for the motifs but also strengthens our understanding of the textiles and baskets available to these people.

Our understanding of prehistoric craft specialization is greatly amplified by study of Castelluccian material from Grotta Ticchiara, excavated and published by Castellana (1997). Here we need simply compare the external and internal designs of footed pots from Grotta Ticchiara (see Lukesh 2006, figs. 15–17). This analysis was facilitated by the development of a digital archive of prehistoric pottery that allows for easy review of images of each item, access to detailed information for each item, selection of subsets of items (based on size, pot shape, site, etc.), and, of critical importance, comparison of up to eight items on a single screen. In essence, this archive facilitates the direct comparison of objects, whether pots or coins. One of the features built into the software allows the selection and display of like material (based on a variety of variables, e.g., shape, decoration patterns, and assemblage type). Selection of classic Castelluccian footed vases and further display of eight of them on a single page presented some very interesting information. The first three pots show little similarity in the decoration schema or style and technique when we look at external decoration. When we select the second image for interior views, the first three pedestalled pots show a remarkable similarity of the internal decoration, both in overall design, individual components, and reflections of a specific hand. It is possible to hypothesize that while the interiors were painted by one craftsman, the outsides were painted by a series of other craftsmen. Similarly one could hypothesize that the interior mattered and the outside didn't. Both such hypotheses give us a basis for further studies and understandings of the Castelluccian potters and way of life and argue for a complex pottery manufacturing environment.

Evidence for workshops of potters and pot painters who share decorative motifs and emulate one another's work (La Muculufa), as well as for potters and pot painters who split the responsibilities for pot decoration (Grotta Ticchiara), expand our knowledge of the social and economic organization of these people and support the concept of confederations proposed by both Holloway and Castellana for the Sicilian Castelluccian peoples. These examples underscore the criticality of the pottery evidence in understanding the dynamics of the populations, not only as one site relates to another, not only as evidence of food and household goods, but also as evidence of organized social and economic structures and relationships among sites and workers. There remains much to be done with the study of Castelluccian pottery manufacture, which we argue was directly related to the commercialization of the world at that time. If we consider the much later world of Etruscan pottery manufacture, we can see possible parallels to the statement of Nijboer: "I will argue that a redirection of the production facilities is an intrinsic component of the centralization processes occurring in Italy from 800 to 400 BC. They are embedded in the transition from village to town, from communal to private property and from tribal to state formation" (1998, x).

That geometric-painted handmade pottery could be attributed to individual artists, that these potters of handmade vessels and painted decoration might form into workshops, sharing decorative motifs and imitating one another, had not previously been widely considered. While up to this point we've been looking at Castelluccian Sicily, if we consider now some wider considerations of Italian and Sicily prehistory we can see that the attribution of pots to specific artists is a development parallel to the close study of prehistoric pots from Southern Italy. In this effort, the mathematical distinction between Protoapennine and Subapennine pottery was developed in the late 1970s using material derived from Holloway's excavations at Tufariello (Holloway *et al.* 1975) as well as measurements of other materials gathered during the summer of 1976 (Lukesh and Howe 1978). What it indicated, as Jean-Claude Gardin wrote in a personal note to one of the authors (Lukesh), is "the claims of hand-made pottery to pattern determinants as much as wheel-made." In effect, it was proven that analysis of the measurements of the pots of very similar aspect could determine which group of pots was under analysis. The early and later Apennine potters (separated by close to a thousand years) produced visually similar pots but with finely distinguished, different mental templates, ones that mathematical analysis of measurements is required to firmly differentiate. In other words, those working in the earlier times produced pottery visually similar to but mathematically differentiable from the later material. These results are a confirmation not only of the individuality of the people but also of strong cultural/temporal distinctions underlying the manufacture of the pottery. And, like the attribution of pots to specific hands, are another step in demonstrating the social complexity of these peoples.

Teglie, thin-bottomed vessels with coarse thick walls whose use is not immediately apparent, offer another window on the possible industries of the Late Bronze Age people (full discussion with references is found in Holloway and Lukesh 1995, 33–36). A review of possible uses and like objects brought the conclusion that these vessels, found on an island in close proximity to salt water, were used to collect salt. The *teglie* from Ustica show no evidence of having been placed on the fire, and the fragility of the *teglie* bottoms argues against this, but they do demonstrate sure evidence of having been placed near fire. One examination of salt in a study of economic prehistory (Nenquin 1961) shows how it can be evaporated with the assistance of indirect heat, not requiring a pot to be placed on an open fire. Analysis of the amount of salt available from evaporation, given the size and number of such vessels, shows it was more than adequate for consumption as well as medicine, animals, food preservation, and tanning of skins. In the Mediterranean climate salt is a necessary part of the diet, since an imbalance or absence can lead to death through a rapid evaporation of water in the body causing dehydration. While we cannot know with this evidence alone the use these people had for salt, close study of the vessels and an understanding of their use in acquiring salt lead us to a better understanding of some of the possible industries during this time.

Another example of developing a broader interpretation of an early culture is the study and subsequent analysis of alari. These objects, well known throughout Sicily and the Mediterranean and found in abundance at Ustica and Monte Grande, are named for a device used to hold wood in a fireplace, yet it is clear that this is not the function. For some time they have been referred to as cult or votive objects with no attempt to suggest how they may have functioned. Efforts following the recovery of a miniature version on Ustica led us to a number of objects recovered in Sicily that helped interpret the history of these objects as well as appreciate their ritual importance (see the final publication of *Ustica II* for full discussion and illustrations; Holloway and Lukesh 2001, 51–53). A female figurine from Camuti attributed to the Castelluccian period has two stubby arms thrust forward and two slight protuberances on the "head," one on each side. Another object, identified as a female alare, no longer has a cylindrical body but a conical body, and has added a handle to its back. Between the two protuberances at the top is a small hole. It is a small step from this figure to the development of the alare as we know it from Bronze Age Sicily. I have suggested that the alare, ubiquitous across Bronze Age sites, easily picked up and set down, open from top to bottom, and continuing in its fashion the long-standing shape of a female figurine, had indeed the commonplace but ritual use of a vessel for offering food to the gods, specifically the outpouring of wine or another liquid before a meal. The miniature alare, worn as an amulet, allowed its wearer to perform a libation, with the familiar goddess shape known from home, perhaps even on the open sea, where carrying the larger alare would be burdensome. That libations could clearly have been made without an alare suggests strongly either the importance of the shape – derived from and evocative of the female figurine – and/or the possibilities of additional ritual activities associated with the alare. Ceremonies associated with the correct positioning of the alare, the order of diverse libations, and even phrases invoked are just a few possibilities that might have enriched the ritual of libation but are lost to us today. There is, unfortunately, at this time no more evidence from which to draw conclusions. And yet, once again, attention to detail has allowed us to move beyond the object to the larger context of the world and the relationships in which it originated.

Round disks made from potsherds were evidently used as counters and routinely found in Bronze Age excavations across Sicily. Such pieces can be used in complex arithmetic operations, and in Europe the counting board or exchequer remained in use well into the seventeenth century. The development of counting using small clay objects modelled in various forms has been argued by Schmandt-Besserat, who helps place their use in the context of the times: "The multiplicity of the counters argues that the first farmers mastered the notion of sets or cardinality but counted concretely. In other words they had no conception of numbers existing independently of measures of grain and animals that could be applied to either without reference to the other" (1999, 191). The quantities found in Bronze Age sites across Sicily, specifically Ustica and Monte Grande, lend strength to the arguments for complex commercial transactions undertaken by these peoples. Those recovered on Ustica were carefully counted and tied to specific findspots. Numbering close to six hundred, they were recovered concentrated along the row of buildings below the site of the hypothesized ruler's headquarters. Most notably, they also become scarce in the strata associated with the latest phases of the site, the period of siege, capture, abandonment of houses, and frenetic repair of the walls, when administration and record keeping had obviously broken down.

The conclusions drawn from these examples are directly related to the serious attention to details as well as to the use, from initial excavations undertaken by Holloway and Lukesh, of the capture of data in computer format, detailed records tied to find locations, and subsequent analysis. Obviously without the easy digital access to measurements and the use of statistical techniques, the existence of templates for handmade pottery could not have been proven. Without the computer records of fine-grain decoration patterns, the amassing of sherds with like patterns for study would have been far more difficult. And in the example of interior and exterior pottery decoration discussed just above, the digital archive – developed directly from the database used and developed over time – provided the ability to easily pull together like material and display it side by side for easy visual comparison.

Finally, without the record keeping of all objects recovered and their findspots across the site, it would not be possible to discuss the implications where counters are found, for example, or of negative evidence – that is, material whose remains are not found or which are found in far more limited parts of the excavation. Here again the underlying systems augmented the archaeological research. While archaeologists look to make contributions to the larger picture of under-standings of prior lives, hoping to write chapters if not books on the social history of mankind, in all cases, this can only be done by the attention to the small and mundane, whether broken pots turned into counters, or undecorated pots, whose measurements demonstrate three thousand years later their common bonds, or geometrical motifs, whose individual parts and workmanship speak of a common hand. I end this piece quoting the man we are honoring in this volume:

> [W]e must also avoid limiting our vision of the past only to the surviving material evidence without acknowledging that the objects are also pointers to technology – and thus to verbally transmitted knowledge – to traditions – and thus to social continuity – to both utility and display – and thus not only to the working life of a community but also to creativity and the diplomacy of men's relations with neighbors and gods at home and foreigners over the horizon. To keep in mind what is superficially missing in the physical record but was present in its creation opens our eyes to many things that in a literate society would be recorded but that with the judicious use of imagination can be recaptured even in the absence of the written word. (Holloway 2000, 2).

Works Cited

Castellana G. (1997) *La grotta Ticchiara ed il castellucciano agrigentino*. Agrigento, Regione Sicilia, Assessorato beni culturali ed ambientali e della pubblica istruzione.

——— (1998) *Il santuario castellucciano di Monte Grande e l'approvvigionamento dello zolfo nel Mediterraneo nell'età del bronzo*. Agrigento, Regione Sicilia, Assessorato beni culturali ed ambientali e della pubblica istruzione.

Castellana, G. and Pitrone, A. (2000) *La cultura del Medio Bronzo nell'agrigentino ed i rapporti con il mondo miceneo*. Agrigento, Regione Sicilia, Assessorato beni culturali ed ambientali e della pubblica istruzione.

Grimes, W. (2007) The many roads not taken in the way to civil war. Review of *Cry Havoc!*. *New York Times*, January 31, 2007, E9.

Holloway, R. R. (2000) The classical Mediterranean, its prehistoric past and the formation of Europe. Paper delivered at the I Congresso Internazionale di Preistoria e Protostoria Siciliane, Corleone, July 1997. Available at http://www.brown.edu/Departments/Joukowsky_Institute/resources/papers/classicalmed/report.html#f4

Holloway, R. R. and Colleagues (1975) Buccino: The Early Bronze village of Tufariello. *Journal of Field Archaeology* 12, 11–81.

Holloway, R. R. and Lukesh, S. S. (1995) *Ustica I, The Results of the Excavations of the Regione Siciliana Soprintendenza ai Beni Culturali ed Ambientali Provincia di Palermo in Collaboration with Brown University in 1990 and 1991*. Archaeologia Transatlantica 14. Louvain, Publications d'Histoire de l'Art e d'Archéologiche de L'Universite Catholique de Louvain 78.

——— (2001) *Ustica II, The Results of the Excavations of the Regione Siciliana Soprintendenza ai Beni Culturali ed Ambientali Provincia di Palermo in collaboration with Brown University in 1994 and 1999*. Providence, Brown University.

Holloway, R. R., Joukowsky, M. S. and Lukesh, S. S. (1990) La Muculufa, the Early Bronze Age sanctuary: The Early Bronze Age village (excavation 1982–83). *Revue des Archéologues et Historiens d'Art de Louvain* 23, 11–67.

Lukesh, S. S. (1993) The La Muculufa Master and company: The identification of a workshop of Early Bronze Age Castelluccian painters. *Revue des Archéologues et Historiens d'Art de Louvain* 25, 9–24.

——— (1999) Early Bronze Age Sicilian geometric decoration: Its origin and relationship to vessel form. In S. S. Lukesh (ed.), *INTERPRETATIO RERUM: Archaeological Essays on Objects and Meaning by Students of R. Ross Holloway*, 1–14. Providence, Center for Old World Archaeology and Art, Brown University.

——— (2006) All knowledge, past and present. *Journal of Electronic Publishing*, Summer, http://hdl.handle.net/2027/spo.3336451.0009.206.

Lukesh, S. S. and Howe, S. (1978) Protoapennine vs. Subapennine: Mathematical distinction between two ceramic phases. *Journal of Field Archaeology* 5 (3), 339–47.

Maniscalco, L. (1989) Ochre containers and trade in the central Mediterranean Copper Age. *American Journal of Archaeology* 84, 537–41.

Nenquin, J. (1961) Salt: A study in economic prehistory. Brugge, Belgium: De Tempel.

Nijboer, A. J. (1998) *Manufacturing and the Market in Early Etruria and Latium: From Household Production to Workshops. Archaeological Evidence for Economic Transformation, Pre-Monetary Exchange and Urbanization in Central Italy from 800 to 400 BC.* Groningen, University of Groningen, Department of Archaeology.

Rouet, P. (2001) *Approaches to the Study of Attic Vases: Beazley and Pottier.* New York, Oxford University Press.

Schmandt-Besserat, D. and Hays, M. (1992) *Before Writing.* Austin, University of Texas Press.

Sjöqvist, E. (1973) *Sicily and the Greeks: Studies in the Inter-relationship between the Indigenous Populations and the Greek Colonists.* Ann Arbor, University of Michigan Press.

Sluga Messina, G. (1983) *Analisi dei motive decorative della ceramica da Castelluccio di Noto (Siracusa), Universitat degli studia di Trieste, Facolta di Lettere e Filosofia, Istituto di Archeologia.* Rome, Edizioni dell'Ateneo.

18

The Greek Entablature and Wooden Antecedents

Barbara A. Barletta

In his treatise *De architectura*, the Roman architect Vitruvius attributes the distinctive forms of the Greek Doric and Ionic entablatures to wooden predecessors. When the Greeks adopted stone for their buildings, architects imitated these earlier forms in the new material. Modern scholars have generally accepted Vitruvius's account of a wooden origin for the Greek entablature, but they have had difficulty in locating specific models for the details. I have explored aspects of this issue elsewhere in conjunction with the origins and early development of the architectural orders (Barletta 2001, esp. 1–20). In honor of R. Ross Holloway and his broad cultural perspective, I take up the problem again here, using comparative material from beyond the Greek world.

Vitruvius's Account

According to Vitruvius, the architectural orders developed very early in Greek history, at a time that we may equate with the Dark Ages or Geometric period, thus between *c.* 1100 and 700 BC. We know from archaeological evidence that during these centuries the Greeks constructed their buildings primarily in perishable materials, that is, mudbrick and wood. The orders are likewise said to have evolved in wood. Vitruvius tells us (*De architectura* 4.2.1–5) that the Doric triglyph originated in boards fastened to the ends of tie beams, which were then decorated with blue wax, and that the metope filled the space between them (Fig. 18.1). Doric mutules represented the projections of the principal rafters below the cornice, while Ionic dentils imitated the projections of the common rafters (Fig. 18.2). Thus, these elements, which had become "ornaments" to Vitruvius, had their origins in functional components.

Modern scholars have expanded the association with wooden forms. Doric guttae are explained as nails or dowels, the taenia as a narrow plank placed on top of the architrave beam to supplement its size, and regulae as planks that partially covered that beam (Gerkan 1948–49, 7–8). The banded Ionic architrave is assumed to represent a series of horizontal boards, stacked one above the other with each projecting slightly beyond that below (Gerkan 1946–47, 17; Kähler 1949, 25). With the subsequent introduction of stone for architecture, these inventions made in wood were translated into the new material (see Hittorff 1870).

Vitruvius's derivation of the "ornaments" of the orders from wooden predecessors might thus explain forms that otherwise make little sense in stone. We know that the Greeks possessed not only an early but also a long tradition of construction in wood (Marconi, this volume). Even with the emergence of monumental architecture in the seventh and early sixth centuries, wood could still be used for major components (Barletta 2001, 125–26). Vitruvius's explanation also fits with both ancient and modern theories that trace a progression of artistic materials from wood to stone, and their renderings from less to more sophisticated. This view of artistic development was particularly propounded by J. J. Winckelmann, the father of art history, and has therefore come to underpin our own understanding of early art. As a result, subsequent scholars have accepted the evolutionary explanation as inherently logical (Barletta 2001, 7–8, 12–18).

In fact, the origins of stone architectural forms in perishable materials have been found also in the architectural expression of other cultures. The plant forms of Egyptian columns have been explained as a translation into stone of plants actually used as supports. The cavetto molding is thought to originate in the terminations of plants lashed together at the top. Perhaps the strongest connection with wooden predecessors is seen in Lycian tombs. The complex representation on house tombs and sarcophagi of projecting and spliced beams is attributed to a "petrification" of actual woodworking forms used in the Lycian house (Bridges 1993, 91).

Problems

Difficulties occur, however, in reconciling the specific forms with their presumed antecedents. This is especially the case with Doric triglyphs. They are found at the same level on

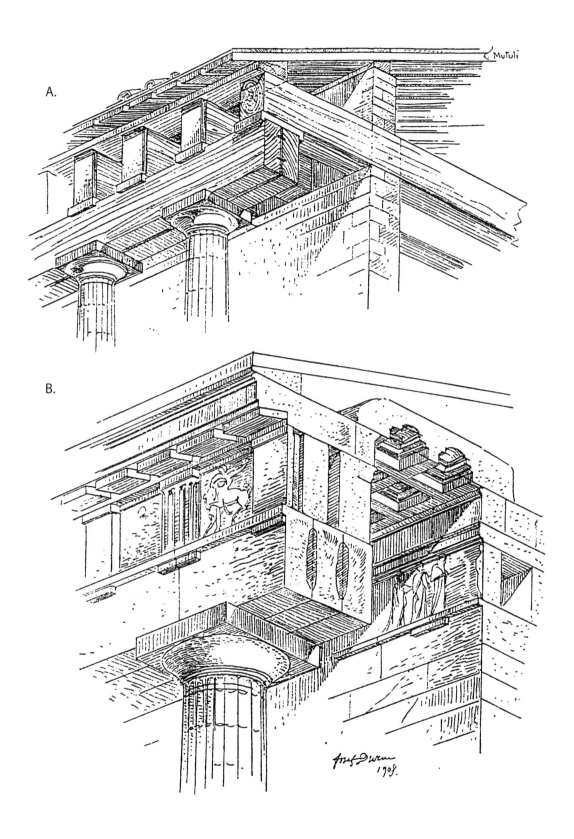

Fig. 18.1 *Doric entablature construction in wood (a) and stone (b) (From Durm 1910, 262, fig. 233).*

Ionic

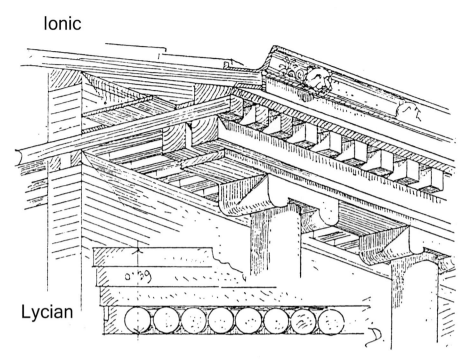

Lycian

Fig. 18.2 *Ionic and Lycian entablature constructions in wood (From Durm 1910, 329, fig. 315).*

all four sides of a building and terminate at the corners in adjacent faces. If these originated in panels covering tie- or ceiling- beams, one would expect them to appear at different heights on facades and flanks. This issue could be resolved if the beams were spliced, but even so, there would be no corner block. Additionally, beams of the size exemplified by triglyphs would be unnecessarily heavy and too closely spaced for their presumed function. It should also be noted that in surviving buildings, the ceiling beams rest at a higher level than the frieze. The mutules above the frieze suffer some of the same problems. As rafter ends, they, too, would have been spaced too closely, and there is no explanation for the guttae on their underside (Gerkan 1948–49, 10).

Vitruvius is not entirely clear regarding the composition of these members. In discussing triglyphs, he states only that the boards were "shaped" as the triglyph was in his time (Morgan 1960, 107). To judge from extant remains, such a wooden member would have been composed of three vertical boards with beveled edges extending most of their height and a horizontal board that united them at the top (Gerkan 1948–49, 8) and served visually as a crown. The taenia, which takes the form of a projecting band along the top of the architrave, as well as the pendant regulae and mutules are all relatively low in height. These would have consisted of narrow boards or planks. Yet scholars have noted the difficulty of producing planks in antiquity (Holland 1917, 147). In fact, the beams used in early buildings may have been unhewn, round logs (Winter 1993, 307).

Vitruvius is less informative about the Ionic entablature, offering wooden antecedents only for the dentils, which he claims imitate the projections of common rafters. As he was well aware (*De architectura* 4.2.1), however, these rafters lie above the other timbers. By contrast, dentils appear below the cornice and thus also the roof timbers. Vitruvius goes on to explain (*De architectura* 4.2.5) that neither dentils nor mutules appeared in the pediments because the rafters that they represented were laid on a slope. In a pitched roof, the common rafters would indeed slope downward, yet dentils project horizontally. They are also found on all sides of a building, which is likewise impossible with the usual type of Greek roof. Some scholars have tried to maintain the wooden background by suggesting that dentils represent the projection of ceiling beams rather than rafters (Gerkan 1946–47, 17, 24; Gruben 1963, 150 n. 123; Dinsmoor 1975, 64). Such beams would project horizontally, but they raise the same problems as noted for triglyphs: unless their joints were spliced, their ends would appear at different levels on the exterior of the building rather than in the uniform level of the dentil course.

While Vitruvius offers no explanation for the two or, more usually, three fasciae found on the Ionic architrave, modern scholars have derived them from a series of wooden boards (Gerkan 1946–47, 17, 21; Kähler 1949, 25). The earliest evidence for an epistyle with fasciae comes from the east porch of the Oikos of the Naxians on Delos, dated *c.* 560 BC, where this member is divided into two unequal bands, the upper less than one-half the height of the lower (Barletta 2001, 115–17). The architrave with three fasciae is first attested *c.* 540 BC in the Temple of Apollo at Didyma, but this articulation appears on only two sides of the building. On the remaining sides this member was smooth. In an earlier (*c.* 560–550 BC), albeit smaller, building from Ionic territory, the Treasury of the Knidians at Delphi, the architrave is likewise smooth. Such evidence speaks against an early origin in wood for the banded Ionic architrave. Moreover, its combination with figural relief in the Didyma architrave raises the possibility that its origins are more decorative than structural.

Various problems in equating the characteristics of the Doric and Ionic entablatures with constructional elements in wood have led several scholars (see Barletta 2001, 145–50) to assume only general inspiration from, rather than direct imitation of, such presumed predecessors. This point is explored further below. First we should ask how closely these wooden elements might have corresponded to the entablature in stone. The answer requires an examination of woodworking in Greece during the time when the entablature was coming into existence, the eighth and seventh centuries BC.

Wood was probably fairly plentiful in the Greek world, at least during early times (Meiggs 1982, esp. 371–99). Yet the Greek climate is not conducive to its preservation (Mols 1999, 69–72; but see Ohly 1953). Thus, we must extrapolate the level of woodworking ability in this period from the few items that do remain and the tools that were available. Such evidence can be supplemented by literary attestations and comparative material from other cultures (especially Egypt) that preserve more documentation.

Tools

The most basic tool for cutting wood was the axe. It was used for felling trees and in the initial preparation of timber. This tool was probably the first used by any people for woodworking and thus has a long history (Goodman 1964, 12). It was known in Greece by the Bronze Age and is mentioned by Homer in regard to Odysseus's construction of a boat (*Od.* 5.234–45). Pliny (*NH* 7.198) likewise assumes an early adoption of the carpenter's axe, attributing it, along with various other tools, to Daidalos as the inventor of woodworking (Richter 1966, 124).

The Greeks also had the saw, which could cut lengths of wood in rectangular and fairly smooth forms. Its use, however, may have been somewhat restricted. According to Meiggs (1982, 112), Homer's omission of the saw in his account of Odysseus's boat reflects actual practice. He argues that the saw was more important to the furniture maker than the shipbuilder. One problem is that saw blades, in iron as well as earlier in bronze, were narrow and could be used only in a pulling motion (Goodman 1964, 115). At least in

Egypt, this technique limited the length of the board produced; it could not exceed the height of the post to which it was fastened, which in turn was approximately the height of the person sawing (Killen 1980, 10). Greeks following this same method also would have been limited in the length of their boards. It is not until the Roman period that we hear of the teeth being set, which allowed the saw to be pushed as well as pulled. This freed the workman from cutting the timber vertically and thus allowed for more accurate results (Goodman 1964, 116) as well as for greater lengths of wood.

Early Greeks were certainly familiar with the adze, which was used to create a fairly smooth and true surface. Aldred (1954, 687) claims that an experienced workman could produce very accurate results with this tool. Yet it was a difficult process, especially because the technique consisted of chipping the surface. Homer's descriptions of Odysseus using the adze to make smooth, flat planks for his boat demonstrate this difficulty (Goodman 1964, 21–22). Nevertheless, probably for lack of a better tool, the Greeks continued to use the adze for this purpose at least into the fifth century BC, to judge from a representation inside a red-figure kylix now in the British Museum, E 23 (Aldred 1957, 232, fig. 207; Goodman 1964, 22, fig. 10; Richter 1966, fig. 609).

In Egypt boards were smoothed further by rubbing them with stones and sand, but this method was not well suited for framing or paneling (Goodman 1964, 39; Ulrich 2007, 41). A superior tool for this purpose was the plane. It was used to shave wood in a continuous manner and could produce shavings the thickness of paper (Ulrich 2007, 41). Although no Greek examples are known (Goodman 1964, 40), tradition holds that the plane was a Greek invention by the craftsman Daedalus. This attribution, however, likely derives from Daedalus's mythical role in later periods. The plane is not mentioned by Homer when he speaks of smoothing a threshold, which Odysseus accomplished with an adze.

At some point the Greeks must have known the plane because, according to Varro (*Ling.* 6, 96), they had a word for it, *rhykane*, from which the Latin *runcina* was derived. A form of this word appears in a text by Biton, who probably wrote in the third or perhaps second century BC (Liddell and Scott 1996, *s.v.* rhykane; Cancik and Schneider 1997, *s.v.* Biton). The plane is mentioned as part of the carpenter's tool kit in the *Greek Anthology* (*Anthologia Graeca* 6, 204–5; Paton 1916, 404–405), but this collection of literary references was assembled very late, in the sixth century AD (Aldred 1957, 228). We cannot, then, be certain when the Greeks began to use the plane. Ulrich (2007, 41) suggests that it was probably employed by the fifth century, as shown by the finely paneled doors of the Classical and Hellenistic periods. There is no evidence to suggest that it existed as early as the eighth or seventh centuries, when the Greek entablature was presumably being formed. Likewise, it may not have been known to the Etruscans. Its use by the Roman period, however, is well attested by literary mentions, remains of the tool, and examples of its products (Goodman 1964, 43–53).

Another important tool for woodworking was the chisel. It could take various shapes and sizes, and therefore assume different functions. The diversity of chisels is demonstrated already by the eighth century BC in a hoard of Assyrian tools found in Egypt (Aldred 1957, 223 and fig. 203). Small chisels that served for engraving as well as sturdier ones that were used for cutting holes and grooves are attested already in predynastic Egypt (Killen 1980, 16). Mortise chisels are known at least from the Old Kingdom (Killen 1980, 17) and are depicted in use in the fifth-dynasty Tomb of Ti at Saqqara (Goodman 1964, 196; Baker 1966, 298–99, fig. 459). These needed to have a thick blade, since they were used in conjunction with the mallet or hammer to make sockets for mortise-and-tenon construction or to lever the remaining chips from a deep hole.

In addition to cutting tools, the Greeks would have had implements for drilling and boring. The bow drill was known to the Egyptians by the Early Dynastic period, if not earlier, and is represented in use in the Tomb of Ti at Saqqara, from the fifth dynasty (Goodman 1964, 160; Baker 1966, 298–99, fig. 459; Killen 1980, 20). It was especially important to the Egyptians because they rarely used nails or screws to secure joints, preferring to reserve small nails or tacks for affixing metal (copper or gold leaf) or veneer to the wooden surface (Aldred 1954, 693; Killen 1980, 11). Instead, from early times they would lash joints together with linen cord or leather thongs or drive dowels through them (Aldred 1954, 692). Dowels were typically cut flush with the surface and hidden from view under plaster or paint, but by the New Kingdom they became a decorative feature in furniture, with their ends elaborated in contrasting materials (Aldred 1954, 693). The Greeks must also have used the bow drill from early times. It was an important tool for ship construction and is probably to be identified with the borer (*teretron*) that Homer mentions in his description of Odysseus building his own boat (*Od.* 5.247; Morrison and Coates 1986, 184–85). The bow drill is the only boring tool shown in use in Greek and Roman depictions, although the auger is mentioned in literature and is known from Roman remains (Goodman 1964, 161, 165; Ulrich 2007, 18–21, 30–32).

The lathe may have been a development of the bow drill (Aldred 1957, 232–33). It is attested by products from the middle of the second millennium BC onward, but no ancient lathe has ever been recovered. We recognize its use in Greek furniture at least by the sixth century BC. It was also applied to architecture for column bases by the second quarter of the sixth century BC, in the Temple of Hera III at Samos and the Temple of Apollo at Naukratis (Dinsmoor 1975, 125, 126 n. 3). The lathe is mentioned by both Greek (Aeschylus, Plato) and Roman (Virgil, Pliny) authors (Aldred 1957, 233; Richter 1966, 124). Indeed, Pliny (*NH* 7.198) attributes its invention to Theodoros, one of the architects of the Hera temple at Samos.

We can thus conclude that the Greek woodworker had available to him the full range of tools known previously in the Mediterranean. Because these were of iron rather than copper or bronze, they allowed for greater efficiency and accuracy than in earlier periods and cultures (Aldred 1957, 228). Their potential application to ancient buildings may be discerned from extant products. Evidence from neighboring regions can be used to supplement that from Greece itself. Such evidence helps to elucidate the techniques of early Greek woodworking and their possible representation in Doric and Ionic entablatures.

Techniques

The Greeks had access to a plentiful supply of wood, which allowed for good-quality as well as large pieces. This was also true for their neighbors along the eastern Mediterranean coast. In Egypt, however, timber was scarce and had to be imported for large projects or fine manufacture already from the third dynasty (Killen 1980, 1). As a result, the Egyptians often compensated with time-consuming techniques, such as the use of plywood and numerous joints (Aldred 1954, 685–86; 1957, 233), which we do not see in Greek works. Another difference is that the Egyptians rarely used nails, whereas the Greeks employed them for furniture as well as architecture (Richter 1966, 125; Winter 1993, 307). Finally, much of our evidence for Egyptian woodworking comes from furniture, which is generally poorly preserved in Greece. Thus, while Egyptian woodworking, because of its relatively good state of preservation (Killen 1996, 13–20), provides a wealth of information about techniques, we must exercise caution in using it to discern practices in Greece.

Perhaps the best evidence for early Greek woodworking techniques comes from the remains of ships. Shipwrecks uncovered in the Mediterranean display construction techniques that remained unchanged over a relatively long time. We have already noted that Homer, writing during the period under consideration here, describes Odysseus's construction of his own boat (*Od.* 5.234–61). This account corresponds closely with the physical evidence (Casson 1971, 217–19). Thus, after cutting and smoothing the planks, he drilled them and fitted them with dowels. This is the method used from the Bronze Age until the second century AD for constructing ships (Morrison and Coates 1986, 184–85; Casson 1994, 31–35). Typically mortises are first worked out roughly with a drill and are then finished with the chisel (Casson 1994, 35). Separately made tenons are hammered into one side and the next plank subsequently fitted onto the projecting tenon. Finally, the planks are drilled and the tenons are secured in place by a dowel on each end.

At least by the fourth century BC, mortise-and-tenon joints were set very closely together, with only four inches or less typically intervening. The tenons themselves were wide (approx. 2 in) and could penetrate halfway into the plank (Casson 1994, 31; see also Casson 1971, 204–5). The result would be very sturdy and tight joints. In fact, it has been questioned whether there was any need—or even room—for caulking. It appears that the wood itself, if sufficiently dry, would have absorbed enough water to create a watertight seal (Morrison and Coates 1986, 185–87; Casson 1994, 31–35). Ships may also have been coated on the hull with black pitch, which would provide an additional seal. This might explain Homer's frequent reference to ships as "black." Wax could be applied as well, as both a sealant and a lubricant (Morrison and Coates 1986, 188–89). When ships were painted, either for camouflage or for decoration, the pigments were mixed with wax in the encaustic technique (Casson 1971, 211–12).

Another method of shell-first shipbuilding, which is well known from Viking ships, was not, however, used by the Greeks or other ancients. This entailed overlapping each plank with the one above and then driving nails or pegs through the double thickness (Casson 1971, 201; 1994, 30). The significance of this so-called clinker-built boat is addressed below.

Greek woodworking techniques may also be discerned from furniture. Few pieces of wooden furniture survive, however, and our knowledge is derived largely from representations in other media. Although furniture required a higher level of craftsmanship and raw material (Aldred 1954, 684), the tools and, at least during the early Greek period, the techniques may not have differed much from those used in shipbuilding or architecture. Thus, a passage in the *Odyssey* (23.195–201) describes how Odysseus made his bed from an olive tree that he smoothed with his adze and drilled, following a procedure similar to that used for construction of his boat. As with shipbuilding, the standard method for joining pieces of furniture was the wooden tenon secured with a dowel (Richter 1966, 125). In thrones and chairs, the tenons and dowels may be seen decoratively protruding through the mortise, as for example in the thrones of Zeus and Hera on the François Vase of *c.* 570–560 BC (Richter 1966, 23, fig. 85). By the fifth century BC, chests or boxes demonstrate the use of paneling, a technique also attested for this period by wooden doors. In Greek furniture, paneling tends to be rather simple, with a rectangular frame surrounding a recessed center. By contrast, on Egyptian chests of the New Kingdom the cabinetmaker would often embellish the panels with additional strips of wood or ivory that were mitered at the corners (Killen 1994, 30–34, fig. 50; 51–53, fig. 60). Mitered joints are known in Egypt already in the third dynasty (Mols 1999, 69).

One can assume that the tools and techniques used by shipwrights and furniture makers would also be known to carpenters. Indeed, in his study of the furniture of Western Asia, Roaf cites similarities with architecture in techniques as well as forms (Roaf 1996, 22–26). If stone architecture imitated wooden predecessors, we might expect to see such correspondences there as well.

Doric Entablature

The modern interpretation of Doric guttae as dowels would seem to find support in the use of dowels by early shipwrights and furniture makers as a means of securing joints. Carpenters must likewise have been familiar with this technique and with the manufacture of such cylindrical pegs. They likely witnessed the close spacing of dowels in the planking of ships, which made the vessels more seaworthy, and one can imagine that when necessary they employed a similar technique in their own constructions. This may be reflected in the series of guttae along the underside of the regula and especially the characteristic three rows of guttae beneath the mutule. Yet for dowels to hold wooden pieces together, they must be hammered into the surface fairly tightly. In the Doric entablature, guttae hang downward from their associated members.

We must ask what purpose guttae, as dowels, served in the hypothetical wooden entablature. They appear in two locations, below the mutule plaques on the underside of the cornice and beneath the regulae, which in turn hang from the narrow taenia. Both mutules and regulae are aligned with the triglyph, and in the case of the former, also with the metope, in the Doric entablature. According to Vitruvius's model, the mutules correspond to the principal rafters, which would naturally rest above and in line with the tie beams and their triglyph coverings. Yet it is not clear why the rafters would require dowels at their ends, since it is unlikely that they were made in pieces. One solution would identify the mutule not as the rafter itself but as a plate or plank affixed to its underside (Mallwitz 1981, 640, fig. 33; Wesenberg 1996, 12) or above (Gerkan 1948–49, 10) with dowels or nails. This interpretation adheres to the spirit, but not the actuality, of Vitruvius's statement. It does not solve the problem, because there is no obvious reason for the application of this additional member to the rafter. Furthermore, nail or dowel holes penetrating the rafter ends, whether or not the hypothetical plate appeared below, would render them unnecessarily vulnerable to moisture.

The function of the regulae is similarly difficult to explain. They appear as short, narrow segments that, according to this line of reasoning, might have been attached to the taenia and perhaps also to the triglyphs by dowels. They offer no clear advantage in protecting the underside of the tie beam or its decorative covering (triglyph), which are already sealed by the taenia and architrave below. Nor can these short segments offer much protection to the architrave itself, which is elsewhere exposed. Dowels inserted into their undersides and extending into the taenia, and possibly even the tie beam, would create the same potential hazards as noted for the rafters. We are left with only one possibility: that guttae served not a functional purpose but a decorative one. If their origins can be found in woodworking, they may mimic the dowels that decoratively protruded from the joints of furniture in both Egyptian and Greek examples. Their use in the Doric entablature would not, then, have been to seal joints but to articulate the vertical alignment of structural members.

The components of the Doric entablature are also difficult to account for in terms of woodworking abilities during the period in question. The construction of regulae and taeniae would require narrow planks. These, along with the series of boards that, according to Vitruvius, comprised the triglyphs, would have been difficult to produce without the plane. As noted previously, Greek woodworkers probably did not acquire this tool before the fifth century BC, when they began to construct paneled doors. Although the Egyptians likewise lacked the plane and were able to compensate somewhat by rubbing surfaces smooth with abrasives, this technique did not allow for a close join (Goodman 1964, 39 and fig. 35) and was also labor intensive and thus unsuitable for large-scale constructions. Without an easy means to produce tightly joining surfaces, it is not clear why the carpenter would have chosen to build up his entablature from narrow pieces of wood. Additionally, the division of the architrave into two parts, with a larger beam below and a smaller taenia above, would seem to present a structural disadvantage.

The triglyphs raise further problems. If we follow Vitruvius's explanation, they would have been formed of three vertical boards with a crowning horizontal. We might expect that the carpenter, like the shipwright, would have aimed for a tight seal between these pieces and therefore would have joined them using mortises and tenons. Here, however, the joints are articulated with grooves, which would have reduced the contact surface and accordingly the area available for carving mortises. On the other hand, Vitruvius suggests that these boards served a decorative purpose, to conceal the ugly appearance of the truncated beam end. Because they are not primarily protective, the carpenters may not have been especially concerned about a tight seal, so long as it was waterproof. For this they may have borrowed a practice from shipbuilders or even from Egyptian woodworkers. Pitch seems to have been used at least as early as the time of Homer, the late eighth century, to provide an additional seal. Wax could also serve this purpose. Both materials were used in Egyptian woodworking to protect and polish the surface (Killen 1980, 10). Vitruvius states that triglyphs were likewise covered with a wax-based paint. It should further be noted that the traditional color

for triglyphs is either black or dark blue, both of which are dominant colors for ships.

Assuming that the difficulties of joining and sealing these panels could be overcome, we still must explain the beveled edges. Perhaps this treatment was intended as decoration. Yet it does not seem to be part of the Greek woodworker's repertoire, to judge from the evidence of furniture. Although remains are limited, extant depictions suggest that the early Greeks preferred right angles to beveled edges and the articulation of a large surface with recessed planes rather than a series of grooves. In later times, especially during the Hellenistic period, furniture becomes more complex and the surfaces more detailed. Yet even then transitions are made with moldings rather than bevels (see Richter 1966, 31 [thrones], 71–72, figs. 377–78 [tables]). The same approach seems to be followed by the Romans, to judge from the furniture in Herculaneum (Mols 1999, 94).

Ionic Entablature

The characteristic elements of the Ionic entablature, consisting of an architrave with either two or three fasciae supporting a dentil course, are also difficult to reconcile with wooden predecessors. Each element required precise workmanship. The relatively small, rectangular dentils might have been executed with an adze, but a plane would allow for more regularity. To execute the dentil course in a single level, saddle joints must have been used. Cutting away half the thickness of each beam for such a joint would have been a time-consuming and questionable task, however. The loss of thickness would have undermined the ability of these beams to carry weight while offering no advantage other than aesthetics. Yet as the projections of common rafters or ceiling beams, the dentils would be expected to appear at different levels of the building.

The plane would have been even more important for executing the stacked boards assumed by modern scholars for the Ionic architrave. Although a similar effect might have been produced by the overlapping planks of later clinker-built boats, this technique is not paralleled in Greek ships or furniture. Furniture makers do employ paneling, but generally of a simpler form and of later date than the prototype wooden entablature. Given the availability of wood in the ancient Mediterranean, it would have been more natural, and structurally more sound, to use one single large beam instead of a series of smaller ones. As already noted, the division of the Doric architrave into two parts is likewise hard to explain under these conditions.

Without the proper tools or traditions, the detailed and regular components seen in the Doric and Ionic entablatures are thus unlikely to have occurred to the early Greek woodworker. Rather, these forms would represent unnecessary and difficult expenditures of time and sometimes even undermine the structural integrity of the entablatures.

Hittorff, J.-I. (1870) in J.-I. Hittorff and L. Zanth, *Recueil des Monuments de Ségeste et de Sélinonte*, 317–66. Paris, Donnaud.

Holland, L. B. (1917) The origin of the Doric entablature. *American Journal of Archaeology* 21, 117–58.

Jacques, C. and Freeman, M. (1997) *Angkor: Cities and Temples*. Bangkok, River Books Co., Ltd.

Jéquier, G. (1924) *Manuel d'archéologie égyptienne: Les éléments de l'architecture*. Paris, A. Picard.

Jessup, H. I. (2004) *Art and Architecture of Cambodia*. London, Thames and Hudson.

Kähler, H. (1949) *Das griechische Metopenbild*. Munich, Münchener Verlag.

Killen, G. (1980) *Ancient Egyptian Furniture 1, 4000–1300 BC*. Warminster, Wiltshire, England, Aris and Phillips Ltd.

Killen, G. (1994) *Ancient Egyptian Furniture II, Boxes, Chests and Footstools*. Warminster, Wiltshire, England, Aris and Phillips Ltd.

Killen, G. (1996) Ancient Egyptian Carpentry, its Tools and Techniques. In G. Herrmann (ed.) *The Furniture of Western Asia*, 13–20. Mainz am Rhein, Philipp von Zabern.

Kjeldsen, K. and Zahle, J. (1975) Lykische Gräber. Ein vorläufiger Bericht. *Archäologischer Anzeiger*, 312–50.

Liddell, H. G. and Scott, R. (1996) *A Greek-English Lexicon*. Oxford, Clarendon Press.

Lloyd, S. and Müller, H. W. (2004) *Ancient Architecture*. Milan, Electa Architecture.

Mallwitz, A. (1981) Kritisches zur Architektur Griechenlands im 8. und 7. Jahrhundert. *Archäologischer Anzeiger*, 599–642.

Meiggs, R. (1982) *Trees and Timber in the Ancient Mediterranean World*. Oxford, Clarendon Press.

Mertens, D. (1984) *Der Tempel von Segesta*. Mainz am Rhein, Philipp von Zabern.

Mols, S. T. A. M. (1999) *Wooden Furniture in Herculaneum*. Amsterdam, J. C. Gieben.

Morgan, M. H. (trans.) (1960) *Vitruvius, the Ten Books on Architecture*. New York, Dover Publications.

Morrison, J. S. and Coates, J. F. (1986) *The Athenian Trireme*. Cambridge, Cambridge University Press.

Ohly, D. (1953) Holz. *Mitteilungen des Deutschen Archäologischen Instituts, Athenische Abteilung* 68, 77–126.

Paton, W.R. (trans.) (1916) *The Greek Anthology*, vol. 1, New York: G.P. Putnam's Son.

Perrot, G. and Chipiez, C. (1883) *A History of Art in Ancient Egypt, 1*. London, Chapman and Hall, Ltd.

Richter, G. M. A. (1966) *The Furniture of the Greeks Etruscans and Romans*. London, Phaidon Press.

Roaf, M. (1996) Architecture and furniture. In G. Herrmann (ed.), *The Furniture of Western Asia*, 21–28. Mainz am Rhein, Philipp von Zabern.

Smith, W. S. (1981) *The Art and Architecture of Ancient Egypt*. Harmondsworth, Penguin Books.

Strathmann, C. (2002) *Grabkultur im antiken Lykien des 6. bis 4. Jahrhundert v. Chr.* Frankfurt am Main, Peter Lang.

Ulrich, R. B. (2007) *Roman Woodworking*. New Haven and London, Yale University Press.

Wesenberg, B. (1996) Die Entstehung der griechischen Säulen- und Gebälkformen in der literarischen Überlieferung der Antike. In E.-L. Schwandner (ed.), *Säule und Gebälk*, 1–15. Mainz am Rhein, Philipp von Zabern.

Winter, N. A. (1993) *Greek Architectural Terracottas*. Oxford, Clarendon Press.

Whereas scholars have accepted Vitruvius's statements because they seemed to offer an explanation for the entablature, our examination demonstrates that these elements find no better rationale in wood than in stone. Moreover, in stone buildings, the components are rendered as complete units, instead of being built of smaller pieces as in the hypothetical wooden entablature. In fact, the creation of an entire triglyph, as opposed to a series of boards, and an architrave, taenia, and regulae in the same block represents a structurally more logical solution.

Stone Construction

At the same time, we cannot overlook the fact that forms and techniques familiar from woodworking were sometimes borrowed for stone constructions. Perhaps the best-known example is the application of the lathe to column bases, as in the Temple of Hera III at Samos and the Temple of Apollo at Naukratis. The late-fifth century temple at the Elymian site of Segesta, in Sicily, which is assumed to have been overseen by a Greek architect, used mitered joints at the corners of its architrave (Mertens 1984, 22). Such a joint would not have been practical for the exterior of a wooden architrave because of its vulnerability to splitting and to the seepage of moisture. It could and often was, however, used in an interior course, in both wood and stone (Ulrich 2007, 130).

Beyond the Greek world, mitered joints, sometimes secured with mortise-and-tenon sockets, may appear in stone door- and window-frames of Khmer temples in Southeast Asia. Our figures illustrate examples from Banteay Srei, built in the tenth century. Although the door frame (Fig. 18.3) has lost its lintel, the jamb on each side clearly preserves the socket for a tenon. The window (Fig. 18.4) shows the mitered corners in an intact frame. As here, windows are often filled with profiled balusters that seem to imitate wooden examples turned on the lathe (Jacques and Freeman 1997, 118). Other elements of decoration at Banteay Srei also seem to be rooted in wood-carving techniques (Jessup 2004, 101). One cannot exclude the possibility that certain aspects of the Greek entablature may likewise have been borrowed from wooden forms. Yet the evidence does not suggest a wholesale translation from wooden predecessors.

One group of monuments that is often cited as exemplifying such a translation from wood is Lycian tombs. Four types were identified by O. Benndorf and G. Niemann (1884, 95–113: house tomb (Fig. 18.5), sarcophagus tomb, pillar tomb, and monumental tomb. Of these, the first two were assumed to derive fairly directly from wooden houses. Indeed, scholars have generally accepted such a faithful translation that they often refer to the house tombs as "petrified" huts. By the time that these stone monuments were built, which is thought to be no earlier than the fifth

Fig. 18.3 *Doorframe at Banteay Srei (Photo: Michael W. Binford).*

Fig. 18.4 *Window at Banteay Srei (Photo: Michael W. Binford).*

century BC (Kjeldsen and Zahle 1975, 347–50; Strathmann 2002, 178–81), the carpentry techniques that they display would have been generally known. Even so, attempts to equate the components of this wooden framework with actual forms have proven problematic.

Although Benndorf and Niemann believed that the originals were fully in wood, more recent scholars have suggested that only the framework consisted of wooden beams and the intervening surfaces were of a more solid material, such as rubble or mudbrick, which would be needed to support the roof (see Kjeldsen and Zahle 1975, 319–23; Bridges 1993, 91–92). The intersection of these beams typically takes the form of a saddle joint, that is, with half of the thickness of each beam cut away in order to overlap and project beyond the intersection (Ulrich 2007, 68–70).

19

Highlights of the Brown University Excavations at the Petra Great Temple, 1993–2006

Martha Sharp Joukowsky

Introduction

The orientalist R. E. Brünnow and the classicist A. von Domaszewski surveyed Petra in 1897–98 and published an ambitious three-volume mapping project in their *Die Provincia Arabia* (1904–9). During World War I, Walter Bachmann, Carl Watzinger, and Theodor Wiegand investigated the city structures under the auspices of the Committee for the Preservation of Monuments of the German-Turkish Army. It was Bachmann who in the 1920s is credited with the identifications of various sites in the central city and designated the names for both the Great Temple and the Small Temple, names that identify the sites today. Figure 19.1 is an aerial overview of the Petra Great Temple site at the close of the 2006 excavations. Figure 19.2 is a plan of the site with the major components identified.

The genesis of the Petra Great Temple excavations can be traced to 1992. Under the sponsorship of Brown University, extensive excavations were launched in 1993 resulting in a tactical and strategic research design and

Fig. 19.1 *Petra Great Temple aerial photograph to south at the end of the 2006 excavations with the (right) Small Temple and (left) Pool Complex (Photo: Artemis W. Joukowsky).*

Petra Great Temple
Brown University Excavations

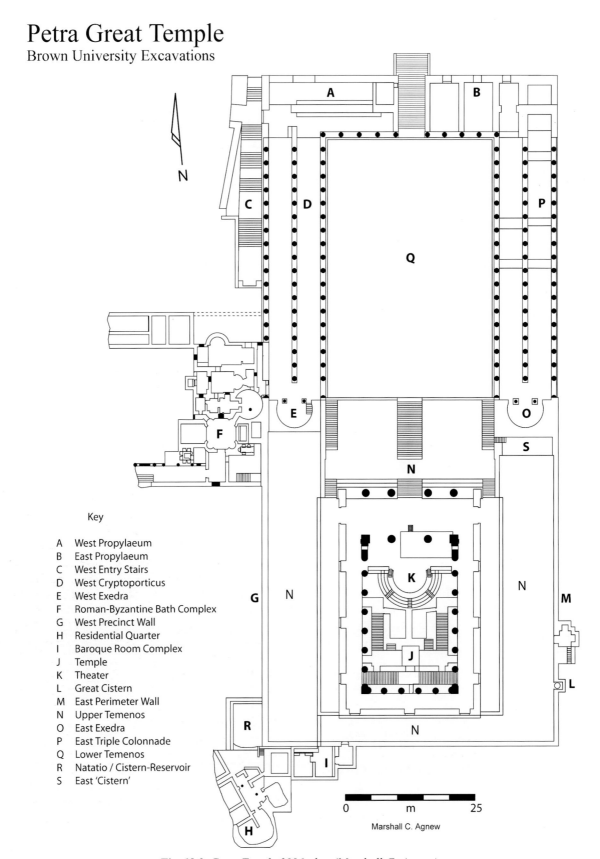

Key

A West Propylaeum
B East Propylaeum
C West Entry Stairs
D West Cryptoporticus
E West Exedra
F Roman-Byzantine Bath Complex
G West Precinct Wall
H Residential Quarter
I Baroque Room Complex
J Temple
K Theater
L Great Cistern
M East Perimeter Wall
N Upper Temenos
O East Exedra
P East Triple Colonnade
Q Lower Temenos
R Natatio / Cistern-Reservoir
S East 'Cistern'

0   m   25

Marshall C. Agnew

Fig. 19.2 *Great Temple 2006 plan (Marshall C. Agnew).*

surveys using the Compass Program and Site Map developed by the Museum of Applied Science at the University of Pennsylvania for a site grid, a topographic map, and recording the step-by-step excavation process with a GIS interface. Since 1993 fourteen successive field campaigns have been conducted annually between 1993 and 2006 in various sectors of the precinct. We are fortunate to have the same data-collection systems in use from the inception of the excavations until the present. In 1998 the first five years of excavation were published (Joukowsky 1998), and to date 206 additional publications have become part of the public record. At this writing, the final excavation publications and specialists reports are under way.

In the earliest season we cleared the temple facade. Thereafter, from 1994 to 1996, site recovery centered on the excavations in all areas of the precinct, and in 1995 ground-penetrating radar (GPR) was used to define the subterranean canalization system. In 1997 the theater was recovered and excavations continued there in 1998. From 1999 to 2000 work resumed in all sectors, and in 2001 the Great Cistern was unearthed. Excavation also took place at the Small Temple, a Roman Imperial cult building. During the 2002 season the Great Cistern excavation continued, but the most significant discovery was the Baroque Room Complex with the remains of its magnificent gilded plaster ceiling. The 2003 campaign concentrated on the definition of the East Propylaeum and three rooms there that lie perpendicular to the principal artery of the central city, the Roman Street. In 2004 we undertook several sondages (test trenches) in various areas, but excavation concentrated in the West Cryptoporticus with the recovery of the West Propylaeum ballista-ball assemblage. Again in 2005 several sondages were excavated to test the stratigraphy in the temple pronaos and the theater orchestra. The West Entry Stairway was excavated, and the bath excavations commenced in earnest. In 2006 the excavation focus was the Roman-Byzantine Baths with a sondage undertaken in the theater seating. Essentially work on the Great Temple structure has been completed, but analysis of the remains, most particularly the architecture, will continue for some time to come.

Our expert Brown University team has been indispensable in recording not only the ongoing excavations but also all the artifacts recovered in our six site databases. Implementation and managing the site have also defined technological advancement for expanding and ensuring the continuity of information access and data preservation. Our databases now support the findings of approximately half a million artifacts, and we are projecting the development of an internet-accessible database. There are now 405,311 fragments registered in the Grosso Modo database. Our architectural fragment database now includes 19,257 registered architectural fragments, coins number 681, and the catalogue of small finds numbers 1,653 artifacts. Ongoing are specialist

analyses of 6,636 glass fragments, 27,656 bones, 810 lamps, and 317,982 ceramics, a sample of which has been examined with Neutron Activation INAA analysis (Bedal 2004; Barrett 2008, 56, Appendix). We have performed chemical analyses on a specimen number of 26,901 stucco plaster fragments and have traced the quarry origins of marble. These indicate the Nabataeans used true fresco secco (Corbeil and Helwig 1999), meaning that no binding medium was detected between the pigments and the plaster base but that the pigments were placed directly onto the wet support. The painted decorative schemes used in the Great Temple decoration have been published by Emily Catherine Egan (2002).

Additionally we have developed the Cave Automatic Virtual Environment (CAVE), the first virtual-reality three-dimensional GIS application for ongoing field archaeological research (Vote 2001). The three-dimensional GIS system, called ARCHAVE, allows users to view and interact with different types of artifacts and architectural finds, in situ, in the context of a CAVE.

The consolidation, preservation, and protection of the enormous Great Temple site have been an integral part of our excavation research design from those early years, and various conservation measures have been undertaken annually. Many of the recovered artifacts from the Great Temple have been selected by museums to be displayed abroad. To promote knowledge of Jordan's extraordinary cultural heritage, the Jordanian government transported a number of our sculptures, including elephant-headed capitals, on a well-publicized international tour of the exhibition *Petra Rediscovered: Lost City of the Nabataeans.* Museums included the Natural History Museum in New York and other venues in the United States, plus the Museum of Canadian Civilizations in Ottawa, Canada. Independently, our celebrated Baroque Room ceiling (Fig. 19.3) and several other artifacts traveled to Berlin and Bonn, Germany, and other examples of our elephant-headed capitals were transported for display to Helsinki, Finland. These expositions promoted a public recognition of Jordan's cultural heritage and the Great Temple for an unparalleled view of a Nabataean historic focus. It is hoped that international support will raise sufficient funds to construct a Petra Museum so that when these objects return to Jordan they will be properly displayed and protected in a museum venue close to the site.

The Great Temple: Stratigraphy and Chronology

I refer to the Nabataean period to cover the earliest mention of the Nabataeans in 312 BC until the Roman annexation in AD 106. Dating accession to the Nabataean throne is fairly well established; however, there are problems in the Nabataean king list (McKenzie 1990, 15) with little-known figures like Aretas I, Rabbel I, and Aretas II, so the

Fig. 19.3 *Baroque Room stucco in situ (Photo: Artemis W. Joukowsky).*

chronology cannot be considered absolute. The Nabataean reign exists for approximately 264 years. The Roman period follows the annexation and extends to the Byzantine period or to AD 325.

We have a paucity of early textual evidence, so what are the benchmarks that can be securely dated? As for the Nabataean period, we have the Ez Zantur ceramic horizons (Schmid 1995; 1996) with beginning and ending dates, so we believe that there are internal cross dates for the deposits. We have a series of closed contexts affirming the construction of Site Phase IV, the Grand Design in the late first century BC; the formal Roman annexation in AD 106; and the devastating earthquakes of AD July 19, 363, and July 9, 551. The continuing construction and destruction of the Petra Great Temple, however, renders a complex stratigraphy, and often partial rebuilding blurs the issue.

A reconstruction of the stratigraphic sequence from the earliest deposits to the latest at the Great Temple is shown in Figure 19.4, which is a summary of the Great Temple Site Phases. Identified are fifteen superimposed strata with the earliest being Pre-Site Phase I, which in many cases was discovered resting on bedrock. We then summarize the data beginning with Site Phase I in the early first century BC and continue with three main architectural phases, Site Phases II–V, representing cultural continuity with major episodes of construction. Site Phases VI–XI, spanning AD post-106 to 551, consist primarily of repairs of collapsed elements, and Site Phases XII–XIV are represented by more collapses and reuse of the area extending into the modern period.

Our excavations have produced this synthesis of the Great Temple stratigraphic sequence for its development. Few chronological correlations, however, can be made for Pre-Site Phase I, which is intriguing but difficult to date because the flimsy architectural remains and cup marks in the bedrock find no link to the strata above it, and the artifact assemblage appears to be mixed. The site at this time may have been a tented encampment, but there is a paucity of evidence to securely assign even this functional reconstruction. We therefore have opted to define Pre-Site Phase I as a prelude to the preparations for the precinct's construction.

The stratigraphic sequence for Site Phases I and II is assigned as preparation of the site for the construction of the early distyle-in-antis temple. This fifty-year span for preparation and building may be questioned, but it is reasoned that Nabataean masons had to spend some time chiseling away enormous amounts of bedrock to place the early temple (30.07 m north-south × 18.36 m east-west) as well as to construct the subterranean canalization system that underlies the entire complex. In other sectors of the precinct, at approximately the same time, monumental walls are constructed, such as the east–west Portico Wall, which delimits the precinct from the major thoroughfare that becomes the Via Sacra, the Roman Street. Thus, in Site Phase II the earliest temple is built and is assigned a mid-first century BC date. This temple is embellished with colorfully stuccoed columns enclosed within fresco-decorated side corridors.

The distyle temple is in use for a few years and then there is a catastrophe of some sort, perhaps an earthquake or

SITE PHASE	DATE	MAJOR CONSTRUCTION -- DESTRUCTION
Pre-Site Phase I	ca. Pre-1st c. BCE	Odd walls and cup marks in bedrock
Site Phase I	ca. Early 1st c. BCE	Bedrock Preparation and Canalization
Site Phase II	ca. Mid 1st c. BCE	Distyle in Antis temple: Portico Wall, Lowest Steps of Central Steps
Site Phase III	ca. Mid-to-Late 1st c. BCE – 1st c. CE	Minor Damage
Site Phase IV	ca. 1st c. BCE – 1st c. CE	Grand Design (Expansion), Tetrastyle in Antis Temple, Full Propylaeum, West Entry Stairway, Nefesh, Lower Temenos Triple Colonnades, Exedrae, Cryptoporticoes, Upper Temenos Great Cistern, East Perimeter Wall, Residential Quarter, Baroque Room
Site Phase V	ca. 1st c. CE	Nabataean Redesign and Repair, Theater Added to Great Temple, Betyls in Propylaeum
Site Phase VI	106 CE and 113/114 Earthquake	Roman Takeover, Damage to Propylaeum West, Repairs to Lower Temenos, Baroque Room Collapse, Temple Doorways and Corridors Narrowed, Bath Complex Constructed
Site Phase VII	ca. Mid 2nd c. CE	Propylaeum Repair, Wall K Razed in East and Rebuilt in West, West Room 1 Constructed, Roman Street Paved, East Propylaeum Rooms 1-3 Constructed, East Exedra Repair, Lower Temenos East-West Cross Walls in East Colonnade, Benches, Temple Doorways Narrowed and Walled-In, Theater Stage Constructed
Site Phase VIII	ca. Late 2nd c. CE	Damage, Abandonment, Collapse, Dumping
Site Phase IX	363 CE Earthquake	Collapse of Propylaeum and Lower Temenos West Triple Colonnade, West Cryptoporticus Collapse, Upper Temenos Added Features
Site Phase X	ca. 4th and 5th c. CE	Abandonment, Fluvial Deposit Accumulates, Lower Temenos Reconstruction of Colonnades with Reused Ashlars, Domestic Secondary Reuse in All Temple Areas
Site Phase XI	Post 551 CE Earthquake	Further Collapse, East Triple Colonnade Collapse, West Entry Stairs Collapse, Temple East Porch Column Collapse, Baths Out of Use
Site Phase XII	Late Byzantine 551 – 640 CE	Abandonment and Robbing
Site Phase XIII	Islamic Period	Series of Major Collapses
Site Phase XIV	Modern Period	Farming of the Lower Temenos by Bedouin, Dumping, Construction of Bedouin Walls, Brown University Excavations

Fig. 19.4 *Chronological Chart of the Great Temple.*

tremors, because a series of collapses are evident. The decision is taken by the Nabataeans not only to rebuild the partially destroyed temple but to elegantly embellish the whole precinct. This is Site Phase IV, our so-called Grand Design, assigned to the last quarter of the first century BC. This expanded Great Temple is the largest freestanding building yet excavated in Petra – its 7,560 m² precinct consists of a Propylaeum, Lower Temenos, and Upper Temenos, the sacred enclosure for the temple proper. Shown in Figure 19.5 is the precinct's virtual-reality representation of this phase. In the Propylaeum and Lower Temenos are east and west (north–south) colonnades under which are crypto-porticoes (vaulted chambers). With 145 columns topped with phenomenal Asian elephant-headed capitals (Fig. 19.6), these triple colonnades lead into semicircular buttressed exedrae. Between the colonnades is a sweeping plaza adorned with

white limestone hexagonal pavers positioned above an extensive subterranean canalization system.

As seen today, this refurbished Grand Design structure has an added tetrastyle-in-antis (four front columns) porch with side anta walls decorated with pilaster reliefs. Measuring 35 m east–west and 42 m in length, a stairway approaches a broad deep pronaos, which in turn leads into the Site Phase II side corridors, which are reused in Site Phase IV. Exterior paved walkways now frame the temple, where sculpted facial fragments and fine, deeply carved architectural elements including pilasters are found. Approximately 15 m in height, the porch columns plus the triangular pediment and entablature hypothetically place the structure's height to a minimum of 19 m.

Beyond the temple proper, a sword deity relief is carved into the bedrock wall of the Upper Temenos above an

Fig. 19.5 Virtual Reality model of Great Temple Grand Design, Phase IV (Eileen Vote).

Fig. 19.6 Elephant-headed capital of the Lower Temenos (Photo: Artemis W. Joukowsky).

underground cistern holding 390,000 liters of water. In the southwest is the Baroque Room Complex, where to our astonishment the massive wreckage of delicately designed, painted, and gilded plaster collapsed (see Fig. 19.3). To the west of this complex is the eleven-room domestic Residential Quarter where masses of figuratively painted Nabataean ceramics and bones are unearthed.

Petra Pool Complex

On a terrace at the same elevation as the Lower Temenos to the Great Temple east and adjoining the Great Temple is the Petra Pool Complex (see Fig. 19.1), excavated and published in 2003 by our former team member Leigh-Ann Bedal. It is an integral part of the Great Temple complex, composed of a large ornamental pool with a rectangular pavilion on an island accessed by a bridge. The pavilion is richly decorated with colored plaster and marble. As suggested by other scholarly researchers (Taylor 2001, 111; Bowersock 2003, 24), this pool paradise may have served for the ancient Middle Eastern water festival known as the Maioumas when water games were held (Segal 1995, 23). Originally identified as the "Lower Market" by Bachmann, the architectural remains document the monumental character of this Pool Complex. Now of certain function, its situation beside the Great Temple attests to its importance. Bedal (2003, 68) places the earliest phase of the Pool Complex to our Phase IV time frame, thus its construction was a major component of the Great Temple's Grand Design. Bedal (2003, 183) states, "The presence of a large formal garden – a virtual oasis – in Petra would have delivered a powerful statement to merchants and foreign delegates entering the city after a long journey through the harsh desert environment."

The Great Temple Theater

In Site Phase V dating to the AD first century, major changes take place within the Great Temple. Walls are built between the columns; four monumental internal stairways are constructed, as well as east and west interior chambers and a central arch. The character of the building is dramatically

Fig. 19.7 *Theater-In-Great Temple to south (Photo: Artemis W. Joukowsky).*

changed, because all of these internal structures provide support for a 620-seat theater (Fig. 19.7) inserted into the center of the building. The focus of the temple has been turned 180 degrees. It would appear that there was a shift to more secular concerns and the temple became a civic building used for more public ritual. At this point there may have been an emerging secularized civic identity and consciousness that defined the community in political as well as religious terms.

In 64–63 BC, before the Roman annexation, the Nabataeans were subjugated by the Roman general Pompey. Nabataea was regarded as a client state of Rome, was taxed by the Romans, and served as a buffer territory against desert tribes. In 25–24 BC Aelius Gallus led an unsuccessful expedition from Nabataea to conquer Arabia Felix – the land of frankincense and myrrh, the kingdom to the south in present-day Yemen. The Roman propaganda of the day made this expedition out to be a success.

The Nabataean period comes to a formal close with the Roman annexation in AD 106. From Ammianus (Amm. Marc. 14.8.13) we know that on behalf of Trajan, A. Cornelius Palma, the governor of Syria, took control of Arabia including Petra and put it under Roman rule – this is one reference to the annexation of the Nabataean kingdom and its incorporation into the Roman province of Arabia. Rome absorbed Nabataea, and Nabataea completely succumbed to Roman hegemony. Dio Cassius (Dio Cass. 68.14.5) tells of Trajan's victory over the Dacians and offers a statement about the Roman annexation of Nabataea by writing, "About this same time, Palma, the governor of Syria, subdued the part of Arabia around Petra and made it subject to the Romans." It has never been clear, however,

from archaeological or historical sources if Cornelius Palma led a military expedition to Petra. The lack of a recorded aggression has suggested that Palma oversaw a peaceful takeover, and Roman coins minted a few years after the annexation inscribed with "Arabia adquisita," not "Arabia capta," indicate a pacific annexation.

The picture might not have been as peaceful as the Roman sources report. At the Great Temple we were astonished to uncover 423 ballista balls averaging 12–18 cm in diameter, 162 arrowheads, two bronze helmet cheek pieces, several javelin points, a scabbard tip, buckles, rings, possible harnesses, as well as nails, spikes and knobs, pins, tacks, fragments of a bracelet and a toggle pin, and four crescent-shaped pendants. The large ballista repository (Fig. 19.8) of the West Propylaeum is assigned to Site Phase VI dating to AD 106, the Late Nabataean period, when there are a number of collapses probably due to Roman aggression. Subsequent researchers will continue to debate this issue, but it is clear that in broad cultural terms the Nabataean period at this time came to a close. Thus, Petra's apogee was from the first century BC to AD second century. Its material culture reached its zenith in the second half of the first century BC, before the Romans established control.

The Roman Imperial Era

As expressed earlier, after AD 106 the world of the Nabataeans was politically Roman. Therefore, we can assume that Petra and Nabataea were completely and formally conquered by the Romans under Emperor Trajan and then became part of Provincia Arabia. It is ironic that Nabataean success was directly related to Roman imperial-

Fig. 19.8 *Ballista ball collection in the West Propylaeum (Photo: Artemis W. Joukowsky).*

ism. Although the Nabataean geopolitical fortunes had changed, in the beginning Roman control seems to have had little effect on the flourishing Nabataean economy. What we do know is that the Roman emperor Trajan constructed forts and completed the 400 km grand highway, the Via Nova Traiana, which extended from Bostra in Syria to Petra onto Aqaba on the Red Sea. Clearly Nabataeans were used as labor for these projects, which helped the Romans achieve a communication network between Arabia and Roman Palestine. We also know that the Roman army absorbed six "Petraean cohorts," Cohortes Ulpiae Petraeorum, a total of 4,500–6,000 soldiers, and that by AD 114 Trajan had granted Petra the title of "metropolis" (mother city), and it served the Romans as the principal center for their southern holdings extending from the Dead Sea to the Gulf of Aqaba.

Nabataean kings were no more, having been replaced by Roman legates or deputies – members of the senatorial rank serving as governors – now that the Roman Legatus maintained order, which clearly manifested the dependence of the now allied city. This is a time when Roman administration consisting of a governor, some generals, and a few senior Roman officials controlled the city. The first governor of the province of Arabia was Claudius Severus (AD 107–115) who organized the building of forts for the Roman legionaries conscripted to keep peace and order. (It may have been he who celebrated Roman imperial worship in the Small Temple. In AD 129 Sextius Florentinus, the Roman governor of Petra, chose to be buried at Petra in an elaborately carved tomb. And in AD 131 the Roman emperor Hadrian (117–138) visited the site and named it after himself, Hadriane Petra. Those native Nabataeans that remained in the city coexisted with the Romans who took advantage of them for Romanization.

The *Periplus Maris Erythraei* of the mid-first century describes the circumnavigation of the Red Sea and the Indian Ocean and their coasts and harbors, and justifies seafaring traffic outsourcing overland routes. With the Roman seafaring trade around Arabia – directly related to the discovery of the monsoons – and the increased influence of Palmyra as an entrepôt, Petra began its decline as a leading trade center. The city, however, did not experience a precipitous collapse but continued to serve the Pax Romana and the Early Byzantines as well.

The Romans took advantage of the commercial ties with Arabia and the Levant. However, with the rise of the Roman monoculture, the decline in trade revenues going into Nabataean hands was restricted and the Nabataean economic base was jeopardized. From the archaeological record, the political and economic realities of Roman control are difficult to analyze, but there can be no doubt that the Nabataeans continued to function under the Romans, although it is probable that many of the elite fled or were exiled to other parts of their former kingdom. Clearly the Nabataeans are assimilated to some degree; however, Nabataean deities continue to be worshipped, the Nabataean script endures and is found on inscriptions dating to the second half of the fourth century, and the Nabataean language continues in use for administrative and legal purposes, although Greek and to a lesser extent Latin are in use as well. The Petraeans are able to carry on their previous lifestyle within the new administrative framework, and cultural continuity appears in AD 106 and thereafter, particularly in the mass-produced pottery and other artifact assemblages resulting in the material record becoming mixed to some degree. Patrich (1990, 165) reminds us: "Hellenization and Romanization did not destroy the Nabataean heritage. The traditional artistic modes of the desert people survived, but from that point on, the parallel manifestations of figurative art were much more obvious than before." The Nabataeans were compelled to obey Roman law. Discovered at Nahal Hever near En-Gedi was the Babatha archive, which dates from AD 93 to 132. These documents are invaluable, because they refer to the Judean Babatha's ownership of property in Nabataea and her desire for legal retribution from the Roman judicial system for herself and her son. Repeatedly, Babatha is ordered to appear before Roman authorities at the law court in Petra. It is obvious that there were continued close relationships between the Judeans and Nabataeans (Glueck 1965, 8–9), although the fortunes of both peoples were now decided by Rome.

During the Roman period the triumph of the Nabataean architectural vocabulary, expressed in the Great Temple precinct, was sadly compromised. In many cases there are signs of building maintenance being carelessly neglected, and this may indicate that to some degree the emphasis has shifted to other sectors of the city. Additionally, there is a subtle shift in material culture as the Roman period continues. For example, the pottery becomes coarser and sandy to the touch and there is a decline in the painting. There also is a general decline in decorative taste. But another artistic effort is highlighted as glass objects become popular and emerge as an imaginative artistic craft with an elegant strength. Figure 19.9 depicts a Roman face vase found in a well conduit in the Great Temple Roman-Byzantine Baths excavated in 2006.

Under Roman rule, Roman classical monuments abound; however, many continue to be embellished with Nabataean motifs. There are many other Roman additions to Petra, including the Tomb of the Roman Soldier, dated to the first half of the first century; this structure is embellished with an elaborately decorated Nabataean traditional triclinium (chamber for ritual meals and meetings, generally with three benches).

The city continued to flourish at least for some time in

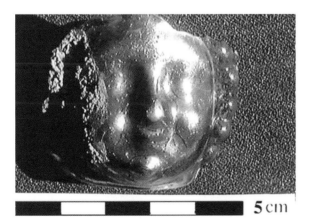

Fig. 19.9 *Glass face vase from the Roman-Byzantine Baths (Photo: Artemis W. Joukowsky).*

the Roman period, with a monumental arch in the Bab as-Siq (which possibly carried an aqueduct) and tomb structures either carved out of the living rock or built freestanding. At some point about this time, a Roman Imperial building, the Small Temple, was constructed adjacent to the Great Temple Roman-Byzantine Baths.

The Small Temple

Just to the west of the Great Temple precinct and just below the Great Temple Roman-Byzantine Baths, the Romans constructed a Roman Imperial Cult building, known as the Small Temple, shown in Figure 19.1. Under the Brown University excavation permit from the Jordanian department of antiquities, our team supervisor, Sara Karz Reid, from 2000 to 2002 excavated the Small Temple. Reid (2006) has published these results.

In building the Small Temple the Romans reconfigured and reshaped the south side of the terrain between the Petra Great Temple and the Qasr al-Bint. Because the Small Temple shares the same alignment with the Qasr al-Bint Temenos Bench, the Qasr al-Bint itself, the Temple of the Winged Lions, and the Temenos Gate, it is surely associated with these structures.

Constructed on a high podium, this imperial cult building is of a Roman prostyle design with six columns across its facade. The interior is decorated with more than 614 fragmentary Roman inscriptions, dedicated to post-annexation Roman emperors. The most important inscription has been dated to the emperor Trajan (Reid 2006, 123–24) from AD 106 to 114, and does refer to his victory over the Dacians. A second inscription (Reid 2006, 131) may refer to the emperor Marcus Aurelius Antoninus, better known as Elagabalus, who ruled from AD 218 to 222, or to his successor Severus Alexander (r. 222–35). A third inscription refers to Emperor Severus Alexander, who elevated Petra to the status of a *colonia*, and has been dated by Reid and Bodel to AD 222. These inscriptions indicate that the Small Temple remained in use at least through the third century.

Although in the third century Petra was elevated to a colony under Severus Alexander, with time, in the third and fourth centuries, the once-flourishing Nabataean caravan towns in the Negev lost their luster and began to wither away as their populations migrated to more important commercial centers. The Romans transported more of their goods by ship from Arabia to Egypt; this trend continued as the main trade routes slowly moved east to the Euphrates and the Persian Gulf, leaving Petra and her caravan cities "out of the loop." With this change in routes, Petra's commercial decline was inevitable. Just as Petra seems to have held on to some of its former glory, its former caravan towns in the Negev, once again, became independent centers of commerce. Pagan temples in the Negev were replaced with richly decorated Christian churches. No longer dependent on once-established Nabataean routes, the

Nabataeans and Petra in particular suffered from economic decline, Bedouin raids, and piracy.

The Roman-Byzantine Bath Complex

Previous probes of a bath complex had been undertaken in 1996, at which time it was hypothesized the scanty recovered features were associated with a bathing establishment. No further excavations had taken place; however, the area was heavily trafficked by mechanical equipment between 1999 and 2004 for the removal of overburden and architectural fragments from the Propylaeum and Lower Temenos West Cryptoporticus.

The 2005–6 excavations ascertain these remains are baths. We discover a platform in the north, and moving north to south, a splash bath, at least two *caldaria*, a *praefurnium*, a *tepidarium* and a *laconicum*. Below the floor level, a partially sunk service corridor extends along the rear of the caldaria and isolates the baths from the Great Temple West Exedra. To the south of the heated rooms is an apsidal vestibule reception room with a frigidarium, an ornamental pool, an elegant well with semicircular cavities for drawing water, an *apodyterium*, toilet, a small cistern, and a columned colonnade fronting on a probable palaestra-gymnasium. This is a small, compact bathing facility, a *balneum*, covering 32 m north–south × 28.4 m east–west, or 908.8 m² as excavated; its plan is presented in Figure 19.10 and an aerial photograph appears in Figure 19.11. As can be seen in the plan, the complex of twenty-two rectangular and square rooms appears to follow the Pompeian type of bath plan (Yegül 1992, 66 *ff.*) with a simple row of windowed, parallel, rectangular rooms overlooking the palaestra to the west.

The Nabataeans held their own concepts of a planned city, and the heart of the city with its Great Temple represented Petra's monumental cult and administrative center. The baths were configured as an up-to-date facility that would propagandize their city as a significant urban center. Baths reflect public traditions and the everyday lifestyles of the time. The concept of the Great Temple baths represents a Petraean political, social, and economic development borrowed from a preexisting Hellenistic-Roman urban tradition (the Herodian Baths at Jericho would have provided a worthy example). The Petraeans borrowed the bath prototype, and the Great Temple's massive West Perimeter Wall was a likely choice for such a complex. The building of the Roman-Byzantine Baths at the Great Temple was a large-scale venture for a well-planned bath system suggesting that the later Nabataean period was a well-organized society with a firm economic structure.

Internal Flow Pattern

From the Roman Road, one possible bath complex entrance in the north is from the West Entry Staircase onto the limestone platform. As yet unknown is how the complex was accessed from the west since that area-district of the baths remains largely unexplored. There is, however, an efficient logic in the arrangement of the rooms that indicates a flow pattern for their usage. It is assumed that most visitors entered the complex from the southwest colonnaded corridor and progressed either to the bathroom (Fig. 19.12) or to change their clothes in the *apodyterium*. From the *apodyterium* the bather would walk into the vestibule to enjoy its ornamental pool or the *frigidarium*, and from the vestibule there was passage either into the *tepidarium* to the east or through the passageway into the vestibules for the *caldaria* (Fig. 19.13). After bathing in the heated rooms, the splash bath was an option for cooling off, or, alternatively, the bather could return to the vestibule for a plunge in the *frigidarium*. Refreshments may have been served in the small court beside the *apodyterium*, which adjoined the well room. Steps would then be retraced to the *apodyterium* to exit through the colonnaded corridor, or there was the option to visit the palaestra either for discussions or for an additional cycle of physical activity. A possible alternative would have been to stroll some 40 m south to enjoy the *natatio*, or swimming pool (originally identified in 2005 as a cistern-reservoir).

Dating the Baths

This blueprint of a small bath plan, a *balneum*, seems to have been conceived and developed in the initial phases before the annexation of Petra by Rome. Two complete lamps (cat. nos. 06-L-4, 06-L-5) were found in the earliest closed deposits under the ornamental pool passageway. Cat. no. 06-L-4 is a Nabataean volute lamp type B with two rosettes of four circles and one rosette with nine petals at the rear of the rim, dated by D. G. Barrett (2008, fig. 4.22) from the beginning of the AD first century through the reign of Malichus II (AD 40–70), and cat. no. 06-L-5 is a locally made round lamp with an ovolos impressed on the shoulder dated to the last third of the AD first century. The closed contexts of these lamps offer us a terminus post quem for the building of the baths. This evidence suggests that in *ca.* AD 70 the baths are constructed.

Most special of the 2006 finds in the baths were ten small, marble, Greek-inscribed fragments found in the caldarium (cat. nos. 06-S-6, 06-S-13), of which there were two joins (as would be expected in Petra, Greek was the lingua franca of the day).

Some of the fragments have drill holes, and preserved bronze dowels used to mount them are still found in the walls. An intact, footed sandstone stele (seq. no. 120A050; l. 0.63 m, w. 0.315 m, thickness 0.18 m) (Fig. 19.14) was unearthed in the columned corridor in secondary reuse blocking the water passage from the well room. This inscribed honorific reads:

Petra Great Temple
Roman Bath Complex
2006 Site Plan

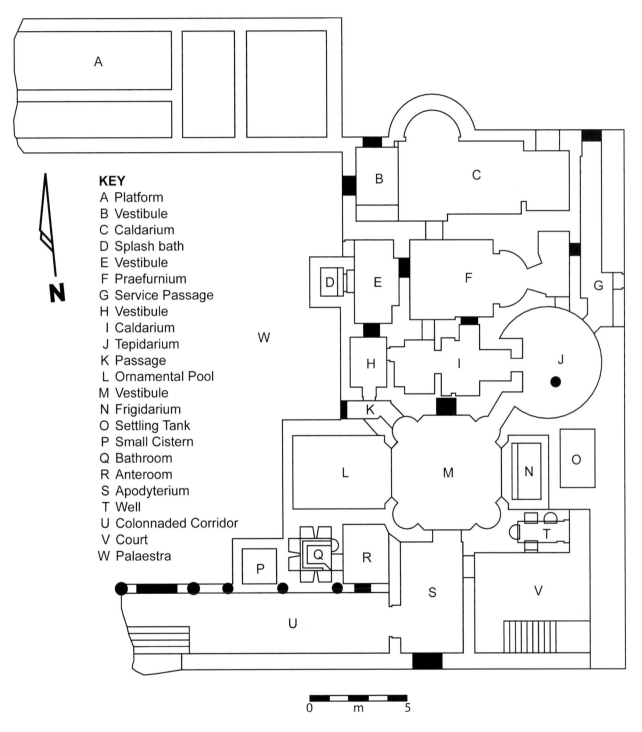

KEY
A Platform
B Vestibule
C Caldarium
D Splash bath
E Vestibule
F Praefurnium
G Service Passage
H Vestibule
 I Caldarium
J Tepidarium
K Passage
L Ornamental Pool
M Vestibule
N Frigidarium
O Settling Tank
P Small Cistern
Q Bathroom
R Anteroom
S Apodyterium
T Well
U Colonnaded Corridor
V Court
W Palaestra

N

0   m   5

Marshall C. Agnew

Fig. 19.10 *Roman-Byzantine Baths plan (Marshall C. Agnew).*

Fig.19.11 *Aerial of the Roman-Byzantine Baths to northwest (Photo: Artemis W. Joukowsky).*

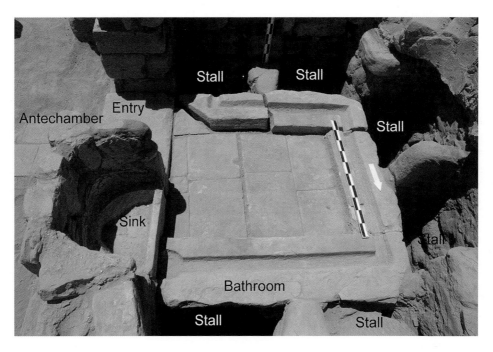

Fig.19.12 *Bathroom in the Roman-Byzantine Baths (Photo: Artemis W. Joukowsky).*

Fig. 19.13 *Caldarium in the Roman-Byzantine Baths (Photo: Artemis W. Joukowsky).*

MAELIVSAVRELIV
THEONSERENVSCV
CONSA[?] fl RO[?] SSO

And the footed base reads:

MUS[?]IARIANAIISIEG
AUGGPR.PR

A provisional assessment of this inscription by Traianos Gagos of the University of Michigan states that the name mentioned is one Marcus Aelius Aurelius Theon Serenus, who also appears in two inscriptions from Bostra as the governor of the province of Arabia from AD 253 to 259. This would place this inscription's date to the mid-third century, and its reuse as a block in the water channel to sometime later. Further interpretation will help us understand more about this individual and whether he governed the province from Petra or Bostra.

The material culture and architecture suggest that the bath installations – *caldaria*, *tepidarium* or *laconicum*, *praefurnium*, cold plunges – and the features present in the formal rooms were constructed at the same time. Frequent modifications, however, took place with the filling in of vaults, the additions of flooring, and the renovation of some of the walls. Reflected in the archaeological record is change, and these changes occurred as a result of the additional modifications or needs of the weakened architecture itself,

Fig. 19.14 *Inscription from the Roman-Byzantine Baths (Photo: Artemis W. Joukowsky).*

or because of earth tremors and the devastating, notorious earthquake of May 19, 363. This earthquake and its tremors so disrupt life in Petra the site never fully recovers and some of the bathrooms are never fully rebuilt. The earthquakes, along with another earthquake of AD July 9, 551, certainly contributed to a more impoverished community, and finally put an end to the Roman-Byzantine Baths and the Great Temple precinct as well.

Now the terminus of the Nabataean rule and the beginning of the Roman period at Petra cannot be seen in isolation, for it is but one aspect of a larger historic picture that recovers some definition at the Petra Great Temple site. The conclusions to our analysis of the Roman-Byzantine bath system can now be reasoned as follows: At the Great Temple there is more continuity from the Late Nabataean period into the Roman period than previously thought. The sequence of the Great Temple Baths is of five consecutive stages. Building begins in Site Phase VI, and the baths are in use until the AD 363 earthquake of Site Phase X. After the earthquake there is a striking change in the character of the baths. Some rooms are no longer used, doorways are narrowed or closed off completely, and there is a dramatic contrast between the late Nabataean working bath and the features that are then reused. Later in Site Phase X it is probable that a kiln may have been constructed over the remains of the southernmost caldarium. Modifications take place and a final collapse occurs with the Site Phase XI earthquake dated to AD 551, after which the site is finally abandoned. To fix a precise date for the termination for the baths' last use is tricky, although it is unlikely that the complex functioned beyond the mid-sixth century and the site's final abandonment. In conclusion, the Great Temple Roman-Byzantine Baths were in use for some four hundred or more years, from *c.* AD 70 to 551; however, the period of active use is gauged from AD 70 to 363, a period of less than three hundred years. By the early sixth century, when Petra experienced a general slump, the bath complex was abandoned.

Now that we have sketched the principal monuments, chronology, and history of our excavations and the Nabataeans in general, we turn our discussion to the Brown University Great Temple preservation program.

Conservation, Consolidation, Preservation, and Protection of the Petra Great Temple

In Petra we live with the environmental uncertainties of flash floods, earthquakes, and erosive action. Conservation is essential for the care and protection of the Great Temple precinct, although these natural disasters will surely continue to threaten the site and cause widespread damage. It is too soon for us to have any feeling of security about either our short-term or long-term Great Temple site conservation efforts or for the future of Petra as a whole.

Often archaeologists leave behind a denuded wasteland, as excavation has brought destruction to many sites while simultaneously destroying the vegetation. In our attempts to excavate the Great Temple, we have tried to control the damage and minimize the effect of the excavations on the environment. It always boils down to the question of attitudes, values, and financial resources. We have attempted to look beyond the immediate survival of the Great Temple precinct for its overall well-being and its future use as an archaeological resource, and, ultimately to preserve and restore the Petra Great Temple as a Jordanian national monument and as part of a World Heritage site.

A battle we have waged at every stage of our fourteen-year excavation process has us pitted against Mother Nature. The Great Temple site demanded the same sorts of resources used by the Nabataeans and their masons, and this has involved a myriad of different challenges. In short, our requirements are similar to those in Nabataean times. We are just beginning to explicate Nabataean culture by addressing the most basic aspects of the physical manifestation of the Great Temple and its precinct, and by isolating the architectural, chronological, and spatial characteristics of the precinct structures in relation to their environment.

Conservation and restoration have multiple values that can be briefly stated as the scientific interest and value of the remains, their aesthetic value, the unique archaeological features and information they provide, the technological acumen of the Nabataeans, and, of course, their tourist merit. Maintaining the function of the Petra Great Temple environment helps to perpetuate the precinct in its setting. Our aim is to consolidate, restore, and preserve a stabilized structure. Conservation is essential to the Great Temple site, which depends upon the proper consolidation of each of the imperiled elements with the ultimate purpose of administering to its requisite care and protection. It also involves the controlled use and systematic protection of natural resources. So often we use the term "consolidation," which is the stabilization and strengthening of architectural elements, for example, by filling the joins between ashlars or pointing the deteriorating mortar between wall components. The ultimate goal is to preserve and protect the site for the future.

From the beginning of our work, our fundamental philosophy has been to treat the site as a fragile and nonrenewable resource requiring protection. Constructed primarily from friable sandstone and degraded limestone, the temple complex is a prime target for material exfoliation as a result of wind and water erosion and the deposition of insoluble salts. This foreseen assumption of potential for structural deterioration makes efforts of consolidation and restoration an ongoing priority. To combat these natural threats a number of measures are taken to reinforce the physical structure of the site.

We formed a conservation management team with vigorous support from Ghazi Bisheh and Fawwaz al-Kraysheh, directors of the department of antiquities of the Hashemite Kingdom of Jordan, and from Suleiman Farajat, director of the Petra National Park. Included also were the directors(s) of the American Center for Oriental Research (ACOR) and our expert restorer, Dakhilallah Qublan, who was responsible for carrying out the various conservation projects. Our conservation-preservation advisory committee has been active since the inception of our project in 1993. Attempting to undertake conservation efforts during excavation and following the completion of each season, annual consolidation plans were proposed to the Jordanian department of antiquities where site-specific measures were outlined, discussed, and problems were addressed. In most cases, solutions were found. This advisory management team maintained a high degree of international cooperation with the Jordanian department of antiquities and a willingness to agree on some forms of control. Thus, as far as the site was concerned, conservation-oriented recommendations were annually exchanged with the Jordanian department of antiquities and ACOR, which monitored the status of many aspects involved with our consolidation-conservation strategies. All parties carefully considered our proposals before a decision was taken to conserve a particular wall, column, or other features such as the wall frescos. At the outset of the 1994 excavations, we organized a long-term plan for site preservation; however, these measures often were impacted by short-term, year-by-year excavation progress that served as immediate temporary expedients to strengthen elements that required specific stabilization. As mentioned above, this labor-intensive, detailed work of consolidation and restoration is performed under the expert direction of site foreman Dakhilallah Qublan with the assistance of some twenty local workmen and the aid of skilled specialists and technicians including architects and conservators, and under the watchful eye of the department of antiquities and Pierre M. Bikai and Barbara A. Porter, directors of ACOR. All of the aforementioned have helped us identify issues, are expert in available resources and materials, and are technically skilled specialists able to perform what is necessary. This group helps to guide our major decisions.

In a continued effort to uphold the principles proposed by the International Council on Monuments and Sites, the International Committee on Archaeological Heritage Management (the World Heritage Convention in 1972), the 1966 Venice Charter, the Hague Convention, and the tenets of the 1956, 1970, and 1985 UNESCO Conventions, we choose to adhere to field treatments to prevent harm to the site and that are reversible. To this end, it is important to note that architectural restoration at the Petra Great Temple is undertaken in a true sense. With elements frequently lacking a clear basis for their reconstruction based on archaeological context, the measures we are taking are geared solely toward the immediate, though impermanent, preservation of the structural integrity of various elements of the precinct. When intact, original stones are reconstituted into temple masonry. In almost all cases, original building materials are used. When fragmentary or robbed out, original constructions are replaced by new stone fills quarried from the Petra bedrock. The conservation of the Petra Great Temple also includes the preservation of in-situ elements that are essentially undisturbed by excavation but require structural protection because of natural process of deterioration such as spalling ashlars and loose mortars. We attempt to carry out restoration so that the structural integrity of the architecture is sustained.

Financial Considerations

From the beginning, it was made clear that the Jordanian department of antiquities would not be able to financially support the provision of conservation measures. This meant that our project had to incorporate conservation plans concurrent with the excavation. As there are no governmental agencies that can care adequately for Petra, this puts the site at risk. Our advisory committee helped us rule on the appropriateness of any proposed consolidation and restoration. We knew that careful planning had to be undertaken if we were to modify the landscape naturally or artificially. In the early years, with deep trenches exposed, we had to set these fragile areas off-limits and protect visitors and animals from falling into them. We also had to carefully plan the means of human access to the site. Each year, once the annual excavations concluded, we proposed a long-term plan and prioritized which projects required immediate attention. Once the short-term annual goals had been met, the longer-term goals of a working plan were resolved by deciding on what the priorities were for consolidation, the detailed documentation for each project, including the mapping out and photographing the areas, and arriving at decisions as to what materials would be needed such as scaffolding, mortar components, numbers of stones that had to be cut and dressed, and finally the schedule for the implementation of the project.

Yearly conservation efforts were made financially possible by two awards (1996 and 1998, respectively) from The World Monuments Fund, a grant from the Samuel H. Kress Foundation through an American Express Award from World Monuments Watch, a program of the World Monuments Fund, and the generous support of the Joukowsky Family Foundation. Since 2000 the Joukowsky Family Foundation has provided subventions for annual conservation expenses. These funds are generously matched several times by special subventions through donations to the Petra Excavation Fund constituted at Brown University.

Although the importance of consolidation and conservation may seem obvious, most excavation budgets are so tight that to be concerned with anything more than excavation is difficult. Since our annual budget is not guaranteed, we have to select our projects carefully, and planning for site conservation has always been in doubt when excavation costs alone have been a cause for concern. Such activities – excavation, conservation, consolidation, preservation, and publication – have always been planned along with our

Brown University annual budgets, although when finances have been tight there have been moments of conflict of interest and financial readjustments between these areas. Each year we had to outline and redefine what we were realistically capable of conserving over the period of time we would be working at the Great Temple.

Conservation Challenges

A planned comprehensive management plan for the protection, conservation, and interpretation of the Petra Great Temple was initiated in 1993 and continues to the present. Primary necessities included two factors: the ecosystem of the site itself, to prevent further strain on the components due to erosion from both soil and water, as well as the careful management of consolidation and restoration of its archaeological components. In order for the archaeological remains to be stable and consolidation measures to be preserved, the recurring processes of soil and water erosion that had been a serious and constant problem had to be curtailed.

In 1993, although the precinct had largely been abandoned, we found the Great Temple site had been exploited by local natives for building, farming, and looting; there was serious deterioration of many of the architectural elements and others were severely eroded. The Great Temple site was deteriorated and had suffered from neglect, as is common in Petra. Individuals who had over many years used the area for farming had replowed the Lower Temenos. Elephant-headed capitals when found on the surface had been carried away as souvenirs – and one still serves as a doorstop in a local Bedouin home.

Preventive preservation of the site is undertaken through the construction of flood channels to divert heavy winter rains away from the complex, the backfilling of trenches to limit exposure of weak structural elements to air and water seepage, and the wrapping of delicate areas with a plastic mesh covered with zinc sheeting secured by sandbags. Protective fencing is also placed around the site perimeter and open excavation areas are partitioned to insure the safety of both visitors to the site and the site itself.

We planned our archaeological investigations as a long-term commitment to the Great Temple, Petra, and to the Hashemite Kingdom of Jordan. Unfortunately, as excavations progressed the extent of new discoveries could not be foretold, and with the continued excavation of the site, the research design including the needs of its architectural elements required expansion and it became essential to organize and direct conservation efforts over an increased area exposed during excavation. Progress for the protection of the site involved a rational planning for public use and access to the site. The long-term benefits have been considerable not only for the aesthetic value of the archaeological remains but also for the public understanding of the Great Temple's architectural statement.

Excavation

Excavation is invasive; it has made the site vulnerable, and our challenge has been to respond to the site's preservation in the most effective ways possible. In 1993 we initiated training in excavation and we have trained some one hundred students from Brown University in excavation methodology, including surveying and conservation. From this group of students many have gone on to graduate studies and are now qualified and respected archaeologists in their own right. Over the years these researchers have devoted at least ten weeks a year excavating, preparing measured drawings, site mapping, writing final reports, and interpreting the site. The tasks range in complexity from the careful removal of debris and documentation to interpretation. But of all these important aspects, team members are also required to recommend and prioritize the specifics of conservation and consolidation of the areas they have been involved in excavating. These recommendations have been integral to our planning as they are then prioritized for the consolidation program. Working painstakingly beside us are local Jordanian workmen who willingly help us to reverse existing damage discovered during the excavation process. They have become expertly skilled in moving architectural fragments with the attendant dangers of imminent collapse. They fill vulnerable cracks in the walls with broken bits of stone to keep the wall ashlars from collapse. They also sweep the site, cut back the weed growth, pick up detritus, and monitor the site's well-being throughout the year. This adds immeasurably to the effort for ongoing site maintenance.

Inherently a destructive science, archaeological excavation raises the issue of on-site efforts of consolidation and restoration. In the act of rescuing the Great Temple architecture and material culture from the dense cover of debris and accumulation, the elements of the site are exposed anew to the threats of air, human contact, and environmental decay. Although excavation can reveal a site, it can be poorly related to the consequences that take place as the site is excavated, and these consequences may provide side effects that are not anticipated, thereby disrupting the overall excavation research plan. A multitude of varying examples of such situations were encountered, for example, when in 2004 the East Propylaeum Room 3 arch was unearthed in a state of collapse and the Lower Temenos West Cryptoporticus walls required support. The Upper Temenos Baroque Room and the Residential Quarter were recovered in 2002 with considerable time-consuming restorative needs, and that same year the Great Cistern was discovered, which required additional, different conservation measures. Our excavation plans had to be flexible and innovative to meet the challenges the excavation posed. In each instance we had to reorganize our excavation research. When we discovered the temple West Corridor west wall – its arched passage entrance was seriously buckled and in a state of imminent collapse – we immediately concluded that its restoration was demanded and its stabilization became a priority. In each instance, the research design needed to be completely adjusted and modifications of the research design had to be put in place so their recovery would be in keeping with the overall site integrity. To the nonarchaeologist these aspects of excavation may seem to be the exception to the rule, but it is striking that in every excavation season at the Great Temple such exceptions have become commonplace. Similar to the step-by-step process of selecting which areas to excavate, our chosen preservation projects have to be the most appropriate and meaningful and priorities must be identified. In spite of these considerations, we have had remarkable breakthroughs that speak for themselves.

One specific set of problems came to the fore when we unearthed the twin *betyls* of the West Propylaeum and the *nefesh* on the West Entry Stairway. Once excavated, they could not remain on-site or they would be stolen, and yet we believed that the public should be able to view them in their original contexts. Once their findspots were documented, they were moved to the tent of our site guard where they would be protected.

Nefesh and Betyls

Along with numerous examples of representational sculpture, our excavations have also recovered aniconic or nonrepresentational sculpture – the *nefesh* and *betyls*. A powerful part of the Nabataean ethnos, both the *betyl* and the *nefesh* are thought to be symbols and embodiments of the god himself. Their iconography is part of the Nabataean visual lexicon. The use of the *nefesh* and *betyls* found at the

Great Temple must have been a reminder of the long-standing nomadic tradition, and their iconography and spiritual meaning became part of Nabataean cultural identity. In particular, the *betyl* demonstrates a visual continuity of ideas – the metaphysical presence of the divine, an icon with sacred power. *Betyls* range from plain rectangular to conically shaped blocks representing the deity – some of them have inscriptions indicating the deity represented. Some of them have eyes and noses and are known as "eye-idols."

At the southwest end of the L-shaped extension of the West Propylaeum's north gallery is a large niche measuring 0.97 m in width and 0.69 m in depth cut into the west face of the Propylaeum West central north–south wall, an extension of the central stylobate wall of the Lower Temenos West Cryptoporticus. In this niche rested exquisitely carved twin aniconic white limestone *betyls* (Fig. 19.15), averaging 0.50 m in height and 0.21 m in width, adhered to the base and rear wall of the niche by a thin layer of plaster. Positioned directly beneath the niche is a bench constructed from medium-sized sandstone ashlars and packed earth resting on the floor of the north gallery. That these *betyls* represent Dushara (the main deity of Petra and the tutelary deity of the Nabataean tribe and its royal dynasty; Wenning 2001, 81) and Al-'Uzza (the goddess) is hypothetical and cannot be proved, but what is clear is that this was a sacred place.

Unearthed in the excavation of the West Entry Stairway on a platform is the remarkable *nefesh* shown in Figure 19.16. The *nefesh* is a sacred Nabataean commemorative monument, carved to consecrate a person or a family, and

Fig. 19.15 *West Propylaeum Betyls in situ to east (Photo: Artemis W. Joukowsky).*

Fig. 19.16 West Entry Stairs Nefesh as excavated (Photo: Artemis W. Joukowsky).

to represent the receptacle of the soul. Often there is no burial associated with it, as in the case at the Great Temple. It serves as a witness to a Nabataean shared belief. It also symbolizes the Nabataean attachment to the aniconic representation of their god in association with an honorific memorial. Patrich (1990, 122) reminds us that the Nabataeans did not use the image of the deceased in their burial monuments but used an architectonic shape to portray their dead. We can imagine they were worshipped in the same manner in the city as they had been in their nomadic lifestyle. Wenning (2001, 87) states: "The Nabataean nephesh is shaped like an obeliskoid pilaster or a pointed cone, often with a blossom/pinecone or a stylized crown at the top. Most of the nepheshes are set upon a base, where the name of the dead person is given . . . Freestanding nepheshes . . . are rare." By their in-situ position in the West Propylaeum and on the West Entry Stairway platform, the *nefesh* and *betyl* are in a high place to view the city surroundings. Both symbolize the presence of the deity, and their location in a public, high, open-air space lends them a theological legitimacy. The prominently located stairway platform serves as a watch place, to make offerings – it is public, a space that sees pedestrian traffic, and it serves a public cult. The presence of the *nefesh* and the *betyl* symbolizes and suggests a conspicuous cultic function for this platform. To a great degree, these are silent sentinels that witnessed a fascinating but enigmatic past. But in their placement, they are far from silent about who witnessed their presence. As they are subject to interpretation, perhaps we can speculate the *nefesh* was a place to remember the honored dead. Unquestionably there is an actual cult of the dead associated with significant religious ritual in Petra; obviously death also plays a prominent role in life. Is the erection of these religious icons

spontaneous and private or does it serve as part of an official act? There are intriguing questions about these aniconic steles that deserve more scholarly attention.

We have carved limestone facsimiles of the *betyls* found in the West Propylaeum, and have reinstalled the reproductions in their original findspot; the originals have been turned over to the Petra Museum. In the West Entry Stairs we commissioned the carving of a replica of the *nefesh*, replacing the original found on the stairway platform. Now the original has been accessioned by the Petra Museum for display, and the facsimile of the *nefesh* has been put on the West Stairway platform. This brief digression about the significant Great Temple aniconic sculpture is important because of the problem resolutions their discoveries had set in motion.

The Lapidaries – Storage for Architectural Elements

During excavation each trench supervisor records all stones that are trench coded, number referenced, and marked with that reference number – this number is carried both to our site architectural fragment database and to their respective lapidary where the stones are stored by type. The objectives in our varied storage areas – lapidaries – are to keep architectural elements in a favorable and separate microenvironment until they can be used for analysis or for restoration. Every architectural element excavated has been numbered, measured, and recorded in our site database. Included in this database are ashlars – the thousands of wall blocks that originally served as the defining building blocks of the structure. There are also arch ashlars, voussoirs, and arch slabs used to embellish the walls as well as doorjambs and threshold blocks and flagstones used for pavements. Other elements include many hundreds of column drums and associated column decorative embellishments such as attic bases, capitals, and capital elements. During our years of excavation architectural fragments have overwhelmed us, and from the first years of our work we established lapidaries for these elements divided by type. By splitting up the architectural fragments by their physical characteristics, we felt we could better manage their storage. We realize as well that some of the most serious conservation problems are associated not with the way these elements have been excavated but with the methods by which they are stored. We make every effort to protect our storage areas.

We have six main areas for architectural storage. Small decorative elements including pinecones, hibiscus flowers, poppies, pomegranates, vines, and the like have been placed in boxes and stored underground at the site, basically returning them to their microenvironment. In a fenced-off area to the west of the temple is our so-called sculpture garden, which is reserved for larger elements such as pilaster blocks, volutes from capitals, bosses, nearly complete capitals, and large domestic implements such as grinders and millstones. We have also utilized the protection of the West Cryptoporticus arched galleries and the East Exedra niches as on-site museum venues. In the West Lapidary is the storage of column drums, and on the West roadway voussoirs and arch blocks are stored along with arch slabs. Another area is reserved only for ashlars that have promise of reuse. And finally there is an area designed for broken and fragmented pieces that have little structural or decorative integrity but that may be used for snecking stone support for other architectural elements. Elephant-associated fragments and the complete, massive elephant-head capitals that we have recovered have been restored, drawn, photographed, and catalogued in our artifact registry. The best specimens have been turned over to the Petra Museum for safekeeping. The few that have been battered have been restored to the tops of columns in the Propylaeum and Lower Temenos.

We use a minimum of mechanical equipment to remove the debris from the site and to lift heavy objects. Rollers (metal pipes) are used dexterously to bring the architectural fragments into position for removal. Because some of these fragments weigh a ton or more, they are cradle wrapped with steel-reinforced straps and lifted by the prongs of the bulldozer and moved to their specifically prepared disposal areas. If the object is highly decorated, it might be swaddled in a blanket or wrapped in foam sheeting before lifting. This system has proved particularly invaluable for our spectacular elephant-headed capitals – one of the crowning achievements of the Great Temple – and pilaster blocks (Fig. 19.17) as well as the more mundane wall ashlars. During restoration, the workers use wooden scaffolding for platforms along with a simple block and tackle to lift heavy architectural fragments such as column drums, capitals, vault slabs, ashlars, and lintels. This reconstruction process can be seen in Figure 19.18. Debris from the site is removed by the bulldozer and trucked to a disposal area reserved by the authorities for our spoil heap.

Conclusion

As this submission has demonstrated, remains of the Nabataean Great Temple(s) attest to an extensive architectural record that Brown University archaeologists (Fig. 19.19) have unearthed. These excavations verify, unambiguously, the sacred and secular character of the site while also reflecting the Nabataean and Petraean architectural and sculptural traditions. Despite the significant change brought about by the Romans, it is possible to reconstruct the site's heterogeneous development in this period with the Roman Imperial Cult building and the Roman-Byzantine Baths. The evidence has helped us establish chronological parameters for the site, and our comprehensive program for preservation underscores the relevant role the Great Temple excavations have played in the remarkable city of Petra.

Fig. 19.17 *Pilaster relief of Fortuna holding a cornucopia (Photo: Artemis W. Joukowsky).*

Fig. 19.18 *Restoration of the West Triple Colonnade (Photo: Artemis W. Joukowsky).*

Fig. 19.19 *2006 Brown University Excavation Team (Photo: Artemis W. Joukowsky).*

Works Cited

Ammianus Marcellinus (1963) Loeb Classical Library (English Translation by J. C. Rolfe), Loeb, 315, Cambridge MA, Harvard University Press.

Bachmann, W., Watzinger, C. and Wiegand, T. (1921) Petra, *Wissenschaftliche Veröffentlichungen des Deutsch-Türkischen Denkmalschutz-Kommandos*, Berlin and Leipzig.

Barrett, D. G. (2008) *The Ceramic Oil Lamp as an Indicator of Cultural Change Within Nabataean Society in Petra and its Environs Circa CE 106.* Piscataway, NJ, Gorgias Press.

Bedal, L-A. (2004) *The Petra Pool Complex: A Hellenistic Paradeisos in the Nabataean Capital.* Piscataway, NJ, Gorgias Press.

Bowersock, G. W. (2003) The Nabataeans in historical context. In G. Markoe (ed.), *Petra Rediscovered: Lost City of the Nabataeans,* 19–25. London, Thames & Hudson.

Brünnow, R. E. and von Domaszewski, A. (1904–1909) *Die Provincia Arabia.* Strasburg, Verlag Karl J. Trübner.

Casson, L. (1989) *Periplus Maris Erythraei.* English translation and edited, Princeton, Princeton University Press.

Corbeil, M-C and Helwig, K. (1999) *Analysis of Fresco Fragments from the Petra Great Temple, Analytical Research Laboratory.* ARL Report 3779, March 19, 1999. Ottowa, Institut Canadien de Conservation.

Dio Cassius (1961–1984) 'Dio's Roman History, LXVIII Loeb Classical Library (English Translation by E. Cary), Cambridge, MA, Loeb, Harvard University Press.

Egan, E. C. (2002) Stucco decoration from the south corridor of the Petra Great Temple: Discussion and Interpretation. *Annual of the Department of Antiquities of Jordan,* 46, 347–61.

Glueck, N. (1965) *Deities and Dolphins: The Story of the Nabataeans.* New York, Farrar Straus & Giroux.

Joukowsky, M. S. (1998) *Petra: The Great Temple, Volume I – Brown University Excavations 1993–1997.* Providence, RI, Brown University, Petra Exploration Fund.

——— (2007) *Petra Great Temple, Volume. II, Archaeological Contexts of the Remains and Excavations, Brown University Excavations in Jordan at the Petra Great Temple, 1993–2007.* Providence, RI, Brown University, Petra Exploration Fund.

McKenzie, J. (1990) *The Architecture of Petra.* Oxford, Oxford University Press.

Patrich. J. (1990) *The Formation of Nabataean Art: Prohibition of a Graven Image Among the Nabataeans.* Jerusalem, Magnes Press.

Reid, S. K. (2005) *The Small Temple: A Roman Imperial Cult Building in Petra, Jordan.* Piscataway, NJ, Gorgias Press.

Schmid, S. G. (1995) Nabataean Fine Ware from Petra. *Studies in the History and Archaeology of Jordan* 5, 637–47.

——— (1996) Die Feinkeramik. In *Petra, Ez Zantur I,* 151–218. Mainz. von Zabern.

Segal, A. (1995) *Theaters in Roman Palestine and Provincia Arabia.* Leiden, Brill.

Taylor, J. (2001) *Petra and the Lost Kingdom of the Nabataeans.* London: I. B. Tauris.

Vote, E. L. (2001) A new methodology for archaeological analysis: using visualization and interaction to explore spatial links in excavation data. Ph.D. dissertation, Brown University.

Wenning, R. (2001) The betyls of Petra. *Bulletin of the American Schools of Oriental Research* 324, 79–95.

Yegül, F. (1992) *Baths and Bathing in Classical Antiquity.* Cambridge, MIT Press.

The Marbles of Three Mythological Sarcophagi at RISD and of Other Sarcophagi Found in Central Italy

Frances Van Keuren

with contributions by L. Peter Gromet

Introduction

Two Roman sarcophagi and a fragment of a third, all located at the Museum of Art, the Rhode Island School of Design (hereafter, RISD), illustrate Greek myths and were reportedly found or purchased in Rome. According to letters from the classicist and dealer E. P. Warren, which are located at the RISD Archives and which date from 1915 to 1921, two of the sarcophagi were found on the site of a lime kiln in Rome (Van Keuren 2005, 170–75). The fragment of the third sarcophagus was reportedly purchased in Rome thirty-four years before the donor, Charlotte F. Dailey, gave it to the RISD Museum in 1902 (Van Keuren 2005, 169–70).

The first sarcophagus to be considered (Figs. 20.1–2) is preserved only on the front side. The front of the lid shows Apollo and Artemis shooting down at the children of Niobe, who are shown on the chest below. All four sides and the lid of the second sarcophagus (Fig. 20.3) are preserved. The front of this sarcophagus shows two scenes from the story of Achilles and Hector – their fight before the walls of Troy and Achilles's subsequent dragging of Hector's body. Only a fragment of the third sarcophagus (Fig. 20.4) survives. However, the female wearing a lion's skin is clearly the Lydian queen Omphale, clad in her lover Hercules's garb.

The identifications of the provenances of the marbles of these three sarcophagi were achieved through analyses of their stable isotopic composition and their texture, color, and maximum grain size. Distinguishing calcitic from dolomitic marble was also important for the fragment (Fig. 20.4). The isotopic analyses of samples of the RISD sarcophagi were made at the University of Georgia by Norman Herz (see Fig. 20.5a, c) and at the University of South Florida by Robert Tykot (see Fig. 20.5b), and observations of the physical characteristics of the marbles were made at the RISD Museum by L. Peter Gromet and

reported to Norman Herz. The Niobid Sarcophagus was determined to be of Carrara marble, the Achilles Sarcophagus of Dokimeian marble, and the Omphale Fragment of dolomitic marble from Cape Vathy on Thassos.

Some design features of the three sarcophagi are consistent with their different marble provenances. For example, the design of the lid of the Niobid Sarcophagus is characteristic of three-sided sarcophagi from Rome, where Carrara marble was shipped for building projects and funerary monuments (see Fant 2001, 167–68, 189). The four-sided decoration of the chest of the Achilles Sarcophagus and the roof shape of its lid (see Fig. 20.3) are standard features of sarcophagi from Dokimeion in Asia Minor. However, another design feature of the Achilles Sarcophagus, the continuous frieze decoration of the chest, deviates from the standard design of Dokimeian chests, whose sides are normally broken up into niches flanked by columns. Furthermore, the arrangements of the sculptured figures from the Achilles Sarcophagus and Omphale Fragment are not typical of sarcophagi from Dokimeion and Cape Vathy, and can otherwise be found only on sarcophagi from Rome.

These examples suggest that the designers of sarcophagi of non-Italian marbles adapted their designs to match designs that were currently popular in Rome, when this was the market for which their sarcophagi were destined (*cf.* Fant 1993, 162, on the differing designs of Marmara sarcophagi that correlate to the different regions where they were found). This thesis is reinforced by the Roman style of two moldings from the front of the Achilles Sarcophagus. An examination of additional sarcophagi from Rome, whose marbles have been demonstrated through analysis to be the same as the RISD sarcophagi, provides further support for the hypothesis that Rome had a distinct iconographic tradition for sarcophagus design, which reflected the international character

Fig. 20.1–20.4 *Clockwise from top: Fig. 20.1, Niobid Sarcophagus, Carrara marble, c. 160–90 AD. RISD Museum 21.076; Fig. 20.2, Unrestored fragment depicting aged nurse, from the chest of the Niobid Sarcophagus; Fig. 20.3, Front side of Achilles Sarcophagus, Dokimeian marble, c. 155–60 AD. RISD Museum 21.074; Fig. 20.4, Omphale Fragment from chest of sarcophagus, Thasian dolomitic marble, c. 200 AD. RISD Museum 02.004 (Photos: courtesy of the RISD Museum).*

Sarcophagus Sample		δ¹³C ‰	δ¹⁸O ‰	Provenance Probabilities
a. Niobid RISD 21.076	Lid	2.24	-2.05	Carrara/Miseglia 92%, Carrara/Collonata 90%
	Chest	2.33	-1.84	Carrara/Collonata 99%, Thassos/Cape Phaneri 93%
b. Achilles RISD 21.074	Lid	1.89	-5.04	Afyon 74%, Usak 56%
	Chest	1.46	-5.16	Afyon 88%, Aphrodisias 39%, Ephesus 37%
c. Omphale Fragment RISD 02.004	Chest	3.54	-4.86	Sardis 15%, Afyon 14%

d. Cape Vathy,
  Thassos
  (quarry sample)
		3.39	-4.86	

Fig. 20.5 *Isotopic compositions are reported relative to the PDB (PeeDee Formation belemnite) standard and have analytical uncertainties of ± 0.04‰ d13C and ± 0.05‰ d18O. Provenance probabilities are reported according to the statistical procedures described in Pentia (1995), using the Stable Isotopic Database of Herz (1992).*

Fig. 20.6 *Niobid Sarcophagus, dated shortly before 150 AD. Vatican, Museo Gregoriano Profano 10437 (Drawing from Robert 1919, pl. 100).*

of her population and exhibited a blending of diverse artistic sources.

Carrara Marble: The RISD Niobid Sarcophagus

Only portions of the front of the first RISD sarcophagus (see Figs. 20.1–2), found in Rome, are preserved (for a recent discussion, see Zanker and Ewald 2004, 77–78). The design of the lid, with a sculptured panel flanked by masks, is characteristic of sarcophagi produced in Rome that were almost always decorated only on the front and left and right sides (Koch 1993, 17–19, fig. 6.1). The marble of both the lid and chest is very light buff colored, fine grained, lacking inclusions, and essentially pure calcite. Isotopic analyses indicate that the lid and chest are most likely made of Italian Carrara marble (Fig. 20.5a). The physical traits of the marble of the sarcophagus are consistent with an identification of the marble as Carrara.

The similarities between the lid and chest in color, grain size, and other aspects of their appearance, coupled with the statistically close isotopic ratios, support the hypothesis that the lid and chest were carved from the same block – a finding consistent with the unified iconography of the two parts. On the sarcophagus lid, Apollo and Artemis shoot at the children of Niobe, who are depicted on the chest below. Apollo shoots from the left edge of the lid and Artemis shoots from the right edge.

Brunilde Ridgway (1972, 102) dates the RISD sarcophagus to *c.* 160–90 AD. Only one other Niobid sarcophagus with the lid preserved depicts the same scheme of Apollo and Artemis shooting down at the Niobids from the lid (Fig. 20.6) (Geominy 1992, 920, no. 32a; Zanker and Ewald 2004, 43–45, 357–59). Like the RISD sarcophagus, this parallel comes from Rome. Found in a late Hadrianic tomb near the Porta Viminalis, this sarcophagus is currently at the Museo Gregoriano Profano in the Vatican. It is dated by Sichtermann and Koch (1975, 49–50) to shortly before the mid-second century, and was found with another sarcophagus that depicts the story of Orestes on both the lid and the chest (Sichtermann and Koch 1975, 52–53, pls. 133.2, 135–40). In the future, it would be valuable to analyze samples from the lids and chests of these additional sarcophagi, to see if the carving of the lid and chest from the same block of Carrara marble, as in the case of the RISD sarcophagus, was standard practice for workshops in Rome that created narrative unity between sculptured lids and chests.

Other Sarcophagi of Carrara Marble

Isotopic analyses demonstrate that workshops in Rome used Carrara marble for sarcophagi for several decades before the RISD Niobid Sarcophagus was carved. The earliest

sarcophagi whose marble falls within the isotopic field for Carrara were found in the second chamber of the Licinian tomb on the Via Salaria in Rome (Van Keuren 2000, 118–21; Van Keuren *et al.* 2003, 88). The earlier of these two sarcophagi is a child's garland sarcophagus with comic masks, whose lid is decorated with hunt scenes (Figs. 20.7–8). The chest of this sarcophagus was revealed to be of Carrara marble, while the lid was found to be of Marmara (*i.e.,* Proconnesian) marble. Grain sizes and electron paramagnetic resonance (EPR) analyses confirm that the

Fig. 20.8 *Right short side of child's garland sarcophagus, with double sets of clamp holes on chest. Museo Nazionale Romano 441 (Photo: courtesy of the Deutsches Archäologisches Institut, Rome, Neg. 04744).*

Fig. 20.7 *Front view of child's garland sarcophagus, chest of Carrara marble, c. 130 AD; and lid of Marmara marble, Antonine date? Museo Nazionale Romano 441 (Photo: courtesy of the Deutsches Archäologisches Institut, Rome, Neg. 1969.2513).*

Fig. 20.9a *Front side of Thiasos Sarcophagus, Carrara marble, late Hadrianic or early Antonine. Museo Nazionale Romano 1303 (Photo by Frances Van Keuren).*

Fig. 20.9b *Detail, Front side of Thiasos Sarcophagus, Carrara marble, late Hadrianic or early Antonine. Museo Nazionale Romano 1303 (Photo by Frances Van Keuren).*

Fig. 20.10 *Left short side of Thiasos Sarcophagus. Museo Nazionale Romano 1303 (Photo: courtesy of the Deutsches Archäologisches Institut, Rome, Neg. 1936.1014).*

chest and lid are of two different marbles (Van Keuren *et al.* 2009, 353–356). The chest can be dated on stylistic grounds to the late Hadrianic period or *c.* 130 AD (Herdejürgen 1996, 118). The presence of two holes for each of the lower attachments of clamps on the right short side of the chest (see Fig. 20.8) suggests that the Marmara lid was not the original one. Furthermore, the lid appears to be later in date than the chest, possibly belonging to the Antonine period (Kranz 1975, 81).

The second sarcophagus from chamber 2 of the Licinian tomb depicts a Dionysiac *thiasos* without the wine god (Figs. 20.9–10, Matz 1968, vol. 4.2, 180–2, no. 73). Initially the lid was thought not to belong with the chest, but the isotopic analyses demonstrate that not only are both of Carrara marble but also they appear to have been carved from the same block (Van Keuren 2000, 119–21). Friedrich Matz (1968, vol. 4.2, 182) dates this sarcophagus to the late Hadrianic or early Antonine period. He includes it, along with Eros sarcophagi and garland sarcophagi (as in Figs. 20.7–8), among the earliest figured sarcophagi produced in Rome (Matz 1968, vol. 4.2, 179). He also notes that the sarcophagus belongs to a small class of sarcophagi that are closely connected in their Neoattic figure types and stylistic treatment to contemporary Attic sarcophagi (for a discussion of a group of decorative reliefs that may have been original Neoattic creations of the early first century AD, see Nulton, this volume). In particular, the cymbal player on the left short side (shown on the right in Fig. 20.10) is a variant of Matz's tympanum player, Neoattic type TH 1 (Matz 1968, vol. 4.1, 18, no. TH1). This same figure type appears on three Attic sarcophagi depicting the same theme of a Dionysiac *thiasos* (Matz 1968, vol. 4.1, 98–99, no. 1, pl. 1; 99–100, no. 2, pls. 2–3; 104–106, no. 8, pls. 10–12).

Since Carrara marble does not appear to have been shipped to the eastern Mediterranean (see below), the sculptor who executed the *thiasos* sarcophagus from the Licinian tomb must have been located either in Carrara or in Rome, where the piece was found. We do not know whether Carrara marble sarcophagi were shipped to Rome in a blank or carved state. J. Clayton Fant stated in an e-mail communication (February 17, 2007), "I'm not aware of any [Carrara] sarcophagus blanks ever found anywhere in the chain from quarry to workshop." The Neoattic figure types on this sarcophagus suggest that its sculptor was either a Neoattic artist living in Italy or an artist in Italy with access to Neoattic models.

Additional sarcophagi at the British Museum have been identified by isotopic analysis as being of Carrara marble. The earliest example, dated *c*. 145–55 AD, is the front panel from the lid of a sarcophagus. The lid shows three pairs of captive Amazons and is first known through fifteenth-century drawings, when it was located in the Roman Forum (Walker 1990, 21–22, no. 14). The next example, dated *c*. 150–70/180 AD, was reportedly found in an ancient tomb at Genzano on the Via Appia southeast of Rome. On this sarcophagus, the lid was revealed to be of Carrara marble, and the chest of Marmara. However, since the chest shows seven of Hercules's labors and the lid the other five, it is believed that both parts were carved at the same time in Rome (Ward-Perkins 1958, 461; Walker 1985, 64–65; 1990, 22–23, no. 15). In an e-mail of February 8, 2004, Susan Walker observed, "It often happened that a chest imported to Rome from Thasos or Proconnesus was given a lid in Carrara on execution of the commission. The lid was often personalised with a portrait or inscription [both lacking in the Genzano sarcophagus]" (*cf.* Walker and Matthews 1988, 123). Since Marmara marble is listed as one of the cheapest marbles in the Prices Edict of Diocletian, issued in late 301 AD (Roueché 1989, 299–300; Corcoran 1996, 228), it makes sense that the bulkier chest of a sarcophagus would be carved of it, while the smaller and frequently personalized lid would be carved of the more expensive Carrara marble.

The latest sarcophagus in the British Museum that isotopic analysis revealed to be made of Carrara marble is a coffin of a female child from the late second century AD (Walker 1990, 17–18, no. 6). This sarcophagus was purchased in Rome in the eighteenth century and belongs to a series of children's coffins that show the deceased child on his/her funeral bed. The series may have been produced by a single workshop in Rome (Koch and Sichtermann 1982, 112–13).

Workshops in Rome clearly used Carrara marble for sarcophagi throughout much of the second century AD. According to Susan Walker and Keith Matthews (1988, 124), "there is evidence to suggest a marked decline in the use of Carrara marble for metropolitan sarcophagi in the third century AD." At the same time, Walker (1988, 30–33) sees during the third century a rise in commissions "given to quarries in Greece and Asia Minor to provide roughed-out chests of traditional Italian shape for decoration at Rome." Specifically, the single eastern quarry represented in third-century sarcophagi from Rome in the British Museum is Marmara (Walker 1988, 30–33; 1990, 13, 18, no. 7; Walker and Matthews 1988, 124).

The use of Carrara marble for sarcophagi seems to have been limited to the western Mediterranean. According to Cornelius Vermeule and Kristin Anderson (1981, 15–16), "marble sarcophagi of the second and third centuries of the Christian era from the Holy Land . . . were imported either from Attica or the coastal cities of Asia Minor." Isotopic analyses have been conducted on seventeen third-century sarcophagi from Roman Palestine. These analyses demonstrate that Marmara, Pentelic, and Dokimeian were the only marbles used (Fischer 1998, 205–30, 238–39, 249–50, 256–57). Mosche L. Fischer (1998, 258) notes an absence of Carrara marble in all analyzed marble finds from Roman Palestine, which include architectural members and sculpture in the round: "As to Carrara marble, it is not surprising that no single artifact seems to be conclusively of this source. This situation reflects the state of matter mainly of the eastern part of the Mediterranean." If the eastern Mediterranean is excluded as an intended destination for Carrara marble sarcophagi, then the decoration that occurs on them should be considered to represent western taste in sarcophagus design. If this assumption is correct, then it may be possible, where thematic motifs first appear on Carrara sarcophagi from Rome, to trace the imitation of these motifs on later sarcophagi that were found in Rome but made of imported eastern marbles. The discussion below of several Dionysian sarcophagi of Thasian dolomitic marble (see Figs. 20.21–26) supports this hypothesis.

Dokimeian Marble: The RISD Achilles Sarcophagus

The Achilles Sarcophagus (see Fig. 20.3) was found in the same lime kiln deposit in Rome as the Niobid Sarcophagus (see Van Keuren 2005, 170–75). Marc Waelkens (1982, 35–36) dates the sarcophagus *c*. 155–60 AD and assigns it to the small grouping within Dokimeian frieze sarcophagi of four examples from Italy (see chart, Waelkens 1982, 9, fig. 7). Physical observations and the results of the stable isotope analyses of the lid and chest confirm that the marble of both is from Dokimeion and demonstrate that Waelkens is correct in including the sarcophagus in his corpus of products from Dokimeion.

Grain size is fine (less than 1 mm) throughout both the lid and chest. There are clear color differences between the lid and chest. The lid is variegated with streaks of pale colors that range from grayish to whitish to reddish beige. The streaks impart diffuse, irregular layering to the lid. In contrast, the chest is mostly whitish marble, with only a very slight reddish-beige tint in places and virtually no gray.

Isotopic analyses of this sarcophagus reveal that the lid

and the chest differ somewhat but are most likely made of marble from Dokimeion (see Fig. 20.5b). The statistically distinct carbon isotope ratios and the different colorations of the lid and chest indicate that they were probably carved from separate blocks. An assignment to Dokimeion is also consistent with the observed grain size and color variegation.

The Asiatic roof shape of the lid is consistent with its marble provenance, because nearly all of the lid's design features are found on lids of the columnar sarcophagi that Waelkens (1982, 35–36, 121–23) assigns to a workshop at Dokimeion. The one alien feature that Waelkens calls attention to is the acanthus leaf decoration on the geison of the lid's front side (see Fig. 20.3). He suggests that this ornament, along with the Lesbian cyma on the socle of the front of the chest, was based on a Roman model. Waelkens hypothesizes that this Lesbian cyma with a pattern of leaves may have been in some cases carved on the socle of sarcophagi after they had been exported from Dokimeion and received in Rome. The molding would have reflected the taste of local Roman customers (Waelkens 1982, 33, 36). That Dokimeian sarcophagi could be shipped to Rome with some architectural details left unfinished is demonstrated by the lid of a Dokimeian sarcophagus from the Licinian tomb, which is dated *c.* 150 AD (see Fig. 20.11).

Studies of moldings support Waelkens's claim that the geison with acanthus leaves and the Lesbian cyma of the Achilles Sarcophagus are characteristic of the buildings of Rome. In particular, the cornice from a Severan colonnade that was added to the north side of the rostra in the Roman Forum has a geison ornamented with acanthus leaves (Wegner 1957, 24–26, pl. 25b). And the plinths of possibly Severan column bases from the north portico, located near Temple A in the Piazza Argentina, exhibit a double Lesbian cyma with leaves that is stylistically similar to the single cyma from the socle of the Achilles Sarcophagus's chest (Wegner 1965, 80–81, pl. 26a–b).

Waelkens (1982, 32) suggests that the richly decorated Dokimeian frieze sarcophagi were made for export to Italy or Pamphylia, and that they were based on models from Rome or Athens. In the case of the RISD sarcophagus, the model for the Achilles frieze does not seem to have been Attic. For one thing, nearly all the Attic sarcophagi depicting the legend of Achilles are later in date than the RISD sarcophagus (see the chronological chart of these sarcophagi in Linant de Bellefonds 1985, 179). Furthermore, most of the Attic sarcophagi with Achilles show earlier or later moments in the narrative.

In the RISD frieze, the walls of Troy are shown in the background. On the left, a beardless Achilles fights a bearded Hector (see Hom. *Il.* 22.306 *ff.*). In the center, Achilles drags Hector behind his chariot (see *Il.* 22.395 *ff.*), while Athena leads the way. On the right is a grieving Andromache. In contrast, five Attic sarcophagi dated between *c.* 180 and 250 AD depict Achilles after the dragging. He stands in a halted chariot, with the body of Hector still attached to its wheel. In a second scene from the same side, Priam is also depicted. He kneels before a seated Achilles and pleads with him to accept ransom for his son's body (Touchefeu 1988, 495, nos. 114–18, pl. 290).

Fig. 20.11 *Back of girl's garland sarcophagus. Baltimore, Walters Art Museum 23.29 (also see fig. 20.16) (Photo: courtesy of the Walters Art Museum).*

Fig. 20.12 *Sarcophagus with Achilles dragging Hector, Pentelic marble, c. 150–70 AD. British Museum GR 1861.2–20.1 (Drawing from Walker 1990, fig. 7, D2).*

Only one Attic sarcophagus depicting Achilles dragging Hector's body may be contemporary with the RISD sarcophagus. This is a weathered sarcophagus from Crete that Walker dates to *c.* 150–70 AD but that Sabine Rogge dates to the late second century. Isotopic analysis has confirmed that this example in the British Museum is Attic Pentelic marble (Fig. 20.12) (Walker 1990, 39–40, fig. 7, pl. 17; Rogge 1995, 110–11, 131–32, no. 17, pl. 42.1). Its depiction of the dragging scene, though, is much simpler than that on the RISD sarcophagus. In addition to Achilles and Hector, there is only a warrior who takes the place of Athena in leading the chariot. On the left is a mound that has been interpreted as the tomb of Patroclus.

Only one lost sarcophagus had a scheme close to that of the RISD sarcophagus (Fig. 20.13). It is known from two drawings (Robert 1890, pl. 21; Wrede and Harprath 1986, 64–65). The sarcophagus was in Rome in the mid-sixteenth century, when the first drawings of it were executed, and was likely found there (Grassinger 1999, 205–6, no. 29). It and the RISD sarcophagus can be proposed to represent the

iconographic scheme characteristic of Achilles sarcophagi that were intended for the market of Rome (Grassinger [1999, 51, 206] suggests a date of *c.* 150 AD for the lost sarcophagus and argues that the scheme of the RISD sarcophagus was derived from a prototype from Rome of about the same date).

As Waelkens (1982, 35) has observed, the friezes on the front and back sides of the RISD Achilles Sarcophagus are executed in different styles. The figures from the front frieze look more refined in their delicate faces and hair, in the drapery folds that wrap around their bodies, and in their more elongated proportions. In contrast, the Cupids in the lion hunt on the back frieze look coarser in execution, with more softly modeled, less detailed faces, hair, and drapery, and with the plump, large-headed proportions of children (Waelkens 1982, pl. 9.1). Significantly, even the lion head antefixes on the lid from the back are more coarsely rendered than those on the front. It is tempting to imagine that the back side of the sarcophagus was executed by sculptors in Dokimeion, while the front was carved by sculptors in Rome, but the figure style of the front is also apparent in the friezes from the two short sides of the sarcophagus (Waelkens 1982, pl. 10.1–2). Also, a unifying feature that is present on all four sides of the chest at the top of the frieze is the egg-and-dart molding. The darts that alternate with the oval eggs are forked at the top, a treatment that can be found on other sarcophagi of Dokimeian manufacture (see Waelkens 1982, pls. 21.2, 22.1) but that does not appear to be characteristic of the architecture of Rome. If this molding was carved in Dokimeion, then it is likely that all four friezes, whose heads partially overlap it, were carved there as well. According to this scenario, Dokimeion's superior sculptors would have been assigned the friezes from the front and the two short sides, while the back would have been relegated to the hands of the less skilled carvers (*cf.* Waelkens 1982, 124–27).

Fig. 20.13 *Lost Achilles Sarcophagus, once in Rome (Drawing from Robert 1890, pl. 21).*

Other Sarcophagi of Dokimeian Marble

Another example of a Dokimeian frieze sarcophagus (Fig. 20.14) demonstrates the phenomenon of a coffin whose design was influenced by its intended destination, central Italy. The sarcophagus is housed at the monastery of Santa Scolastica in Subiaco, a Roman site whose ancient name was Sublaquem and which is located in Latium about 70 km southeast of Rome. Matz (1968, vol. 4.2, 194–95, no. 78) lists the piece as the only example of a Dionysiac sarcophagus from Asia Minor. Waelkens (1982, 34, no. 4) identifies it as Dokimeian on the basis of its Lesbian cyma, which he compares to that of a garland sarcophagus from Turkey (1982, 27, no. 29). The marble of the garland sarcophagus (Afyon Museum no. 3315) was revealed to be Dokimeian through isotopic analysis (Stowell Pearson and Herz 1992, 285). Waelkens dates the Dionysiac sarcophagus

Fig. 20.14 Carrying of drunken Pan from right short side of Dionysiac Sarcophagus, Dokimeian marble, c. 150–55 AD. Subiaco, Santa Scolastica (Photo: courtesy of the Deutsches Archäologisches Institut, Rome, Neg. 1985.1210).

c. 150–55 AD, while Boardman (1997, 935, no. 222) follows Matz in accepting the slightly later date of 160–70 AD.

Waelkens concludes that the Dionysiac sarcophagus in Subiaco deviates from standard Dokimeian sarcophagi because of its intended destination of Rome and its adherence, therefore, to Roman models. That Roman models were used is strikingly demonstrated by its three-sided decoration and its resultant lack of decoration on its back side, and by the unusual decoration on its right short side. This side exhibits a scene that Boardman (1997, 935) describes as Pan "carried by a satyr or Erotes." Here the goat-legged god is carried by a satyr and two Erotes. The distinctive feature of the scene is the position of the drunken Pan. He is shown from a frontal position, with his goat legs carried horizontally and his torso angled upward so he can lean on his helpers. There are only three other sarcophagi that depict the same scene (for two of them, see Boardman 1997, 935, nos. 224–25). The earliest example is a fragment from the central front part of a garland sarcophagus in Naples (Fig. 20.15). Over the central garland is the god Pan, carried by three Erotes. The scene is arranged very similarly to that on the Subiaco sarcophagus, except that the figures are laid out in mirror-image fashion. Helga Herdejürgen (1996, 108, no. 46) dates the Naples sarcophagus fragment *c.* 135 AD and notes how the right, garland-bearing Eros resembles the central Eros on the child's garland sarcophagus from the Licinian tomb (see Fig. 20. 7). The resemblance lies in the pose of the two Erotes, who are both shown in a profile view as they move to the right and lift their heads, right arms, and right feet. If the Naples sarcophagus, like figure 20.7, was executed in Italy and made of Carrara marble, then we would have here an example of a scheme that originated in a workshop in Italy and was then picked up by a Dokimeian workshop.

This elegant Eros type on figure 20.7 and the Naples sarcophagus is not known on garland sarcophagi that were made at Dokimeion (see Waelkens 1982, 13, fig. 9). After

Fig. 20.15 Garland sarcophagus with drunken Pan depicted over central garland, c. 135 AD. Naples, Museo Nazionale 6677 (From Matz 1968, vol. 4.1, pl. 28.2; courtesy of the Museo Nazionale).

columnar sarcophagi, garland sarcophagi were most frequently produced at Dokimeion (see Waelkens 1982, 9, fig. 7, for a chart of numbers of examples of the different Dokimeian sarcophagus types). Their production extended more than a century from the Claudian period until *c.* 165 AD (Waelkens 1982, 7). Lynn Stowell Pearson and Norman Herz analyzed four examples of garland sarcophagi with Gorgon heads that Waelkens includes in his catalogue of garland sarcophagi from Dokimeion (Waelkens 1982, 23, no. 19, 26–27, nos. 28–29, 29–30, no. 36). In all four cases, the isotopic analyses confirmed that the sarcophagi are made of Dokimeian marble (Stowell Pearson and Herz 1992, 284–85). Two of these sarcophagi appear to be from Rome, while the other two are from Turkey.

The earlier of the two Roman examples (Figs. 20.11 and 20.16) comes from the same second chamber of the Licinian tomb as figures 20.7–10 (Van Keuren 2003, 88). It is a child's sarcophagus that was produced *c.* 150 AD (Waelkens 1982, 26–27, no. 28). Significantly, the sarcophagus was sent unfinished. In particular, the left portrait head from what must have been intended to be the front (Fig. 20.16) was not completed. Including portrait heads on the sarcophagus seems to be a reflection of a desire in Rome for remembrance of the deceased, perhaps shown on the right, and family members (the mother being the left unfinished diademed bust?). Other unfinished details can be found on the lid of the back of the sarcophagus (Fig. 20.11). The bracket in the center and the antefixes are all unworked. The second dolomitic garland sarcophagus is also believed to be from

Rome and was also a child's sarcophagus. It is dated *c.* 160 AD and is in the Casino Rospigliosi in Rome (Himmelmann 1974, pl. 24a; Waelkens 1982, 29–30, no. 36; Stowell Pearson and Herz 1992, 285, fig. 4; Isik 1998, 293, pls. 119.1–2, 5). On a damaged short side of this sarcophagus, the garland decoration is replaced by three standing figures – a man, a woman in a doorway, and a second woman. Perhaps we are again dealing with a deceased, here the woman in the doorway, and family members.

Dokimeian columnar sarcophagi from Rome also appear to reflect the interest of the Romans in portraiture. A fragment from the center of the front of a Dokimeian Muse sarcophagus was reportedly found in the late eighteenth century in "I giardini di Pompeo," Rome. That its marble is Dokimeian is supported by isotopic analysis (Walker 1990, 51–52, no. 66). Walker (1988, 33) argues that the head of the deceased, which stylististically resembles monumental relief sculpture of Rome from the late Antonine period, was left unfinished until the sarcophagus reached Rome. According to Walker, "this may represent an attempt to convey a Roman type, if not an individual portrait."

Marble from Cape Vathy on Thassos: The RISD Fragment with Omphale from a Chest

The marble provenance of the sarcophagus fragment with the head of Omphale in Hercules's lion skin was more difficult to determine than those of the other two RISD sarcophagi. The isotopic analysis was inconclusive, as the

Fig. 20.16 *Front of girl's garland sarcophagus, Dokimeian marble, c. 150 AD. Baltimore, Walters Art Museum 23.29 (also see fig. 20.11) (Photo: courtesy of the Walters Art Museum).*

statistics of possible calcitic marble provenances demonstrate (see Fig. 20.5c). However, a letter from John Herrmann in the curatorial file reported that an analysis of a sample of the fragment by electron-beam microprobe in 1991 at the Museum of Fine Arts, Boston, indicated it was dolomitic marble. He concluded that the sample was from "the Cape Vathy region of Thasos" (for his publication of the analysis, see Herrmann and Newman 1995, 83, table 3), which is the only major source of dolomitic marble in antiquity. We further confirmed the dolomitic character of the marble by applying dilute hydrochloric acid to a few small flakes taken from the fragment, which failed to effervesce.

Herz (1992) reported that his stable isotope database of ancient quarries contained a field sample from Cape Vathy with results very close to those of the sarcophagus fragment (see Fig. 20.5d), thereby confirming its identification as Cape Vathy marble. Significantly, analyses by Eric Doehne of further samples from Cape Vathy resulted in the recent publication of an expanded quarry field, within which our analysis results now fall (see Tykot *et al.* 2002, 190, fig. 3).

Two papers delivered at the ASMOSIA 7 conference on Thassos concerning the cargo from a wreck found at Torre Sgarrata near Taranto reveal that nine blank sarcophagi, each with a rectangular shape and rectangular interior cavity, were made of dolomitic marble from Cape Vathy (for the abstracts, see Calia *et al.* 2003; Gabellone *et al.* 2003; see also Antonelli 2002, 89–111). The RISD fragment appears to be from the same type of rectangular sarcophagus and is contemporary with the wreck, both being dated *c.* 200 AD (for dating of the sarcophagus, see Ridgway 1972, 103). Thus, it is argued that the sarcophagus from which the RISD

fragment originated was shipped blank from the Cape Vathy quarry and was only decorated once it reached its destination. That this destination was Rome is suggested by the donor, Charlotte F. Dailey, who claimed she purchased it there in 1868 (Van Keuren 2005, 169–70).

On the fragment, Omphale faces front, although her incised pupils show that she is looking to the viewer's right. A low-relief woman to the viewer's left of Omphale, shown in profile, looks in the same direction, while lifting up her right hand to her cover her face. If this second figure is correctly interpreted as Omphale's attendant and if her gesture is one of shock, then Hercules should be restored to the right and her shock would reflect her dismay at seeing him in Omphale's feminine attire. According to Ovid (see *Fast.* 2.305–58), he exchanged attire with the Lydian queen in preparation for their participation in Bacchic rites. Lucian, whose writings fall in the reign of Marcus Aurelius (161–80 AD), describes a comparable painting with Omphale "wearing *his* lion's skin and carrying *his* club, pretending to be Heracles, and him dressed in saffron and purple, carding wool and being beaten by Omphale with her slipper, and, most shocking of sights, with his clothing loose and hanging off his body and the masculinity of the god reduced to an unsightly femininity!" *(How to Write History* 10, Macleod 1991, 209).

The only other sarcophagus with the Omphale myth that also presents the figures in a continuous frieze is also from Rome (Fig. 20.17). It is a fragmentary *lenos* (a sarcophagus with an oval shape) in the Vatican that was found in the catacomb of Praetextatus (Boardman 1994, 49, no. 40, pl. 37). Matz (1968, vol. 4.1, 142–45, no. 41) dates this sarcophagus to the early third century AD, a dating that

Fig. 20.17 *Front of a lenos with Omphale, early third century AD. Vatican, Magazines (Photo: courtesy of the Deutsches Archäologisches Institut, Rome, Neg. 03258).*

would make it roughly contemporary with the RISD fragment. On the *lenos*, Omphale stands on the left edge of the front side, garlanded and decked out in Hercules's lion skin and holding his club in her raised right hand. She looks down and to the viewer's right, at the drunken and fallen Hercules, who can be restored under a large lost lion's head ornament. With his surviving right hand, Hercules tugs on a paw of his confiscated lion skin.

Current research suggests that *lenoi* such as these were shipped in an unfinished state to Rome, which is the only known location where they were used (Herrmann 1999, 63). Unfinished *lenoi* were found in a shipwreck at San Pietro near Taranto (Walker 1985, 62–64), and isotopic analyses revealed that they are made of dolomitic marble from Cape Vathy (Herrmann 1999, 63). Unfinished *lenoi* have also been found in the Thasian quarries of Cape Vathy and Saliara (Wurch-Kozelj and Kozelj 1995) and in quarries on Marmara (e-mail communications from Nusin Asgari of February 18, 2004 and October 15, 2008; a book on her "Proconnesian survey" is in preparation). Given all this evidence, one can hypothesize that similar to the RISD fragment, the Vatican *lenos* did not receive its final decoration until it reached Rome.

Although the Omphale myth, with the queen in Hercules's lion skin and with figures arranged in a continuous frieze, appears only on the RISD and Vatican sarcophagi, a Roman origin for their frieze decoration receives support from interpretations of contemporaneous events in Roman history. Representing a female deceased in the guise of Lydian Omphale may have been seen as a compliment to the contemporary Syrian empress, Julia Domna (Kampen 1996, 240). That Julia Domna may have been likened to Omphale in the capital of Rome is suggested not only by her eastern origin but also by the policies of her husband, Septimius Severus (Palagia 1986, 149). Severus constructed a huge temple in Rome that was dedicated to the joint cult of Hercules and Bacchus (Cass. Dio, *Roman History: Epitome* 77.16.3). Some scholars have identified this temple as the colossal ruin on the Quirinal hill (Santangeli Valenzani 1991–92; 1996). Severus's identification with Hercules is demonstrated by a medallion that was minted in Rome in 202 AD and that shows Severus wearing the head of Hercules's lion skin as a helmet (Gnecchi 1912, pl. 152.6). Also, in order to emphasize the continuity between the Antonine and Severan dynasties, Severus claimed to be the brother of Commodus, the last of the Antonine emperors (Cass. Dio, *Roman History: Epitome* 76.7; and inscriptions from Ostia in Dessau 1887, 25–26, nos. 112–14; Wickert 1930, 631, no. 4381). Commodus not only dressed up as Hercules but also frequently donned female dress (SHA *Comm.* 9.6, 13.4; Herodian 1.14.8). Thus, his mistress Marcia is likely to have played the part of Omphale (Vermeule 2000, 22; SHA *Comm.* 11.9, on Marcia portrayed as an Amazon), and Julia Domna may have done the same.

Other Sarcophagi of Dolomitic Marble from Cape Vathy, Thassos

The Omphale Fragment at RISD does not represent the only sarcophagus from Rome whose marble has been revealed to be Thasian dolomitic. John Herrmann and Richard Newman, who analyzed the Omphale Fragment, conducted hundreds of additional analyses to determine which sculptures in major collections worldwide were executed in dolomitic marble from Thassos. The analysis techniques that they used were X-ray diffraction or electron-beam microprobe, and in some cases isotopic analyses were also carried out (Herrmann 1999, 58; Tykot *et al.* 2002, 191–92, table 1). When the figural types on sarcophagi from Rome and environs that they determined to be of dolomitic marble are examined as a group, some interesting trends can be observed (for the analysis results of the seven sarcophagi in the Museo Nazionale Romano, see Herrmann and Newman 1995, 82, table 3; 1999, 301; Herrmann 1999, 69, appendix 3).

The earliest sarcophagus of dolomitic marble dates to the Trajanic period. It was found in Ostia and is now in the Museo Nazionale Romano (Giuliano 1981, 148–50). The Greek inscription on the sarcophagus tells us that the deceased was an Ephesian named Titus Flavius Trophimas, who was skilled in all the arts (*pánmousos*). The inscription also states that the sarcophagus was provided for Trophimas by two friends, who are shown to the left of the inscription practicing their crafts of shoemaking and rope making. Trophimas is depicted to the right of the inscription. He assumes the role of an Isiac initiate, wearing a *perízoma* or loincloth and holding forked percussion sticks and a flute (see Fleischhauer 1964, 125, fig. 71; Andreussi 1996; Hurschmann 1996). His dancing pose, with bent right leg and body angled to the viewer's left, is close to that of Matz's *thyrsophoros* or figure type TH 66 (Fig. 20.18) (Matz 1968, vol. 4.1, 45, no. TH 66; *cf.* the Isiac dancer in the painting from Herculaneum, Witt 1971, pl. 26). Yet all the sarcophagi Matz cites as exhibiting the *thyrsophoros* type are Antonine or later in date. The early appearance of a similar figure type on Trophimas's sarcophagus suggests that such motifs, derived from the repertoire of Neoattic sculptors (see Nulton, this volume), were first utilized for sarcophagi of Greek artisans of central Italy, and then gained favor on sarcophagi of the Roman elite (for the possible use of Attic models by Ostian sarcophagus carvers, see Agnoli 2002, 212).

Another early dolomitic marble sarcophagus in the Museo Nazionale Romano was produced *c.* 120–50 AD. It was found in Rome and contained the body of a ten-year-old girl named Flavia Sextiliane (Giuliani 1981, 184–86; Huskinson 1996, 64, no. 9.23). The name of the deceased is inscribed on the front of the chest, on a shield that is borne by two flying Erotes. Additional Erotes decorate the segmented lid. Those left and right of the central tympanum seem to be

Fig. 20.18 *Matz, figure type TH 66 (From Matz 1968, vol. 4.1, 45, fig. 66).*

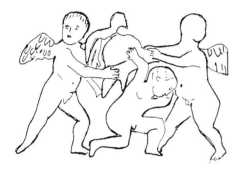

Fig. 20.19 *Figure group from Eros Sarcophagi showing Erotes with helmet (From Bonanno Aravantinos 1998, 79 Typentaf. II.3).*

related to the series of figure types and groups that decorate later Eros sarcophagi from the Antonine and Severan periods (Bonanno Aravantinos 1998). The left Eros kneels as he lifts what may be a sword in a sheath; behind him is a small shield. The right Eros exhibits a kneeling pose with both arms raised that is very close to the pose of an Eros figure type who kneels to take up the burden of a helmet (see the central Eros in Fig. 20.19). On the later sarcophagi, the kneeling Eros forms part of a three-figure group, while on this sarcophagus he appears alone. The hypothesis has been proposed that the groups of Erotes on the later sarcophagi were dervied from the Eros frieze, which was added to the interior of the temple of Venus Genetrix, the Forum of Caesar in Rome, during a Trajanic restoration (Floriani Squarciapino 1950, 114; Rizzo 2001, 224). If this theory is correct, the sarcophagus with the single kneeling Eros may represent the first borrowings from the temple frieze.

Two sarcophagi in the Museo Nazionale Romano belong to the later series of Eros sarcophagi and are made of dolomitic marble. One is known to come from Rome, and the other has an unknown provenance. Both are Antonine in date, were used for children's burials, and show Erotes making arms (Giuliano 1981, 59–61, 159–61; Blanc and Gury 1986, 1018, no. 541, pl. 715; Huskinson 1996, 42, 49, nos. 6.27, 6.29; Bonanno Aravantinos 1998, 89, nos. 11–12, pl. 36.2–3). Both sarcophagi exhibit the same motif on the center of the chest, of a shield that is held up by an Eros on one or both sides. This motif was very likely derived from the Trajanic frieze from the temple of Venus Genetrix, for it appears on a well-preserved section of the frieze (Fig. 20.20) (Floriani Squarciapino 1950, 109 *ff.*; von Hesberg 1981, 1074–75). Since the probable model for the Erotes with a shield was a temple frieze in Rome, the sarcophagi demonstrate the strong influence that art of the capital

Fig. 20.20 *Trajanic interior frieze with Erotes from Temple of Venus Genetrix, Forum of Caesar, Rome (Photo: courtesy of the Deutsches Archäologisches Institut, Rome, Neg. 1958.972).*

Fig. 20.21 *Front of Indian Triumph Sarcophagus, Thasian dolomitic marble, c. 170–90 AD. Baltimore, Walters Art Museum 23.31 (Photo: courtesy of the Walters Art Museum).*

Fig. 20.22 *Detail of front of Indian Triumph Sarcophagus. Baltimore, Walters Art Museum 23.31 (Photo: courtesy of the Walters Art Museum).*

exerted, even on sculptural workshops in Rome using non-Italian marbles.

Several Dionysian sarcophagi from Rome were revealed to be of dolomitic marble. One example is the Indian Triumph Sarcophagus from the third chamber of the Licinian tomb, now located at the Walters Art Museum in Baltimore (Figs. 20.21–22) (*Sarcophagus with the Triumph of*

Dionysus). The proposed date for this sarcophagus is *c.* 170–90 AD (Matz 1968, vol. 4.2, 231–33, no. 95; Van Keuren 2003, 92). Figures from this sarcophagus appear to be derived from figure types on earlier Dionysian sarcophagi. In particular, the tympanum player from the front of the sarcophagus (shown on the upper right in Fig. 20.22) belongs to Matz's figure type TH 27 (Matz 1968, vol. 4.1, 30, no.

Fig. 20.23 *Dionysian Sarcophagus, Thasian dolomitic marble, early Severan date. Museo Nazionale Romano (Photo: courtesy of the Deutsches Archäologisches Institut, Rome, Neg. 1936.1016).*

TH 27), which he suggests was derived from the same late Classical prototypes as his Neoattic figure type TH 1 (see the cymbal player from the Thiasos Sarcophagus, Fig. 20.10, made of Carrara marble).

Another Dionysian dolomitic sarcophagus from Rome, now at the Museo Nazionale Romano, shows the wine god in a chariot drawn by two centaurs (Fig. 20.23) (Matz 1968, vol. 4.2, 257–58, no. 117; Giuliano 1981, 119–21). To the right of his chariot is a tympanum player of Matz's type TH 27, which is the same figure type as the tympanum player in figure 20.22. This sarcophagus appears to be later in date than the Baltimore sarcophagus, being assigned by Matz to the early Severan period.

These two sarcophagi with figure type TH 27 seem to illustrate George M. A. Hanfmann's (1971, 398) summary of Matz's beliefs:

> If I understand Matz correctly, he believes that the adoption of these designs and types was essentially accomplished by the "Neo-Attic" workshops of the earlier Empire. The sarcophagi

sculptors of later ages (*e.g.*, the Antonine "Baroque") did not go back directly to Hellenistic originals of Pergamene Baroque but restyled to their taste the designs already included in the "Neo-Attic" tradition (1, 14 *f.*).

I offer the further suggestion that models of Neoattic figural types were preserved for extended periods of time in the workshops of sculptors in Rome who specialized in carving particular types of marble.

Two additional Dionysian sarcophagi, both from Rome and of dolomitic marble, are located in the Museo Nazionale Romano. They appear to be contemporary, since they both have been dated *c.* 170–80 AD. Each one shows Dionysus in a chariot drawn by centaurs, and exhibits Matz's Dionysian figure types. One shows a flute player in front of Dionysus's chariot who belongs to Matz's type TH 36 (Fig. 20.24) (Matz 1968, vol. 4.1, 33, no. TH 36; vol. 4.2, 251–52, no. 108; Giuliano 1981, 64–66). While this figure is not identical to Matz's type TH 27 (see Figs. 20.22–23), her ecstatic pose is close to that of type TH 27. The second

Fig. 20.24 *Dionysian Sarcophagus, Thasian dolomitic marble, c. 170–80 AD. Museo Nazionale Romano 128577 (Photo: courtesy of the Deutsches Archäologisches Institut, Rome, Neg. 1965.1129).*

Fig. 20.25 Front of Dionysian Sarcophagus, Thasian dolomitic marble, c. 170–80 AD. Museo Nazionale Romano 214 (Photo: courtesy of the Deutsches Archäologisches Institut, Rome, Neg. 1936.1018).

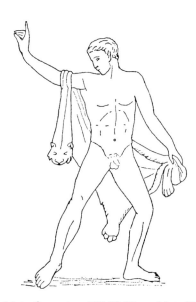

Fig. 20.27 Matz, figure type TH 18 (From Matz 1968, vol. 4.1, 25, fig. 18).

Fig. 20.26 Detail of Ariadne from front of Dionysian Sarcophagus. Museo Nazionale Romano 214 (Photo: courtesy of the Deutsches Archäologisches Institut, Rome, Neg. 1936.1019).

Dionysian sarcophagus depicts the wine god discovering a sleeping Ariadne (Figs. 20.25–26) (Matz 1968, vol. 4.3, 399–400, no. 225; Giuliano 1981, 123–25; Gasparri 1986, 555, no. 191). The satyr directly to the viewer's right of Ariadne, who holds a *lagobolon* in his left arm as he lunges to the right, is Matz's figure type TH 18 (Fig. 20.27) (Matz 1968, vol. 4.1, 25, no. TH 18). While Matz does not identify the figure as belonging to the same type, the satyr who

supports Silenus on the right front section of the Thiasos Sarcophagus (see Fig. 20.9b, of Carrara marble) exhibits a very similar lunging pose. It is noteworthy that this lunging pose appears on sarcophagi of two different marbles, one Italian and the other the non-Italian Thasian dolomitic. Outline drawings would be an easy method of transmitting figure types from one workshop to another in Rome.

The final dolomitic sarcophagus from central Italy was discovered in Ostia and is currently located in Munich (Fig. 20.28; Gabelmann 1986, 733, no. 65; Sichtermann 1992, 116–17, no. 54; Herrmann and Newman 1995, 83, table 3). Dated *c.* 170–200 AD, the sarcophagus shows the goddess Selene visiting the sleeping Endymion. The dating of the sarcophagus would make it either contemporary with the Ariadne sarcophagus in Rome (see Figs. 20.25–26) or later than it. In any case, the sleeping figure of Endymion is

Fig. 20.28 *Detail of Selene and Endymion Sarcophagus, Thasian dolomitic marble, c. 170–200 AD. Munich, Glyptothek 189 (From Sichtermann 1992, pl. 54.2; courtesy of the Glyptothek).*

compositionally close to that of Ariadne. Note in particular the similar placement of the lowered left arm with the left hand grasping the drapery, and the similar raising of the right arm to rest on the head. The flat treatment of the bared torsos is also similar, as is the arrangement of the drapery so that it covers the genitals. These similarities suggest that sculptors working in Rome and the vicinity in dolomitic marble may have had standard figure types that they could adapt to similar mythological situations, such as a vulnerable, sleeping character who is approached by an active seducer. The adaptation is evident here in the way Endymion's eternal sleep has resulted in his being given a more horizontal position than Ariadne, who will soon wake up to the sound of Dionysus's noisy entourage. Michael Koortbojian (1995, 101–2) has already suggested such a phenomenon of multivalent figure types. Now that the marbles of Roman sarcophagi are being identified through reliable analytical techniques, a stronger case can be made for the transferal of figure types from one myth to another within the same or related workshops.

The foregoing sarcophagi from Rome that have been demonstrated through analysis to be of dolomitc marble show that figure types were apparently copied from sarcophagi of other marbles, notably Carrara, and then became stock types that were used over extended periods, not only for illustrations of the same themes but also for depictions of narratives with similar but not identical story lines.

Conclusions

The results of a combined isotopic and iconographic study of three RISD sarcophagi demonstrate significant con-

nections between their marble provenances and their overall forms; but for the two sarcophagi of non-Italian marbles, the intended destination of Rome seems to have determined the type of decoration that was applied. The Achilles Sarcophagus was made of Dokimeian marble and utilized a standard Dokimeian roofed lid, but the continuous frieze decoration on the chest departs from the standard columnar design of Dokimeian chests. Instead, the frieze decoration on its front follows Roman models, as do the base molding on the front of the chest and the geison on the front of the lid. However, the egg-and-dart molding with the split tops of the darts, which crowns all four sides of the chest, is characteristic of sarcophagi made in Dokimeion, and suggests that the friezes that overlap it were all actually carved in Dokimeion.

The RISD Omphale Fragment was carved of dolomitic marble from Cape Vathy on Thassos. This fragment is one of only two depictions on sarcophagi of Omphale in Hercules's lion skin, the second being a *lenos* from Rome. The recoveries of blank sarcophagi of Cape Vathy marble from shipwrecks and unfinished *lenoi* from shipwrecks and eastern quarries suggest that the importation of unfinished pieces with final decoration to be done in Rome was a common practice. It is proposed that in both instances of the depiction of the Omphale myth, imported marble was carved in Rome, under the apparent influence of Severus's identification with (and worship of) Hercules and possibly Julia Domna's association with Omphale.

The Niobid Sarcophagus was carved of Carrara marble. As would be expected for a piece of Italian marble, the sarcophagus has a Roman form, with a sculptured panel and masks on the lid. The isotopic analyses of the lid and chest, as well as the unified design in which the gods Artemis and Apollo appear on the lid and their victims the Niobids on the chest, provide strong evidence that the lid and chest were carved from a single block of Carrara marble.

Like the three RISD sarcophagi, additional sarcophagi from central Italy that were executed in Carrara, Dokimeian, and Thasian dolomitic marble were produced during the second century AD. The earliest sarcophagus, that of Ephesian Trophimas, was made of Thasian dolomitic marble in the early second century AD. The seemingly Neoattic pose of the dancing figure of Trophimas demonstrates the early introduction in central Italy of Neoattic figure types, on sarcophagi of imported marble. Neoattic influence is again evident in the Carrara marble *thiasos* sarcophagus from the late Hadrianic or early Antonine period. Later Dionysian sarcophagi from Rome, dated to the late Antonine and early Severan periods and made of Thasian dolomitic marble repeat earlier Neoattic figure types from the late Antonine and early Severan periods. For example, the leaning satyr who supports Silenus on the front of the Carrara marble *thiasos* sarcophagus is transformed into the lunging satyr to the right of Ariadne on a Thasian sarcophagus. These examples demonstrate the interconnections between workshops in Rome, even those working in different marbles. The means of transmission of figure types may have been line drawings. Interconnections can also be suggested within workshops that specialized in a particular marble such as Thasian, as in the case of the evident adaptation of the sleeping Ariadne, a figure type which, slightly altered, became the endlessly slumbering Endymion.

Sarcophagi from Rome of imported marbles and with non-Dionysian subject matter reflect the influence of monuments and trends in Rome. In particular, Thasian dolomitic marble sarcophagi depicting Erotes with arms utilize figure groups that initially appeared on the Trajanic frieze in the temple of Venus Genetrix. Sarcophagi of Dokimeian marble were shipped to Rome with portrait heads unfinished, a practice that reflected the Roman desire to commemorate the specific appearance of the deceased and surviving family members.

As more analyses of the marbles of Roman sarcophagi are carried out, more clarification will be achieved about what marbles were being used for sarcophagi in central Italy, and for what durations of time. Also, when the figural decoration of sarcophagi is examined in conjunction with the analysis results, more interconnections within and between workshops, beyond those tentatively proposed in this article, will be revealed.

Acknowledgments

L. Peter Gromet at Brown University made the observations and wrote the descriptions of the marbles of the three RISD sarcophagi. He also contributed the discussion of the analysis techniques and the interpretations of the analysis results. Furthermore, he made valuable suggestions on my iconographic arguments. Donato Attanasio at ISM-CNR in Rome conducted electron paramagnetic resonance analyses on Museo Nazionale Romano 441 (Figs. 20.7–8). Gina Borromeo at the Museum of Art, the Rhode Island School of Design, facilitated the research on the three RISD sarcophagi presented in this paper and helped with the examination of the style of the Achilles Sarcophagus. Also, Susan Walker at the Ashmolean Museum at Oxford, John H. Oakley at the American School of Classical Studies at Athens, and R. Ross Holloway at Brown University read and offered most helpful suggestions on the paper. Asen Kirin and Gilbert Head from the University of Georgia and Susann Lusnia from Tulane University helped me with parts of the argument.

I also wish to thank the University of Georgia Research Foundation and the Samuel H. Kress Foundation for their generous support, which enabled me to attend the ASMOSIA 7 conference, where a preliminary version of this paper was presented. The Center for Archaeological Sciences at the University of Georgia granted funds for the isotopic analyses of the three RISD sarcophagi, and the RISD Museum engaged the Boston conservator Kent Severson to take samples of these sarcophagi for analysis.

Works Cited

Agnoli, N. (2002) Officine ostiensi di scultura funeraria. In C. Brunn and A. G. Zevi (eds.), *Ostia e Portus nelle loro relazioni con Roma. Acta Instituti Romani Finlandiae* 27, 193–212.

Andreussi, M. (1996) Isis (S. Sabina). In E. M. Steinby (ed.), *Lexicon topographicum urbis Romae* 3, 114.

Antonelli, B. (2002) *Herculis Nodus: Il Relitto di Torre Sgarrata (Taranto)*. Taranto, Comune di Taranto.

Blanc, N. and Gury, F. (1986) Eros/Amor, Cupido. *Lexicon iconographicum mythologiae classicae* 3, 952–1049.

Boardman, J. (1994) Omphale. *Lexicon iconographicum mythologiae classicae* 7, 45–53.

——— (1997) Pan. *Lexicon iconographicum mythologiae classicae* 8, 923–41.

Bonanno Aravantinos, M. (1998) Sarcofagi romani raffiguranti eroti con armi. In G. Koch (ed.), *Akten des Symposiums "125 Jahre Sarkophage-Corpus" Marburg, 1995,* 73–96. *Sarkophag-Studien* 1. Mainz am Rhein, Philipp von Zabern.

Calia, A., Giannotta, M. T., Lazzarini, L., and Quarta, G. (2003) The Torre Sgarrata wreck: Characterization and provenance of white marble artefacts in the cargo. In *ASMOSIA 7: Seventh International Conference, Thassos, Greece, 15–20 September 2003, Book of Abstracts,* 34. Athens, Laboratory of Archaeometry, NCSR "Demokritos;" French School at Athens.

Corcoran, Simon (1996) *The Empire of the Tetrarchs: Imperial Pronouncements and Government AD 284–324*. Oxford, Clarendon Press.

Dessau, H. (1887) *Inscriptiones latii veteris latinae.* Corpus Inscriptionum Latinarum 14. Berolini, apud G. Reimerum.

Fant, J. C. (1993) Ideology, gift, and trade: A distribution model for the Roman imperial marbles. In W. V. Harris (ed.), *The Inscribed Economy: Production and Distribution in the Roman Empire in the Light of* Instrumentum Domesticum. Journal of Roman Archaeology Supp. Ser. 6, 145–70. Ann Arbor, University of Michigan.

——— (2001) Rome's marble yards. *Journal of Roman Archaeology* 14, 167–98.

Fischer, M. L. with contributions by Peral, Z. and Grossmark, T. (1998) *Marble Studies: Roman Palestine and the Marble Trade.* Constance, Universitätsverlag.

Fleischhauer, G. (1964) *Etrurien und Rom. Muiskgeschichte in Bildern, Band 2: Musik des Altertums. Lieferung 5.* Leipzig, VEB Deutscher Verlag für Musik.

Floriani Squarciapino, M. (1950) Pannelli decorativi del tempio di Venere Genetrice. *Atti della Accademia Nazionale dei Lincei. Memorie* ser. 8, vol. 2, 61–118.

Gabellone, F., Giannotta, M. T., Monte, A., and Alessio, A. (2003) The Torre Sgarrata wreck (South Italy): Marble artefacts in the cargo. In *ASMOSIA 7: Seventh International Conference, Thassos, Greece, 15–20 September 2003, Book of Abstracts,* 41. Athens, Laboratory of Archaeometry, NCSR "Demokritos;" French School at Athens.

Gabelmann, H. (1986) Endymion. *Lexicon iconographicum mythologiae classicae* 3, 726–42.

Gasparri, C. (1986) Dionysos/Bacchus. *Lexicon iconographicum mythologiae classicae* 3, 540–66.

Geominy, W. (1992) Niobidai. *Lexicon iconographicum mythologiae classicae* 6, 914–29.

Giuliano, A. (ed.) (1981) *Museo Nazionale Romano: Le Sculture* I, 2. Rome, De Luca.

Gnecchi, F. (1912) *Medaglioni romani, volume terzo: Bronzo.* Milan, Ulrico Hoepli.

Grassinger, D. (1999) *Die antiken Sarkophagreliefs,* vol. 12.1. *Die mythologischen Sarkophage, Erster Teil, Achill, Adonis, Aeneas, Aktaion, Alkestis, Amazonen.* Berlin, Gebr. Mann.

Hanfmann, G. M. A. (1971) Review of F. Matz, *Die dionysischen Sarkophage* (1968). *Art Bulletin* 53, 397–400.

Herdejürgen, H. (1996) *Die antiken Sarkophagreliefs,* vol. 6.2.1. *Stadtrömische und italische Girlandensarkophage: Die Sarkophage des ersten und zweiten Jahrhunderts.* Berlin, Gebr. Mann.

Herrmann, J. (1999) The exportation of Dolomitic marble from Thasos. In *Thasos: Matières premières et technologie de la préhistoire à nos jours, Actes du Colloque International 26–29/9/1995, Thasos, Liménaria,* 57–69. Athens, French School at Athens.

Herrmann, J. and Newman, R. (1995) The exportation of dolomitic sculptural marble from Thasos: Evidence from Mediterranean and other collections. In Y. Maniatis, N. Herz, and Y. Basiakos (eds.), *The Study of Marble and Other Stones used in Antiquity: ASMOSIA 3 Athens: Transactions of the Third International Symposium of the Association of the Study of Marble and Other Stones used in Antiquity,* 73–86. London, Archetype Publications.

——— (1999) Dolomitic marble from Thasos near and far: Macedonia, Ephesos and the Rhone. In M. Schvoerer (ed.), *Archéomatériaux: Marbres et autres roches. ASMOSIA 4 Bordeaux–Talence 9–13 octobre 1995,* 293–303. Bordeaux, Centre de Recherche en Physique Appliquée à l´Archéologie (CRPAA); Talence, Maison de l'archéologie.

Herz, N. (1992) Provenance determination of Neolithic to Classical Mediterranean marbles by stable isotopes. *Archaeometry* 34, 184–95.

Himmelmann, N. (1974) Ein kleinasiatischer Sarkophag in Rom. In *Mélanges Mansel,* vol. 1, 45–52. Ankara, Türk Tarih Kurumu Basimeri.

Hurschmann, R. (1996) Perizoma. In H. Cancik and H. Schneider (eds.), *Der neue Pauly: Enzyklopädie der Antike* 9, 590–91. Stuttgart and Weimar, J. B. Metzler.

Huskinson, J. (1996) *Roman Children's Sarcophagi: Their Decoration and Its Social Significance.* Oxford, Clarendon Press.

Isik, F. (1998) Zu Produktionsbeginn und Ende der kleinasiatischen Girlandensarkophage der Hauptgruppe. In G. Koch (ed.), *Akten des Symposiums "125 Jahre Sarkophage-Corpus" Marburg, 1995. Sarkophag-Studien* 1, 278–94. Mainz am Rhein, Philipp von Zabern.

Kampen, N. (1996) Omphale and the instability of gender. In N. Kampen (ed.), *Sexuality in Ancient Art: Near East, Egypt, Greece, and Italy,* 233–46. Cambridge and New York, Cambridge University Press.

Koch , G. (1993) *Sarkophage der römischen Kaiserzeit.* Darmstadt, Wissenschaftliche Buchgesellschaft.

Koch, G. and Sichtermann, H. (1982) *Römische Sarkophage.* Munich, C. H. Beck.

Koortbojian, M. (1995) *Myth, Meaning, and Memory on Roman Sarcophagi.* Berkeley, Los Angeles, and London, University of California Press.

Kranz, P. (1975) Review of M. Honroth, *Stadtrömische Girlanden* (1971). *Gnomon* 47, 77–82.

Linant de Bellefonds, P. (1985) *Sarcophages attiques de la nécropole de Tyr: Une étude iconographique.* Paris, Editions Recherche sur les civilisations.

Macleod, M. D. (1991) *Lucian: A Selection.* Warminster, England, Aris & Phillips.

Matz, F. (1968) *Die antiken Sarkophagreliefs,* vols. 4.1–4.4. *Die dionysischen Sarkophage.* Berlin, Gebr. Mann.

Palagia, O. (1986) Imitation of Herakles in ruler portraiture: A survey, from Alexander to Maximinus Daza. *Boreas: Münstersche Beiträge zur Archäologie* 9, 137–51.

Pentia, M. (1995) Carbon and oxygen isotopic ratio bivariate distribution for marble artifacts quarry assignment. *Romanian Journal of Physics* 40 (2–3), 369–79.

Ridgway, B. S. (1972) *Classical Sculpture.* Providence, Rhode Island School of Design.

Rizzo, S. (2001) Indagini nei fori Imperiali. *Mitteilungen des Deutschen Archäologischen Instituts. Römische Abteilung* 108, 215–44.

Robert, C. (1890) *Die antiken Sarkophagreliefs,* vol. 2. *Mythologische Cyklen.* Berlin, Grote'sche Verlagsbuchhandlung.

——— (1919) *Die antiken Sarkophagreliefs,* vol. 3.3. *Einzelmythen.* Berlin, Grote'sche Verlagsbuchhandlung.

Rogge, S. (1995) *Die antiken Sarkophagreliefs,* vol. 9.1.1. *Die attischen Sarkophage, Erster Faszikel, Achill und Hippolytos.* Berlin, Gebr. Mann.

Roueché, C. with contribution by Reynolds, J. M. (1989) *Aphro-

disias in Late Antiquity. Journal of Roman Studies Monographs 5. London, Society for the Promotion of Roman Studies.

Santangeli Valenzani, R. (1991–92) NEOS UPERMEGETHES. Osservazioni sul tempio di piazza del Quirinale. *Bullettino della Commissione Archeologica Comunale di Roma* 94, 7–16.

———— (1996) Hercules et Dionysus, Templum. *Lexicon topographicum urbis Romae* 3 (H–Z), 25–26. Rome, Quasar.

Sarcophagus with the Triumph of Dionysus. http://www.thewalters.org/works_of_art/itemdetails.aspx?aid=21 (5 February 2007).

Sichterman, H. (1992) *Die antiken Sarkophagreliefs,* vol. 12.2. *Die mythologischen Sarkophage, Zweiter Teil, Apollon, Ares, Bellerophon, Daidalos, Endymion, Ganymed, Giganten, Grazien.* Berlin, Gebr. Mann.

Sichtermann, H. and Koch, G. (1975) *Griechische Mythen auf römischen Sarkophagen.* Tübingen, Ernst Wasmuth.

Stowell Pearson, L. and Herz, N. (1992) Isotopic analysis of a group of Roman Gorgon sarcophagi. In M. Waelkens, N. Herz, and L. Moens (eds.), *Ancient Stones: Quarrying, Trade and Provenance: Interdisciplinary Studies on Stones and Stone Technology in Europe and Near East from the Prehistoric to the Early Christian Period,* 283–85. Leuven, Leuven University Press.

Touchefeu, O. (1988) Hektor. *Lexicon iconographicum mythologiae classicae* 4, 482–98. Zurich and Munich, Artemis.

Tykot, R. H., Herrmann, J., van der Merwe, N. J., Newman, R., and Allegretto, K. O. (2002) Thasian marble sculptures in European and American collections: Isotopic and other analyses. In J. Herrmann, N. Herz, and R. Newman (eds.), *ASMOSIA 5: Interdisciplinary Studies on Ancient Stone, Proceedings of the Fifth International Conference of the Association for the Study of Marble and Other Stones in Antiquity, Museum of Fine Arts, Boston, 1998,* 188–95. London, Archetype Publications.

Van Keuren, F., with assistance of Trillmich, W., Trillmich, C., and Ghezzi, A., with appendix by Anderson, J. C. (2003) Unpublished documents shed new light on the Licinian Tomb, discovered in 1884–1885, Rome. *Memoirs of the American Academy in Rome* 48, 53–139.

Van Keuren, F., Attanasio, D., Gromet, L. P., and Herz, N. (2009) Multimethod Provenance Investigation of Eight Roman Funerary Monuments from the Licinian Tomb and the via Ostiense, Rome. In Philippe Jockey (ed.), *Marbres et autres roches de la Méditerranée antique / Interdisciplinary Studies on Mediterranean Ancient Marble and Stone. Actes du VIIIe colloque international, Proceedings of the VIIIth International Conference, Association for the Study of Marble and Other Stones used in Antiquity (ASMOSIA), Aix-en-Provence, 12–18 juin 2006, Aix-en-Provence, 12–18 juin 2006,* 351–367. Paris, Coll. L'atelier méditerranéen, éd. Maisonneuve & Larose, Maison méditerranéenne des sciences de l'homme.

Van Keuren, F. (2000) Late-nineteenth-century restorations of sarcophagi from the Licinian Tomb, Rome. In L. Lazzarini (ed.), *ASMOSIA 6: Interdisciplinary Studies on Ancient Stone. Proceedings of the Sixth International Conference of the Association for the Study of Marble and Other Stones in Antiquity. Venice, 2000,* 117–26. Venice, Laboratorio di Analisi dei Materiali Antichi.

———— (2005) Archival history of three mythological sarcophagi at the RISD Museum. *Marmora: An International Journal for Archaeology, History and Archaeometry of Marbles and Stones* 1, 169–86.

Vermeule, C. C. (2000) Livia to Helena: Women in power, women in the provinces. In D. E. E. Kleiner and S. B. Matheson (eds.), *I Claudia II: Women in Roman Art and Society,* 17–27. Austin, University of Texas Press.

Vermeule, C. C. and Anderson, K. (1981) Greek and Roman sculpture in the Holy Land. *Burlington Magazine* 123 (934), 7–19.

von Hesberg, H. (1981) Archäologische Denkmäler zu den römischen Göttergestalten. *Aufstieg und Niedergang der römischen Welt* 2, 17.2, 1032–99.

Waelkens, M. (1982) *Dokimeion: Die Werkstatt der repräsentativen kleinasiatischen Sarkophage.* Berlin, Gebr. Mann.

Walker, S. (1985) The marble quarries of Proconnesos: Isotopic evidence for the age of the quarries and for *lenos*-sarcophagi carved at Rome. In *Marmi antichi: Problemi d'impiego, di restauro e d'identificazione. Studi miscellanei* 26, 57–65.

———— (1988) Aspects of Roman funerary art. In *Image and Mystery in the Roman World: Three Papers Given in Memory of Jocelyn Toynbee,* 23–36. Gloucester, Alan Sutton.

Walker, S. (1990) *Catalogue of Roman Sarcophagi in the British Museum.* Corpus Signorum Imperii Romani. Great Britain 2, fasc. 2. London, British Museum Publications.

Walker, S. and Matthews, K. (1988) Recent work in stable isotope analysis of white marble at the British Museum. In J. C. Fant (ed.), *Ancient Marble Quarrying and Trade: Papers from a Colloquium Held at the Annual Meeting of the Archaeological Institute of America, San Antonio, Texas, December, 1986.* British Archaeological Reports International Series 453, 117–25.

Ward-Perkins, J. B. (1958) Roman garland sarcophagi from the quarries of Proconnesus (Marmara). *The Smithsonian Report for 1957,* no. 10377, 455–67.

Wegner, M. (1957) *Ornamente kaiserzeitlicher Bauten Roms: Soffitten.* Cologne and Graz, Böhlau-Verlag.

———— (1965) *Schmuckbasen des antiken Rom.* Orbis antiquus 22.

Wickert, L. (1930) *Inscriptiones latii veteris latinae: Supplementum ostiense. Corpus Inscriptionum Latinarum* 14.

Witt, R. E. (1971) *Isis in the Graeco-Roman World.* London, Thames and Hudson.

Wrede, H. and Harprath, R. (1986) *Der Codex Coburgensis: Das erste systematische Archäologiebuch.* Exhibition Kunstsammlungen der Veste Coburg. Coburg, Coburger Landesstiftung.

Wurch-Kozelj, M. and Kozelj, T. (1995) Roman quarries of Apse-Sarcophagi in Thassos of the second and third centuries. In Y. Maniatis, N. Herz, and Y. Basiakos (eds.), *ASMOSIA 3 Athens: Transactions of the Third International Symposium of the Association of the Study of Marble and Other Stones used in Antiquity,* 39–47. London, Archetype Publications.

Zanker, P. and Ewald, B. C. (2004) *Mit Mythen leben: Die Bilderwelt der römischen Sarkophage.* Munich, Hirmer Verlag.

21

Women's Desire, Archaeology, and Feminist Theory

Natalie Boymel Kampen

One of the best things Ross Holloway taught his students was to keep rethinking problems that might seem "finished." I take my lead from him.

In the past two decades Praxiteles's *Aphrodite of Knidos* and other statues of nude Aphrodite have become the focus of a good bit of scholarly interest and rethinking (Fig. 21.1). Much of it is fascinating and provocative, especially since it extends the range of approaches to Greek monumental sculpture beyond the customary methods of formal analysis, copy criticism, and iconography into new questions about meaning and reception. In this paper, I argue that, with one very recent exception, the majority of new scholarship about the Knidia's meanings has taken on reception primarily in terms of a conversation between Praxiteles's intentions and the responses of male viewers. This has led to some important new interpretations of men's responses, but it has limited other avenues, particularly those that concern ways that women might have understood the statue and others like it and might therefore have been capable of interpretations that not only resembled but also differed from men's. I proceed by talking a bit about the nature of the interpretations that have appeared recently, and discussing the kind of evidence they use and the theories and methods on which they draw. Then I propose some alternatives to these interpretations based both on different theoretical assumptions and on the belief that no interpretation of a statue can be wholly convincing without serious consideration of its archaeological context or the ensemble of objects that circulated around it (Kousser 2005). I do not propose the definitive new interpretation precisely because I believe that different viewers brought a variety of interpretations and readings to the statue, and that these readings made for a constantly shifting image open to multiple fantasies and desires. And, in any case, until some of the recent findings from the Knidos excavations have been fully published – a number are in preparation – my suggestions remain provisional (Şahin 2005).

Fig. 21.1 *Aphrodite of Knidos, front view of the Belvedere type. Vatican Museo Pio-Clementino, inv. 4260 (Photo: Monumenti Musei e Gallerie Pontificie).*

I begin, however, by acknowledging a recent paper (Seaman 2004) that attempts to reconstitute a sense of the original appearance and setting of the *Aphrodite of Knidos*. Seaman takes what has been a long tradition of formal analysis and combines it with the more recent questions about reception to move what has been a stalled discussion. Her examination of the various forms of evidence gives more space to the literary and to the question of the appearance of the statue than the reader will find here, where epigraphical material is given a bit more priority, but her conclusions are generally in harmony with those below. By reexamining the many versions of the Knidia, large and small, stone, bronze, and terracotta, she proposes that there was not an original and a later variant from which all other versions were slavishly copied, and she suggests that the dominant elements found in most versions included the boyish back, the face with a faint smile, the head turned to the left, and a small water jar from which drapery was being lifted. The last point may be arguable given that lifting up and putting down are not gestures clearly distinguishable from simply holding something, but the rest of the description and the awareness of multiple versions seem absolutely right, as does the reminder that none of our literary evidence suggests a connection between the Knidia and a specifically Knidian version of the Aphrodite cult. Thus Seaman opens up the discussion to accommodate not only her sense of the complexity of Praxiteles's ideas but also her belief in the statue's association with love and marriage, with ritual bathing and erotic magic. This in turn frees the discussion from the domination of debates about the statue as ashamed or anxious, as the Knidia's hand covers her *aidos,* and it allows us to think more seriously about how both male and female viewers understood the statue and its many larger and smaller echoes. It is at this point that a reconsideration of the scholarship on viewing and reception and a discussion of the role of feminist theory in helping us to understand the relationship of the female viewer to the female body open up.

Theory and the Male Viewer

Both feminist thought and Michel Foucault are to be thanked or blamed (depending on your point of view) for the fact that the Knidia seems to play an important role in every recent book on Greek art and culture (*e.g.*, Blundell 1995; Havelock 1995; Spivey 1996; Stewart 1997; Osborne 1998; Beard and Henderson 2001). Whereas she was a long-standing favorite for scholars of *Kopienkritik*, at the heart of discussions of the nude, of Praxiteles, and of the style of the fourth century, she has also become the subject of reception analysis as it is produced mainly by Anglophone scholars in the United States and Britain. Perhaps because of the conjunction of interest in Foucault and Lacan as well as of Laura Mulvey and other feminist reception critics,

whom I discuss below, much work on the *Aphrodite of Knidos* has focused on the way Pliny the Elder (*HN* 36.21–21) and Pseudo Lucian (*Amores* 13–14) discuss the statue; these texts are at the center of developing theories of male viewing practices and men's sexual desires. In his *History of Sexuality* Foucault takes up the Pseudo Lucian passage as a way to think about the mutability of sexual desire and about the nature of sexual behavior and discourse in a period he defines as coming before the modern pathologization of the male homoerotic (Foucault 1988, 211–27) (Fig. 21.2). The passage, which brings a group of men to Knidos as tourists interested in seeing the famous statue, involves a discussion, a parody of philosophical debate, about the

Fig. 21.2 *Aphrodite of Knidos, back view of the Belvedere type (Photo: Monumenti Musei e Gallerie Pontificie).*

relative merits of love between partners of same or of different sex. The statue, viewed from the front, is the object of desire for the proponent of heterosexuality, whereas the view from the back provokes expressions of rapture from the proponent of same-sex lovemaking. Indeed, the latter compares Aphrodite's flanks to those of a beautiful boy, Ganymede.

Many commentators before and after Foucault have read the passage in Pseudo Lucian along with Pliny the Elder's story about the young man who became so obsessed with the Knidia that he hid in the sanctuary all night. Pseudo Lucian also tells this story. One can still, they say, see the stain left on the Parian marble thigh by the youth who blurred the lines between woman and goddess, statue and mortal, artifice and love object. The two texts are wonderful sources of information for ways to talk about male desire and sexual preferences, and about the Hellenistic and Roman culture in which both touristic and voyeuristic desires come into play. The passages explore male desire without reference to ritual practice and without acknowledgment of the statue as representing a goddess not just an idealized hetaera.

I cite only a small sample of the recent discussions of the Knidia to show briefly the way this Foucauldian interpretive strand takes up the use of these two texts; nevertheless, all the recent discussions of the statue comment on the combination of nudity and pose and ask to whom the statue speaks and in what ways. For Robin Osborne, in an article of 1994 that compares the possible reception of the Knidia to that of the Archaic kore, the Aphrodite really has nothing to say to a female audience (87), based as she is on the evocation of male desire, on a conversation between men about the female body that is really about their own desire. Unlike the kore with her direct stare and outstretched hand, her rich clothing and her ability to evoke the marriageable maiden, to Osborne the Aphrodite offers no access to the female gaze that seeks a model or a mirror (89). His argument is based on a sense of the social and political changes that occur at the end of the sixth century, but he leaves undiscussed the possibility of equally important changes resulting from the Peloponnesian wars, changes that may have made the later fourth-century world different from its predecessors. Interestingly, his position on the statue has some similarity to the earlier one articulated on formal grounds by Gerhard Rodenwaldt (1943) in the 1940s and later by Adolph Borbein (1973) in the 1970s; fourth-century statues are understood by both to exist in a world of their own, separated from the viewer by their distant gazes, their remote and self-contained quality. This, although neither suggests it, leaves the way open for the kind of conversation that Eve Kosofsky Sedgwick (1985) would include in her description of homosociality, as men create bonds between them through the use, discursive or actual, of women's bodies. Osborne sees this homosocial conversation as less automatic and totalizing in the case of the Archaic kore than

the Knidia. Whether his argument is correct is another matter, but what is important here is his insistence on the Knidia's availability to the male viewer and his belief that the statue does not speak to the female viewer.

For Sue Blundell (1995), whose book on women in Greece gives rather little space to the visual arts, an erotic response is consciously generated by the sculptor who offers the Knidia as caught unwilling by a voyeuristic spectator. She presents the interesting notion that the voyeur captures the goddess's attention and thus leaves the viewing male safely unseen and able to look all he likes. Despite the admission of the danger of being caught looking at the goddess, a danger implicit in the need for a deflection of her glance, Blundell's Aphrodite is still vulnerable and can be assaulted, spied on, and laughed at by the male viewer. And as Osborne (1998, 95) too points out, Aphrodite again exists within a context that "eclipsed and silenced women as much in life as in art." The narrative that the statue initiates for the viewer is always, for these writers and for others such as Nigel Spivey (1996) and Nanette Salomon (1997), about men. The female body is merely a pretext for men's fantasies and their conversations with one another.

Andrew Stewart (1997, 97–106), although he uses the same materials and the same basic argument about the central importance of the artist's intentions and the male viewer's desire, proposes the possibility that male desire cannot necessarily always be fulfilled. His comments on the thwarted voyeur have to do with the depiction of the uncarved genitals of Aphrodite, which permit no penetration by eye or penis; in this way he proposes allowing the goddess to retain some of her power, for it is not simply her gaze that, if returned, might prove terrifying in its divine anger but also her body's ability to refuse access that lets her remain a goddess after all (Stewart 1997, 104). Nevertheless, for him Aphrodite remains reactive, embedded in a network of male gazes.

All of these readings of the Knidia are influenced by feminist versions of reception theory, but all of them tend to obscure important components of the politics of the theory. Whereas Laura Mulvey's seminal 1975 article, "Visual Pleasure and Narrative Cinema" (1989a), proposed a normative male viewer for the Hollywood narrative films she was investigating, there was more to the theory than this aspect of it, and the author herself (1989b), along with many other theorists, most notably Ann Kaplan (1983) in her article "Is the Gaze Male?," rethought the original article in order to make space for resistant female viewing. In the original paper, Mulvey (1989a) suggested that the films were addressed intentionally to male viewers and that the only positions for female viewers were either as if male, therefore denying their own differing experiences and possible responses, or as if masochistic, in the roles of women whom the films forever objectified, victimized, or stereotyped. In revising the theory several years later, Mulvey (1989b) and others recognized the power of all viewers, male and female, to reconfigure what they see for their own purposes, to operate, at least to some degree, in opposition to hegemonic norms of viewing. This provides the possibility for fantasy and desire built on experiences that viewers do not share with Hollywood filmmakers, that women do not share with men, and so on. In other words, the theory seems to have been appropriated by writers in classical archaeology in a rather ossified form.

Even feminist attempts to think about the Aphrodite, both Blundell's and Salomon's, have tended to preserve this reliance on Mulvey as well as on the Roman testimonia. In Salomon's case, an essay published in 1997 argues that the statue does have female viewers, and it speaks to them as Osborne's does not. But the author positions the female viewer as abject, building on Mulvey's original theory, and sees the statue as a lesson in feminine vulnerability and bodily abasement that remains in operation for centuries thereafter. At one level, this theory, like those of the other authors I've been discussing, has considerable merit. For indeed the normative viewer, the viewer presumably intended in the unknowable mind of Praxiteles, was a Greek male citizen. Apparently his desire mapped onto that of the artist, and the statue did become the object of their homosocial conversation, a place for questions about sexual-object choice, about fantasy, about the relationship between sight and sex, as between artifice and reality. And from this point of view, the move to imagine the statue as a lesson in abjection makes sense because the female viewer exists here as an extension of male desires and practices, and she is always previously constructed as in need of control, in need of abasement. The power of her sex, as sexual object but also as mother, is thus contained both through the vulnerability of the statue to the male gaze and through the construction of a female viewer to whom the statue teaches shame.

One of the virtues of Seaman's discussion of the Knidia, referred to above, is its rejection of the notion of abjection and its willingness to imagine multiple categories of viewers. Although she does not engage with feminist theory (indeed, her main, if understated, interest in theories is really in those of art history and archaeology), she uses close examination of the images to reject the idea of the frightened or ashamed figure. The gesture she identifies as pulling up the drapery from the water jar becomes not an element in a narrative of voyeur and goddess trying to hide but rather a part of the imagery of the powerful goddess's bath of ritual purification. Whether before marriage or after sexual intercourse, the ritual bath associated with Aphrodite at numerous sites becomes a way to open up viewing to a wider audience because both brides and hetaerae or prostitutes will have experienced this kind of purification rite. The goddess is thus a figure full of ritual power and erotic allure in this reading, one that permits women as well as men access to the figure.

Feminist Theory and the Female Body

Feminist theory can take this expansion of the audience further. The notion of the statue as a vehicle for the construction of particular kinds of femininity in all the readings of the past few decades is especially interesting in light of the work of the gender theorist Judith Butler. Writing on performativity in the context of contemporary U.S. culture, Butler suggests that men and women become masculine and feminine in a culture by the repeated performance of gender.

> If the body is not a "being" [by which I understand Butler to mean not an a priori and fixed entity] but a variable boundary, a surface whose permeability is politically regulated, a signifying practice within a cultural field of gender hierarchy and compulsory heterosexuality, then what language is left for understanding this corporeal enactment, gender, that constitutes its "interior" signification on its surface? . . . I suggest that gendered bodies are so many "styles of the flesh." These styles are never fully self-styled, for styles have a history, and those histories condition and limit the possibilities. Consider gender, for instance, as a corporeal style, an "act," as it were, which is both intentional and performative, where "performative" suggests a dramatic and contingent construction of meaning. (Butler 1990, 139)

Butler's reading of the body and of gender as constantly coming into being implies both historical constraints and a dialectic between interior and exterior forms. She sees gendered personality (interiority) as manifesting itself on the body in conversation or in struggle with historical forces, and the interior identity as shaped by repeated bodily practices of gender. Repetition is crucial: "As in other ritual social dramas, the action of gender requires a performance that is repeated" (Butler 1990, 140).

Although Butler does not deal with this, visual representation is central to that repetition. The nude Aphrodite as monumental marble, as small bronze or marble statuette, as cheap terracotta, and as image on a coin repeat the form, distribute it widely, make it constantly accessible to the repeated seeing, touching, verbalizing, and worshipping by women and men of every stratum (*e.g.*, Marcadé 1969, 233–34). The repeated image becomes a kind of inevitability and may thus achieve the status of the ideal form of female beauty and desirability for its period and place.

Through the repeated image, the female body learns to perform femininity, the male to perform masculinity, through both the social and the artistic repetitions, through social and visual practices. The male body learns what it is not, what it desires, what it must not be (though perhaps it secretly yearns to be) through looking at the nude Aphrodite, writing and reading about her, thinking about her. As Butler (1993, 12–16) and others have suggested, what the individual cites shapes her or his identity and that of the community. Citation, in the sense of a conscious or an unconscious reference, is part of the very process of performativity as

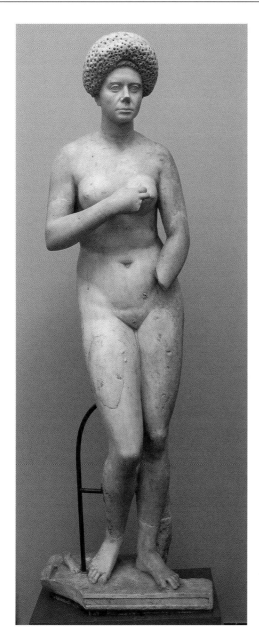

Fig. 21.3 *Roman statue of a woman in the guise of Aphrodite, later first century CE, from Lake Albano. Copenhagen, Ny Carlsberg Glyptotek, inv. 711 (Courtesy the museum).*

in fact Butler (1993, 93–119) herself has indicated one in her later, autocritical rethinking of the theory of performativity of gender. She, like Mulvey, has asked where in this theory there is space for change, for resistance or reassessment; clearly, it is not enough to imagine human beings as automata following social directions inevitably, unquestionably, always. Individuals and communities have and continue to negotiate bodily and psychic practices, as when ideas about same-sex behavior and its meanings and public manifestations change. If we combine this perception of the possibility of resistance and change in the performativity of gender with an acknowledgment that women's experiences are often quite different from those of men, we can follow Seaman and further open up the possibility for new thinking about the meanings of the Knidia.

Women at Aphrodite Sanctuaries

If women's experiences can be different from men's, and we have ample evidence for this among Greek citizens in this period, and if those experiences are never static but are capable of change, and here too, especially after the Peloponnesian wars, there is evidence, then why would we not imagine women having historically specific responses to the Knidia that differ from as well as resemble normative male responses and that might build on historically specific experience? Even before we can approach this question, we need to establish the presence of a varied population of women at Aphrodite sanctuaries, to ask whether domestic uses of Aphrodite imagery indicate a more private context for worship or are decorative objects or collectibles, and to imagine women as worshippers of a goddess rather than voyeuristic or masochistic tourists or working girls before a porn queen's image.

Here the importance of archaeological ensemble becomes very clear. Although both traditional and revisionist interpretations of the Knidia remain rooted in the isolated individual statue in a museum, and in the elite literary corpus, no matter what its historical relationship to the object, this seems the least promising path on which to continue. Granted, and this becomes painfully clear as we go on, the site of Knidos and the sanctuary of Aphrodite there offer little help to the interpreter (I thank the many people who provided information about current work on Knidos and Aphrodite statues; they are too numerous to name here but among them are Andrew Stewart, Phillip Kendrick, and Ian Jenkins). Some of the small finds have been lost or are unlocated, some are in museums in Bodrum and Izmir, some from the early days of excavation are in collections in western Europe; most remain uncatalogued and unstudied. The picture is, however, beginning to improve. Since the mid-1980s both German and Turkish teams have been working at Knidos. Ceramics are being catalogued by Ursula Mandel and others in Germany, and many of the terracottas

Butler proposes it (Fig. 21.3). So the statues in their multiplicity and replication provide a source for the citation of men's desires, which can find form, embodiment, in the Aphrodite of Knidos. So, too, these many renditions of the Knidia and other Aphrodites act as the source for citations for women's conceptions of desirability, sexual power, and bodily presentation.

Butler's theory can be used in a variety of ways, one of which Salomon shows us, another of which scholars such as Stewart reveal. But I think there are several other directions in which one might take this kind of theory, and are being published by Mustafa Şahin. Further, Ian Jenkins is publishing the sculpture from the nineteenth-century excavations. And finally, some of the inscriptions from the site, although probably a fraction of what is still to be excavated or located, have been catalogued by Wolfgang Blümel (1992). Given the state of the work on the site, it might seem premature to venture further than a critique of previous literature for its neglect of female viewers. However, I suggest that we cannot proceed with a discussion of the reception of the Knidia by women or men unless we risk trying to imagine the site's archaeological ensemble. Without the possibility of small finds, inscriptions, plantings, and the architecture that still remains under debate, the statue will continue to stand isolated from both worshippers and historical context.

To begin with the idea that brides and married women as well as prostitutes and hetaerae worshipped Aphrodite at her sanctuaries from, say, 350 through to the end of the first century BC, we can look at the inscriptions that indicate dedications by and for women at those sanctuaries, and here I consider a sample of the evidence from Greece, the islands, and Asia Minor but not from the West (see also Strabo 8.6.20 for the temple prostitutes of Corinth).

A sample of the inscriptions indicates that women made dedications at the sanctuaries in far smaller numbers than men did, that most inscriptions are about priests rather than about private dedications, and that the inscriptions are very unevenly distributed geographically, in part because of the state of excavation and publication of many sites. The most frustrating is, as I mentioned, Knidos itself. The collection is extremely small and it cites no more than one or two inscriptions securely connected with Aphrodite. One inscription concerns a dedication by a priest of Aphrodite and a group of men (Blümel 1992, no. 612) and the other indicates the anonymous dedication of a relief to Aphrodite and Peitho (Blümel 1992, no. 242). So neither testifies to women as dedicants here.

At other sites there is more information. For example, near Knidos, in the neighborhood of Cos, a third-century inscription gives a list of men and women who contributed to a fund for construction of a temple to Aphrodite (Paton and Hicks 1891, 277–79), a second-century statue base that seems to be from the sanctuary of Aphrodite Ourania in the agora of Elis records a dedication of a wife and daughter to Aphrodite (*Supplementum epigraphicum graecum* [hereafter *SEG*] 49 [1991], no. 387), and from Amorgos, *c.* 300, comes an inscription that reads as follows:

> The boundary of the houses and gardens adjoining the houses put up as security to Nicesarete for her dowery, consecrated and dedicated to Aphrodite Ourania in Aspis by Nicesarete, wife of Naucrates, and her guardian Naucrates, and according to the wills deposited in the temple of Aphrodite and with Eumonides the archon and with the official Ctesiphon. (Finley 1951, 155)

Most Aphrodite inscriptions lack adequate provenience, but some of the inscriptions from Old Paphos do come from the sanctuary of Aphrodite, often from the temple area itself, although they may of course have been moved there (for inscriptions found in the sanctuary area, see Mitford 1961, nos. 21, 41, 63, 85, 88, 92, 97,103–4). Among the numerous examples of dedications concerning women from Old Paphos are inscribed bases dedicated by women for their husbands and their children as well as by parents for their daughters; many of these are datable to the third century. Thus, a mother sets up a statue for someone named Aristonactis (*SEG* 20 [1964], no. 190; Mitford 1961, no. 31, restores as Aristonaktos, a son); Socratis dedicates a statue for her daughter sometime after 163 (*SEG* 20 [1964], no. 202; Mitford 1961, no. 63, restores as Sokrates, masculine); Ptolemaeus honors his wife (and daughter?) in a third-century dedication in the name of Aphrodite Paphia (*SEG* 20 [1964], no. 247), the priests of Aphrodite Paphia honor a *strategos* and his wife and children just before 100 (*SEG* 13 [1956], no. 584), and Diogenes erected a statue of Creto the daughter of Kleon who are both recorded on a marble base of the later third century (*SEG* 20 [1964], no. 189).

So we have at least some evidence for women who are not prostitutes as worshippers of Aphrodite at sanctuaries. The terracottas provide equally interesting possibilities. In the terrace sanctuary area of Knidos, at least one terracotta fragment of a nude female figure in a polos has been interpreted by Şahin (2005, 72–73) as a fifth-century Aphrodite, and the numerous figurines representing veiled female heads and figures he sees as brides. From the Hellenistic period come fragments that could be Aphrodite draped and semidraped (Şahin 1995, 86–88), but so far no replicas of the Knidia from this area have been published. However, finds of terracotta statuettes of nude or seminude Aphrodite uncovered with marble statues of the goddess and altars from domestic structures in Hellenistic Priene (Prittwitz und Gaffron 1998, 113–14) suggest that there may also have been communities in which domestic worship of the goddess was conducted by men and/or women. Marble statuettes from Delos seem to confirm this (Seaman 2004, 535). Graves also reveal substantial finds of terracotta statuettes of the Knidian and other Aphrodite types, especially in Greece and the Aegean. Married women and daughters are honored and are named as dedicants in the Aphrodite temples on Delos in the later fourth and third centuries, and a number of offerings of sacrifices, of jewelry and statues, are made by women from rich families and by named priestesses (Bruneau 1970, 331–48). A rather racy statue of Aphrodite with Pan (Fig. 21.4) came from a room in the Establishment of the Poseidoniasts of Berytus at Delos dated to the second and first centuries (Marcadé 1969, 393–96, pl. L: MN Athens inv. 3335; Bruneau 1978a, 134). The Poseidoniasts were businessmen who are known to have participated in the

Fig. 21.4 Aphrodite with Pan, from the Establishment of the Poseidoniasts of Berytus at Delos, front view. Athens, National Museum, inv. 3335 (Courtesy the German Archaeological Institute in Athens).

but much of it is literary rather than dedicatory. Nossis's poem on Polyarchis, for example (*Anthologia Palatina* 6.332), says, "Let's go to the temple of Aphrodite to see how her statue is intricately worked from gold. Polyarchis set it there, with the great wealth she won from her own body's splendor." This is in accordance with the other material about dedications made on the basis of women's earnings from their beds and so forth, mainly from the Greek anthology. As Vinciane Pirenne-Delforge shows in her 1994 study of Archaic and Classical manifestations of Aphrodite, the evidence is not, however, the same as the suggestions in comedy that prostitutes had an official cult role at sanctuaries of Aphrodite.

It may never be clear whether one or another sort of figurine or statue type was associated with or meant to appeal to dedicants who were married women, married men, and so forth, and indeed one would not be surprised if everyone used more or less the same kinds of objects as ex-votos. The only thing that does seem clear is a picture of regular use of large numbers of mold-made terracotta figurines as inexpensive ex-votos and of small bronze and marble statuettes, of replication and dispersion of forms connected with known statue types such as the Knidia, and of the presence of Aphrodite figurines in tombs, houses, and sanctuaries of many different deities.

What Does a Woman (Worshipper) Want?

At this point it makes sense to ask what the various people who make dedications and honor gods and goddesses want from them. Presumably they all want a share of whatever the deity's power can confer, and in the case of Aphrodite, that power is sexual; it is about desire and fulfillment. Now, let us assume that, although philosophers and writers of new comedy, novels, and pastorals had complex responses to sex and both mockery and yearning were part of those responses, their writings cannot be taken as unmediated indications of responses of the worshippers of a sexual goddess. How then should we think about Aphrodite? Many worshippers were interested in the goddess's power to make someone want them, to make them sexually attractive, and even to allow them to keep a partner with whom to have children and to have the sexual responses necessary to conceive those children. Prostitutes and courtesans presumably wanted someone to want them enough to provide them a source of steady income and protection, even eventually a way out of the sex business, but perhaps unmarried and married women alike had some similar motives. Might we imagine that women who had little choice in whom they would marry, who might at best have veto rights over parental choices, and who were young and inexperienced in sex would need the help of the goddess to guide them? Would not mothers and daughters want the goddess to help counter the fears of a young woman about

festivals of Poseidon and of Apollo and whose building contained a statue of Roma and an inscription indicating worship of Aphrodite Astarte who is attested elsewhere at Delos, as is Isis Soteira Astarte Aphrodite Euploia, in dedications by men and women from places such as Ascalon and Sidon (Bruneau 1978b). The indications are, then, that men and women regularly celebrated Aphrodite in a variety of contexts, and that the women included wives and daughters as well as priestesses.

There are a number of pieces of epigraphical evidence that suggest prostitutes and metics as worshippers as well, to be traded into a new home with strangers around her? Even more crucial, this is a society in which husbands and wives live apparently rather separate lives and where there is little premium on affection in marriage, despite the literary and visual evidence for the growth of a certain romantic sensibility in the later fourth and third centuries. Would a woman need Aphrodite's help in making her attractive enough to keep her husband kind to her and loyal to her and their children? Might not, then as now, sexual attractive-ness provide a certain protection to a wife, the old saw about wives for procreation, hetaerae and prostitutes for pleasure notwithstanding. Given that some texts propose that both husband and wife needed to experience orgasm in sex in order to conceive, might also a bride as well as her groom have sought the help of Aphrodite in their sexual relations (Fantham et al. 1994, 186)?

The Knidia, as do so many statues, forms a locus of desire and fantasy, for women as well as for men; she acts as a model and a way to imagine desire. So we go beyond Butler's primary statement about the performativity of gender and move into desire and fantasy as modes that transform as well as reinforce the gendered body and spirit. The goddess does not have to intend to do this, nor does the artist have to intend her to do so. Once she stands before viewers, she cannot control them beyond a certain point; then (within historical limits) they may resist, challenge, or drift into thoughts of their own. Then mothers and daughters may imagine themselves loving the goddess, making her the repository of their own yearnings, may imagine them-selves calling upon her for her help as Peitho and rescuer. Does the allure of the goddess, in the Knidia so mysterious and so open to diverse interpretations, permit the bride, the wife, and the courtesan all to have their hopes of comparable allure, of a bodily and sensual power like that of the goddess? If the fourth-century bride and wife are to be instructed in a suitable bodily form and readied for its performance in order to receive the fantasies of men, then that should not preclude their own (perhaps overlapping) fantasies. Even for women with little power or authority of their own, with little control over social ideology or even their own marriages, allure, like romance, could provide a kind of payoff for willing participation in the system. To be a beloved as well as an honored wife and mother is a conceivable hope for women attending Aphrodite in a world that was changing in ways that affected them as much as it did men.

This inquiry into women as worshippers of Hellenistic Aphrodite suggests that we need multiple interpretations of the Knidia that are rooted in acknowledgment of the multiplicity of viewers. This means that the goddess, her ambiguity of pose and demeanor reinforcing this need, can indeed be understood through the lens of male desire, homosocial and heterosexual alike, and it means that for some viewers touristic and voyeuristic motives are primary. Masochism and abjection are possible, but so is a kind of

glorious modeling of the desirable woman in her own interests as bride, wife, mother, and as prostitute or courtesan as well. Whether the statue was intended to evoke male desire, to suggest the marriage bath, or to hint at the uncovering of sacred things in a process of mystic revelation, it requires study that attends not to some universalizing reception theory but to the particularities of time, place, and social locations of worshippers. I conclude by asserting that it is possible to study women's desire even in a world in which it was so seldom articulated by women themselves.

Works Cited

Beard, M. and Henderson, J. (2001) *Classical Art: From Greece to Rome*. Oxford and New York, Oxford University Press.
Blümel, W. (1992) *Die Inschriften von Knidos. Inschriften griechischer Stadte aus Kleinasien* 41. Bonn, Habelt.
Blundell, S. (1995) *Women in Ancient Greece*. London, British Museum Press.
Borbein, A. (1973) Die griechische Statue des 4. Jahrhunderts v. Chr. *Jahrbuch des Deutschen Archäologischen Instituts* 88, 43–212.
Bruneau, P. (1970) *Recherches sur les cultes de Délos à l'époque hellénistique et à l'époque imperiale*. Paris, E. de Boccard.
——— (1978a) Deliaca (II). *Bulletin de Correspondance Hellén-ique* 102 (1), 109–71.
——— (1978b) Les Cultes de l'établissement des Poseidoniastes de Bérytos à Délos. *Hommages à Martin J. Vermaseren I*, 160–90. Leiden, Brill.
Butler, J. (1990) *Gender Trouble: Feminism and the Subversion of Identity*. New York and London, Routledge.
——— (1993) *Bodies That Matter*. New York, Routledge.
Fantham, E., Foley, H. P., Kampen, N. B., Pomeroy, S. B., and Shapiro, H. A. (eds.) (1994) *Women in the Classical World: Image and Text*. New York and Oxford, Oxford University Press.
Finley, M. I. (1951) *Studies in Land and Credit in Ancient Athens 500–200 BC*. New Brunswick, NJ, Rutgers University Press.
Foucault, M. (1988) *The History of Sexuality 3: Care of the Self*. New York, Vintage Books.
Havelock, C. M. (1995) *The Aphrodite of Knidos and Her Successors*. Ann Arbor, University of Michigan Press.
Kaplan, E. A. (1983) Is the gaze male? In E. A. Kaplan *Women and Film*, 23–35. New York, Methuen.
Kousser, R. (2005) Creating the past. The Vénus de Milo and the hellenistic reception of classical Greece. *American Journal of Archaeology* 109, 227–250.
Marcadé, J. (1969) *Au Musée de Délos*. Paris, E. de Boccard.
Mitford, T. B. (1961) The Hellenistic inscriptions of old Paphos. *Annual of the British School at Athens* 56, 1–41.
Mulvey, L. (1989a) Visual pleasure and narrative cinema. In L. Mulvey *Visual and Other Pleasures*, 14–26. Bloomington, Indiana University Press.
——— (1989b) Afterthoughts on "Visual Pleasure and Narrative Cinema" inspired by King Vidor's "Duel in the Sun (1946)." In L. Mulvey *Visual and Other Pleasures*, 29–38. Bloomington, Indiana University Press.

Osborne, R. (1994) Looking on – Greek style. Does the sculpted girl speak to women too? In I. Morris (ed.) *Classical Greece: Ancient Histories and Modern Archaeology*, 81–96. Cambridge, Cambridge University Press.

——— (1998) *Archaic and Classical Greek Art*. Oxford and New York, Oxford University Press.

Paton, W. R. and Hicks, E. L. (1891) *The Inscriptions of Cos*. Oxford, Clarendon Press.

Pirenne-Delforge, V. (1994) *L'Aphrodite grecque. Kernos,* Suppl. 4. Athens and Liege, Centre International d'Etude de la Religion Grecque Antique.

Prittwitz und Gaffron, H.-H. von. (1998) *Der Wandel der Aphrodite*. Bonn, Habelt.

Rodenwaldt, G. (1943) Theoi rheia zoöntes. *Abhandlungen der Akademie der Wissenschaften zu Berlin*. Philologisch-historischen Klasse 13. Berlin, Akademie der Wissenschaften.

Şahin, M. (2005) Terrakotten aus Knidos: Erste Ergebnisse. Die Kulte auf der Rundtempelterrasse. *Istanbuler Mitteilungen* 55, 65–93.

Salomon, N. (1997) Making a world of difference: Gender, asymmetry, and the Greek nude. In A. O. Koloski-Ostrow and C. L. Lyons (eds.) *Naked Truths: Women, Sexuality and Gender in Classical Art and Archaeology,* 197–219. London and New York, Routledge.

Seaman, K. 2004 Retrieving the original Aphrodite of Knidos. *Rendiconti della Accademia dei Lincei* ser. 9, 5, 531–94.

Sedgwick, E. Kosofsky (1985) *Between Men: English Literature and Male Homosocial Desire*. New York, Columbia University Press.

Spivey, N. (1996) *Understanding Greek Sculpture: Ancient Meanings, Modern Readings*. London, Thames and Hudson.

Stewart, A. (1997) *Art, Desire and the Body in Ancient Greece*. New York and Cambridge, Cambridge University Press.